THE ORIGINS OF COURTLINESS

Mercurius

C. STEPHEN JAEGER

◊

THE ORIGINS OF COURTLINESS

◊

CIVILIZING TRENDS AND THE FORMATION OF COURTLY IDEALS 939–1210

UNIVERSITY OF PENNSYLVANIA PRESS · PHILADELPHIA

THE MIDDLE AGES
a series edited by
EDWARD PETERS
Henry Charles Lea Professor
of Medieval History
University of Pennsylvania

Design by Adrianne Onderdonk Dudden

Library of Congress Cataloging in Publication Data

Jaeger, C. Stephen.
  The origins of courtliness.

  Bibliography: p.
  Includes index.
  1. Courts and courtiers.   2. Courtly love.
  3. Chivalry.   4. Civilization, Medieval.   I. Title.
  GT3520.J34   1985   940.1   84-15276
  ISBN 0-8122-7936-0

  Printed in the United States of America

Frontispiece from Staatsbibliothek, Munich, clm. 10268 (Michael Scotus, *Liber introductorius*), fol. 85r.

For my Mother, Kathryn Jaeger

CONTENTS

PREFACE

The idealizing that romantics and Victorians brought to their understanding of the Middle Ages has made that period a natural target
for the moderns' love of debunking. Arguments that deflate our image of medieval life have a much greater power to persuade than do
any that seem to reflect the tinted picture of Camelot painted by
Tennyson and Sir Walter Scott. The American intellectual is especially prone to see himself as the antagonist of Europeans on this
score. We have a strong tradition of deflating the Middle Ages,
which began with Mark Twain. For Americans, to see clearly the
quality of life that really prevailed in that period means to strip away
a veil of sentimentality and lay bare a much cruder reality beneath
it. My daughter recently wrote a report on the Middle Ages in her
fifth-grade history class. In the entry on the period in her *Britannica
Junior* she found the following observations:

This was the age of chivalry. Knights mixed high idealism with cruelty.
Lords expressed noble and romantic beliefs in flowery language, but treated
their serfs and slaves with inhumanity. . . . People were led to beautiful visions on the one hand and to indulge in low foolishness on the other. . . .
The Middle Ages were not ideal and life was not peaceful and charming, but
neither were they a time of utter darkness. . . . Civilization did not stand
still in the Middle Ages, for history is a continuous development.

This may be popular scholarship, but, like the last squeezing of the
grapes, it distills for us the essence of popular conceptions of what
is "medieval": an age whose "high idealism" is undercut by its basic
"cruelty"; its "noble and romantic beliefs" and "flowery language"
a camouflage for its "inhumanity." Civilization certainly would have
stood still in the period, the passage implies, if some blind momentum of "continuous development" had not goaded it into motion, as
if progress had only been possible because the cart of history pulled
the sluggish horse of the Middle Ages.

This book did not arise as an answer to that kind of sentiment,

but in the post–T. H. White, post-Tolkien years in which it was conceived, researched, and written, I was often exposed to movies and
novels in which the coarse sensibilities of the age loomed large in
the author's or director's overall conception of his work. It was perhaps unavoidable that I came to see a book about the refinement of
courtiers and kings in part as a refutation of a popular tradition that
insists on depicting medieval kings as bullies with atrocious table
manners and dirty clothes.

But popular conceptions aside, a kindred skepticism is also common among scholars in America and Europe. Currently this is fos-
tered as much by Marxist *Ideologiekritik* as by post-structuralist on-
slaughts on the relationship between idea and reality, words and
things.

It is important to distinguish between the romantic/Victorian
idealizing of the Middle Ages and the idealism that was an actual
motivating force in the period. This book is a study of court ideals and
their effect in educating human sensibilities, their civilizing influence.
I have tried to arrive at something like an objective historical judgment of the origins and nature of courtly and chivalric ethical ideals,
their actual social context, and their transmission from one class to
others. I hope that I have found high ground beyond the misty visions
of romantics and the hypercriticism of skeptics, a position that frees
our view of the social and ethical ideals of medieval courts from the
distortions of enthusiast and debunker alike.

Just as big a problem, however, is to recover the reality of those
ideals from the distortions they suffer in the best sources representing
them: courtly literature, Arthurian romance, the romances of antiquity, troubador love-lyric, and Minnesang. The aesthetic-ethical world
of Arthurian romance is not completely detached from contemporary
life. The ideals of that world originated in a particular social context as
held and practiced values. But courtly literature is a hindrance to recovering that context. Here the origins of medieval courtesy are three
and four times transformed, sublimated into the airy, unreal atmosphere of chivalric fairy tales, and hardly any path leads from that literature back to the social reality that nurtured it. Courtly literature is
not a mimetic mirror but, rather, a mask hiding the reality that produced it, and it cannot be the point of departure of this study. It
comes at the end, just as in terms of intellectual history it came at the
end of the civilizing trends which shaped medieval courtesy.

A great deal of Latin literature depicts the court life of the tenth to
the twelfth centuries, or arose in response to that life. This literature is
my point of departure: panegyric, chronicle and annal, ethical and didactic writings, and above all, the biographies of bishops. The reader

will certainly want to ask why these works and why the figure of the bishop lend themselves to the study of court life and values. I hope to answer this in my first chapter, but as a kind of emblem of the answer I have taken as my frontispiece a medieval drawing showing a figure in the robes of a bishop. It is not a portrait of any particular bishop. It represents the pagan god Mercury. What conception of that god can have led the illustrator to depict him in the clothes of a Christian pastor? It was undoubtedly Mercury's role as a bringer of education and a representative of the ideal goals of an education: eloquence and the ethical guidance of life. Mercury was in a sense a patron god of civilizing, and the closest approximation to this role for the medieval illustrator was a bishop. He carried out this office not only in his diocese but also, and perhaps more importantly, at court.

I have incurred many debts in the course of writing this book. My work on it began in 1979 when a Fulbright Research grant made possible a stay in Münster, West Germany. I am grateful to the Fulbright Commission for their support of my work. In Münster I was fortunate to have the resources of the Institut für Mittelalterforschung at my disposal, and I would like to express my gratitude to Professors Friedrich Ohly, Peter von Moos, and Karl Hauck for their generous hospitality. In the past four years I have presented sections of this work in the form of lectures and articles. My debts to the many colleagues and friends who have offered advice and guidance are great. Rather than pay them back piecemeal and unevenly here, I shall take recourse to whatever is the author's equivalent of bankruptcy and give up all my collected assets in the form of this book. Such as they are, they are much richer for the help of many donors.

The *Mittellateinisches Wörterbuch* is a reference work of particular importance for my study. I would like to thank Dr. Theresia Payr of the Bavarian Academy of Sciences, who with patience and understanding sent me many references from the still unpublished materials for the dictionary.

My work would have been much worse and progressed much more slowly without the generous help of the Bryn Mawr College Library staff. I am particularly grateful to Anne Denlinger and Gertrude Reed. I am relieved to be able at last to show proof to Bryn Mawr's inter-library-loan librarian, Bob Zaslawsky, that I made some use of all those books he ordered for me. To him and to Joan Hodgson of the University of California at Santa Cruz I am especially thankful. I would also like to express my thanks to Professor Hubert Heinen for helping me read proofs and for his many helpful suggestions.

Thanks are due to the following journals and publishers for allowing me to use materials from previous publications: *Speculum*,

Journal of English and Germanic Philology, and the Kümmerle Verlag, Göppingen.

Since I completed the manuscript of this book two works of particular interest and importance on the beginnings and nature of the chivalric ideal have come to my attention: Georges Duby's collection of essays *The Chivalrous Society* (Berkeley: University of California Press, 1977), and Maurice Keen's *Chivalry* (New Haven: Yale University Press, 1984). Both place the emergence of chivalry in a field of forces bounded by the values of the feudal lay aristocracy on the one hand, and Christian-monastic-ecclesiastical values on the other. Duby places particular stress on the movement for the peace of God and the authority over the waging of war which the church gained through that movement; Keen stresses the crusading ideal and the religious complexion of knighthood as presented in the romances and in the rituals of chivalry. Neither of these scholars argues that the origins of courtliness lie in these two areas and, in fact, the code of courtly behavior which is the subject of my book plays only a very peripheral part in these two important studies. However, both Duby and Keen recognize the central role of that code in the formation of chivalric ideals, and their silence on the beginnings of courtesy confirms that many factors obscure the actual origins of the code. The feudal nobility was a distinct class; the monasteries and the church under the reform were distinct spheres. But courtliness was borne by a class that stood between the secular and the religious realms.

Duby and Keen bring forward much testimony connecting chivalric ideals with Christian-monastic ones. These clearly play a part in the shaping of one aspect of the chivalrous knight, and Keen finds much interesting evidence in romance. But central to the shaping of chivalric ethics are ideals revived from classical antiquity. I look forward to the work that studies carefully the medieval myths of the Roman origins of chivalry and that will teach us to regard medieval chivalry as a neo-classical institution. Whatever it owes to monasticism and the crusade ideal, the chivalric ideal owes a great deal to the "renaissance" spirit of the twelfth century, a spirit which also accounts in large part for the birth or rebirth of courtliness.

ABBREVIATIONS

AHR	*American Historical Review*
AKG	*Archiv für Kulturgeschichte*
AQDG	Ausgewählte Quellen zur deutschen Geschichte des Mittelalters: Freiherr vom Stein Gedächtnisausgabe
ATB	Altdeutsche Textbibliothek
AUF	*Archiv für Urkundenforschung*
BAR	British Archaeological Reports
BBSIA	*Bulletin bibliographique de la société internationale Arthurienne*
Bibl. rer. germ.	Bibliotheca rerum germanicarum, ed. Ph. Jaffé
BKMR	Beiträge zur Kulturgeschichte des Mittelalters und der Renaissance
BLVS	Bibliothek des litterarischen Vereins in Stuttgart
CFMA	Classiques français du moyen âge
CSEL	Corpus scriptorum ecclesiasticorum latinorum
CTSEEH	Collection de textes pour servir à l'étude et à l'enseignement de l'histoire
DA	*Deutsches Archiv für Erforschung des Mittelalters*
DNL	Deutsche Nationalliteratur
DGQ	*Deutschlands Geschichtsquellen im Mittelalter*
DVJS	*Deutsche Vierteljahrsschrift für Literaturwissenschaft und Geistesgeschichte*
EETS	Early English Text Society
GRLMA	*Grundriss der romanischen Literaturen des Mittelalters*
GRM	*Germanisch-Romanische Monatsschrift*
Hist. Jb.	*Historisches Jahrbuch*
HV	*Historische Vierteljahrschrift*
HZ	*Historische Zeitschrift*
JEGP	*Journal of English and Germanic Philology*
LB	*Lebensbeschreibungen einiger Bischöfe des 10.-12. Jahrhunderts,* trans. Hatto Kallfelz. AQDG, vol 22. Darmstadt: Wissenschaftliche Buchgesellschaft, 1973.
LThK	*Lexikon für Theologie und Kirche*
ME	Middle English
MGH, SS	Monumenta Germaniae Historica, Scriptores
MGH, SS rer. Germ. in us. schol.	Monumenta Germaniae Historica, Scriptores rerum Germanicarum in usum scholarum

MHG	Middle High German
MIÖG	*Mitteilungen des Instituts für österreichische Geschichtsforschung*
ML	Middle Latin
MPH	Monumenta Poloniae Historica
MTU	Münchener Texte und Untersuchungen
OF	Old French
PBB	*Beiträge zur Geschichte der deutschen Sprache und Literatur*
PL	Patrologia Latina
RF	*Romanische Forschungen*
RS	Rolls Series
RTAM	*Recherches de théologie ancienne et médiévale*
WDF	Wege der Forschung
ZfK	*Zeitschrift für Kirchengeschichte*
ZfdA	*Zeitschrift für deutsches Altertum*

THE ORIGINS OF COURTLINESS

INTRODUCTION

T HE CIRCUMSTANCES that call forth "classical" periods of literature and art vary widely from one age to the next. The Renaissance of the fifteenth and sixteenth centuries grew out of political turbulence, an atmosphere of unbridled self-assertion and ruthless competition among men. This at least is the picture drawn by Jacob Burckhardt in his *Civilization of the Renaissance in Italy*. Human individuality had lain numbed in a kind of magical enchantment that medieval Christianity had cast over it. Its release led to arbitrariness and ruthlessness in the wielding of power. The notion of god-given institutions faded, and the individual ruler could shape and exploit the state unfettered by piety, charity, the fear of hell, or the hope of heaven. The state emerged from the chaotic political circumstances of fourteenth-century Italy as a "work of art," formed by human ingenuity and will. This same eruptive awakening called forth also the art of the Renaissance, which Burckhardt sees as parallel to political craft, both of them responses to the unchaining of man's will and creative forces. Burckhardt's model linked ruthlessness and violence with titanic creativity, and that echoed a widespread conviction of his dispirited age that all vital cultures are in their origins Dionysian.

The flowering of literature that began in the second half of the twelfth century and maintained its vitality into the first decades of the thirteenth had a very different background. It was the expression of a movement aimed at taming the reckless assertiveness of the European feudal nobility, at limiting its freedom in manners and morals, at restraining individual willfulness, and at raising this class from an archaic and primitive stage of social and civil life to a higher stage, imbuing it with ideals of modesty, humanity, elegance, restraint, moderation, affability, and respectfulness. If in the fifteenth century violence and arbitrariness nourished art, in the twelfth it was a rebellion against those forces. In the courtly period the urge to representation allied itself with the forces of civility, urbanity, and refinement.

This book is a study of the civilizing process that preceded the flowering of courtly literature in the twelfth century and introduced the ethical ideals that have come to be called "chivalric." The term is misleading if taken to refer to the class in which the ethical ideals of the chivalric knight in romance actually originated. These were native to another social class: the educated members of courts, the *curiales* who served kings, bishops, and secular princes, and the entire class of men who aspired to that position. The ethical and social values that guided their lives at court are the narrower subject of this book.

The dates in my title, 939 and 1210, give the outer limits of my study. The danger of drawing distinct borders is that it arouses the impression that they exist, that developments in cultural and intellectual history can be sliced like a pie and served up in neat segments. These dates mark important points on a continuum. The forces that produced courtly ethics were present in Carolingian court culture, and these forces could not have articulated themselves as they did from the eleventh century on without ideals of courtesy, urbanity, and statesmanship inherited from ancient Rome. Nor did the end of this development occur in 1210. It maintained its momentum through the end of the Middle Ages and into the modern period, giving the definitive stamp to western notions of the gentleman and of courtesy. It is safest to say: I have set as the borders of my study the years 939 and 1210. Its subject flows energetically past those boundaries at either end.

In 939 or thereabout Otto the Great summoned his younger brother, Brun, to his court. Brun was about fourteen years old at the time. He became chancellor, and in 953 he was raised to the archbishopric of Cologne. Brun was a handsome, highly educated, and talented young man with a clear eye for the practical necessities of administration and politics. He had a pedagogic bent that made itself felt in the documentary style of Otto's administration and, if we are to believe his biographer, in the intellectual life of the court itself. Under his influence the court was transformed into a kind of school of philosophy and the liberal arts.[1] But as if this bent transmitted itself to the kingdom at large, we notice a burgeoning of cathedral schools during the days of Brun's influence at court. By 950 Magdeburg was known as an illustrious school. By 952 the school at Würzburg was in full blossom; by 953 Cologne; by 954 Hildesheim; by 956 Trier.[2] There is a direct connection between the royal court and the rise of these cathedral schools. The king had found a purpose for this institution, and it was surely his brother who helped to shape its goals. Otto had faced rebellion in the early years of his rule, and in these unrests he had learned that the loyalty of the bishops in his kingdom was not unshakable. An institution to educate and prepare young men for loyal service to the kingdom was one answer to this instability. In his brother he found the perfect architect and administrator of a new program of education which had a major role to play in the formation of the Ottonian "imperial church system." The educational goal of the cathedral schools was no longer the training of clerics in pastoral duties but rather the training of talented young men, noblemen close to the king above all, for state administration. Here a humanistic education became an essential part of preparation for service to the empire; the curriculum was adapted to the requirements, both human and practical, of an office.

The year 1210, the other terminus of our period, marks the death of the German narrative poet Gottfried von Strassburg who by then had brought his version of the romance of Tristan and Isolde about three-quarters of the way to completion. The hero of this romance is the epitome of the courtly chivalric gentleman, though in many ways he is quite different from the typical knight/hero of Arthurian romance. He is above all an artist and intellectual who possesses many talents and attainments, among them chivalric prowess. The models that guided the poet in representing his hero in this way are something of a mystery. Modern commentators are fond of calling Tristan an "artist figure," though Gottfried himself called him a "hoveman" and certainly any reader, say, from the Renaissance, familiar with the types of aristocratic society, would have recognized in him a courtier.

In what follows I will try to show the coherent development linking 939 with 1210. I referred above to this development as a "process of civilizing," echoing the title of Norbert Elias's important study of court society from the Middle Ages to the eighteenth century.[3] Elias's book had an odd fate. First published in 1939, it received hardly a mention in the scholarship on court society and courtly literature before the 1960s. It was rediscovered in the wake of the trend to sociology and sociological studies of literature in the late sixties and seventies and is now into its second edition and sixth printing. Elias's general argument on the dynamics of change in aristocratic society— the social and psychological mechanisms that commend moderation and restraint, in short, the mechanics of civilizing—is still authoritative, and his is decidedly the voice to agree or take issue with. The sociologist was able to come to grips with what literary historians could explain only in a general and inexact way: that medieval courtesy had its roots in the social context indicated in the phrase *court society*, that is, in the real conditions of "courtly" life. Simple as it sounds, it represents a major shift in perspective on the subject. Traditional historians of medieval culture and literature derived notions of courtesy, naturally enough, from the best-known sources describing it: courtly romance and lyric. The world of vernacular courtly literature is the world of knights, combat, adventure, and amours in Celtic fairy tale landscapes, the sublime dream world of "chivalric" society. The natural assumption was that this dream reflected some social reality. From this assumption arose the idea that *courtoisie* sprang more or less spontaneously to life in France, along with the literature of courtly love, an expression of ideals current among the French lay nobility, the chivalric class. The evidence on the beginnings of courtesy as an actual social phenomenon in Europe (as opposed to a literary phenomenon) does not confirm this traditional explanation; on the contrary, it urges us to rethink and revise it considerably. Courtesy and "chivalric" ideals were nurtured in the conditions of court life. This is the simple and compelling lesson of Elias's book, and it is entirely in accord with the historical evidence.

What we learn from the Latin sources on courtesy bears out Elias's model over long stretches. But his notions of the originating forces behind the civilizing process do not hold up well. He gives first priority to mechanisms inherent in the structure of court society. In doing so, he steps boldly—and against the stream—into a flow of traffic dominated by intellectual and cultural historians, who tend to give predominance to great men and ideas in the development of civilized life. It will be worthwhile quoting him at length:

The transformation in the direction of civilizing, and with it to some extent also the growing reliance on reason, does not occur in some hermetic sphere of "ideas" or "thoughts." Here one is dealing no longer only with transformations of "knowledge," with developing "ideologies," in short with changes in the contents of consciousness, but rather with changes of the entire human posture, of which structures of consciousness, and particularly habits of thought, form only a small part, a single sector. This process has to do with transformations in the entire economy of the soul through all its regions from those where the ego guides in all lucidity to those where the guiding forces are unconscious impulses. . . .

. . . In the light of studies of intellectual history and the sociology of knowledge, thoughts and ideas appear as the predominant forces in the conduct of human life. And the less conscious forces, as well as the structured network of drives and emotions in its entirety, remains more or less in the dark.

But any investigation that regards only the consciousness of men, their reason and ideas, without concern for the functioning of human drives, for the direction and form of human emotion and passion, is limited from the outset in its effectiveness. . . . (2:388)

Leafing through the standard depictions of the intellectual development of the west one often gains the impression that the authors are under the spell of a vague conception that the progress of human consciousness towards reason, the change from magical-traditional forms of thought to more rational ones, has its cause in the emergence of a series of genial and especially clever individuals. Such illuminati, the arguments seem to run, by virtue of their exceptional intelligence, taught western man to use his innate reason properly. (2:397–98)

The strictures of a monarchical, aristocratic society impinge on the entire psychic economy of its highest members in a variety of ways, Elias argues. "Civilizing" is in its origin a response, among the circle close to the king, to these strictures. The forms and values of that circle become diffused through aristocratic society, and eventually through society at large. The basic stimulus to restraint and moderation, to the stifling of impulsiveness and passion, to the rational channeling of drives, is, according to Elias, conflict, competition, vying at close quarters with men of exceptional personal qualities for the favor and attention of the king. The negative counterpart of this conflict is the fear of social degradation and of the attempts by others to assert their superiority. One's guard is constantly up; intrigue, foresight, manipulation, and wit ward off the thrusts of the rival. The conditions of the inner circle of the ruler's court engender caution, discretion, and calculating foresight. The courtier becomes the master of his every word and act, of his diction and gestures, of the motion of his eyes and the tilt of his head, all of which, when uncontrolled, provide rivals with ammunition against him. Outbreaks of passion and impulsive confession of sentiments actually felt likewise open a man to attack and "degradation." Hence the mask and the disguise become major psychic vestments of the courtier. This produces a refinement and sensitivity unimaginable to men who live in more natural circumstances. One element of this growing refinement, one among many, is the evolution of ethical values and educational ideals. This is, generally stated, Elias's argument.

He is far from denying the importance of ideals and of the exceptional individual in the process of civilizing. He only doubts that they set this process in motion. Rather they are its products. He sees ethical codes as the articulation of successful strategies of conduct which arise as a response to circumstance, and as a means of transmitting these strategies to future courtiers via education. This process of conscious formation and articulation of strategies is what Elias calls "formation of the super ego" ("Über-Ich-Bildung"). The idea which Elias opposes—that civilizing forces originate in particular values transmitted by gifted individuals—cannot explain why the same tendency to refinement produces similar forms of behavior in aristocratic social structures wherever these occur. The courts of China and Japan, and of Arabia and Europe, generated comparable social types and ideals of civilized life. This must have its explanation in forces inherent in the structure of the societies themselves.

Comprehensive as Elias's study is, precise and draftsmanlike as his description of the mechanics of change is, there is much to disagree with. The sources he knows best and cites most are postmedieval—more a disappointment to the medievalist than a fault of the presentation. But even so, the work is light on primary sources and heavy on theory. There is a powerful bias built into the method. He uses Freudian categories to analyse the relations between society and the individual, and these categories urge on him the priorities marked out above: the real motivating and guiding forces in social transformation must lie in the preconscious realm, in the "economy of impulses" ("Triebhaushalt"). The "formation of the superego" and resulting genesis of ethics are secondary responses, even though they dominate the consciousness and the cultural records of civilizing. But it is more the presuppositions of his method than the realities of social development in the Middle Ages that urged on Elias this ranking.

My study deals with men and ideas. This perspective was not chosen by methodological predisposition, but was thrust on me by the testimony of my sources. To the objection of a sociologist that the methodological predisposition lies in the documents themselves, if not in my mind, I would reply that the sources are not so limited, not so exclusively the product of a collective, unified superego. The sources are rich and varied: biography, history, chronicle and annal, polemics against the court, and imaginative literature. To some extent their authors were idealizers and myth makers, but they represent a whole spectrum of attitudes and points of view. Some of the best testimony to the civilizing of Europe in the Middle Ages comes from the opponents of this trend. They see and represent the movement at its lowest, most material and shallow, and in doing so they offer a reliable corrective to the idealizing tendency in the majority of the sources. There is much in the following study that confirms Elias's "Theory of Civilizing,"[4] but there is much that contradicts it.

My study encourages us to see a system of education and its curriculum as the most important element in the process of civilizing. The founding of this system is traceable to a man remarkable for his learning, his pedagogy, and his statesmanship, Brun of Cologne. He handpicked many of the most prominent men in the Ottonian imperial court and church, trained them for state service, and promoted their advancement to the highest positions of power and influence in the empire, and he perpetuated his principles of choice in a system of cathedral schools. All of this precedes by an entire century that train of social changes in which Elias locates the birth of the civilizing process in the Middle Ages: the growth of population and the resultant tightening of the network of interdependencies in the kingdom and at court; the growth of wealth and the development of a money economy; the increasing flow of goods and the trade in territories that require large central administrations. Unless it is possible to transport these developments back in time by a century, some basic revisions of Elias's ideas on the origins of civilizing forces are necessary. Elias sees courtesy as a product of certain social changes, a response to conditions. I maintain just the contrary: courtesy is in origin an instrument of the urge to civilizing, of the forces in which that process originates, and not an outgrowth of the process itself.

The essential act that set the civilizing process in motion in the medieval West was the allying of the apparatus of government with a system of education. Let us take as the formula and symbol of this alliance "Otto the Great and Brun of Cologne": Otto the possessor of political foresight conceiving institutions to attain ends; Brun the shaper of one of those institutions.

‹›

Courtesy is one example of a civilizing force, a specific historical-ethical phenomenon. Subordinating it to the broader category "civilization" reflects, I believe, its actual place and function in intellectual and social history. But "civilization" and "civilizing" are big and hard words, and I want to offer some definition of them by referring to a myth of the origins of society told by Castiglione in his *Libro del Cortegiano*. It is appropriate to have in front of us some notions of the beginnings of civil life drawn from the "literature of civilization" itself.[5] Castiglione's work will be one of our most useful points of orientation on the subject of courtiers and courtesy, and so the myth is of particular interest, coming as it does from the milieu in question, if not from the same period. It is a point of departure that will help us define some terms and clarify some problems. The myth is brought into the dialogue as an argument for the natural origin of virtue, and runs as follows:[6]

Prometheus stole from Minerva and from Vulcan that artful knowledge whereby men gain their livelihood; but they did not yet know how to congregate in cities and live by a moral law, for this knowledge was guarded in Jove's stronghold by most watchful warders who so frightened Prometheus that he dared not approach them; wherefore Jove took pity on the misery of men who were torn by wild beasts because, lacking civic virtues, they could not stand together; and sent Mercury to earth to bring them Justice and Reverence,[7] so that these two might adorn their cities and unite their citizens. And he ordained that they should not be given to men like the other arts, in which one expert suffices for many who are ignorant, . . . but that they should be impressed upon every man; and he established a law that all who were without justice and reverence should be exterminated and put to death as public menaces.

The myth wants to root the civic virtues in the Absolute: they are "god-given." But we can translate this into natural terms by seeing Jove as an aboriginal ruler and Mercury (who for Castiglione is a representative of eloquence and learning, not merely a messenger) as an educator. The myth implies a political constellation. I hope the reader will eventually be persuaded that it is more than a self-fulfilling hermeneutic game if I suggest that in Castiglione's myth we have fully the mythical counterpart of the historical diad, Otto and Brun: a ruler and an educator. The mission of Mercury is to bring about social organization, the integrating of man into an order maintained by justice and respect for the rights of other men. The original stimulus to this organization is the need for protection and security: men are "torn by wild beasts" in the primal state of disorder. The means of accomplishing this integration is the implanting of civic virtues. Justice has its external counterpart in law, Reverence in "the moral law," a code of civic, courteous, respectful behavior. The compassion of Jove and the mission of Mercury can be read as a mythical statement of the beginnings of the process of civilizing. But the union of men attained in this way is only society, not civilization.

One of the main points of the myth is to distinguish between arts, in the broadest sense of the word, τέχναι, and civic virtues. The former precede the latter, but do not remove man from the primal state of chaos. The arts by themselves give activity and livelihood to each individual, but they do not unite men. Let us call this state of man equipped with the gifts of Prometheus "culture," and define it as the free exercise of any human skill or talent aimed at bettering the condition of man. This includes all forms of "cultivation," tilling the soil, cooking, making tools, and all else included among the *artes fabricae* (those stolen from Vulcan). It also includes learning, skill in speech (from Minerva), and finally the arts in the narrower sense: music, painting, sculpture, and literature. Culture precedes society. In this state men can protect themselves as individuals, since Vulcan's skills are at their best in the forging of weapons. Still they are torn by beasts, because they cannot stand together.

In the state of culture, there are heroes, artists, the great individual living in splendid autonomy and enjoying the freedom to exercise his skills and talents. Castiglione had a clear conception of the distinction between the cultural and the civic, and his clarity allows us to recall a distinction that in our day is so blurred by the hypertrophy of culture and the atrophy of civilization that the two terms have lost their clear contours and often are used interchangeably.[8] Note that Castiglione, the Renaissance humanist, has a clear ranking of the two: in the Promethean world the state of culture is lawless and dangerous; the titanic men of that primal time are torn by animals, as if suffering vicariously the punishment of their patron demigod, Prometheus. Their prerogatives are stolen by a trickster-titan from the gods. But the civic virtues are given out of compassion by the gods themselves. The "secrets" of the arts are poorly guarded, since the thief manages to steal them easily. But the secrets of communal life are held under so jealous a watch that Prometheus is frightened even to approach the sanctuary. The myth ends with a warning to those titanic individuals who do not receive or do not respect the gifts of Jove: exclusion and death.

The society formed in this way has three basic needs: to provide for its people, to defend itself, and to perpetuate its institutions and values. Failing this the society will dissolve. But to consolidate requires that the order ordained by Jove must subjugate the individuals favored by Prometheus and equipped with his gifts: no provisions without agriculture, no defense without weapons and warriors, no continuity and tradition without education and art. But culture does not enter easily into a subservient state. It clings to its primal freedom. The wish dream of the cultured man is that civilization will dissipate before his skill "like fog before the sun." He will even go so far as to scorn the advantages of justice and reverence, glorify his loneliness and suffering, and cast the idealizing veil of the titanic and the Promethean over them. The warrior wants nothing more than to exercise force unrestrainedly, the artist to work and create unhampered by the restraints of society and unpestered by civic responsibility. These classes seek emancipation as strongly as society seeks their subjugation. This struggle is apparent within the soul of each member of society but also in the greater theater of society and the interrelations of its various groups. The public man longs to withdraw and devote himself to studies and art. This urge in a ruler was apparently a real source of instability in the state. At least the motif occurs in the literature of civilization with some persistence: Prospero abandons his state to tyranny in order to indulge in his secret studies.[9] A *Fürstenspiegel* from the early thirteenth century, the *Somnium morale Pharaonis*, which we will discuss later, is directed against the *rex curiosus*, the king so given to speculation and study that he neglects the business of state.

The process of civilizing aims at educating the individual groups of society in law and civility. It is essential for its functioning that the structure of society itself maintain the legal and the moral order, that a complex system of punishment and reward be built into this structure. The dynamics of such a system are the subject of Elias's *Prozess der Zivilisation*. It turns the prohibitions of the law into prohibitions imposed on the individual by himself, establishes an ordering of priorities in the soul of each individual based on the renunciation of autonomy and of unlimited self-assertion. When a society educates its members to the extent that all groups within it willingly make this renunciation, but especially the warriors and artists, then we can speak of civilization, and no longer merely society. I stress the importance of education and willing renunciation because the alternative means by which a society commonly subjugates the individual is force and repression.

So then, we can define civilization for the purposes of this study as a social order in which the warrior class and the intellectual/artisan/artist class are won for the cause of society, willingly place their arts in its service, and regard this service as an ideal. To bring it to a formula: civilizations arise when culture willingly serves society. We could apply the definition to a good many historical situations, but let us turn to the one at hand, the beginnings of civilizing in Europe.

‹›

We are concerned above all with three classes or groups of society: the educator/statesman, the warrior, and the artist. The ruler is of peripheral interest, but in many ways this figure is a refraction of the educator/statesman, since the latter educates the ruler and can represent him in historical texts according to his own image. Most important for the process of civilizing is the educator/statesman. His creed is restraint, moderation, self-control, the subjection of passion to reason, humility based on a sense of personal greatness; it is also wit, love, reverence, affection, eloquence, and friendship. His every act, word, gesture, and facial expression has political meaning, is the result of conscious choice, and works to further strategies and long-range plans. His qualities allow him to conduct affairs of state in calm and to bring them to a conclusion with a minimum of conflict. They also bind men to him in loyalty and affection and form the personal terms of a social contract: they spell the renunciation of violence and arbitrariness in favor of law and the common good.

The warrior in his native and uncivilized state has no use for these virtues and can even regard them as corrupting. His creed is heroism and honor. The stifling of conflict and the mastering of passion is not in his interest. Violence and hot-headedness offer him greater advantages than restraint and reason.

The subject of this book is the emergence of a class of educator/statesmen from that original alliance, Otto and Brun, the genesis of values and ideals which sprang from that alliance, and their spread to the warrior class. But the process that occurs on the level of society repeats itself in the soul of each individual. If we were a society of ants or bees, that would not happen. Statesmen and warriors exist as identifiable social groups, though their qualities are mixed in varying permutations in the soul of each individual. If that were not so, then statesmen would tend to sterile effeteness, warriors to self-destructive violence and endless cycles of revenge. But whatever the innate teleology of character and destiny in each individual, nature also implants the seeds of other forms of life, and it is the task of education and social pressure to arrange rankings. In observing the civilizing process of the tenth to twelfth centuries, we see the establishing of an ideal inner hierarchy, which places the statesman mentality above that of the warrior. The statesman generates an ethic, a set of civic virtues, and this ethic is transferred gradually—via instruction—onto the class of knights, a class prepared by many factors to receive and accept this influence. Civilized man at his best emerges when the warrior tendency in his soul, alive, energetic, and able when necessary to break through the brittle shell of civility that contains it, willingly subjects itself to the ethos of the statesman. The hero of romance embodies this ideal balance, and in particular the hero of Gottfried's *Tristan*.

The third class or group is the artist. First we should observe that court society always tends to produce an aestheticising of manners. The basic act of the civilized man is to structure his conduct, cultivate and tailor his manner, and guide his action toward preconceived ends. The exercise of office becomes performance; political and civic activity becomes a work of art. An outward expression of this tendency is to be seen in the elaborate ceremonies that are such a striking feature of Byzantine and oriental courts.[10] In the West during the Middle Ages and the Renaissance, this tendency is embodied in the courtier. Court life also produces an intense refinement in sentiment and emotion, the ability to detect subtle shades of meaning and expressions of intention and sentiment in the most minute gestures. Individuals and groups invent subtle and private codes as a means of lifting the mask momentarily either to signal genuine feeling or to put forward another mask as a strategy of deceit. The context in which this tendency to refinement of emotion and communication culminates is the clandestine love affair, a pastime as pervasive in the life of the courtier as is combat in the life of the warrior. A result of these two tendencies is that human conduct at court tends to structure itself according to aesthetic principles; gesture and speech and the whole economy of human interactions fall into rhetorical categories. There develops what might be called a "poetics of conduct." In Elizabethan

England, manuals of court behavior and etiquette could provide the model for books of poetics; decorum, elegance and "style" in behavior could be seen as analogous to the same qualities in verse.[11] And conversely, the speech and posturing, the posing, feinting, dissimulation, and irony of characters at court can be regarded and analysed as a network of rhetorical strategies.[12] Where the forms of experience are so close to forms of expression, they invite representation more powerfully and compellingly than life in less artificial surroundings. The psychological narrative and the love lyric are the appropriate vehicles for the courtly cult of emotion.

But whereas the lyric gave vent to the subjectivism of court society, to the cult of the ego, the romance had a pedagogic function to fulfill. It put forward an ideal model of the civilized warrior. The courtly romance was the single most powerful factor in transmitting ideals of courtesy from the courtier class in which they originated to the lay nobility. The artist in our scheme does not constitute an independent class, like warrior or statesman; he has no clear social profile in the Middle Ages, being now cleric, now knight. He is, in the civilizing aspect of his art, a metamorphosis of the educator/statesman. His activity is subordinated from the outset to the process of civilizing; this is the stimulus that produced the form.

I intend to view the blossoming of courtly literature in the second half of the twelfth century as a result of the process of civilizing that preceded it. Erich Köhler's statement of the general social presuppositions of this period suits rather well the abstract scheme I have presented above:

Great periods of art, the formation of what might be called "classical" phases, rest on the socio-cultural alliance of two or possibly several social groups. The causes of such creative alliances are partial, but vital, constellations of self-interest of an economic and political nature.[13]

The alliances and the progressive knitting of social groups, that is, the transference of values and ideals from one to the other which concerns us here, crested in the great vernacular literature of France and Germany in the twelfth and early thirteenth centuries.

‹›

This book has two parts. The first deals with "courtiers." Here we face a difficulty in the choice of terms, which I have avoided until now by referring to this group generally as "educator/statesmen." The period itself and the relevant sources provide us with three terms for these men: *curialis, capellanus,* and *clericus.* We can find any of these three terms applied in our sources to the men whose lives and values are the object of this study. But the first two become misleading when translated into English. "Courtier" for *curialis* is so laden with associations from the Renaissance as to conjure that Protean universal man in state service whom Castiglione described. "Chaplain" for *capellanus* is rendered misleading by the common use of the term in modern ecclesiastical parlance. It calls to mind the clergyman in his capacity as religious advisor, and this function plays only a very minor part in the political and cultural influence of the men in question here. *Clericus* is the most encompassing of these terms. It refers generally to clergy living outside the monastic life. It embraces students, teachers, clergy of parish and cathedral churches, court clergy, bishops, and archbishops. These men wore the tonsure and clerical robes, or were supposed to. It is a much broader, more diverse group than that with which I am dealing, namely, the educated men in court service as advisors, tutors, servants, and chaplains of the king. Not all of the men in this class were clerics, and not all of the clerics were religious. "Courtier," for *curialis*, is the most useful and most accurate term. It focuses on the social context and resonates with the whole field of words generated by that context: court, courtesy, courtliness, and so forth.[14] The courtier described by Castiglione is a much richer figure than the medieval *curialis*, but it is an idealized construct. The reality of the Renaissance courtier may not have been all that far from that of his medieval counterpart. The blurring of contours that occurs by referring to *curiales* as courtiers is justifiable in that there is a direct historical development linking the medieval figure to his counterpart in the Renaissance. The ethical and social foundations of the Renaissance courtier lie in the milieu under consideration here. Hence there is some educational value in applying this term in this context. May it serve to overcome the notion that the courtier is a creation of the Renaissance!

The term courtier has the further advantage that it is purely worldly. The educated members of the court were by and large *clerici*. Where should they have gotten an education if not in the church as clerics? But they were not first men of God and servitors of the faith, even though they often had religious duties at court. We can form a general picture of the character of the *curialis* by calling to mind Thomas Becket as chancellor for Henry II of England. He was a witty, debonair gentleman, who entertained lavishly, dressed splendidly, and won the favor and affection of all men. He was well educated in booklearning, but also in courtly pursuits and pastimes: hunting with dogs and birds, for instance. At some point he must have learned combat on horseback, since he served Henry in the campaign against Toulouse in 1159, leading an army of seven hundred men and fighting with success. His loyalty to God and the church cannot have been pronounced at this point. If it had been, the king probably would not have promoted him to the archbishopric of Canterbury. A quip ascribed to Archbishop Manasses of Rheims characterizes this class at its most defiantly worldly: "The archbishopric of Rheims would be a pleasant thing if it did not oblige one to be singing masses constantly."[15] Christian ideals, taken over into the worldly life and assimilated to ancient Roman ethical ideals, had an important role to play in forming a medieval ethic of state service. But the religious life did not for the most part determine the conduct, behavior, and loyalties of *curiales*.

The second part is entitled "Courtesy." Whereas the first part deals with men and a social context, the second deals with the ethical values that guided their activities and with the diffusion of these values from *curiales* to other classes of society. My point of departure in both parts is a series of what might be called sociological word studies, that is, examinations of contemporary terminology and concepts, the ethical vocabulary of courtiers. This opens to view an extensive Latin vocabulary of courtesy, gives us access to the phenomenon in historical and biographical writings, and makes possible a study of the development of courtesy prior to its representation in courtly literature.

I have used the words "courtesy" and "courtliness" interchangeably. They translate the Middle Latin *curialitas*, the Old French *courtoisie*, and the Middle High German *hövescheit*. Since the difference between "courtesy" and "courtliness" in modern English is not registered in the medieval vocabulary, I have thought it best to preserve the ambiguity of the original terms by ignoring the differences between the modern English words.

PART ONE

◇

COURTS AND COURTIERS

◊ 1 ◊

THE COURTIER BISHOP

The Structure of the Court

T HE WORD "court" evokes the picture of a royal residence where the king, surrounded by his family and advisors, receives guests, ambassadors, and petitioners, and administers the land. But royal courts in the earlier Middle Ages looked quite different. The German king exercised his authority while traveling about the country. He was received along with his entire retinue in the residences of loyal bishops and secular nobles, who owed him hospitality as a form of feudal service. Also there was a series of royal palaces (*Pfalzen*) set at various places throughout the land to accommodate the king and his entourage. Particular locations such as Aachen, Speyer, and Goslar could become favorites of particular kings, but there was no single residence. The composition of the king's retinue was also not fixed. There was a constant coming and going of dukes, counts, bishops, and archbishops who sought the king to transact business, receive favors, and render advice. It is perhaps least misleading to say that the household of the king with its attending vassals and guests at any given time and place constitute his court.

Courts in the Middle Ages, like the administrative staff of modern governments, were structured according to the wishes and needs of the ruler, not according to constitutional law. The structure of a medieval court in the earlier period is marked by divisions of duties rather than by strict demarcation of offices. Within these limits it is possible to point to some general institutional divisions and to some offices, the titles of which remain consistent over long periods of time, even if the nature and duties of the offices are extensively transformed.

We are well informed about the court of Charlemagne through the household book *De ordine palatii* written in 882 by Archbishop Hincmar of Rheims for the young King Karloman.[1] This work is a good point of departure, since the Carolingian court provided the model for royal courts in Europe generally. We can take it from Hincmar's book that the two basic divisions of the household are the chapel on the one hand and the secular court offices on the other.

Of the many secular offices the four most important were chamberlain (*camerarius*), seneshal (*senescalcus*), butler or steward (*buticularius*), and marshall or constable (*marescalcus, comes stabuli*).[2] These offices all have their origins in the menial duties of the household, as is still evident in some of the titles: the root meaning of *marescalcus* is simply "stable boy." In the title *comes stabuli*, or "count of the stable," the rise in dignity of the office is evident, though the charming incongruity in the idea of having a count attend to the stables shows also a reluctance to gloss over the original area of responsibility when the importance of the office outgrew that context. The particular duties of these offices are not of any importance for us (see the detailed notes of Gross and Schieffer in their edition of *De ordine palatii*). We should just note that the time when these officers swept the stables and made the beds was centuries past by the age of Charlemagne. Each of them by then had a staff to attend to his particular area of jurisdiction. The officer himself, invariably a high and powerful noble, presided over that staff from a lofty distance and spent his time at court as a counselor and executive officer of the king.

There were two tendencies in the secular offices that we should note. First, the head of each office, as his wealth and power increased, gradually formed his own household separate from the court, a household which itself tended, as it grew, to divide into the same various divisions of the greater, royal household. The court offices were constantly moving toward a purely ceremonial status, so that at any particular time there were two sets of court officers: those princes of the realm who had the ceremonial titles of court office and lived outside the king's household, and those who resided with the king and oversaw the household duties. The second tendency was for these offices to become hereditary, or at least for their holders to want to make them hereditary. At no time in our period was the inheritance of court offices the rule. Rather, the ability of particular families to retain court offices depended entirely on their stature and influence. This situation produced tensions between the ruler and the families of his officers when he sought to break a family's hold on the office. The count of Hainault in the early thirteenth century, Baldwin VI, found the conflict among holders of office and contenders such a nuisance that he asked his chaplain Gislebert of Mons to draw up a list of court offices with the names of the present officers.[3]

The other major division was the chapel. This comprised the entire staff of clerics attached to the household. The court chapel originated in the Carolingian dynasty.[4] Among the duties of chaplains was the care of the household relics, and this is the duty from which the name of the office and its officials derives. The most important of the relics of the Carolingian dynasty was the cape of Saint Martin, the *cappa*, or, with diminutive ending, *capella*. The thing guarded gave its name to the entire treasury of relics, then to the sanctuary where they were kept, finally to the group of clerics in charge of it. They were *capell-ani*, the *-an-* suffix meaning generally in Indo-European languages "keeper of" the thing indicated in the stem.

The head chaplain bore the title *Apocrisarius*, and Hincmar describes him as the papal legate at court, generally a bishop or deacon, with broad diplomatic and administrative duties. Of far greater importance ultimately was the office of chancellor, the immediate subordinate of the head-chaplain, according to Hincmar, and in charge of the scribes and notaries of the court. In the earlier Middle Ages there was no chancery separable from the chapel; this is a phenomenon of the twelfth century.[5] In Carolingian times individual chaplains divided their time between religious and secretarial duties.

The chaplains were the educated members of the court. They enjoyed an unusual legal status as "spiritual vassals" of the king. Like other vassals, they owed him *servitium*, and their activity in the chapel was part of it. They were not subject to any episcopal or abbatial authority, but lived according to special rights and privileges.[6] They were, in short, clergy living outside of the church hierarchy.

Transformation of the Chapel in Ottonian Times

The natural tendency of court officers to emancipate themselves from direct service at court and to step into high positions in the kingdom had its counterpart in the chapel in the progression from chaplain to bishop. Service to the king in his court had been an avenue to a bishopric since late antiquity and this continued in Carolingian times. But the frequency of this route as well as its political importance increased dramatically under Otto the Great and his successors.[7] Otto sought to break through a cycle that plagued central authority throughout the Middle Ages: the political unification produced by threats from external enemies gave way to political fragmentation as soon as those threats receded. The feudal nobility tended to fall away from the emperor, resist the obligation of rendering him service, and fortify their own domains into autonomous principalities as soon as they no longer required the central authority to keep peace in the empire.

One genial response of the Ottos to this tendency was to create a new network of political alliances by building up the office of bishop into that of a mighty feudal lord, conferring domains and titles of nobility on its occupant. The result was the integration of the church into the political power structure of the empire, and the creation of a new class of aristocrat: the "spiritual prince" (*geistlicher Fürst*). The Ottos seated their own relatives and close friends in vacant bishoprics. This of course created irregularities in the procedure of electing bishops. The election of a bishop was reserved by canon law to "clergy and populace." But the king enjoyed an ill-defined right, legitimized only by the appeal to custom, to approve episcopal elections and give them official sanction by investing the bishop elect with ring and staff.[8] The Ottos made broad use of this "right." They were effective in putting forward and seating their own candidates in vacant bishoprics; they managed to prevent the seating of candidates whom they opposed, and were willing to exercise this power—Otto III at least— even in cases where the diocese held the privilege of free elections.[9] In this way the bishopric became a powerful political instrument in the hands of the emperors. The judicious choice of men to fill vacant bishoprics allowed a succession of emperors to create a buffer against the traditional political opposition of the feudal nobility. It was also a convenient feature of this reshaping of the imperial power structure that the office of bishop was not hereditary; these prelate-princes could not found dynasties and forge small kingdoms for themselves and their families, as the lay nobility could.

The court chapel had a major role to play in this development. It provided the pool of talented men close to the king whose talents, loyalties, and qualifications could be closely observed by the king. Future prelates were groomed at court for political/ecclesiastical service to the empire as bishops. The royal chapel became a "school for imperial bishops."[10] Under these new circumstances it was inevitable that the criteria for selection of chaplains and the emphasis in expectations changed. Fleckenstein observed a transformation in the composition of the chapel under Otto the Great. The chapel tripled in size during Otto's thirty-seven-year reign. A specific constituency accounted for the increase: clerics of high nobility attached to a cathedral. The number of monks in the chapel decreased. This shift is significant for several reasons. First, the contemporaries would have regarded the increase in the number of members of the nobility as an indication of a rise in the quality and distinction of the institution. Second, the decrease in the number of monks is a clear indication to us that the influence of monasteries and monastic schools was on the wane. Finally, the shift in the composition of the chapel demonstrates the increasing role the cathedral schools assumed in preparing young men for service in the chapel and in the kingdom. It is possible to dis-

tinguish specific stages of this shift. Before 953, the year in which
Brun assumed the archbishopric of Cologne, Otto's policy with regard
to the seating of bishops did not differ markedly from that of his
predecessor, Henry I. In 953, appointments, particularly in Lorraine,
but also elsewhere in the kingdom, suddenly began to fall predomi-
nantly to former pupils of Brun from the cathedral school of Cologne.
Then in 967, two years after Brun's death, just as suddenly and dramatically, the chapel took over the task of supplying candidates.[11] Evidently Brun transformed the cathedral school of Cologne into the testing and training ground for future bishops. Upon his death, this
function, which during his lifetime had proven its value, was taken
over by the court chapel, and from this point on the sequence in the
career of many an aspiring bishop was set: cathedral school, court
chapel, episcopacy.

As a result the chapel was transformed. Under the Carolingians it
had been an ecclesiastical institution in which the head chaplain functioned in the role of abbot or bishop, pastor to the other members.
Chaplains were responsible for the religious life of the court, and with
the exception of scribal functions their duties did not extend far beyond this. Under the Ottos, on the other hand, the chapel came increasingly to attract talented, highly educated men of high nobility.
They were friends, advisors, and educators to the king. Ordinarily
they numbered poets, scholars, and artisans in their ranks, and they
largely determined the cultural life of the court. The nature and requirements of the new court chapel produced, or at least greatly
swelled the numbers and importance both at court and in the kingdom, of the educated aristocracy. The higher ranks of chaplains constituted a cultural and political elite. The creation of an educated elite
at court which enjoyed a measure of intellectual freedom made for ex-
traordinary possibilities not foreseen by the rulers who conceived and
implemented an "imperial church system."

These, briefly, are the forces that brought into prominence the figure of the "courtier bishop" (*episcopus curialis*). The term comes from
the church reformer Petrus Damiani, who applied it with contempt to
bishops who had gained their office by service at the king's court:

[Episcopi], qui ecclesiae militando promoti sunt, vocantur ex more pontifices;
ita qui famulando principibus fiunt, dicantur a curia curiales.[12]

Those bishops who are promoted for service to the church are customarily
called "pontiffs." And so let those who advance by serving princes be called
"courtiers" from "court."

This figure was of major importance in the politics, culture, and civilizing of Europe in the precourtly period. He combines in himself the

three major strains of medieval European culture: the traditions of the indigenous tribal nobility, Christianity, and the educational tradition of classical antiquity.[13] If cultural historians have nonetheless paid little attention to the courtier bishop, it is in part because of various misconceptions about the figure himself and about the nature of his *vita*. One misconception has been the assumption that a cleric had to be a pious churchman in order to become a bishop. Friedrich Heer points to this factor as a hindrance to understanding the political role of the imperial bishop.[14] He was first an administrator, statesman, and diplomat. If, having assumed the office of bishop, he also turned out to be a pious and saintly churchman, so much the better. But piety was not a requisite quality of the position in the same way that statesmanship and administrative skills were. In late antiquity the old Roman senatorial nobility could regard a bishop's office as practically a hereditary right (e.g., the case of Sidonius Apollinaris). And the notion that a bishopric could be all but a prerogative of the aristocracy and the ruler's favorites lasted well beyond the Middle Ages. Stendhal in his *Charterhouse of Parma* can still have a court intriguer map out a career for a talented young nobleman which had a tradition of more than a thousand years behind it:

"Note . . . that I do not intend to make him an exemplary priest, like so many you see. No, he is a great noble first and foremost; he can remain perfectly ignorant if it seems good to him and will none the less become a bishop and archbishop, if the prince continues to regard me as a man who is useful to him."[15]

The only idea in this passage that owes more to Stendhal's cynicism than to the realities of a certain ecclesiastical career is that the future bishop could afford to be ignorant.

Another misconception that has tended to obscure the real nature of this figure is the assumption that the ideals of the office, if not the social and political realities of it, were orthodox Christian ones. Of course an orthodox ideal of the episcopate existed. Its classical formulations were Saint Paul: 1 Tim. 3:2–7; and Gregory the Great, *Regula pastoralis*. But as we shall see, the qualities that were appropriate in a court chaplain and future bishop in the Ottonian-Salian imperial church had little to do with this orthodox ideal of the bishop but were, rather, hardly distinguishable from the qualities appropriate to the character and obligations of a courtier serving the king.

The new requirements of court service which emerged from the particular circumstances of the Ottonian-Salian court chapel produced an ethic of state service based, not on conventional notions of the episcopacy, but rather on the education and values of the courtier bishop. It reflects the hybrid nature of that figure: both imperial courtier and prelate. This ethic and its native context—the court service of educated clerics—shapes an ideal courtier, a figure that in many ways is the prototype of the Renaissance courtier. Some of the conceptions of this ethic were to surface in the etiquette of *courtoisie* in vernacular literature, projected onto the figure of the chivalric knight. The following chapters are devoted to observing this ethic at work in the men who embodied it, and to recovering and formulating its central conceptions. But we begin with a look at the best sources.

Vitae episcoporum

The *vitae* of bishops who came to their office via service at the royal court regularly contain a description of the court service of the young cleric. These passages are vivid revelations of court life and manners. They show us typical careers, only slightly idealized. From them emerges a type of the aristocratic cleric as royal servant and future bishop in the imperial church.

We should distinguish the episcopal biography as a genre from hagiographic legends and saints' lives. The latter are popular works that blend legends from oral tradition about a saint's life and activity with available commonplace legends and tales of miracles.[16] The bishop's *vita*, on the other hand, stands in the tradition of ancient rhetoric and historiography and of the biography of late antiquity. It tends to idealize its subject to some extent, but the ideal models are quite different from those of the saint's legend. Whereas the saint's legend spoke to the masses, the episcopal *vita* spoke to the educated aristocracy and reflects in large part its values.[17] The cleric in imperial service identified more closely with the model of the Roman statesman than with any Christian martyr, though this could change if, as in the case of Thomas Becket, the cleric's relation to the emperor cooled after his entrance into the episcopacy. But at court the educated aristocracy kept classical-humanistic, Ciceronian ideals alive, found a social context for these in service to the empire, and amalgamated them with Christian virtues. It is this amalgam of classical and Christian ideals of the active public life which is reflected in the descriptions of a court cleric and future bishop in the *vitae*.

Another consideration important for my purposes is a development within the bishop's *vita*. In Merovingian and Carolingian *vitae* the beginning chapters, describing the period prior to the cleric's promotion to church office, tend to a stereotypical idealizing of the future bishop according to monastic-ascetic ideals. In the *vitae* from the Ottonian-Salian period this is no longer true. With the exception of the earliest biographies—such as those of Brun of Cologne (d. 965; *vita* ca. 968) and Ulrich of Augsburg (d. 973; *vita* between 982 and 993)—the description of the character and activities of a future bishop becomes almost wholly secularized. The young cleric may well be praised for his *pietas* and *sanctitas*, but these virtues play almost no role in the life of the future bishop before his rise to office, as described in his *vita*. This posed a problem for the biographers of courtier bishops who became saints. The biographers of Otto of Bamberg and Thomas Becket, for instance, must show the development from a worldly court servant and administrator into saint and, in Becket's case, martyr. The biographies of these two, and of many others with similar careers, fall into two parts and represent two distinctly different types: the courtier-cleric prior to becoming bishop, and the man of the church thereafter.[18]

Bishops' *vitae* are a secularized form of Christian biography. Their style could be characterized generally as realistic; the perspective of the biographer, in contrast to that of the hagiographer, might be called objective. The classical statement of a commitment to "realistic" depiction is by Abbot Norbert of Iburg in his Life of Benno II, bishop of Osnabrück (d. 1088).[19] He rejects the method of those biographers who make saints out of their subjects, inventing tales of their miracles; instead he claims to describe the man as he actually was, not omitting his vices or exaggerating his virtues:

Nec enim imitanda hic videtur quorundam magis temeraria quam religiosa assentatio, qui in eorum, quos describunt, tantummodo laude versantur et non tam, quid egerint, attendere videntur, quam quid egisse debuerint. . . . Itaque non eum verbis sanctificare contendimus . . . sed eius vitam sine fuco . . . depromimus.

Nor does it seem appropriate here to imitate the flattering tendency of some who, impelled more by arrogance than religion, are to such an extent obsessed with the praise of those whom they describe that they seem more concerned with what they ought to have done than with what they actually did. . . . And so we will strive not to sanctify him with our words . . . but to depict his life without obfuscation.[20]

Herbord of Michelsberg, author of *Dialogue on the Life of Otto of Bamberg*, admonishes the participants in the dialogue to remain objective in describing Otto's life, "lest we should seem to have magnified things out of all proportion to the truth out of love for him."[21] Repeatedly authors of bishops' Lives avoid the reproach of flattering their subjects,[22] and though this may be a *topos* of medieval historiography,[23] it appears to have real power to guide the observation of a biographer. Adam of Bremen's famous description of the life of Adalbert of Bremen is neither the legend of a pious saint nor the idealized *vita* of a man of the church. It is the tragedy of a courtier who neglected his first duty to the church in order to pursue the vainglory of worldly fame and power at the court of King Henry IV. Part of the reason Adam attains something like "objectivity" in his portrayal of Adalbert is that he shrinks from flattering a man whom flattery had driven to ruin. What was possible in the legend of a saint—stylization of the man's youth according to models of sainthood, montage of conventional, interchangeable episodes and tales of miracles—was clearly not appropriate in the *vita* of a bishop.

Nonetheless there is an element of fictionalizing in the *vitae*, though in the descriptions of the youth and court service of the future bishop it is wholly different in nature and intent from hagiography. There is a tendency in some biographies to romanticize the early life of the bishop, that is, to stylize episodes in his youth according to models from contemporary secular fiction. We will see several examples later in this chapter. But these are fairly rare. The descriptions of the future bishop's court service project a model of the courtier-cleric that shows him an ideal embodiment of the demands and expectations of life at the royal/imperial court. It is very misleading to suppose, however, that because of the use of conventional literary elements in these descriptions they are only a collection of empty *topoi* and that no useful conclusions about contemporary court life can be drawn from them. In order to answer this objection—one which holds considerable power over the minds both of literary and cultural historians—I have drawn broadly on sources outside the genre of episcopal biography which offer a corrective to the stylizing in the *vitae*. Also, my third chapter is devoted to the large body of polemics against court clerics which views from a negative perspective the qualities and patterns of behavior seen as ideal in the *vitae*. This again corroborates the usefulness of the *vitae* as sources on the values of court servants, since writers do not polemicize against empty *topoi* and purely literary schematizations, but rather against real conditions perceived as abuses.

I have drawn for the most part on the Lives of German bishops, but the worldly clergy formed a class whose values were not limited by national boundaries. While national differences did exist in the conditions of court service and certainly impinged on the lives of courtly clerics, the ethical values of courtiers were not similarly bound. Even though there are good reasons for thinking that the native context of these ethical values was the imperial courts, their diffusion in Latin texts shows that we are justified in treating them as a common

European phenomenon. I have referred to this phenomenon elsewhere as "courtly humanism," and I will use the term in what follows to describe this international culture of educated, worldly clerics.

The Type of the Courtier-Cleric

In spite of the sense of individual character and destiny that the bishops' biographers generally evince in describing their subjects, a model of the future bishop emerges from the opening chapters of the *vitae*. There are typical characteristics and typical careers.

The following scheme can serve as a pattern for describing the person and development of a chaplain/bishop prior to his assuming church office. He is of high nobility. In the rare instance that a non-noble became chaplain/bishop (as did Gerbert of Aurillac, Anno of Cologne, and Benno II of Osnabrück), his nobility of mind, spirit, and manners is praised. His inborn potential or his promise (*indoles*) as well as his personal gifts are apparent from his earliest days: physical beauty, quickness of mind, ease of speech, and graceful manners. His parents send him to school, *litteris imbuendus, moribus instituendus*. He excels in his studies and swiftly leaves all his fellow students behind. At school he shows himself to be diligent, learned, wise, and eloquent, friendly to all men and beloved of all. He is taken into the service of a bishop and becomes head of the school, then provost. The bishop makes him his confidant and personal advisor. Various lords, secular and ecclesiastical, compete with each other for his services. The king hears of this gifted young man and makes his acquaintance, perhaps while the young cleric is on a diplomatic mission at the king's court. In the *vita* there is often a description of the young man's appearance and his character and virtues before he enters the king's service. These attributes can occasionally explain his acceptance into the royal chapel. He is tall, handsome, and well-proportioned. His character and conduct (*mores*) are praised, then his virtues: he is discreet and wise (*discretus et prudens*), farsighted, diligent, and skilled (*providus, strenuus, sollertus*), but at the same time humble, meek and gentle, patient, and pious (*humilis, mansuetus, patiens, pius*). Other personal qualities frequently mentioned are *gravitas, moderamen, affabilitas, amabilitas*. The king makes him his chaplain, perhaps over the objections of the bishop, to whom he has become indispensable. At the king's court he wins the favor of the entire court by his good manners, affability, and gentleness. He wins the special affection and favor of the king, who takes him into his confidence and seeks his advice on all matters. Then, when a bishop dies, the king casts about for a successor and hits upon our man, perhaps with the help of some miraculous urging. After initial refusals ("canonical reticence"), he is raised to the bishop's seat.

This scheme is not a prescribed or obligatory sequence of events and set of virtues. It is an attempt to consolidate some of the most common qualities and the most common experiences of a chaplain/bishop. It applies rather neatly to the youths of some of the greatest bishops from the tenth to the twelfth century: Bernward of Hildesheim, Meinwerk of Paderborn, Anno of Cologne, Benno II of Osnabrück, Otto of Bamberg, to mention only a few. What produced the unity of this scheme? Certainly not elements of a hagiographic-legendary tradition; these play almost no role in it. Elements of a literary-biographic tradition are definitely present, but these are limited almost exclusively to rhetorical schemes already known in antiquity and to elements borrowed from historiography and biography of antiquity or early Christianity. I cannot name a single instance of a bishop's biographer citing, quoting, or even alluding to another work of the same genre composed within two hundred years of his own. Such use of works of the same genre occurred to any extent only when an author borrowed from previous works on the life of the man whose biography he was writing, and this was done, not to follow tradition, but simply to compile available pertinent sources. Even though the biographers had a sharp sense of the personality of their subjects, the actual qualities they observed cannot be granted much of a role in the above scheme, since it includes only typical characteristics. On the other hand, it is wrong to distinguish too sharply between the personal qualities of a human being and the qualities appropriate to the office he holds. The descriptions of courtier bishops are stylized according to the actual requirements and expectations of that dual position: courtier and bishop. We learn from a man's catalogue of virtues not how he "really" was but how he ought to have been, according to his social position. Furthermore, these requirements exercised an influence, not only on the men composing the biographies of courtier bishops, but also—and in the first place—on men aspiring to the bishopric. It is this factor, I believe, that accounts foremost for the unity of the above scheme: it reflects the actual stages in the career of a typical courtier bishop; it reflects the actual qualities appropriate to the position. The type of the medieval courtier and the prototype of medieval courtesy originated in the requirements of an office. In my commentary on the scheme, I single out qualities and events that are illustrative of this assertion. At this point I am presenting conceptions and *topoi* of description as if they had no history. In a later chapter I will return to them in a different context and attempt to set them more clearly within a tradition.

EPISCOPAL BEAUTY

An impressive appearance was all but a requirement for a bishop.[24] It is a commonplace in the *vitae*. Here are some of the epithets: Adalbero II of Metz (d. 1005): "corpore plus cunctis sui temporis venustus, statura decorus, forma elegans, oculis amantissimus"; Gunther of Bamberg (d. 1065): "vir tam corporis elegantia quam animi sapientia conspicuus." Lampert of Hersfeld reports that this same bishop so far surpassed other mortals in "formae elegantia ac tocius corporis integritate" that in Jerusalem great crowds gathered around him wherever he went in order to marvel at his beauty.[25] Anno of Cologne (d. 1075): "Erat . . . preter virtutes animi et morum gloriam corporis quoque bonis ornatissimus, statura procerus, vultu decorus" (Lampert, *Annales*, p. 328 [1075]). Norbert of Xanten, archbishop of Magdeburg (d. 1134): "forma et habilitate corporis beneficio naturae gaudens"; Philip of Heinsberg (d. 1191): "corpore pulcherrimus."[26] The biographer of Ulrich of Augsburg points to Ulrich's impressive appearance as a factor in the two major steps in his rise to the bishop's seat: he is accepted into the service of Bishop Adalbero of Augsburg "propter nobilitatem parentum et bonam eius indolem et formositatem"; and the king (Henry I) accepts the nomination of Ulrich as bishop, "intuens herilitatem staturae illius, et comperiens doctrinae suae scientiam."[27] Certainly physical beauty will be attributed to monks and rulers, but it was not in any sense regarded as a qualification for either of those states. It could be regarded as a qualification for a bishop. Ugliness or puniness could be raised as an objection against a candidate. The election of Bardo, formerly abbot of Hersfeld, to archbishop of Mainz in 1031 was opposed by "evil and envious men" who, says his biographer, scorned his monkish background and "disgusting appearance."[28] Hiltdolf of Cologne (d. 1078), who must be numbered among the most wretched and inglorious bishops of the earlier Middle Ages, stood up badly in comparison with his mighty predecessor Anno ("statura procerus, vultu venerandus"). When Henry IV proposed Hiltdolf as archbishop, people and clergy rejected him as "homo statura pusillus, vultu despicabilis, genere obscurus," possessing neither virtues of body nor virtues of mind appropriate for a bishop (Lampert, *Annales*, p. 342 [1076]). His lack of *statura* became a legend. He is said to have cut off the end of Anno's crozier in order to accommodate it to his own size. Anno appeared in a dream and drove him from the bed he had occupied.[29] Physical beauty and stature were considered desirable qualities in a man of the world. The parents of Adalbert of Prague decide on a worldly career for him "prae nimia pulchritudine" (MGH, SS 4:582, ll. 14–15). They appear as such in the earliest tract prescribing the qualities of court servants and royal advisors, Hincmar's *De ordine palatii*. A court minister, Hincmar writes, should be "nobili corde et corpore" (chap. 4, p. 66).

EDUCATION

The education of a courtier bishop is a rich topic. The *vitae* are a mine of information on the history of education in the Middle Ages and on the development of the cathedral schools. A good education, a sharp and practiced mind, knowledge and eloquence are qualities praised in every *vita*.[30]

We noticed earlier that the emergence of the courtier bishop was preceded by shifts within the court chapel and that one of these shifts was the change from the monastery to the cathedral school as the institution for educating chaplains. This shift occurred, in Germany, as a result of the need to educate clerics in both court and imperial service. Fleckenstein has shown that the cathedral school began to loom large in the education of royal chaplains in the second half of Otto I's reign. The men of stature in the chapel after this point received their education in the cathedral schools. This development is important, since it indicates that an institutional basis existed for the cultivation of the qualities and talents that crystallized into the type of the courtier bishop. If the cathedral schools provided a preparation for court service and the office of imperial bishop, then certainly ideas must have been formed and propagated there of the qualities appropriate for those positions. Since we find a clear picture of those qualities in the *vitae*, it stands to reason that we are formulating an ideal maintained and inculcated at the cathedral schools.

The contents of such an education will occupy us at length later. For now, it is relevant to note that descriptions of education in our period regularly link letters with manners. Bernward of Hildesheim was sent to school, "literis imbuendus, moribus etiam instituendus"; Wazo of Liège, as schoolmaster, exercised the disciplines "tam morum quam litterarum."[31] Anno of Cologne applied himself at school to all things that would "sharpen his mind and ennoble his manners" ("Quicquid ad exercendum ingenium, quicquid ad nobilitandos mores"—MGH, SS 11:468, l. 8 ff.). The guidance of life and nobility of manners regularly appear as an element of clerical education in this period, and while this did not distinguish Ottonian-Salian times from Carolingian,[32] the contents of the term *mores* and notions of the proper conduct of life changed considerably.

Most important, an education was tied specifically to the preparation of a courtier bishop. Otto I summoned his brother Brun "e scolis in palatium" (*Vita Brun.*, chap. 5, *LB*, p. 186). This route into the court and bishopric was typical, and this phrase "from the schools into the palace" had the widest resonance among the clergy throughout our period; it marked the obligatory stages in the career of an aspiring imperial bishop.

MORES

Praise of a man's *mores* is an obligatory topic of medieval biography. *Mores* are learned, or learnable, qualities, acquired at school along with *litterae*, as we just observed. "Proper conduct" is a more accurate translation than "character" or "morals," though the term includes both an internal disposition to the good and the outward bearing that brings it to expression. Such formulations as *probitas morum*, *nobilitas morum*, *honestas morum*, and *boni mores* were commonplace, and in no way specific to the milieu under consideration.[33] But a formulation that has a specific and important meaning in a courtier bishop is *elegantia*, *venustas*, *gratia morum*. There is a whole complex of court manners and ideals expressed by these and other related terms, such as *suavitas morum* and *amoenitas morum*. The terms themselves have in common a shift in *mores* from the ethical to the aesthetic sphere. In this alone we might suspect the influence of the court. When manners become aestheticised, we begin to approach the artificial atmosphere of court life and etiquette, and the courtier ideal of "the self as a work of art" will not be far behind. We will study the meaning and social function of these terms here and in a later chapter in as much detail as the sources allow.

Otto of Bamberg possessed these qualities in abundance. At least each of his three biographers ascribes them to him.[34] The anonymous biographer, a monk of Prüfening, says that all the prelates of Poland "marveled at the elegance of his *mores*."[35] Ebo says that the abbess of Niedermünster placed all the affairs of the monastery in his hands, "having observed the elegance of his person and his mores" (1.3, p. 12). According to Herbord of Michelsberg, he won the favor of the "great and powerful" of Poland not only through his talents and virtues, but also with the help of his physical elegance ("suffragante sibi eciam corporis elegancia"—3.32, p. 198). It occurs very early as a quality of a court cleric. Notker of Liège, chaplain of Otto III, was, according to the brief sketch of his personality by Anselm of Liège, "very distinguished for the elegance of his manners,"[36] and praise of the quality persists well beyond our period.

It is possible to determine with some exactness the social context, the meaning, and the provenance of these terms. The last two I will reserve for a later chapter. The original social context in our period is *idoneitas*, "suitability" for service in the royal chapel. We could not hope for a more lucid illustration of this connection than the observation in the biography of Meinwerk of Paderborn that Meinwerk was judged worthy of service at the king's court because of the elegance of his manners: "Meinwercus autem, regia stirpe genitus, regio obsequio morum elegantia idoneus adiudicatur evocatusque ad palatium regius capellanus efficitur."[37] ("Now Meinwerk, born of the royal family, is judged suited for the royal service because of the elegance of his manners, and, called to the palace, he is made a royal chaplain.") Elegance, beauty, or grace of manners consistently appear as qualities which attract the admiration and wonderment of lords secular and ecclesiastical and which qualify the cleric who possesses them for court service. Bernward of Hildesheim was sought after by several lords who admired his "grace of manners": "fit . . . inter episcopum et comitem de tantae indolis iuvene religiosa concertatio, ut uterque pro morum gratia illum sibi adoptare intenderet" ("there ensues . . . an honorable contest between the bishop and the count for a youth of such great promise, so that each of them strove to win him over because of his grace of manners."—*Vita Bern.*, chap. 3, *LB*, p. 278). The earliest occurrences of the term in the context of entry to the royal chapel are in Germany, but it occurs in France as well. Marbod of Rennes relates in his *Vita Licinii* (written before 1096) that in his youth Licinius (bishop of Angers, d. ca. 610) left school to seek service at the court of King Clotarius, who willingly received him "because of his close family ties, his dignified and excellent appearance and his elegant manners."[38] This passage brings us close to a sharp focus on the determining factors for entry to the court: nobility (or blood relations with the king), impressive appearance, and "beauty or elegance of manners." This last quality endears a cleric to the ruler and bespeaks promise of a rise to high office. The author of the *vita* of Altmann of Passau (written between 1130 and 1140) describes Hartmann, Abbot of Göttweig:

Erat enim summo religionis studio deditus, prudentia tam saeculari quam spirituali eximie praeditus, copiosa disertus eloquentia, morum exuberans elegantia. Unde principibus totius regni erat acceptissimus, et ipsi regi Heinrico V familiarissimus, qui et eum in archiepiscopatu Iuvavensi sublimare disposuit.

He was devoted to the highest study of religion, exceptionally gifted with wisdom in matters secular and spiritual, articulate and eloquent, abounding in elegance of manners. For this reason he was highly sought after by the princes of the realm and in fact enjoyed high favor with King Henry V, who also intended to raise him to the archbishopric of Salzburg.[39]

Agnes of Poitou, wife of Henry III, sought Ulrich of Zell for her personal chaplain "because of the harmonious suaveness of his delectable manners": "famulum Christi speciali dilexit affectione. Illius etenim delectabilium morum conventa suavitate, suis eum obsequiis voluit adhaerere." [40] By the end of the twelfth century this quality was cultivated by courtiers in general, clerical and lay, as a criterion of acceptability in royal service. A passage in the *Gesta Danorum* of Saxo Grammaticus lays out clearly the complex of entry into court service and the role of "beautiful manners" in the career of a courtier. Writing on the fringe of Europe, Saxo—chaplain of the archbishop of Lund, educated in France or Germany or both—was familiar with the language and customs of the European courts. In the passage in question, written probably in the last decade of the twelfth century, he describes the early tribulations of Iarmericus (the Ostrogoth Ermanaric, in Saxo's version, son of the Danish king Sywardus). A hostage to Ismarus, king of the Slavs, Iarmericus is released from prison to become a farm laborer. Here he distinguishes himself for administrative ability and becomes master of the king's slaves. He is then taken into the close circle of the king's retainers:

Ubi cum se *iuxta aulicorum ritum* egregia morum amoenitate gessisset, brevi in amicorum numerum translatus primum familiaritatis locum obtinuit ac veluti quibusdam meritorum gradibus fretus ab infima sorte ad spectatum honoris fastigium concessit. . . . Grata omnibus Iarmerici indoles erat.[41]

Since in this position he bore himself with so excellent a charm of manners, *as is the custom of courtiers*, he was raised to the circle of the king's friends and swiftly obtained the highest degree of favor, and as if borne on by successive degrees of merit he passed from the lowest state to the pinnacle of esteem and honor. . . . This promising youth Iarmeric was pleasing to all.

Here the central role of "charm of manners" in a courtier's career is quite evident. It is represented as a quality or mode of behavior customarily cultivated by courtiers. This is so in harmony with the testimony of other texts on *elegantia morum* that we can accept Saxo as a reliable witness and conclude that charm, beauty, and elegance of manners are qualities that endear courtiers to lords, qualify them for service at court, and propel them into high favor and influence at court.

VIRTUES

The list of virtues that characterized future bishops in royal service is long and varied. The biographers were keen observers and had a view of the strengths and weaknesses of their subjects that was generally unclouded by the urge to sanctify them. Still, it is possible to filter out some characteristics, relying on frequency and confirmation from nonbiographical sources, which clearly constituted requisite or desirable qualities in royal, clerical administrators.

The virtues fall into three categories: (1) Religiosity: *pietas* or *sanctitas, studio religionis deditus*. These occur in bishops' catalogues of virtues, but the biographers rarely report incidents that illustrate them. (2) Virtues connected with the exercise of administrative duties: *discretione providus, auctoritate gravis, acumen ingenii, strenuitas, diligentia, moderamen, facundia, eloquentia, sollertas*, and *astutia*. (3) Personal qualities: *gravitas, compassio, moderamen, mansuetudo, humilitas, probitas, patientia, amabilitas*, and *affabilitas*. In general, the qualities of the courtier bishop produce an odd blend of virtues from the active and contemplative life: authority and humility, zealousness and compassion, gravity and affability. The biographer of Meinwerk of Paderborn framed Meinwerk's catalogue of virtues with precisely this counterpoint of balancing virtues in mind. According to the biographer, Meinwerk tempered his gravity with affability; he was

discretione providus, actione precipuus, moribus approbatus, virtute perfectus, humilitate communis, compassione singularis, mansuetudine lenis, auctoritate gravis, patientia amabilis, vindicta pro zelo iusticie terribilis. (*Vita Meinwerci*, chap. 5, p. 8)

The passage should be translated with the adversatives that are implied in the original: he was "foresighted in judgment" and at the same time "a master of action"; humble, compassionate and gentle, and yet "grave in his authority"; "amiable in his patience," but "terrible in his zeal for exacting just vengeance." Here virtues from the Benedictine rule are combined with qualities appropriate to men in state service. In the *geistlicher Fürst* we encounter an ideal of understated human greatness for which this age was indebted above all to the Ciceronian ideal of the statesman. The mighty Heribert of Cologne "protested his inferiority, whereas he was superior to all men" ("superior cunctis inferiorem se aliis protestans"). Conrad of Constance pursued humility the more eagerly the more exalted his position: "quanto magnus sit, eo magis sectetur humilitatem."[42] Brun of Cologne "though at the highest pinnacle of nobility was humble and

gentle" ("in maximo nobilitatis fastu humilis et mansuetus erat"—
Vita Brun., chap. 11, *LB*, p. 194). Ulrich of Zell humbled himself the
more deeply the higher he was raised above others: "tantum in se est
humiliatus, quantum super alios exaltatus" (MGH, SS 12:255, ll. 21–
22). Variations on this formula recur like leitmotifs in the *vitae*; it
clearly formulates a central characteristic of the courtier bishop. We
are probably right in seeing in these formulations an aristocratic ideal
of restraint and deference inspired above all by Cicero, *De officiis* 1. 26:
those are right who urge that "quanto superiores simus, tanto nos
geramus summissius." But there is a danger of underestimating the
intermingling of Christian influences with the classical. Ecclesiasticus
3:20 gives the advice, "Quanto maior es, humilia te in omnibus."
Nevertheless, patterns of behavior are not generated by classical or
biblical allusions alone apart from a social context in which the virtue
lives and functions.

Like human beings, virtues adapt to the circumstances into which
they are placed. Affability in the context of pastoral care and the
bishop's love for his congregation is one thing; as a virtue that governs
the relations of a court cleric to the ruler, it is something quite different. What constitutes the originality in the type of the court cleric is
neither the accession of individual virtues nor the combination of traditional ones, but rather it is the transformation that virtues traditional in the office of bishop undergo when these are placed in the
context of court service.[43] Although many of the virtues mentioned
above deserve commentary, I will concentrate on three which illustrate especially clearly this transformation produced by the circumstances of court life and which open to view patterns of behavior typical at a ruler's court.

Mansuetudo

Mansuetudo is gentleness of spirit, a placid, benevolent passivity
shown to friends and enemies alike. Associated virtues are *humilitas*,
patientia, and *modestia*. The *vir mansuetus* suffers abuse without murmuring; he knows no anger or resentment. Lampert of Hersfeld can
praise Bishop Gunther of Bamberg for meekly tolerating insults from
his own servants (*Annales*, p. 104 [1065]). It sounds like saintly long-
suffering and Christian self-denial. But again, probably the first line
of influence is antiquity. Cicero had held up Ulysses as a paragon of
affability for tolerating insults from his servants to achieve his ultimate ends (*De officiis* 1. 113). John of Salisbury devotes a long chapter
of his *Policraticus* (3. 14) to praise of this quality. He gives many examples of ancient statesmen, philosophers, and emperors suffering

abuse and insult patiently. There are no examples from the Bible or
Christian hagiography. This is not to say that this pattern of behavior
had no place in the Christian life. But in the context of state service
and of virtues appropriate to men in the highest state office, it is important to recognize the very distinct difference between Christian
self-denial and aristocratic deference. The former is based on the individual's conviction of his true wretchedness; the latter on the individual's sensitive awareness of his own greatness. Also we must not
imagine that Cicero's formulation of aristocratic deference somehow
generated this kind of behavior in the medieval courtier. Deference is
a constant of aristocratic society. Marcel Proust observed it in the
French nobles of his time and described it in terms that would not be
out of place applied to a medieval courtier:

there was still at this period between any smart and wealthy man of that section of the nobility [namely, the highest] and any smart and wealthy man of
the world of finance or "big business" a strongly marked difference. Where
one of the latter would have thought he was giving proof of his exclusiveness
by adopting a sharp, haughty tone in speaking to an inferior, the great gentleman, affable, pleasant, smiling, had the air of considering, *practising an affectation of humility and patience*, a pretence of being just one of the audience, *as
a privilege of his good breeding.*[44]

Certainly for the Middle Ages, Christian humility will have been a
nurturing and legitimizing factor, if not an originating one.

   Mansuetudo is anything but a heroic virtue in the conventional
sense. It can form a contrasting pair with the warlike spirit of the ruler
or knight. Otto of Freising gives a long description of Rainald of
Dassel and Count Palatine Otto of Wittelsbach as imperial legates of
Barbarossa in Italy. After a long list of qualities that the two have in
common, he distinguishes them by opposing Otto's "gladii severitas"
to the *mansuetudo* appropriate to Rainald as a cleric: "prope moribus
equales, preter quod uni ex officio et ordine clericali necessaria inerat
mansuetudo et misericordia, alteri . . . gladii severitas dignitatem ad-
diderat."[45] But it was a ruler's virtue in antiquity and the Middle
Ages.[46] The development in ethics which marks the civilizing of Europe perhaps more clearly than any other is the gradual filtering of
this virtue through the ranks of the lay nobility. *Mansuetudo* is the
civic virtue par excellence. Its opposite vices, wrathfulness and
vengefulness, entangle societies and social groups in destructive net-
works of conflict and make impossible the peace and tolerance necessary for civilized interaction. *Mansuetudo* is one of the dominant
themes of medieval ethical writings: be slow to anger, tolerate wrongs
for the sake of a more distant goal, do not seek revenge.[47] Gottfried

von Strassburg made the opening episode of his *Tristan* into a mirror of this virtue, showing how the father of the hero is brought low because of his inability to accept wrongs and to compromise with the men around him (cf. *Tristan* 269 ff.). The relevance of such preaching to a hot-headed, ungovernable chivalric class is evident. How much more relevant and necessary this virtue is to the tight inner circle of advisors and ministers to a king. Here a group of ambitious, talented, proud men is thrown together, in direct competition with each other for favor. Always in this situation, open conflict is proscribed.[48]

"Gentleness of spirit" had a particular role to play in making self-assertion possible in these circumstances. We might say that at court it represented a strategy of self-assertion. We have a lucid example of this in an incident from Walter Daniel's Life of Ailred of Rievaulx.[49] The famous Cistercian was in service at the court of King David of Scotland from his fourteenth to his twenty-fourth years (1124–33). He became steward of the royal court, a personal advisor to the king, and was placed in charge of the business affairs, internal and external, of the court. The king planned to procure a bishopric for him, but in 1133, Ailred entered the Cistercian monastery of Rievaulx, where he later became abbot. His biographer describes him with formulae common in the *vitae* of courtier bishops, though he injects monastic elements that are foreign to the German *vitae* (e.g., Ailred falls into a mystical ecstasy while serving at the king's table). The king loves him ("Rex vehementer amabat eum"; "amore complexus est"—chap. 2, p. 2), and places many officials under his authority. He becomes "as it were a second lord, an alternate prince" (ibid.). Ailred pleases all men in all things. He knows no rancor or resentment against any man, and though in a position to do harm to many, he does good to all. Such an abundance of affability and benevolence (*benignitas*) meets in him that no abuse, no slander can provoke him to anger or revenge. He is loved by all, except that he has a particularly unpleasant enemy, a certain "thick-skinned and stiff-necked knight, blunthearted and utterly untameable" ("miles durus et rigidus valde stolidique cordis et penitus indomabilis"). This knight hates and envies Ailred because he is loved by the king and by all the court. He begins to work secretly against him, telling "envious words and idle tales of detraction," but is ignored. Finally his anger breaks out in public, and he reviles Ailred openly before the entire court, uttering imprecations which the biographer shrinks from relating. To the knight's charge that Ailred is unworthy to enjoy such intimacy and esteem from the king, Ailred responds, composedly and patiently, *mansuetissima elocucione*, "You say well, excellent knight, and everything you say is true; for, I am sure, you hate lying and love me. Who indeed is worthy to fight for King

David, or to serve him as he should be served? I know only too well, and hold myself in deep displeasure, that I am a sinner, and have failed much in my service." Ailred's superior bearing and gentle eloquence win the affection and trust of the king even more, and he begins to place important business in his hands. But also he wins over the knight, who broods long over his own humiliation and Ailred's victory. In the end they become firm friends (see chap. 3, p. 5 ff.).

The incident is of course highly embroidered. The stance of suffering contumely to turn it back on the offender may well be adapted from Cicero's *De amicitia* (21.77), which certainly Ailred and presumably his biographer knew well. But that a knight is assigned the role of boorish slanderer is significant both in the sociology of court life in the twelfth century and in the context of the cleric's biography.[50] In this scene the Christian/classical virtues of *mansuetudo, patientia* and *humilitas,* borne by *eloquentia,* are transformed into weapons of the active life, instruments for asserting a superior form of humanity over the rough-cut warrior boorishness of the knight. The irony of the pointed comments ("you hate lying and love me") shows that the stance of humble self-denial is a calculated one. In the intrigue-filled atmosphere of the court, the cleric, who could not bear arms and hence could not reach for his sword in the face of insult, had the superior weapons of intellectual suppleness and long-suffering. In this scene we can observe the contest between knight and cleric as a sociological reality. The confrontation must have been common in court life. And this same opposition produced the love debates of noble ladies in Middle Latin and Old French poetry comparing knight and cleric as lovers. In both fields of confrontation—court life and love—the cleric was normally the victor, not only because clerics depicted the contest, but because the nature of court life itself favors the stifling of conflict, not the open airing of it. In this field of battle, composure, submissiveness, irony, and a fine and gentle bearing were much more effective weapons of self-assertion than headlong assaults. The first rule of court behavior is: maintain unbroken cheerfulness, calm, and amicability. Even disputes must be resolved within the confines of this rule. This requires wit, eloquence, and the mastering of impulse, not weapons. Ailred's stance of humble self-denial makes him master of the hot-headed knight. This virtue is a close relative of the "humility" lauded by David Lloyd in the splendid and powerful Cardinal Wolsey: "To be humble to superiors is duty; to equals is courtesie; to inferiors, is nobleness; and to all, safety; it being a virtue that for all her lowliness commandeth those souls it stoops to."[51]

In the scene just discussed we also see the social circumstances that would have commended an ideal of elegant, gentle courtesy to a warrior class. It is a good illustration of the circumstances that lead to what Elias calls "Verhöflichung der Krieger." The taming of the *miles indomabilis* and his subsequent friendship with Ailred show clearly the forces that produce the knighthood's willingness to appropriate for itself a clerical ideal of gentleness, or at least to recognize its superiority.

The virtue of *mansuetudo* also functioned within a strategy of courtier self-display. In the hot-house atmosphere of court life the *curialis* faces the real dilemma of having to display the talents and skills that win him the favor of the ruler without arousing envy among his competitors.[52] The solution to this dilemma was to set up a counterpoint between the brilliance of the talents and the self-effacing humbleness with which they are put forward. This solution produced an important courtier virtue. We can observe it at three stages in its development.

1. THE CHRISTIAN VIRTUE

Baudri of Bourgeuil describes an incident in the life of Saint Hugh (archbishop of Rouen, d. 730) at the court of Charlemagne. (The anachronism is due to Baudri's uncritical rendering of his source.) One day a debate takes place at court on theological questions. Hugh sits silently and listens as others put forward their opinions. Soon the issue is clouded and the debate at an impasse. Then the others turn to Hugh and demand his response. When he finally speaks, he does so with such wisdom that all hang on his words; they marvel at his knowledge and declare that the Holy Spirit has spoken through him. The incident is reported to the emperor, and Hugh's bearing so pleases him that he begins to love him more dearly and to heap honors on him.[53] What pleased all and won the favor of the emperor was not only that Hugh possessed great wisdom but also that he concealed his understanding, great as it was, until forced to speak. It is a specific instance of the more general dialectic of greatness and humility expressed in Cicero's phrase "quanto superiores, tanto summissius." Modesty and self-denial stand here in the same relation to intellectual self-assertion as gentleness and patience do to impulsive assaults in Ailred's contest with the boorish knight. In both instances restraint wins the day and captures the ruler's favor.

2. THE RETICENT PRODIGY: CALCULATED UNDERPLAYING OF TALENTS

The stage at which the Christian virtue becomes wholly secularized is seen in the arrival at court of the young prodigy Tristan in Gottfried's version of the romance. After Tristan has struck awe into the Cornish hunting party by a dazzling display of hunting skills, he apologizes, saying that he has now done the best he was capable of; had it been in his power, he would have served them better (3045–48). When the awestruck hunters ask him who he is, he claims to be the son of a merchant, though both he and the reader are aware that he is the son of the lord of Parmenie (3096–3102). At King Mark's court, Tristan listens to the performance of a musician, the best they have at the court. He comments on the performance in a way that indicates he knows a thing or two about music. When asked by the musician whether he himself can play, Tristan replies that he once could, but now has grown so rusty that he dare not (he is only 14 years old at the time!). When he finally takes up the instrument, after much urging, he plays so skillfully that the entire court is in raptures. The king asks him whether he knows other instruments. Tristan answers no. The king presses him further. Tristan relents: he knows all sorts of instruments, but not as many as he would like to know. And besides, he has not been at it for long, only seven years or so. The instrument that he plays best, the *sambjut*, has never even been heard of in backwoods Cornwall. The court breaks into new and fervent acclaims of Tristan's almost superhuman endowments (3656 ff.). Since Mark has heard him sing songs in French, Latin, and English, he asks Tristan whether he knows other languages. Tristan replies that he knows some others "tolerably well" ("billiche wol"). Then he is addressed in the various languages known at court—Norwegian, Irish, German, Scottish, and Danish—and handles himself in each like a native. The courtiers can only gasp in admiration (see 3690–3720).

There are other examples, but the pattern is clear: in each there is a calculated underplaying of his skills, accomplishments, and social standing—all the things from which he ought to derive status and preferment at court. The result is that the awed admiration for his skill is increased in his onlookers by the secondary admiration for his nonchalance. By first concealing, then bagatellizing great talents, he magnifies them and multiplies the harvest of honor he collects from the wondering court. To bring this pattern of behavior into sharper focus, Gottfried gives us a look into King Mark's thoughts as he observes the child prodigy at work: "He marvelled that he [Tristan] could so well conceal such courtly accomplishments and such good skills of which he himself was perfectly aware":

> nu Marke der sach allez zuo
> und saz allez trahtende,
> sinen vriunt Tristanden ahtende

und wundert in des sere,
daz er so höfsche lere
und also guote liste,
dier an im selben wiste,
also verhelen kunde.

(3576–83)

Clearly it is not only the talents themselves, but the strategy within which they are presented, which captivate. Tristan's success is immediate: he becomes master huntsman, chief musician, and the king's favorite and private minstrel, and he is showered with gifts and preferment. At the same time he is beloved of all; there is no anger or resentment; he becomes, as Gottfried calls him, "a beloved courtier" ("ein lieber hoveman"—3487).

The pattern is essentially the same as in the scene from Baudri's Life of Saint Hugh, but the great difference is that the effect was calculated in Tristan's performance. What was a virtue has become a stratagem.

3. *SPREZZATURA* IN THE RENAISSANCE COURTIER

Castiglione gives us something like a theoretical pronouncement on this pattern of behavior. Count Ludovico da Canossa, the proponent of the perfect courtier in the *Libro del Cortegiano*, stipulates that the courtier must at all costs avoid affectation in the display of attainments. He can do this by practicing in all things a certain disdainful attitude toward his own accomplishments ("una certa sprezzatura"), "which conceals all artistry and makes whatever one says or does seem uncontrived and effortless. . . . grace springs especially from this, since everyone knows how difficult it is to accomplish some unusual feat perfectly, and so ease in such things excites the greatest wonder." And, "So we can truthfully say that true art is what does not seem to be art, and the most important thing is to conceal it" (1. 26, trans. Singleton, p. 43).[54] That is, the courtier treats his own best accomplishments as if they amounted to nothing, as though he had acquired the skills involved with no effort whatsoever. *Sprezzatura* aims at arousing in the observer the impression that if the courtier can perform something so difficult with such ease, he could with effort accomplish a great deal more. The stance is perfectly apparent in young Tristan's apologies for his awesome skills and his protestations of discontent with his own accomplishments. The scenes discussed from the Life of Saint Hugh and Gottfried's *Tristan* suggest that Castiglione was giving a new name to a courtier's virtue that had long since been discovered and cultivated at European courts.

Affabilitas—Amabilitas—Benignitas

There is a broad complex of virtues in the *vitae* whose focus is the amiability of the courtier. Some of the formulae are *affabilis, amabilis, omnibus carus, gratus, gratiosus, omnibus gratus.* We frequently encounter some variant of Saint Paul's *omnibus omnia factus sum,* though applied to a court cleric it rarely is the virtue of the proselytizer; *ut omnes salvos facerem* (1 Cor. 9:22). The quality of affability appears to have been obligatory in a courtier bishop. It or some variant characterizes virtually every bishop whose *vita* is considered here. Some examples: Brun of Cologne: "Arridebant ei omnia" (*LB*, p. 182); Franco of Worms (d. 999): "cunctis affabilis erat, cunctis benignus extitit" (MGH, SS 4:833, 1. 35); Adalbero II of Metz: "Omnibus omnia factus . . . universis non modo clericis et laicis. . . . Hunc omnis sexus et aetas, hunc omnis ordo et conditio . . . miro affectu mentis venerabantur ac diligebant" (MGH, SS 4:661, 1. 17 ff.); Bernward of Hildesheim: "Deo gratae et hominibus acceptae indolis gratia domno episcopo . . . omnique congregationi dignus et familiaris efficiebatur, propinquorumque dilectioni probatissimus habebatur" (*LB*, p. 276); Meinwerk of Paderborn: "omnibus carus et amabilis, aspectu et colloquio affabilis" (*Vita Mein.*, p. 6); Anno of Cologne: "cunctorum oculis gratiosus, omnium animis amabilis" (MGH, SS 11:467, ll. 22–23); Otto of Bamberg: "omnibus gratus" and "se multa opportunitate ac modestia duci aptavit et toti curie gratum fecit" (Herbord, p. 198) and "Tanta . . . industria et bonitate se . . . gessit, ut ab omnibus curialibus amaretur" (ibid., p. 202); and Rainald of Dassel: "hilaris, affabilis" (Acerbus Morena, p. 168), and "iocundus et affabilis omnibus" (MGH, SS 16:464, 1. 51).

These virtues had a role in the bishop's office and in the Christian life in general, which I will point out in a later chapter. But, again, at the courts of the Ottonian-Salian kings they took on quite a different complexion. Here affability and amiability find a broad social context and a distinct social function, but both context and function are not only foreign to the Christian significance of the virtues; they are directly contrary to it. In court life affability was connected with what was a central concern in the life of the courtier: winning and maintaining the favor of the lord and his court. It was a token of success in court life to make oneself beloved of all. This applied to laymen and clerics alike. In the *Ruodlieb*, the main character, a land-owning nobleman, impresses the king by his talents in fishing, then wins the affections of the entire court by his manners ("affectans sese cunctis"— 2. 50). The favor of the lord is the overarching concern of Castiglione's *Libro del Cortegiano*, the goal at which all the courtier's attainments aim. And it is simply a fact that the favor of the ruler is the prime mover of court life. Affability and amiability are prominent means of winning it. The biographer of Burchard of Worms tells that Burchard's brother and predecessor as bishop of Worms, Franco (d. 999), so enjoyed the trust and intimate friendship of Emperor Otto III that while still a youth he participated in the king's important councils and was privy to his secrets:

Cunctis affabilis erat, cunctis benignus extitit. . . . ab imperatore multum honoratus et carus prae aliis habitus, illius consilio. . . rem publicam in pace regebat.

He was affable to all, he was benevolent to all. . . . Greatly honored by the emperor and beloved above others, it was by his advice . . . that the emperor governed the republic in peace.[55]

It would be entirely in the spirit of this passage to translate the first phrases causally: *Because* he was affable and benevolent to all, and *because* he was loved and preferred by the emperor, the kingdom could be governed in peace with his counsel. This biographer and many others saw a direct connection between affable manners, the affection of king and court, and high position and influence. The sequence of events by which a talented courtier rose to preferment often had its beginning in his affability. The biographers have a keen eye for this sequence: a cleric, called to the court, wins the affection of all by his affability, dazzles all by his talents, is taken into the inner circle of the king's advisors, becomes his most intimate friend and counselor, finally governs all the business of the court, ruling at the emperor's side, or even in his stead. Bernward of Hildesheim "was received most benevolently [by the Empress Theophanu] and in a short time attained to the highest degree of favor with her" ("benignissime suscipitur atque in brevi summae familiaritatis locum apud illam obtinuit"—*LB*, p. 278); Meinwerk of Paderborn: "because of his impeccable conduct, both his royal majesty and the host of nobles revered him" ("cum irreprehensibiliter conversaretur, et regalis celsitudo et procerum multitudo eum reverabatur"—*Vita Mein.*, p. 8); and "Meinwerk . . . standing fully in the king's attention, passes from favored to favorite, and is made his inseparable companion in business both public and private" ("Meinwercus . . . regi . . . notissimus, de karo fit karissimus, factusque est ei in negotiis publicis et privatis comes irremotissimus"—ibid., p. 15); Anno of Cologne "once accepted into the court, . . . swiftly attained the highest place of familiarity and favor with [the king], surpassing all clerics who resided within the palace gates" ("in palacium assumptus, brevi apud eum [Henry III]

pre omnibus clericis, qui in foribus palacii excubabant, primum gratiae et familiaritatis gradum obtinuit" Lampert, *Annales,* p. 328 [1075]);
Arnold of Mainz (d. 1160): "ascending from the lowest rung to the
highest height through the whole scale of dignities, . . . adorned in
the splendor of princes, the most illustrious chancellor of the imperial
court administered his office at the emperor's side like a second emperor" ("ab extremo ungue usque ad supremum calculum per dig-
nitatum gradus ascendens . . . ut splendore indutus principum, im-
perialis aule illustrissimus cancellarius, quasi alter imperator in latere
imperatoris imperii prestaret officio").[56] In this context also we can
place that passage from Saxo telling how Iarmericus rose in a brief
space of time to the highest degree of favor with his king because of
his administrative skill and his *amoenitas morum* (above, p. 34).

It is worthwhile to recall now the historical circumstances of the
court chapel after Otto I, as I sketched them in earlier. The Ottos increasingly drew bishops from the ranks of their chaplains and chan-
cellors, building the episcopate into an important instrument of imperial politics by filling vacancies wherever possible with men strictly
loyal to the emperor. Under these circumstances it lay in the nature of
the position of court chaplain and future bishop that his relation to
the emperor or king was an extraordinarily close and personal one.
The love and trust of the emperor amounted to prerequisites for preferment at court and advancement to a bishop's seat.[57] In the *vitae* after
Otto I we no longer encounter the miraculous selection of a bishop
common in Carolingian Lives. Gone are the days when the emperor
appointed a lowly and obscure servant to a vacant seat because he
saw a marvelous light breaking from the man's body as he slept.[58]
While the Ottonian and Salian biographers no longer feel obligated to
testify to the sanctity of a courtier bishop as young man, virtually
every one attests to his affability and trustworthiness. Otto III seems
particularly to have cultivated close relations with his chaplains. Petrus Damiani tells of the cleric Tammo, brother of Bernward of Hildesheim, that he was so beloved of the emperor and on such close terms
with him that they wore the same clothes and at table ate from the
same bowl, joining their hands together when they met in the dish.[59]
The relationship of the chaplain to the king is regularly described with
the vocabulary of friendship, love, and blood relationship. Otto III
"very much loved" Burchard of Worms ("valde illum dilexit"—MGH,
SS 4:833, l. 23); Meinwerk of Paderborn showed Henry II the "flames
of his intimate love" ("flammas dilectionis intime"—*Vita Mein.*, p. 17);
Henry IV embraced Otto of Bamberg "as if he were his only son" (Ebo
1. 3, p. 12). This introduction to the vocabulary of favor in the courts
suggests that favor was won on two accounts: personal charm and

service to the emperor, affability and loyalty. The man in favor had the affection and love of the ruler. A swift rise in stature was the result.

Moderamen—Moderatio—Mensura

The king's court in the period of the investiture controversy was for a cleric the eye of the hurricane. He stood in the middle of conflicting forces in which he often found himself bound to both parties. Herbert of Bosham tells that Thomas Becket and his predecessors barred any cleric with obligations to the king from the archbishop's household, because in times of dissension such clerics were "placed between the hammer and the anvil."[60] The ability to function between hammer and anvil without being crushed was useful. Adaptability and conformity were necessities of life. This ability was the virtue of *moderamen*. It is well illustrated by Archbishop Christian of Mainz. He was chancellor to Frederick Barbarossa, and the emperor placed him in this important diocese during a time of schism. The former occupant, Conrad, later archbishop of Salzburg, had a serious falling out with the emperor, who drove him from his see. He sought refuge with the pope in Rome and won his support. The emperor was excommunicated, and the see was left without a pastor. The choice of a new archbishop fell on Christian for reasons which his catalogue of virtues will make apparent:

Instituit ergo dominum Christianum, sue quidem curie cancellarium, loco domini Conradi Bavari, virum utique mire prudencie, in rebus ambiguis et arduis subtilissimi consilii et velocissimi inventorem. Erat eciam vir mire paciencie in adversis; nulla in prosperis superbia extollebatur, vultus benignitate omnibus graciosus et aliis honestis moribus adornatus. Hunc ergo, quia tam ecclesiasticarum quam secularium personarum favorem cognovit habere, constituit episcopum Maguntinensem.[61]

He appointed the chancellor of his court, Christian, in place of Conrad of Bavaria. The former was a man of remarkable wisdom, who in hopelessly entangled situations could in a twinkling produce the most shrewd and incisive advice. He was moreover of marvelous equanimity in adversity, while prosperity could not raise him up to arrogance. For the placidity of his countenance he was beloved of all, graced with other honorable qualities. The emperor, then, appointed this man, who knew how to retain the favor of both lay and clergy, bishop of Mainz.

The schism was at length settled by the intercession of Christian, who arranged the seating of Conrad in the archbishopric of Salzburg. We find men in this class with incredible skill in reconciling opposites and weaving their way through difficult affairs. Heribert of Cologne as chancellor of Otto III accompanied the emperor to Italy, and while the emperor put down sedition in Rome by violence and the sword, Heribert remained in Ravenna, reconciling adverse forces "mansuetudine modificante et iustitia" (MGH, SS 4:742, l. 43). The whole region was pacified merely by his moderating presence ("moderamine suae conversationis"—ibid, p. 743, l. 26), and this persuaded Otto that Heribert was a fit candidate for the archbishopric of Cologne.

Probably the classic example of episcopal *moderamen* in this period is Benno II of Osnabrück. At the height of the conflict between Henry IV and Gregory VII, he left for Rome to have his episcopacy, which he had received from the hand of the king, confirmed by the pope. His biographer praises his ability to reside among the enemies of the king and yet retain the loyalty of both sides: "Tanto enim se toto illo turbine bellorum prudentiae veritatis et fidei utrobique moderatione librabat, ut in utraque semper ei parte sine suspicione et timore conversari liceret" (*Vita Benn.*, chap. 17, *LB*, p. 408). His ability to balance and reconcile conflicting parties was put to the test dramatically at the synod of Brixen in 1080, called by Henry to depose Gregory and place the bishop of Ravenna in the papacy. Here, no reconciliation was possible; only a choosing of sides. But Benno hit on an ingenious if undignified solution. On the day of the decisive discussion, he found a hollow place at the back of the altar in the church where the meeting was to take place, and he crept into this hiding place—though it was not easy to do—and covered it with a curtain hanging before the hollow. There he spent the day of deliberations, emerging only after the decisive vote had been taken. His fellow bishops were struck with wonder and amazement at the stratagem; the king, after assuring himself of Benno's future loyalty, gently reproached him, and Benno continued his moderate path, retaining the friendships of both popes and the king at the same time! (chap. 18, *LB*, p. 410 ff.).[62]

We are hard put to come to terms with this "virtue" and other qualities that permitted clerics to serve both church and state; they are difficult to reconcile with our conceptions of character and loyalty. Benno is the opposite of a Thomas Becket, who in the contest of church and state passed from the former to the latter and back again, holding strong, if shifting loyalties and leaving an implacable and powerful enemy in his wake. Benno was a cool-headed mediator, who remained loyal to irreconcilably opposed parties through the most trying and divisive crises. His brand of *moderamen* is perhaps not a heroic quality in the crude sense of simple loyalty. But there is a higher sort of heroism represented by it. It is the virtue of the peacemaker who guides turbulent affairs of state toward a calm and conciliatory end. When confrontation and rupture become inevitable, it is only consistent in a Benno of Osnabrück that he should still refuse to take sides, but rather head for shelter. Benno's feat lived on in the memory of the church at Osnabrück. In the early twelfth century an altar with a hollow back was erected there, "as if to render thanks to the insensate wood" (ibid., p. 412).

‹›

If I have treated the type of the courtier bishop as if it had no history prior to the tenth century, it is because I want to establish firmly that it is rooted in social circumstances, in the circumstances of court life in general, and in particular in the social and political circumstances of the royal chapel of the Ottonian-Salian kings. The type certainly had antecedents. Sallust described the young Jugurtha in formulae that we encounter repeatedly in the *vitae*: *decora facie, ingenio validus, omnibus carus* (*Jugurtha* 6. 1). Merovingian and Carolingian bishops were described in terms which recur in the *vitae* of their Ottonian successors. It is striking that the type has next to nothing to do with the orthodox model of the bishop as formulated by Gregory the Great in his *Regula pastoralis*.[63] The Ottonian royal chapel in its relation to the imperial church was the social matrix that brought forth an ideal type: the mighty, skillful royal advisor who is the darling of the king and court and the humble servant of all men. The cathedral schools responded to the requirements of an office by formulating an educational ideal, drawing on models in antiquity, Christian tradition, the traditions of the bishop's office, and the imperial courts. But we can say decisively that this type was not derivative in the sense of a stylized and conventional scheme with no roots in contemporary social and political life.

REPRESENTATIVE FIGURES (I):
OTTO OF BAMBERG

ANY OF the bishops whose *vitae* are cited above could serve as exemplary figures. But the ensemble of qualities and typical experiences that constitute the type of the courtier bishop is perhaps best represented in Otto of Bamberg. Otto's life is richly documented, and his court service, first with Judith, wife of Duke Wladislaw of Poland and sister of Henry IV, then with Henry IV himself, lasted fourteen years, from 1088 to 1102.[1]

Otto was born in Swabia of noble but poor parents. He was "an elegant lad" ("elegantem hunc filium"—Ebo 1. 3, p. 9). It was apparent from his earliest days that he was a "magni meriti vir" (*Vita Priefl.* 1. 1, p. 6). His elder brother, a knight, inherited his father's possessions, and Otto was sent to school. Having mastered grammar and studied the poets and philosophers, and lacking the wherewithal to continue his studies, he left Germany for Poland, where he knew there was a "dearth of literate men" (Herbord 3. 32, pp. 196–97). In Poland he soon had learned the customs and the language so well that he passed for a native (*Vita Priefl.* 1. 2, pp. 6–7). The three major biographers give widely differing versions of his early activities in Poland. Herbord tells that he took over a school for boys and was soon rich and honored, "omnibus gratus." He began to serve "great and powerful men," who favored him for his knowledge of letters and of the Polish language, for his frugal and chaste life, and also for the "elegance of his appearance" ("suffragante sibi eciam corporis elegancia"). He was well suited for diplomatic missions between "great men" (Herbord 3. 32, pp. 197–98). According to Ebo, the young Otto who was "pleasing and honorable to all for the gravity of his manners and the splendor of his modest conduct" ("morum gravitate et modesti habitus nitore cunctis acceptus et honorabilis"), went to Poland as chaplain of Judith upon her marriage to Wladislaw. He served her most faithfully and made such a name for himself that the noble and powerful men of the region positively competed to have their sons accepted into his tutelage. He became wealthy "in gold and silver."

Judith frequently sent him, laden with magnificent gifts, on missions to her brother Henry, and the authority and circumspectness with which he carried out his legations excited the admiration and wonder of the emperor (Ebo 1.1, p. 10). According to the monk of Prüfening, he taught young boys, won the love and affection of all wise men, and became so widely known that all the prelates of the land loved him sincerely, not only for his splendid eloquence, tenacious memory, sharp mind and learning, but also for the elegance of his manners. He served these lords and won high favor with them. He also won the favor of Duke Wladislaw and served him on diplomatic missions (1.3, pp. 7–8). Herbord says that Otto came to the attention of Duke Wladislaw while on such a mission. He found great favor with the duke and with his entire court. The service of such a cleric, so the duke thought, must do honor to his house (3.33, p. 198). At this point Herbord relates a romanticised version of Wladislaw's courtship of Judith. It was inspired by a brief episode in the Prüfening *vita* and is worth relating not because it is historically accurate but because it shows how romance motifs could accrete around the figure of the gifted court cleric. The first wife of the duke had died several years after Otto entered his service. After a period of mourning, Otto and the great men of the land meet together to discuss the question of a new marriage. Otto urges a match with the sister of the German emperor, a match that would bind the power and nobility of German lands to the duke in ties of friendship. Word of Otto's speech comes to the ears of the duke. He summons Otto, who tells him of the greatness of Germany and its emperor and of the beauty and nobility of the emperor's widowed sister, whom any man would be fortunate to marry. The advice is accepted by the duke and all the princes of the land, in whose estimation Otto rises greatly. Otto is chosen as head-emissary and is sent off with great pomp and circumstance to Germany. He wins the bride, and the wedding is celebrated (see Herbord 3.33, pp. 198–200). Almost certainly Herbord's model for this episode was the "bride quest" of epic poetry. Otto was not the only courtier bishop whose life and activity lent itself to a literary representation. Benno of Osnabrück had so distinguished himself in Henry III's campaign in Hungary that popular tales and songs were composed about him in the vernacular ("populares fabulae et cantilenae vulgares"—*Vita Ben.*, chap. 6, LB, p. 382). One version of the youth of Thomas Becket romanticizes the meeting of his parents, making his mother into a daughter of the emir of Palestine, whom Gilbert Becket met while being held prisoner by the emir during a crusade. They fall in love, and when he returns to England, she follows and eventually finds him, aided by the only two words of English she knows: London and Gilbert.[2] What a pity that no "court-cleric romance" was composed and that none of the "Bennoiad" has survived.

Upon the return of the wedding party to Poland, Otto becomes Judith's chaplain. He is regularly sent as an emissary between Poland and Germany, transforming the court of the emperor and that of the duke "as it were into a single republic" (Herbord 3.33, p. 200). The emperor takes note of this gifted man, heaps rewards on him, and wins him for his service, explaining to his disappointed sister that "such a cleric is necessary for the imperial court" (ibid.). Ebo depicts Judith giving in to the request of her brother reluctantly, "hardly enduring" separation from Otto and weeping copiously upon his leave taking (1.3, p. 12). At the royal court, Otto so conquered the emperor by the nobility of his bearing ("nobilitate morum") and his sincere loyalty, that the emperor embraced him as his only son, making him his private secretary and chancellor, and placing all that was precious in the palace in his charge. He also placed him in charge of the building of the cathedral at Speyer (Ebo 1.3–5, p. 12 ff.). Otto was loved and honored by all members of the court. He was dear to the greatest and the least and governed all things in the king's house "like a second Joseph" (Herbord 3.35, pp. 201–2).

At this point both Ebo and Herbord tell the anecdote of Otto and the repairing of the king's psalter. One day Henry takes Otto aside to a more private place ("secrecius eum compellans"), so says Ebo (1.6, p. 15), and asks him whether he knows the psalter well and can sing it to him. Yes, replies Otto, to the king's delight. He bids Otto sit by his side when no one else is about, and together they sing the psalms. Herbord says that whenever the king read and prayed in private, Otto was there to discuss and meditate on the texts with him. Seeing the king pleased by this, Otto continues presenting hymns, psalms, and prayers and readings from Scripture through the year. Otto is always at hand to bring the emperor his psalter, because "in his skill and shrewdness he thought he should neglect nothing which could win him the favor of his lord." We want to note this perplexing phrase and return to it later: "Nichil enim Ottonis sollercia negligendum putabat, quo sibi gratiam domini conciliare valeret" (3.34, p. 201). Otto notices that the book is torn and soiled from use. He sets about repairing it. The king one day asks for it, and Otto is at hand with the restored book. "Not this one," says the emperor, "I want my psalter." "This is it," says Otto. "This is well done, replies the king, loving him in his heart more than his words indicated" (ibid.). The king is less restrained in Ebo's version. He is "struck dumb" ("obstupefactus") by the splendor of the restoration, and when he finds out that it is Otto's work, he embraces him lovingly and calls out: "Just as you . . . have restored my psalter, replacing its old cover with a new one, so also I shall raise you to new heights of honor, replacing your pauper's clothing." From that time on he sought an opportunity to promote Otto to a bishopric (Ebo 1.6, p. 16).

‹›

In these episodes the ideal of the courtier bishop is recorded so clearly and so uncritically that the presentation is occasionally startling. An idealized picture of Otto as royal advisor and courtier emerges from all three versions. In each of the *vitae* Otto's early career stands under the sign of *captatio benevolentiae*, the winning of favor. The biographers do not focus on stages in a rise to sainthood but rather on stages in a worldly career. Otto arouses love and amazement in his lords for his elegant ways, his appearance, his skill as diplomat and administrator, and his attentive, loyal service. He is constantly in the eye of "the rich and powerful," the "greats" and the "magnates" of the land. Powerful lords and prelates court him at every stage of his career. They delight when he enters their service; they weep when he leaves it. Here he steps into the role of a figure much admired among the court clergy, the "vir expetibilis." We recall that various lords had competed for the service of Bernward of Hildesheim, drawn to him by his "grace of manners."[3] Likewise the "optimates" of Saxony had fought in honorable contention over Benno II of Osnabrück, and his fame made him "expetibilis" even to foreign lords.[4]

Ebo and Herbord also focus sharply on the degree of intimacy that Otto enjoyed with the emperor. Henry speaks with Otto in private ("remotis aliis") and makes Otto the partner of his "orationes privatae." Herbord explains Otto's actions in the episode of the book repair by stating that Otto, skilled and shrewd as he was ("Ottonis sollercia"), feels he should leave no stone unturned in winning the favor of his lord, and this consists in bringing him his book, repairing it, and taking part in his private meditations. But while the book is a psalter and the sessions are devoted to prayer, neither Herbord nor Ebo praises Otto's *pietas* and *sanctitas*. It is not pastoral care and religious instruction of the king that impress them, but rather it is Otto's skill in winning the favor of the ruler. The trivial service of repairing the book therefore can become a central episode in Otto's rise to preferment. Much more striking is the fact that Ebo depicts this episode as the explanation for Otto's rise to the bishopric. It is obviously an apocryphal explanation, suggested to Ebo by the rhetorical *translatio* of the new bound book to Otto's "renewal" and elevation. In earlier *vitae* the rise to the episcopacy is regularly motivated by miracles, or the intercession of God. Here a courtier's skill and devotion pave the way. It is significant that Ebo, a Michelsberg monk and priest, who apparently advocated the Hirsau reform,[5] can envision the rise to the bishop's office in this way. To such an extent had the model of the courtier bishop become entrenched and legitimate that it could be put forward uncritically by a monk favoring the church reform. He must have opposed the practice of clerics' serving the king in order to attain church office, but he did not bring this conviction to bear on his account of Otto's court service.

Clearly neither Ebo nor Herbord regarded it as their task to depict Otto as a pious man and future saint in their accounts of his court service. They described a gifted and highly successful courtier, even allowing glimpses of the worst side of that figure to slip into the depiction.

◇ 3 ◇

CRITICISM OF THE COURT

T O ILLUSTRATE that no sin goes unpunished, the church reformer Petrus Damiani tells the following story. A cleric of the church of Cologne is fording a river, when suddenly a man appears next to him, takes hold of the reins of his horse, and stops him. It is Saint Severin, once archbishop of Cologne, now a spirit wandering the earth. The cleric, struck dumb by the apparition, recovers sufficiently to ask what so famous a man is doing in this sorry place. "Take my hand," the saint replies, "and you will learn my story by feeling rather than by hearing." They clasp hands and proceed. But the cleric at once notices that the saint's hand is hot. The heat increases and becomes so intense that the flesh begins to melt away. Soon the cleric holds in his hand only bare bones with small pieces of flesh clinging to them. "Why is so terrible an affliction visited on a man so revered by the church?" he asks. The saint replies that only one thing was found punishable in him: that as a cleric at the king's court, he took so keen an interest in the affairs of state that he neglected chanting the liturgy at the prescribed hours. For this sin he now suffers, and he begs the cleric and his fellows to pray for him so that he can be redeemed and enter heaven (PL 145: 578–79).

The clerics who read or heard this anecdote might have accounted themselves lucky if they felt only their hands threatened by its message. Flames as hot and unrelenting threatened the souls of most of them, according to the picture drawn in the large body of writings that attack the court service of clergy. The position itself was precarious, to serve the king with the hope of attaining preferment in the church: "Ecclesiastica quippe deserunt, dum Ecclesias concupiscunt," in the terse formulation of Petrus Damiani (PL 145:463B). These clerics lived outside the church hierarchy, yet sought high positions in the church. This state of affairs had provoked criticism ever since the office of court chaplain was established.[1] The potential for conflict with the church was acute. Objections against court service by clerics were voiced, to be sure, even against the revered Brun of Cologne.[2] But these objections were muted by recognition of the legitimacy of rendering unto Caesar the things that are his. If Caesar is divinely appointed to head church and state, so much the narrower the corner into which orthodox reservations against the practice are forced. But the church reform considerably widened their field. Court service came under serious attack during the investiture controversy in the polemics of the reformers who opposed secular interference in the affairs of the church. The first independent tract directed specifically against the court clergy was Petrus Damiani's *Contra clericos aulicos*, written around 1072 (PL 145:463–72). But polemics against court clergy were not tied specifically to the reform movement, though this was a nourishing factor wherever such polemics appear throughout our period. By the middle of the twelfth century what might be called an independent satirical form had developed, the "court satire."[3] The most prolific center of such criticism was the court of Henry II of England.[4] John of Salisbury, Peter of Blois, Gerald of Wales, Nigel Wirecker, Herbert of Bosham, and Walter Map are a few of the more illustrious writers who attacked Henry's court either directly or indirectly. These writings develop a set of common topics and themes; the objects of attack are limited and consistent. By stretching the definition somewhat, one can even speak of *topoi* of court criticism. But above all these writings are a response to social realities: the writers looked first at conditions at court, then called on sources in antiquity or contemporary writings for their formulations. These writings affirm the reality and central importance in court life of those values and ideals treated in the previous chapter by representing them from the negative perspective and depicting them in the worst light. The type of the court cleric is not an idealized literary construct if we find polemics against it. As I said earlier, writers do not polemicize against literary fictions or conventional ideal schemata, but against social realities perceived as wrongs.

These writings provide a corrective to the idealizing of almost any other representations of court life in the Middle Ages. They paint a picture of the court which makes it seem little better than hell itself. It is likened to the ocean, where men suffer shipwreck, or to the infernal regions. Courtiers are likened to dogs and serpents; they are called parasites, backbiters, and flatterers, men whose only motive is ambition, whose only interest is in raising or maintaining their positions by supporting the whims of the king; they are called enviers, intriguers, and manipulators, who conceal the emptiness and malice of their minds behind a gloss of good manners and affability. The life of any court has two faces: the one is elegant, urbane, courtly; the other murderous, treacherous, swollen with stifled hatred. These texts focus unrelentingly on the latter.

A thorough study of court criticism in the twelfth century is still to be written. Uhlig's impressive work which treats the period as a way station to the later Middle Ages and Renaissance will be the indispensable foundation for such a work. But the study that brings court critical writings into focus with the testimony of romance, biography, and chronicles would have to focus more directly on the large body of writings from this period. Here I can only pick out a few motifs that bear directly on my topic.

Ambition

Gregory the Great had warned in his *Regula pastoralis* that a man who actively seeks the office of bishop is not qualified for it; shunning honor and advancement puts forward a man's qualifications for the bishopric. This warning appears not to have been a hindrance to attaining office in the imperial church. Benzo of Alba, in his panegyric to Henry IV, can speak unvarnishedly in praise of "the royal chaplains steeped in sighs for the [episcopal] ring they hope to be granted" ("regales capellani longa suspiria trahentes pro anuli beneficio").[5] But the prescript of Gregory was not forgotten. Every candidate came humbly and unwillingly to his office. "Ambition Unmasked" is a good title for an anecdote told by John of Salisbury. An ambitious monk paid the king (which king, John does not remember) a sum of money to grant him a vacant abbacy. Called before the electing body, the monk, "eliciting more avid support by a show of modesty, shunned the burden of office, refused the honor and publicly professed himself unworthy of such a position." "It is clear that you are unworthy," the king replied, "since you have already paid for the office with so great a sum of money."[6] Here modest self-denial, a quality that was seen as a virtue in our ideal courtier, is seen as an unacceptable stratagem, one under attack. And indeed, many of those virtues praised highly in our courtier bishops look quite different viewed through the negative optics of court criticism. John of Salisbury paints a scathing picture of the ruthless seekers of office, hovering vulturelike around incumbents:

Hi sunt qui crebris muneribus visitant potestates, laterales et familiares eorum sollicitant, ecclesiarum primis se commendant, applaudant omnibus et etiam magnarum domuum non modo officiales sed ciniflones rogant ut, cum locum viderint, meminerint sui. Hi sunt amici omnium et qui non se sed amicos in se desiderant promoveri. Hi sunt qui vitam scrutantur alienam, negligunt suam, infulatorum annos dinumerant, canis letantur, phisicos et genelliacos de fatis praesidentium consulunt, librant humores et quasi in statera appendunt elementa vivacium. . . . Debiles etate vel morbo concutiunt, etiam sinceros criminibus incrustant simulatis, et quasi heredipetae vacillantium cathedris insidiantur turpique interveniente commercio occupatarum sedium saepe illicitas impetrant cessiones.

These are the ones who with lavish gifts visit potentates, soliciting their ministers and familiars, commend themselves to the leaders of the Church, applaud everyone; and in great houses they ask not only the high officials, but even the hair dressers, to keep them in mind, should they see a vacant position. These are the friends of everyone, who seek not their own promotion but that of their friends through themselves. These are the ones who keep close scrutiny over the lives of others, though not over their own. They count the years of men of distinction; their hearts leap up at the sight of grey hairs; they consult with physicians and horoscope casters on the fate of those in office; they take inventory on the life fluids remaining in them, placing in the scales as it were vital elements of the living. Those frail with age or sickness they startle and shock; they smear the innocent with false crimes, and like heirs at the bed of a failing man, they lay in wait around bishops. By intervening with dubious means, they can often force retirement from occupied positions. (*Policraticus* 7.19, ed. Webb, 2:172)

We hear distinct echoes of our type in this passage: the man who applauds all and is the friend of all is cultivating *affabilitas* and *amabilitas*, making himself *omnibus carus*. A passage from Innocent III's tract *De contemptu mundi* makes even clearer that the attack on ambition has as its object qualities we observed as ideals in the preceding chapter:

Ambitiosus semper est pavidus, semper attentus, ne quid dicat vel faciat quod in oculis hominum valeat displicere, humilitatem simulat, honestatem mentitur, affabilitatem exhibet, benignitatem ostendit, sub- et obsequitur, cunctos honorat, universis inclinat, frequentat curias, visitat optimates, assurgit et amplexatur, applaudit et adulatur.

The ambitious man is always nervous, always on guard, lest he say or do something that could appear displeasing in the eyes of men. And so he dissembles humility and honesty, puts on a show of affability and benevolence, is compliant and servile, does honor to all men, bows to all, frequents court, visits princes, stands up and embraces them, praises and flatters. (2.26, PL 217:727A)

And he does all this so that men will think him suited for office, praise and approve him ("ut judicetur idoneus, ut reputetur acceptus, ut laudetur ab hominibus, et a singulis approbetur"—ibid.). These texts show us that affability, amiability, humility, and modesty were in fact the qualities by which men sought and won favor at court. Both those who accepted and worked within this system of preferment and those who looked in from the outside, disapprovingly, saw them as such.[7]

Mansuetudo has this same double face: it is a virtue and a vice at the same time, an endearing quality and a form of wheedling self-ingratiation. In a later tract the chameleon, "a naturally gentle animal," is made the symbol of the courtier and favor-seeker: [the chameleon is] "animal naturaliter mansuetum, licet quando infirmatur se esse simulet mansuetum. Eos designat qui in domibus regum sunt et . . . voluntatibus omnium se conformant."[8]

It is an effective critic who exposes as vices those very virtues professed by his enemy. In the courtier bishop at his best, these virtues of amiability, gentleness, and adaptability were forms of aristocratic deference, the submissive bearing of the man who wields great power. The eyes of the court critic rested on the lower ranks of court clerics and saw only swarms of office-seekers. Naturally the virtues appropriate to office appeared as wretched, ambitious servility. They had no eyes for the image of the Roman senator behind the facile courtier. Here we see perhaps for the first time in medieval Europe the dual optic through which court life and the figure of the courtier have since been viewed: a splendid center of urbanity and school of virtue peopled by gifted and skilled statesmen; a theater of intrigue and villainy swarming with ruthless, fawning flatterers.

Miseriae Curialium

"The miseries of courtiers" is a phrase coined by Peter of Blois (PL 207:48B). It became something like a *topos* and served a later court critic, Aeneas Silvius Piccolomini, as the title of his anti-court tract.[9] Peter of Blois spoke from experience. He had begun his court service in Palermo as the tutor of the young Prince William II, but he rose too fast to too high a position and was thrust out by the intrigues of the local courtiers, who could not tolerate an outsider in such intimacy with the prince. He sought and failed to find a position in France, again because of "envy and intrigue." In England at last he was active at the court of Henry II. Some time after leaving the court, he wrote a letter to his former colleagues warning against the dangers of the court and urging them to leave. This is his Epistle 14, one of the most important documents of court criticism in the Middle Ages.[10] He entered the court, he says, driven by a spirit of ambition, and immersed himself totally "in the waves of civil life" (43A). He knew that court life is the death of the soul, that it is damnable in a cleric to devote himself to court or to secular affairs (43B). But between his own ambition and the flattering promises of the prince, he was caught in a trap, in which he became a hardbitten conspirator against his own body and soul (43C). But then God sent a sickness to scourge him and remind him what he owed Him, and he left the court. Now he writes to the royal chaplains to convert them from court life. There they labor and toil so greatly that were they to do the same in the service of Christ, they would earn martyrdom. But these "martyrs of the world" suffer tribulation only to gain entrance to hell, a place very much like the court (44B–C). Courtiers are in danger. This is a persistent theme of the letter. Death lurks around every corner, broken limbs and sickness are the reward of enormous efforts. But for courtiers lulled in the sweet hope of rewards these things lose their sting: "They delight in ardors; what is heavy grows light, what is bitter turns sweet, and our martyrs, though they are weak, do not feel their toil, and though they are avaricious do not count the cost" (45A). He stresses particularly the danger of death. The letter ends with the solemn warning,

Vita nos fugit, mors instat, hostis insidiatur ut rapiat, et non est qui eripiat . . . quia curia plena est laqueis mortis.

Life flees from us, while death is close behind, the enemy lies in wait to snatch us away, and no one is there to free us . . . for the court is filled with the snares of death. (51B–C)

Peter could rise to heights of sermonizing eloquence on this theme. Here a passage from a poem/dialogue between an advocate and an opponent of the court life. The opponent:

> Quid te iuvat vivere
> si vis vitam perdere?
> In anime
> dispendio
> nulla est estimacio:
> si vis ut te perhennibus
> absorbeant suppliciis
> mors et inferna palus,
> confidas in principibus
> et in eorum filiis,
> in quibus non est salus.[11]

What use to you is living if you mean to throw your life away? In the expense of spirit there is no dignity. If you want to be swallowed up in lasting torment by death and the marsh of hell, then put your trust in princes and in their sons—salvation is not to be found there.

How great is the gap that separates the realities of court life from the extreme view in these turgid admonishings? It is difficult to find reliable testimonies. Clearly the court critics gave a grossly distorted picture of the evils of the court. And even if we find great numbers of them agreeing that court life is the death of body and soul, it says little about the real dangers of the court. The many stories of abominations at the court of Henry IV may throw some light on Peter's dire warnings. The king is said to have arranged the murder of anyone who spoke against him or criticized him. If he desired another man's wife or daughter, he took her and had the survivors killed. A counselor of his, Konrad, was waylaid on a mission and killed secretly. No one knew why, but it was suspected that he had slept with the king's mistress. These ugly stories come from Bruno of Merseburg's *Saxonicum bellum*[12] and must be regarded as revealing more about the author's imagination than about Henry's morals and the tenor of life at his court. They are bald attempts to discredit a political foe; their basis in reality is no doubt fairly narrow. On the other hand, Burchard of Worms set up a law for the government of the episcopal court in response to bad conditions prevailing there. In the article setting forth punishments for murder the writer complains about the *homicidia* that occur almost daily among the members of the court, who behave to each other like wild animals ("more belvino"). In one year, he writes, thirty-five servants of the church were murdered by their comrades, and the latter all but boasted of their deeds.[13]

Fear, anxiety, and suffering are the lesser miseries of courtiers which recur regularly in the anti-court polemics. Various word plays attest to the persistence of these ideas. *Curia curarum genetrix* is a common proverb.[14] The word "court" (*curia*) is derived from "blood and gore" (*cruor*). To remain there (*morari*) is to die (*mori*). Courtiers are branded in Peter of Blois' Epistle 14 as "men whose lives are lost, torturing themselves with labors, crucifying themselves with cares" ("Perditae vitae homines se laboribus torquent, cruciant curis"— 46C). Ambition is one of the causes of this suffering: "perpetuis cruciatibus affliguntur, cum sibi praeferri plurimos . . . videant" (Aen. Silv., *De mis. cur.* 9, p. 31); the snares of envy, slander, and intrigue, another. Walter Map tells of the steward of his household, a good and god-fearing man, who was crushed by the petty harrassments he suffered from other and worse members of the house. John of Salisbury reports that Thomas Becket as chancellor of Henry II frequently came to his former lord, Archbishop Theobald of Canterbury, with tears in his eyes, lamenting that the constant afflictions and treacheries to which his position exposed him had extinguished his will to live.[15]

I think it likely that the stress in these writings on the courtier's willingness to tolerate tribulations and contumely has its roots less in any objective condition of court life than in the held ideals of the courtiers themselves. This bearing was dictated by the virtues of *mansuetudo* and *patientia*. These virtues made possible the calm execution of state business. Open conflict was avoided, and the economy of honor was ignored in favor of the dogged resolve to serve well and assert oneself in circumstances where impulsive outbreaks were short-sighted and ill rewarded. Here I believe is the middle ground between the idealizing of *mansuetudo* that we encounter in the *vitae* and the carping of critics against the blind and suicidal urge of the *curialis* to tolerate the toils of the court at all costs. An incident in the reminiscences of Aeneas Silvius Piccolomini bears out this interpretation. This places us in the mid-fifteenth century, well beyond our period, but the conditions of the cleric's service at secular courts still apply; so do, it will be apparent in the following example, the ideals of gentleness and long-suffering. Aeneas served Emperor Frederick III as secretary and protonotary in his chancery. For a time the chancellorship was exercised by a Bavarian, Willhelm Tacz, who hated all Italians. He insulted Aeneas outrageously. As the lowliest of all the court servants, Aeneas was generally despised and made the butt of jokes. But "he bore everything calmly" ("aequo animo tulit omnia"). One of his fellows, a lover of the gentler muses ("mansuetiores musas") encouraged him to take heart, to persist, and he did so. At length the chancellor, Caspar Schlick, returned and bestowed his favor on Aeneas, whom he found "talented, industrious, and able to stand hard work." His stocks at court rose steadily, until he was in the position of temporarily assuming the chancellorship, and his old enemy was soon forced out. This happened, Aeneas comments, "so that all might know that meekness is easily exalted and pride still more easily brought low."[16] It was this cleric who, in the name of meekness, had borne much contumely in his court service, who later wrote a tract on the miseries of courtiers, complaining of the "unending tribulations" in the service of princes that seem to him intolerable (*De mis. cur.*, p. 26).

Intrigue

There is a grotesque inversion of values that occurs in court life. Whatever can be put down to a man's merit can also be turned to his discredit. The good is made bad and the bad becomes good. Everything allows of a negative construction, virtue included. And in a situation where all favor flows from the prince, the man who has the prince's ear is in a position to create the "truth" to his own liking and his own ends. This is the logic of the *invidus* and the *detractor*, a scourge of court life second only to the flatterer, according to the critics. The manipulation of favor to further one's own ends, that is, intrigue, was a common pastime of courtiers; to make one man fall in favor and another rise. Intrigue was a second-line means of attaining princely favor. The first was merit, virtue, and loyal service. When this first line failed the ambitious but incompetent courtier could bring low the man of merit in the hope that his own star would rise. Hence the common complaint that it was precisely the best men at court who were singled out for attack: "Ubique . . . qui illustrioribus clarescunt meritis acrius invidiae toxicato dente roduntur" (*Policraticus* 7.24, ed. Webb, 2:215).

Intrigue was also the means for settling conflict consistent with that important law of court life: maintain unbroken cheerfulness and amicability. Hence the constant warnings against false friendship at court:

> Pacis habent vultus odii secreta, venenum
> Fraudis amiciciam tenui mentitur amictu.
> Occulit immanes animos clemencia vultus.
> Pectoris asperitas, risu pretexta sereno,
> Interius fervens laqueos innodat et hamos
> curvat in insidias.[17]

The placid face conceals secret hate, the poison of deceit cloaks itself in the tender embraces of friendship. Behind the benevolent countenance lurks the soul of a monster. Masked in a serene smile, a fierceness raging within the breast lays its traps and hangs out its hooks as snares.

It is a truism of court life that all public acts and words are a mask; to reveal one's true sentiments and intentions is the act of a naive fool. Life is divided into two levels, and the man who cannot maintain this double life has no place at court. Cunning under these circumstances could be almost a positive quality, at any rate an ambivalent one. This ambivalence is indicated in the medieval vocabulary of cunning. Latin *ars* and MHG *list* share the double meaning of skill and cunning. The cleric at court was in an especially precarious position. His obligations to the church tended to loosen his sense of loyalty to the king. A whole body of writings in the tradition of *contemptus mundi* taught him distrust of the world. The temptation must have been strong to regard his presence at court as a form of pious fraud. This stance would not be inconsistent with Christ's own words: "Behold, I send you forth as sheep in the midst of wolves: be ye therefore wise as serpents, and harmless as doves" (Matt. 10:16). The biographers of Thomas Becket regularly draw on this logic to justify the saint's service as the king's chancellor. His famed worldliness places them in a predicament. One of the biographers says quite forthrightly, "It is not easy to explain how he maintained this role of twin man [or two-fold man], a man of the church and of the court" ("Exinde qualiter geminum virum gesserit, ecclesiasticum scilicet et curialem, non est facile explicare").[18] John of Salisbury describes Becket's "two-fold" ways at some length in his poem, *Entheticus de dogmate philosophorum*. He says that Thomas, having perceived the evil state of affairs at court, sought to remedy things by *ars*:

> Ut furor illorum mitescat, dissimulare
> Multa solet, simulat, quod sit et ipse furens.
> Omnibus omnia fit, specie tenus induit hostem,
> Ut paribus studiis discat amare Deum.
> Ille dolus bonus est, qui proficit utilitati . . .[19]

In order to tame their madness, he is wont to dissemble often; he feigns madness himself; he is made all things to all men; in appearance he plays the part of the enemy, so that he [i.e., the enemy] will learn to love God with a zeal equal to his own. This is a good deceit, a useful expedient . . .

Thomas' service to the king was secret service to the church. He only dissembled loyalty to Henry, the better to further the affairs of the church and win its officers to pious ways. This becomes a standard explanation for his court service. We notice a familiar phrase in the above passage: "omnibus omnia factus est." It is a term of high praise in the courtier bishop. Here of course, in the context of pious deceit, it takes on a slightly different complexion, or rather another aspect inherent in this "virtue" becomes visible. Striking as John's praise of Becket's secret service to the church is, it is outbid by some lines of Herbert of Bosham explaining Becket's role as chancellor:

O quam magna, quam admirabilis in aulae ingressu nostri juvenis condita discretione industria! O singulare in virtutibus et operibus discretionis officium! haec quippe auriga virtutum, dissimulatrix operum oculis intentionum, totius denique sapientiae et scientiae condimentum, qua plerumque non minus sapienter quam scienter dissimulatur quod agitur, et agi putatur quod non agitur. Qua etiam instruente persaepe fit ut ex caritate contra caritatem, contra legem pro lege, et contra pietatem pro pietate fiat.

Oh how greatly and admirably did our youth labor with secret discretion upon his entrance into the court! Oh performance of duty unique in its virtues and works of discretion! This charioteer of virtues, skilled at concealing from view the motivations of his deeds, in short, an ornament of all wisdom and knowledge by which often he dissembled no less wisely than knowingly what was being done, so that one thought that that was happening which was not really happening and that what was happening was not in fact happening. And by the instruction of these virtues things were done again and again contrary to charity but out of charity, against the law but for the law, contrary to piety but for the sake of piety. (*Vita Thomae*, RS 67:3:173)

Adaptability and "being all things to all men" are in themselves ambiguous qualities; a mild form of dissembling is inherent in them. Circumstances could conspire to bring out a less harmless form of dissembling from this same matrix of idealism. Here then is the negative side of that most prevalent complex of virtues in the system of values of a courtier bishop: affability, amiability, and adaptability. They made for civilized, charming and sophisticated conduct of social life, and they could on occasion be the mask for deception, now pious, now impious.

"Leave the Court"

In Lucan's *Pharsalia*, Pompey seeks refuge and a place to reconsolidate his fortunes after his terrible defeat in the civil war. His fleet approaches Egypt, and when the news of its imminent arrival reaches the court of the young King Ptolemy, he takes counsel on how to receive this guest. One advisor, an expert in evil and tyrannical ways, urges him to forget all bonds of loyalty, all obligations that tie him to Pompey, and to refuse aid to a man whom fortune has abandoned. Kings weaken their power, he argues, when they give ear to considerations of law, justice, and humanity. "Leave the court if you wish to remain virtuous" ("Exeat aula,/Qui volt esse pius"—8.493–94). The saying became proverbial in medieval ethical writings, and it abounds in the anti-court polemics.[20] Of course the medieval writers paid no attention to the context from which the saying was lifted. For them it was not cynical advice appropriate to a malevolent, unscrupulous counselor, but rather sound good sense which gave a pithy formulation and the authority of antiquity to a sentiment regularly preached by the Church. State service cannot have appeared wicked by nature to a Roman author or statesman; leaving cannot have been regarded as an act of piety. It was the duty of a citizen; the ardors, trials, and treacheries of state service were to be faced with the virtues of *fortitudo* and *constantia*. Indeed public life was seen as producing these virtues. Plutarch points out that ambition and contention were prescribed in the Spartan constitution as spurs to virtue; even more, that strife in public affairs is a cosmic principle:

The natural philosophers are of the opinion that, if strife and discord should be banished from the universe, the heavenly bodies would stand still, and all generation and motion would cease in consequence of the general harmony.[21]

So high a value could be placed on these forces which were to be viewed by medieval churchmen as the sum of worldly evil and skulduggery.

Lucan's "exeat aula" was read straight by the authors of anti-court polemics.[22] Herbert of Bosham warns of court life in his biography of Becket,

Exeat ergo aula necesse est qui hujus serpentis aulici virus metuit, qui tox-icum fugit. Quia si forte non pungit ipse, ab alio tamen punctus inficitur; et eo quidem periculosius quo latentius, quo ignoratur quis punxerit. (RS 67:3:177)

Anyone who fears the venom of the court serpents and who flees their poison must leave the court, since if he himself shrinks from striking, he will be stung and infected by another's bite. The more secret, the more concealed the serpent's identity, the more dangerous his sting.

"Leave the court" became the proper, legitimate stance for the cleric serving the king. And the misunderstood or misapplied dictum of Lu-can was often transposed into action. Archbishop Conrad of Salz-burg, for example, was, in his youth, a chaplain at the court of Henry IV. But when he saw the conditions at the court, "barren of all human and divine decency, full of filth and turpitude," he began to criticize the emperor and urge him to improve his life. The women of the court, beautiful and high-born abbesses and nuns, held the highest favor, and ecclesiastical offices were filled at their pleasure. Conrad's complaints inflamed the king against him; he became the object of se-cret intrigues and finally left the court.[23] Walter Map's steward, re-ferred to above, exemplifies this pattern. He complained to his lord that the harrassments of the court had surpassed his power to resist, and he left his service with the words, "I cannot by myself prevail against all of them. I would prefer to place all things into your hands than to be tormented by these constant squabbles. Farewell!" ("Non possum ad omnes solus; malo vobis omnia resignare quam his dis-trahi rixis; vale"—*De nug. cur.*, p. 10). Gerald of Wales included a large dossier of texts warning against the court in the prologue to *De principis instructione.* He had himself been lured to the court of Henry II by vain and empty promises. Once there, he found that his Welsh origin made him the butt of ridicule, and, the promises of the king proving empty, he finally left the court, inveighing against its "fallacias decipulas et dolos" (Prol., RS 21:8:lix).

In short, a whole apparatus of social forces worked to dissuade the cleric from court service, and these found support in classical and Christian texts against the service of princes.

‹›

It would be quite against my intentions if this chapter were seen as unmasking or debunking the idealism of the bishops' *vitae*, confront-ing the "ideals" of the former with the "reality" of the latter. The major works of court criticism were written for reasons that were often not admirable. Their authors were either forced or driven from the court or otherwise frustrated when they failed to attain their ambitions. John of Salisbury, for example, wrote the *Policraticus* in exile. The intriguing Arnulf of Lisieux had apparently denounced him to the king; he fell from favor and was forced to leave. Peter of Blois bounced from one court to the next and ended his career ungloriously as subdeacon at Bath. Gerald of Wales retired to a life of study, driven out by the envy of Henry's courtiers. Uhlig gives many examples of this same constellation and concludes, "Grundsätzlich ist zunächst persönliches Ressentiment als Triebfeder anti-höfischer Äusserungen zu veranschlagen" (*Hofkritik*, p. 175). Hence these writers are highly suspect as witnesses to the realities of court life. The complaints of disgruntled failures castigating the lowest abuses and the worst men have no more claim to representing reality than do the idealized pictures drawn by the biographers of bishops.

The other main motivation for composing anti-court tracts in the eleventh and twelfth centuries was advocacy of the church reform and the Gregorian party against Henry IV. This was the motivation of Petrus Damiani and the biographer of Conrad of Salzburg. Ecclesiastical and political considerations worked together to produce all those unsavory stories of Henry and his court in Bruno of Merseburg's *Saxon War*. Bruno's belief in his cause lifted all barriers that hold an author to the mere truth and permitted him to put down salacious fabrications to discredit a political enemy. This kind of writing is closely related to the detraction and slander often attacked by court critics.

Court life was dangerous and held many temptations. This does not distinguish it from public life in any political system. Power and favor flowed from a single person. This made the dangers more acute, the incentives to intrigue more intense, and the fall from favor absolute. The dangers of court life may themselves have been a stimulus to the formation of an ethic of public service, a set of ideals to guide the lives of the clerics who chose to sail those perilous waters.

In a sense, Herbord and Ebo, as biographers of Otto of Bamberg, were better witnesses to court life and the role of the courtier than were John of Salisbury and the court critics, who held sharp biases against the court and its head. It is best to say that these two different kinds of sources are complementary distortions of court life, the one representing it at its best, the other at its worst.

REPRESENTATIVE FIGURES (II):
ADALBERT OF BREMEN

I N A BISHOP'S biography a certain critical stance is practically obligatory. The writer nods his head toward the bishop's failings, and in this way he bears witness to the errors a man entangled in worldly business is inevitably heir to. But the tone generally is panegyric; the author marvels at the good in his subject, and anything low or corrupt laid to his charge is discreetly filtered out or put down as the envious slander spread by the enemies that a man in high position is bound to make. A work remarkable for releasing itself from this conventional tone of praise is Adam of Bremen's history of the Church of Hamburg-Bremen, or rather that part of it devoted to Archbishop Adalbert, whose administration lasted from 1043 to 1072. Adam himself regarded the telling of Adalbert's life as a perplexing undertaking. He begs the indulgence of his readers if in the telling of so manifold a tale of so many-sided a man he has waxed prolix; the debt he owes to the truth overrides the rule of brevity.[1] He represents Adalbert as a "problematic nature," a man whose life is not governed by a harmoniously functioning economy of virtues and weaknesses. He describes Adalbert's many talents, his rise to prominence and power, and the protracted conflict between good and bad fortune that ended in the degeneration of his mind and character. It is, in short, biography in a tragic mode, and as such is one of the most remarkable pieces of writing from the Middle Ages. It is rivaled only by Abelard's autobiography for precision of psychological observation and for uncompromising revelation of the responses of the inner man to hostile circumstances.

The work has also inspired some fine commentary by modern readers.[2] What I have to add to these is a reading of the biography that makes use of some of the ideas formulated in the preceding chapters.

Adalbert is in a much more profound sense a representative figure than Otto of Bamberg. Otto appeared in his three biographies as a courtier bishop stamped from a mold, provided with a model career and a set of conventional courtier virtues as happily trimmed to his external circumstances as those of a heroine in a musical comedy. Adalbert is represented as a much more complex figure. Central to Adam's biography is conflict arising out of the archbishop's character. Far from casting a veil of idealizing over this conflict, he relentlessly exposed the psychology of character that led to the demise of his subject. It is this honesty of the biographer that could make of Adalbert a figure who suffered—of internal necessity—and succumbed to the real tensions that must have beset many a courtier bishop in the imperial church. These tensions Adam depicts with a style and sensibility tutored by a knowledge of Roman historians. In his treatment of Adalbert the perspective of the bishop's biographer enters an unlikely partnership with that of the court critic.

The *Gesta Hammaburgensis ecclesiae pontificum* is distinguished from other works of its genre only in its third book, the biography of Adalbert.[3] Adam was a writer of genius, clearly, but he unfurled it only on one occasion. The demands and expectations of genre generally sing lullabies to individual genius, coaxing it to sleep. The talent for incisive psychological analysis in historical writings slumbered comfortably from late antiquity to the Renaissance, and if Adam arose apologetically from this bed of mediocrity which the genre *Gesta pontificum* had prepared for him, it is because of the dubious fate and character of Adalbert. History and literature of course would be much poorer if all men were saints; this is obvious. The problematic in Adalbert sharpened Adam's vision and analytical powers, but his vision was also guided by other circumstances. Midway through his third book he points out that the archbishop made it a habit never to elevate men close to him to the episcopate. Adam was *magister scolarum* at the church of Bremen in the later years of Adalbert's administration, and the prelate had a special affection for Adam ("me dilexit"—chap. 64, p. 212). The position of *magister scolarum* had been a springboard to the court chapel and episcopate for many courtier bishops from the tenth century on, but not for Adam of Bremen. We have seen various examples of clerics impelled by frustrated ambition to paint a negative picture of the court and its representatives, and this may have been a factor in Adam's case. But while his depiction has much in common with that of the court critics, the general posture of the latter is absent: spiteful baring of fangs. Adam reports the tragedy of a revered prelate with compassion, impelled to castigate the circumstances that brought it about by shock and wonderment at the man's failings.

Another strong factor guiding Adam's vision is the fear of flattery; it hedged him in on one side as much as did the fear of detraction on the other:

In quo littoris accessione vix aliquem portum video inpericiae meae. Ita plena sunt omnia scopulis invidiae detractionumque asperitatibus, ut ea, quae laudaveris, adulatione carpant, quae vero delicta reprehenderis dicant fieri ex malivolentia. (Chap. 1, pp. 142–43)

Approaching this shore, I hardly see any haven for my inexperience. Caught between the crags of envy and the whirlpools of slander, what you praise is put down to flattery, while reprimands are said to be motivated by maliciousness.

And at the end of the work, as Adalbert dies alone, unprepared, still nursing illusions of worldly glory to come, Adam is tempted to embroider, perhaps by conjuring up a repenting speech and some mourners. But no, to the end he stays true to his resolve not to flatter:

Eheu quam vellem meliora scribere de tanto viro . . . Videtur . . . mihi periculosum esse, ut talis homo, qui, dum viveret, propter adulationes perditus est, ei nos scribentes aut loquentes post mortem adulari debeamus. (Chap. 64, p. 212)

How I long to write things more favorable to so great a man. . . . But it seems to me . . . precarious and improper to flatter after his death—in writing or speaking—a man who in life was driven to his ruin through flattery.

Here a conventional stance clothes a genuine sentiment. All the conventions of hagiography and panegyric tugged at him, as much as the understandable impulse of a beloved retainer to mitigate a scene so pitiful. But a real moral hesitation gave strength to the conventional posture: I shun flattery. In general it is the peculiar gift of Adam of Bremen that he fills conventional schemata and categories of judgment with life. He is not "original" in the modern sense, but the *topoi* and conventions within which he operates are imposed on a reality that is observed, experienced and, above all, felt.

Adalbert as a young man possessed qualities common to the best men in his station. He was wise, noble, handsome, eloquent, and restrained (chap. 1, p. 143). His early career took him from Halberstadt to Hamburg as chaplain to Archbishop Hermann, then back to Halberstadt as provost. Probably before his elevation to the see of Hamburg-Bremen he served in the chapel of Henry III.[4] As provost he shows himself

nimirum vir genere nobilissimus . . . ingenio acri et instructo, multarum artium suppellectile; in divinis et humanis prudentiae magnae et ad ea, quae auditu vel studio collegit, retinenda et proferenda memoriae celebris, eloquentiae singularis. (Chap. 2, p. 144)

a man of the most noble lineage . . . with a sharp and learned mind, the master of many arts and skills; his wisdom in things human and divine was immense, his memory in retaining what he had heard or read was remarkable, his eloquence in expressing them unique.

He was humble, but his humility was of a questionable nature, Adam says, in that he showed it only to those beneath him in station. To the "princes of the world" and to his peers he would not humble himself in any way. He was "so affable, so generous, so hospitable, so desirous of divine and human glory in equal measure" that he transformed Bremen into a second Rome (chap. 23, p. 167). In short, he was a mirror of the ideal bishop, even more, of the ideal human being.

But an abundance of virtues, no matter how good in themselves, produce an imbalance in the psychic economy when they are not tempered with discretion and moderation. Adalbert lacked both: "he was ignorant of moderation"; "he exceeded measure" ("ignorabat modum"; "mensuram excessit"—chap. 36, p. 180); "disdaining the golden mean of his predecessors, he scorned custom" ("floccipedens auream decessorum mediocritatem vetera contempsit"—chap. 9, p. 150). Exercised without moderation his virtues became the means of his demise, not of the sensible conduct of life. His pride in his own nobility exceeded all measure, and he sought to erect great edifices to it: "aliquid magnum vel se dignum cogitavit ubique nobilitatis suae monimentum relinquere" (ibid.). Nothing could be ordinary for Adalbert. His dress and manners and the whole atmosphere with which he surrounded himself at Bremen and Hamburg were outlandish and extravagant. He accounted himself a descendant of Otto II and Theophanu and hence had a love for the Greeks, "whom he sought also to imitate in dress and manners" (chap. 31, p. 174). Hamburg, which Adalbert loved particularly, was to be built up in pomp and splendor: "He sought to make everything grand, everything marvelous, everything glorious, in matters both divine and human" (chap. 26, p. 170). He called many clerics, selecting especially those able to please the people with their sonorous voices. The performance of Christian ritual took on forms exotic and unknown to Adam. The church became a theater projecting that image of the Old Testament God coming in "thunders and lightnings and a thick cloud" and striking the people in the camp of Moses with fear and trembling (cf. Exod. 19:16): "et propterea dicitur fumo delectatus aromatum et fulguratione luminum et tonitruis alte boantium vocum" (chap. 26, p. 170) ("for this reason he is said to have delighted in the smoke of spices, the flashing of lights, the thunderings of voices booming out on high"). The world of his diocese was made to represent the temperament of its pastor. Adalbert wanted to impress and strike amazement in the world, to inspire awe, and so these unconventional rites performed to the glory of an Old Testament God were also celebrations of Adalbert, monuments to his greatness.

He could not live like ordinary mortals. This addiction to the grand, the glorious, and the exotic, was the vice that confounded all his other virtues. If these could have been compounded harmoniously, Adam says, they would have formed a truly blessed man. But vainglory, desire for fame, and an excessive vaunting of his own greatness brought down envy and hatred on him and made all his undertakings seem motivated by self-aggrandizement. For all his prudence, he lacked any sense of the weight of the resentment accumulated in those whom his grand ways offended: "in principio introitus sui, cum esset vir superbissimus, arrogantia sua multos sibi mortales fecit contrarios" (chap. 68, p. 216) ("in the beginning of his career, being boundlessly inflated with pride, he turned many men against him by his arrogance").[5] His nobility and thirst for glory raised him above the consideration of others. It is a bent of mind that does not distinguish him from many of the feudal nobles of his age, some of his great enemies among them. But Adalbert was a bishop, not a duke or count sitting secure and self-sufficient within the walls of his castle, holding in his own hands the power to deflect all the effects of his arrogance.

Adalbert was oddly suspended between the mentality of the duke and the mentality of the bishop. But the alliance of mentalities, far from doubling his resources, had the opposite effect: it paralyzed him. The general and the courtier in him were always squabbling, and many victories were lost as a result. His incapacity to deal with the forces he called up against himself was one of his basic failings. His earliest efforts in the church were aimed at freeing it from the influence of the local Saxon dukes. Duke Bernhard of Saxony was not well disposed to him as a result. He envied and suspected Adalbert for his "nobility and wisdom" and considered him a spy sent by the king to feel out the weaknesses of the duke. All this and Adalbert's extravagant ways called down on him the implacable hate of the duke. He vowed that the archbishop would never have a happy day in his office so long as he and his sons lived. Adalbert's response was oddly timorous and reflected nothing of the nonchalance appropriate to high nobility. The threat gradually wore him down; he became a prey to fear, anger, and anxiety ("ira et metu anxius moliri [coepit]"— chap. 5, pp. 146–47). His thoughts were all bent on plotting the harm of the duke. Adalbert exhausted himself in the assertion and display of his greatness and nobility, and nothing was left for the defense of it. What a lucid illustration of this dubious investment of resources that his first act in Bremen after his confirmation is to pull down the old city wall and use its stones to extend the basilica, as if the defense wall and towers were of little use! ("quasi minus necessarium"— chap. 3, p. 145). This tearing down of a defense wall to erect a magnificent if vulnerable building is the perfect external counterpart of Adalbert's psychic expenditures: he piles all his stones into monuments for his ego, and none are left for defense. Threats are nothing to a man with weapons; but they produce fear and anxiety in a man who looks within and finds his resources gone. Adalbert is like the tyrant who melts down his cannons and guns to make bronze lions as monuments to his courage and magnificence. But when the enemy is at the gates and the arsenal is empty, fear and anxiety (and, one hopes, a dawning sense of his own stupidity) is the only intelligent response.

Adalbert, in anguish of soul, turned to the royal court for help. From then on all his efforts were concentrated on consolidating his position with the king. Only in the favor of the king could he find help and counsel. At this time the tensions were set once and for all that determined the course of his life: his efforts to free and restore his church to magnificence made him the life-long enemy of the local feudal nobles; to oppose this enmity and find an alternative route to glory, he cultivated the king's favor and threw all his efforts into the business of the royal court.

Adalbert, like Otto of Bamberg, was a master of the courtier's art, the winning of favor. He has this in common with Otto of Bamberg, and had only this one soul resided in his breast, he might have become that *vir beatus* Adam glimpsed in him smothered by vainglory and excess. We want to observe his rise to favor at court and his skill at establishing himself in the highest position of influence. He undoubtedly had served Henry III in his chapel, and had won his favor, since he was elevated to the archbishopric during his reign. But Adam's account is silent about Adalbert's early relations with the court. After provoking the enmity of the dukes, Adalbert was tireless in his efforts for the king:

Proinde visus est tantos in curia labores tolerasse, tantas ubique terrarum expeditiones sponte cum suis desudasse, ut infatigabilem eius viri constanciam miratus cesar ad omnia publicae rei consilia virum habere maluerit vel primum. (Chap. 5, p. 147)

As a result, he bore so many tasks and tribulations and toiled willingly at so many foreign expeditions to all parts with his retinue that the emperor marveled at his indefatigable constancy and favored him as the first in the counsels of the empire.

This passage is noteworthy for anticipating the vocabulary of the theme *miseriae curialium*. Peter of Blois was to marvel deprecatingly at the industry of courtiers who, in the expectation of royal largess and favor, sweat in the king's service "in labore et aerumna" (ep. 14, PL 207:44B; cf. 2 Cor. 11:27); these men, whom he calls "martyrs of the world," throw their lives away in cares and tribulations: "se laboribus torquent, cruciant curis" (46C). If the king comes to them with some mission, no matter how impossible, "at once you volunteer. You speak grand words and promise deeds yet grander" ("sponte te offers, magna dicis et majora promittis"—46D). Aeneas Silvius would caution any man seeking service at the court to first ask himself, "an tolerare labores . . . contumeliasque valeat sustinere" (*De mis. cur.* 3, p. 26).

Adalbert's "diligence" was interpreted by contemporaries as flattery of the king. Lampert of Hersfeld says that Adalbert first gained influence with the king "by frequent colloquies, by service and by flattery" (*Annales*, p. 88 [1063]), and that he later gained the regency "through conniving" ("regem callidis subreptionibus suum fecerat"—p. 134 [1072]). He insinuated himself into the king's favor, says Bruno of Merseburg, not to root out the weeds of vice with the hand of episcopal authority, but to water their seeds with flattery (chap. 5, p. 16). When he vied with Anno of Cologne for the position of favor and influence with the boy King Henry IV, Adalbert is said to have striven with all the finesse he could muster to ease out Anno and make himself the tutor of the king: "Cuius [i.e., Anno's] absentiam Adelbertus . . . aucupatus . . . omni arte circa aulicos molitur, ut regis eruditio et paedagogium sibi committeretur."[6] It is a neat illustration of the characters of the two men that the position of favor captured by Anno through kidnapping the young king was won back by Adalbert through subtle wheedling ("omni arte").

So high did Adalbert rise in favor through his tireless efforts and counsel that Henry III nominated him for pope in 1046. But in an untypical act of deference, Adalbert turned down the nomination in favor of his own candidate, Suidger of Bamberg. Adalbert became Henry's "inseparable companion and supporter in all things" ("illi individuus comes vel cooperator in omnibus"—chap. 27, p. 171). His fame and influence were at a high point. His authority with both the pope and the emperor was so great that nothing was undertaken in state affairs without his counsel (chap. 30, p. 173). Through his wisdom the course of the state was set and wars won; enemies were proud to be conquered by him; the Byzantine emperor and the French king paid homage to him. His missionary work in the North advanced successfully to the point where he could envision himself as Patriarch of the North.[7]

But far from securing him at the pinnacle of power, all Adalbert's courting and winning of the king planted the seeds of his ruin, which Adam locates squarely in his lust for favor. To satisfy this appetite he drew great crowds of followers to his retinue, most of whom Adam regarded as worthless rabble. But a teeming court was part of Adalbert's plan to win glory. Crowds of followers he deemed necessary to gain the esteem of the world. If anyone entered the king's court and found favor there, at once Adalbert sought to win him for his own retinue (see chap. 37, p. 181). He lavished money on this throng, and his diocese was "mercilessly ravished" by taxes that he levied to support his extravagances (chap. 36, p. 180). Earlier he had expended his best and most praiseworthy efforts on his church. Its interests had originally driven him to seek favor at court. Here he was capable of doing much good. But he lost sight of this goal: the church became a source of income and an instrument for cementing his position at court. This foolish neglect of priorities is a clear symptom of his moral corruption, and Adam has a decisive explanation for it:

Cuius morbi causas cum diligenter et diu perscrutarer, inveni sapientem virum ex illa, quam nimium dilexit, mundi gloria perductum ad hanc mollitiem animi. (Chap. 36, p. 180)

Pondering long and deep on the causes of this degeneracy, I have concluded that this wise man was driven to such weakness of spirit by the worldly glory which he loved beyond measure.

Another odd inversion occurs in Adalbert's relation to his own retinue. Adam brands them as parasites, hypocrites, and flatterers. There were actors, doctors, alchemists, and dream interpreters among them. With this retinue, Adalbert, stamped as a flatterer by his enemies, proved himself totally susceptible to flattery. Friends and strangers alike could coax him out of his consuming fits of anger through praise. His soothsayers told him fantastic stories—told to them by angels, they claimed—of his coming glory, the advent of a new golden age in Bremen. Further angelic whisperings had him driving all his enemies from court, becoming pope, living to a ripe old age. And Adalbert believed it all. He no longer put any faith in those who told him the truth; the few honest men remaining would have been wise to leave and preserve their integrity, Adam comments, quoting Lucan's "exeat aula" (chap. 37, p. 181). Consistent with his growing gullibility was his penchant for superstition. He searched through Scripture to find confirmation of messages brought him in dreams and signs. He consulted auspices before undertaking journeys. In later chapters Adam must defend him from the reproach of practicing magic and sorcery.

Another result of Adalbert's thirst for praise was that he gave great banquets and showed lavish hospitality, the better to gain men's favor. Presiding over these affairs, he delighted in criticizing eminent men, attacking them for avarice or foolishness or disloyalty to the king. The result was that, in absurd contradiction of his intentions, he gained the hatred of all men, great and small (chap. 39, p. 183). For the sake of worldly glory he foreswore all the virtues that had been his in the beginning.

Adalbert's morbid need for approval and praise is a consistent thread in Adam's narrative. He would spare no efforts to gain approval, and even his efforts to win the king's favor are placed in this light. Fame and glory were far more prominent motives than influence and power. And another theme of the narrative, the dukes' hatred and Adalbert's morbid reactions, is embedded in this psychological complex. He made mortal enemies of the dukes and then failed to placate them in spite of many attempts. It is as if what was denied him by the dukes had to be compensated for in the adulation of his court. Adalbert vented his rage and anxiety at their plottings through those calumnies he directed at the nobles in general: "quorum invidia, simultates et odia, itemque insidiae, obprobria et calumpniae traxerunt archiepiscopum ad omnia . . . offendicula" (chap. 40, p. 184). Ultimately the dukes' hatred drove him to insanity. The mechanism of self-affirmation became disordered in Adalbert. When approval beckoned from without he took foolish and degenerate measures to lure it, ruining his diocese and cultivating flatterers; when it was denied, he responded with anger, resentment, and vilification. In this way flattery and detraction become rampant in Bremen, spreading like a plague from its original place of infestation, the bishop's *mores*.

These two—flattery and detraction—are of course prominent categories of court criticism. It is hard to imagine that any other medieval writer could have given more depth and more precise formulation to the psychological mechanisms that underlie these phenomena. Here we see how Adam fills conventional schemes with life, deriving the man's entire story from his character, as he had promised in the beginning of the narrative.[8]

The moral of this development is perfectly clear, though it remains implicit in the events of the narrative: the man who needs and courts the favor of others ends by gaining the hatred of all. Punishment in kind is meted out to one of the central courtier virtues. To be all things to all men, to be pleasing and affable, in short the epitome of the courtier's art, ends in the opposite of its true goal when motivated by vainglory and ambition. Another keen observer and critic of court life, John of Salisbury, dissected these same psychological mechanisms, or ones closely related, in his polemics against Epicureanism in the *Policraticus*. Epicureans are men at court who want only happiness and pleasure as the ground tone of their existence (7.15, ed. Webb, 2:154). But the happy life cannot be attained through pleasure, since the pleasure-seeker requires for the realization of his goals wealth, power, and esteem. The man who seeks these things is the easy prey of hypocrites and flatterers, since he puts aside virtue and with it the means of distinguishing right from wrong. By his quest for glory he earns the wages of confusion and death ("omnia, quae militare videbantur ad gloriam, confusionis stipendium et mortis acceptura sunt"—7.22, ed. Webb, 2:203). The man who spurns the search for glory and cultivates virtue cannot be deceived by flatterers (ibid.). John's words again and again strike directly at the sort of court follower Adalbert became in Adam's story. In John's satirical "garden of epicureanism," the fourth stream is the one that nourished Adalbert's vainglory: "The fourth swells up with deception in seeking to appease its hunger for celebrity and esteem through the quest of eminence." ("Quartus ab appetitu celebritatis et reverentiae, dum eminnentiam quaerit, fallaciter intumescit"—7.16, ed. Webb, 2:342.) This ambition reaches, not its desired goal, but the opposite. The man who would wield great power finds himself a slave at the very pinnacle of worldly success; the man who courts fame and favor grows vile in the swollen pride of his vainglory: "Hinc est quod . . . potens et praesidens in summo fastigio servit . . . et famae procus et gratiae in toto tumore inanis gloriae vilescit" (7.24, ed. Webb, 2:413–14).

Adam's tale of Adalbert's "Glück und Ende," as Misch aptly calls it, can be understood within categories which the contemporary, or near contemporary depictions of court life, positive and negative, present us with: ambition, flattery, intrigue, detraction, "leave the court." The role that Adam assigns to the court in Adalbert's life has not been emphasized as it deserves. After all, it is the court of the king and Adalbert's dogged pursuit of the king's favor on which Adam squarely places the blame for Adalbert's corruption and the ruin of his diocese: "Itaque ex illo tempore nostram ecclesiam omnes calamitates oppresserunt, nostro pastore tantum curiae intento negotiis" (chap. 33, p. 176). ("And so from that time on our church was oppressed by all sorts of calamities, while our pastor was intent only on the business of the court.") No warnings could hold him away from the accursed court: "At ille parvipendens omnium voces . . . totus in curiam vehemens et in gloriam preceps ferebatur" (chap. 46, p. 190).

The *exeat aula* theme is sounded again when Adam observes that Adalbert ignored the examples of wise and great men who fled the court as if it were a form of idolatry: "Felix, inquam, si . . . infelicem curiam aut nunquam vidisset aut raro visitasset" (chap. 54, p. 199).

He considered it his duty to the church to endure the toils of the court, and even to face dangers and death ("pericula et mortem subire"—chap. 54, p. 200). And yet with the church at its lowest point—famine conspired with the depredations of the nobles and of the archbishop's retinue—still Adalbert thought only of the court: "Ita intento ad curiam pastore nostro sanctissimi vicarii eius dominicum ovile vastantes more luporum in episcopio grassati sunt" (chap. 56, p. 203). ("And so with our pastor intent on the affairs of the court, his most holy vicars prowled through the episcopate, ravaging the lord's sheepfold like wolves.") Death itself could hardly distract him from the court: "rei publicae negotia tractavit usque ad extremam exitus horam" (chap. 63, p. 211).

These passages and many others conveying the same state of affairs illustrate how Adam cast the court in the role of antagonist and wicked corrupter of his hero. The core and moral intent of Adam's narrative can be stated in the phrase "courtier's tragedy." Of course its themes are much more generally locatable in Christian tradition: the fall of pride, the dangers and treachery of vainglory. But in Adam's narrative the specific social context of these vices is the king's court.

I pointed out earlier the complex of tensions decisive in Adalbert's career: the diocese, the court, the feudal nobles. We observed his neglect of the church and his fall from standing there. This fall continued and the decline and growing disorder in the diocese became so terrible that Adam shudders to relate it (p. 190). At the same time it became increasingly evident that that cornerstone of his existence, the king's favor, was likewise not unshakeable. The master maneuverer was himself vulnerable to intrigue. Anno of Cologne and a number of bishops and high noblemen, united by a dense network of resentments against Adalbert, banded together to drive him from his favored position.[9] The conspirators met with the king in Adalbert's absence at Tribur in 1066 and demanded that the king either expel him from the court or yield the government of the empire to them. The king gave in, and Adalbert was driven from the court "as a magician and seducer" (chap. 46, p. 191). The accusation was useful for prying the favorite from his position of influence with the king. We will encounter it again. But with Adalbert it was both effective and credible.

He had only one alliance, with the king. Here his influence was absolute; he was the chief counselor and tutor of the young Henry, and he became regent of the empire, *consul* as Adam calls him. To Henry he was affable, cajoling, and avuncular,[10] the former friend and close ally of his father. If these factors consolidated his influence with the king, they also opened him to the reproach of seduction and sorcery: the king's affection for Adalbert could be made to appear as the result of spells cast by an arch-wizard. Courtiership and influence over those in power may well appear to men affected adversely by them to be a form of evil magic. Moreover, Adalbert was anything but a courtier to Anno and his allies. Anno was of low nobility. He was a stern, forceful, and unrefined politician, "a man of atrocious bent of mind," Adam calls him (chap. 33, p. 177). These qualities cannot have failed to call forth scorn in Adalbert, in so many ways his opposite. And Adalbert, after initial, hollow shows of friendship, would not have concealed from Anno his sense of superiority. At least he did not conceal it from many superior in rank to Anno. Anno can have had little understanding of the finesses of the courtier and the effects that the courtier's art could produce on a yet malleable ruler, and in his plain vision of human affairs, he may well have actually perceived the ties that bound the king to his rival as being of a suspicious, irrational origin. Moreover there was Adalbert's own bent toward superstition. Adam swears solemn oaths that the many rumors of Adalbert's practicing magic were false (chap. 62, pp. 208–9). His assurances are more fervent than the truth requires. After all, if Adalbert hearkened after prophecies and consulted auspices, he believed he could put his ear to the workings of fate, and if his ear, why not his hand?

When the dukes saw their enemy forced from his position with the king, they were not slow to press their advantage and exploit his momentary vulnerability. After an initial barrage of contumely and secret plots, Magnus, son of Duke Bernhard, gathered a troop of knights and rode into Bremen to attack the person of the archbishop. But he escaped and fled to an estate in Goslar, where he spent a wretched six months in exile and isolation, stripped of both the court and diocese, his enemies triumphing on every score.

A humiliating peace with the dukes was arranged, and Adalbert returned to Bremen. But he was often absent, for as much as two years at a time. Now the worst disorder set in. Among the populace there was reversion to paganism and open scorning of morality and the rites of the church. Adalbert prescribed stiff penalties: arrest and confiscation of goods. But in his absence greedy bailiffs exploited the situation to line their own pockets: they arrested the innocent on

scant cause and stole their goods. Adalbert himself lived "by plunder-
ing the poor and the church's goods" (chap. 56, p. 202). Murder became rampant among the clergy; all the bonds of order were dissolved; and as if nature itself conspired with social disorder, a famine
struck the city and left people dead in the streets. With many other
appalling details, Adam paints the picture of total collapse of the social and moral order. And amidst all this chaos, the now half-mad
archbishop sat in his palace revelling in the blandishments of his flatterers. The external disorder clearly mirrors the psychological dis-
orientation of the man in whose hands alone order resides.

Nonetheless Adalbert managed, by further acts of quasi-magical
courtiership and by lavish expenditures, to restore himself to his previous position at court. But to no avail. He was broken in body and
mind, and his behavior became increasingly erratic:

Siquidem mores viri, licet semper a communi mortalium habitudine dissen-
tirent, circa terminum vero inhumani intolerabilesque et alieni a se ipso videbantur. (Chap. 61, p. 207)

Although this man's behavior certainly had always been at odds with normal
human habits, toward the end it took a turn to the inhuman, intolerable and
bizarre.

Death took him unawares, while he was still intent on the business of
the court and still filled with hope for the present life. It was in his
nature to grasp for some last subterfuge and subtle intrigue to out-
maneuver this last enemy. Lampert of Hersfeld expresses his struggle
with death in just these terms. Adalbert had long since urged his doctors to apply their "most highly refined ministrations, as if by guile he
could thwart nature" ("diu per exquisitissimas medicorum operas
morti obluctatus . . . quasi naturam arte eludere posset"—*Annales*,
p. 134 [1072]). In the end he was still surrounded by mountebanks
and prophets filling his willing ears with tales of a coming golden age,
of his enemies prostrate at his feet, of long life and health. These flattering prophecies drowned out the ominous warnings of imminent
death made by a seeress who had appeared in Bremen some time before his death (chap. 63, p. 210). He died alone, and Adam perorates
on the theme of *vanitas*:[11]

O fallax humanae vitae prosperitas, o fugienda honorum ambitio! Quid tibi
nunc, o venerabilis pater Adalberte, prosunt illa, quae semper dilexisti, gloria
mundi, populorum frequentia, elatio nobilitatis? Nempe solus iaces in alto
palatio, derelictus ab omnibus tuis. Ubi sunt autem medici, adulatores et
ypocritae, qui te laudabant in desideriis animae tuae . . . ? Omnes, ut video,
socii mensae fuerunt, et recesserunt in die temptationis. (Chap. 65, p. 213)

Behold how deceptive is human felicity, how much the ambition for honors to be shunned! Worldly glory, throngs of guests and exalted nobility, these things which you loved so, what good are they to you now, o venerable father Adalbert? See how lonely you lie in your high palace, abandoned by all your court. Where now are all your doctors, your flatterers and hypocrites, who lauded the desires of your soul . . . ? All of them were your companions at table, and now, I see, they have turned away in the day of your trial.

‹›

If Adalbert of Bremen is a representative figure, then what does he represent? Certainly a flawed or dissonant or contradictory character must explain his destiny in some measure. But personal and psychological eccentricities cannot by themselves explain his historical and cultural role. Nor can the picture of him that emerges from his biography be explained in terms of inconsistencies of judgment by Adam of Bremen.[12] One must agree that Adam did not produce a unified picture. But he was in the predicament of an undergraduate writing an essay on a book that is beyond his comprehension. The categories of understanding and judgment at his disposal are not sufficient to encompass the complex work, and so he falls to summarizing the plot, dealing with various episodes on varying terms. The *diversitas* of Adalbert had just this effect on Adam.

If we judge Adalbert as a representative of that station in which he was successful and effective from beginning to end, then he was first and foremost a courtier. As an archbishop he was worse than a failure; as a feudal lord, he fought his battles mainly with intrigue, that is, with a courtier's strategy. And yet at his lowest point as pastor and prince in 1069, he was able to regain his position as chief counselor to the king, and in 1071, one year before his death, as regent of the empire: "in summa rerum gloria positus" (chap. 60, p. 206). His head was filled with thoughts of state business to the hour of his death.

In courtiership Adalbert distinguished himself from others of his station. Otto of Bamberg and Thomas Becket, for instance, both of them arch-courtiers, shuffled off that dubious coil in passing from the court to the cathedral. Both became bishops and servants of the church. But for Adalbert the period of court service never ended; there was no transition from courtier to pastor. And the church itself was merely a second-best court and kingdom for him, a stage and showplace for nobility, splendor, and magnanimity.

But it must also be observed that Adalbert was a terrible courtier, his successes with the king notwithstanding. In him we can see the results of a courtier's lack of *moderamen* and of his failure to be "all things to all men." The essence of *cortegiania* is to inspire benevolence and reconcile conflicts, to win favor by subordinating passion and desire to reason, to use that favor to guide the state and the prince according to principles of reason and the common good. When this is the goal, then the courtier is a great statesman, and courtliness represents a civilizing force working at the highest level of power. But to Adalbert the results of affability were attainable only within a limited sphere and the results of *moderamen* completely beyond his grasp. Ambition and self-interest overshadowed reason, and his government became a tyranny. Here the other side of his character stood in the way of the courtier. He was a great nobleman from a distinguished family, possessed of exuberant pride and arrogance, given to unrestricted self-assertion. The favor won by the courtier dissolved in the hate inspired by the haughty lord. In the end we judge Adalbert best if we see him as caught between two medieval *Lebensformen*: on the one hand the land-owning nobleman of the archaic period of feudal society whose values were wealth, high birth, high spirits, warrior prowess, and love of honor; on the other the courtier bishop.

For all his exoticism, there is something primitive about the figure of Adalbert of Bremen. His byzantine habits and style were surely not over-refinement and decadence. Just the opposite. His character having been shaped in an archaic stage of the civilizing process, he is thrust into a more advanced and refined stage, and he parades about in the clothes and manners appropriate to it. Civilization, like capitalist society, has its *nouveaux riches*, and the effects of civilized forms of life and the obligations they impose can be as disorienting to the newcomer as hordes of money to the fledgling entrepreneur. Adalbert's association and successful dealings with a North only recently emerging from paganism encourage me to think that here, a century or two before, he might have found a social context favorable to his dual nature. As *goði* his nobility and cunning would have complemented each other. He would have found much to admire and identify with in a figure like Snorri the priest of *Eyrbyggja Saga*. Here even the lowest of his qualities, superstition, would have been in its element, and the reproach of wizardry would have turned into something he dearly loved, praise.

THE DEFENSE OF THE COURTIER

B ALDESAR CASTIGLIONE begins the second book of his *Libro del Cortegiano* with a polemic against carping old fools who see only the evils of modern courts. The courts of their own day, these men say, were peopled by virtuous men and women who enjoyed chaste and modest pleasures. But now they see the courts filled with "envy, malevolence, corrupt manners, and a most dissolute life given over to every kind of vice" (2.2, trans. Singleton, p. 92). Castiglione answers that senility has blinded these men to the good in courts; those who have lost the ability to enjoy the pleasures of the mind and body are apt to see in the pastimes of the younger generation only dissolution. But the dissolution is in the mind of the beholder. And in like manner the erosion of their faculties produces a blind spot in their perception of the Good. Of course there are many wicked and evil men at courts, but this is a symptom of the presence of virtue. Good arises as a counterbalance to evil: "Who does not know that there would be no justice in the world if there were no wrongs? No magnanimity, if none were pusillanimous? No continence, if there were no incontinence? . . . No truth if there were no falsehood?" (ibid.). In the beginning of his fourth book, Castiglione explains the good that the ideal courtier works, the ideal goal toward which all his individual talents and skills tend: it is to win the favor of the prince to such an extent that he can speak the truth with no fear and thus use his position of trust to guide the ruler along the path of virtue and rational governing of the state. The courtier in this position teaches the prince the advantages of justice, liberality, gentleness, magnanimity, and the other virtues appropriate to a good ruler; he warns him against vice, slander, and flattery (see 4.4–5).

Castiglione is the intellectual architect of good courtiership, and in the sections just referred to he is the defender of this art against its many attackers, who were not all senile and foolish. The Middle Ages produced no comparable defense of the courtier and his role in court life. Only criticism of the court and its clerical officials could legitimately make its appearance in the authoritative form of the written word. The standard, shallow interpretation of Lucan's "exeat aula" was symptomatic of a judgment of the court so unshakeably established that court critics could anticipate little opposition to their branding courtiers as unscrupulous scoundrels, who either threw off their virtue upon entering the court, or were stripped of it in the course of their stay. The sanctioned stance for the man of virtue at court was to grin, bear it, and leave as soon as possible: "like a prisoner he tolerated the court of King Henry rather than staying there out of any love for it," says the biographer of Ulrich of Zell (MGH, SS 12:251, ll. 26–27). This statement and the description of Ulrich's court service have exemplary, orthodox character. Both Henry III and his wife, Agnes of Poitou, loved Ulrich dearly, and he instructed Agnes in the good life by example and precept. He won the love of all and was a teacher of virtue to the entire court (p. 254, l. 27 ff.). Here is the model of the courtier nearly as Castiglione envisioned him, making use of a favored position to instruct the ruler and his court in virtue. But neither of Ulrich's biographers has a good word to say about the court, nor do they take Ulrich's activities as a model of good courtiership. Just the contrary, his exemplary behavior is illustrated when he leaves the court to keep his virtue intact. Common sense would commend to the modern observer the thought that, if the center of government teems with ambitious, venal characters it might not be a bad idea to have some men of principle at the ruler's side. But conservative Christianity generally was blind to any good in court service in our period.

But men of principle did stay at court and regarded it potentially as a school of virtue and their own activities as good and, if not orthodox, at least legitimate and justifiable. They had an ethic of state service to guide them through the difficulties of court life (this is the subject of a later chapter), and they had an idealizing conception of their duties at court. In this chapter I want to reconstruct the elements of this *apologia* from the fragments of it that have survived.

Peter of Blois' heated attack on his former colleagues at Henry's court in his Epistle 14 did not go unanswered. They responded in high dudgeon defending themselves against his charges. Their letter, alas, has not survived. But it elicited a conciliatory answer from Peter, and this letter, his Epistle 150, presumably summarizes some of their main arguments (PL 207:439–42). It is one of the rare testimonies to pro-court sentiments from the period.

Peter is chastened by their anger and begs their understanding. He wrote against the court and its members during a period of illness, he says. This made all the precious things of the world appear vile, all pleasures painful. But he wrote out of love for courtiers, not hate. The life of the court is indeed fraught with dangers, and rare is the man who escapes its snares to rise to eminence. But he does not condemn this life altogether. Courtiers can do much for the good of the state and the well-being of their fellow men. They can aid the poor, advance the cause of religion, work for fairness, enlarge the church, and perform numerous acts of compassion. But they must avoid the vices of the courtier: envy, slander, venality, and vengefulness. He goes so far as to declare service of the king a sanctified activity: "Fateor quidem, quod sanctum est domino regi assistere" (440D), and he cites biblical precedents. The association of upright clerics with kings and princes is not only a tolerable but a desirable activity, for the lives of kings can be disposed to the good and to salvation when they follow the precepts of religious men and the advice of wise men. He ends this defense in a crescendo of praise for the courtier. Since antiquity men have found it laudable to find favor in the eyes of princes, he says quoting Horace: "Principibus placuisse viris non ultima laus est" (441B; cf. Horace, Ep. 1.17.35). "And so I deem the service of the king and the care of the republic not only laudable but even glorious, so long as one thinks not of oneself but is all things to all men" ("Non solum ergo laudabile, sed gloriosum reputo domino regi assistere, procurare rempublicam, sui esse immemorem, et omnium totum esse"—441C).

He sees the court service of the cleric justified in terms similar to those which Castiglione was to use: at their best they guide the state and the prince along the path of virtue. Earlier in his Epistle 14 he had cited a similar goal as the self-justification of courtiers. Asked why they follow the court knowing that it is contrary to God and salvation, they reply, white-washing their ambition, by reference to ancient examples: for the instruction and correction of kings, they say, for example, Moses was sent to Pharaoh (PL 207:46C). Here again we glimpse a fragment of a justification of court service that did not survive in any detailed formulation; here again we see that the instruction of kings is a major element of this ideal.

Peter of Blois ends his Epistle 150 responding to the anticipated bemusement of the recipients: first they heard how wretched and dangerous court life is; now how splendid it is. But even the best philosophers have contradicted themselves, he explains, and he makes himself a successor to Solomon in this respect. For our purposes it is important to note that his antagonism to court service was challenged, and that he backed away from it. This tells us something about the strength of the sanctioned view of the court. It did not have the authority of orthodoxy. The feelings of the harshest court critic were ambivalent. All court critics wrote in the lap of orthodoxy. We learn from Peter of Blois' Epistle 150 that they would have represented the court and the courtier's duties differently if they had written from the context of the court, where they would have been accountable to high-minded courtiers who possessed a conception of the value and dignity of their position. The letter also shows us that the courtiers knew how to defend themselves. Otherwise no challenge would have been issued to Peter's Epistle 14. They were tied to the court not just by ambition but also by a sense of obligation. Peter of Blois refers ironically to the chaplains of Henry's court as "professores mundi" (Ep. 14, 44C), and this can only mean, "men who commit themselves to the world."[1] Behind the sarcasm we can infer a sober reality. The formulation finds an echo in some lines from Gottfried's *Tristan*. In a polemical passage against the abuse of love among his contemporaries, Gottfried speaks of

> wir, die zer werlde haben muot,
> swie so er si boese oder guot.
> (12257–58)

We who set our mind on the world, whether this be good or evil.

Gottfried is one of our best witnesses to the courtier mentality in the twelfth and early thirteenth centuries. Here he corroborates what we inferred from Peter of Blois' term *professores mundi*, that men at court were capable of making a commitment to that life, a commitment that put aside the question of the unorthodox judgment of it ("swie so er si boese oder guot").

Aeneas Silvius Piccolomini also affords glimpses of an unwritten "courtier manifesto." Here also the context is the author's answer to a position taken by men who defend their court service. Some men, he writes, think that in serving kings they can promote the public good, serve the state, look after widows and orphans, and succor the needy and the afflicted. To these men he must respond, lest the stupider position seem the wiser. They must be ignorant of the workings of the court to hold such a high-minded view. At court men promote only their own interests; no man is capable of practicing virtues in that atmosphere (*De mis. cur.* 28, p. 51). Aeneas answers another position on which Peter of Blois is silent, one which implies a powerful and, we might say, humanistic defense of the court. He says that opposing envy, vice, and ambition at court should be left to the most courageous of men, to those who possess divine and human wisdom in the highest degree. Ordinary mortals submerge in the waves of vice. But the few who do survive and effect virtue at court earn so much the greater merit:

Durum est ambitionem fraenare, avaritiam compescere, invidiam domare, iram cohibere, luxuriam coartare, dum semper inter ista verseris. Si quis tamen sibi a Deo creditum talentum novit, vincere ut ista possit, et . . . si potest ignem ingredi, et non uri, non illum curiam sequi prohibeo; nam meritum tanto grandius assequetur, quanto periculosius militavit. (*De mis. cur.* 31, p. 54).

Hard it is to rein in ambition, suppress avarice, tame envy, stifle wrath, and cut off vice, while standing in the midst of these things. But if any man feels that his God-given talent equips him to conquer them and . . . to stand in fire without being burned, this man I will except from my prohibition of the court, since his merit is so much the greater for being wrested from great dangers.

But he quickly adds that he doubts such a man can exist. Still, here we have, indirectly transmitted, something like a breath of ancient attitudes toward state service. It is only for the strong; it builds character; it is a school of virtue. Envy and ambition are positive forces, counterbalances to virtue, to use Castiglione's term; the greater the evils of the court, the more magnificent and admirable the virtue of the men who withstand and overcome them. I find this attitude formulated in a positive sense only in one text in the Middle Ages, again Gottfried's *Tristan*. The hero, now the king's favorite, is the object of a court intrigue. King Mark's barons are threatening him and plotting against his life. (We will look at the scene in detail later.) Tristan goes to the king and asks permission to leave the court; he is no longer equal to its threats and dangers. Mark responds with a speech on the positive value of facing danger:

> ir aller niden unde ir haz
> nu so dir got, waz schadet dir daz?
> hazzen unde niden
> daz muoz der biderbe liden:
> der man der werdet al die vrist,
> die wile und er geniten ist.
> wirde unde nit diu zwei diu sint
> reht alse ein muoter unde ir kint.
> diu wirde diu birt alle zit
> und vuoret haz unde nit.
> wen gevellet ouch me hazzes an
> dan einen saeligen man?
> diu saelde ist arm unde swach,
> diu nie dekeinen haz gesach.
> (8353–66)

Now by God what harm does the envy and hate of them all do you? A good man must face hate and envy. A man increases in worth as long as he is envied. Virtue and envy are to each other like a mother to her child. Virtue incessantly gives birth to envy and nourishes it. Who is there on whom hate falls more directly than a man blessed by fortune? But bliss and fortune are contemptible when they have never faced hatred.

Commentators of *Tristan* have recognized the conventionality of this speech.[2] Its dominant theme is "envy strikes the heights," and we can find numerous parallels in contemporary sources. Very striking and out of season is the sentiment, "diu saelde ist arm unde swach,/ diu nie dekeinen haz gesach." Observers of court life were unanimously convinced that its vices consumed virtue and turned it into its opposite. Here is a voice that argues for the positive value of hate and envy, of the dangers and miseries of the court. They are the fires that test and temper virtue, and the virtue that has not been thus tempered is worthless.[3] This sentiment appears unique when placed against the chorus of voices arguing for the cloistering of virtue. A court critic, and many readers of *Tristan*, would dismiss these words as the blandishing speech of a weak king who fosters vice, a speech filled with just the alluring sort of sentiment held up to a courtier to keep him in the bonds of the court and prevent him from leaving to preserve his integrity. Such promises and blandishments were made by kings; the references to them are legion. But grand regal promises are normally of gold, fiefs, money, horses, prebends, and so forth. These are the allurements of the court. The promise of honor, virtue, and dignity to be gained in the fight against court vices places Mark's speech in a tradition of defense of state service which began in antiquity, continued faintly in the Middle Ages, and was revived by Castiglione.

Models: Joseph in Egypt

The court cleric could appeal to various biblical precedents to anchor the legitimacy of his own station: Moses serving Pharaoh, Daniel serving Nebuchadnezzar and Belshazar, and David serving Saul. The one to which I find most frequent reference, however, is Joseph in Egypt.[4] Saint Ambrose had held up the figure of Joseph as a model for the Christian administrator in his *De officiis ministrorum*,[5] and this had set a convention. The appeal in the Joseph story for the courtier cleric is self-evident. The patriarch was sold into slavery in the land of Egypt as a young man. Here he is guided through dangers and pitfalls by the help of God. Eventually he becomes head of Potiphar's household and finally Pharaoh's chief counselor and overseer. "Exile in Egypt" becomes a standard circumscription for worldly service; Pharaoh for a king or ruler; Joseph for the skilled court servant. Ebo praises Otto of Bamberg for winning the affection of all and governing the affairs of Henry's court "like a second Joseph" ("quasi alter Joseph curam gerens universorum"—3.36, p. 202). Walter Daniel refers to Ailred at the height of favor with King David as "noster Joseph" (chap. 3, p. 5). He praises Ailred's wisdom in confounding the intriguing knight, and comments, "It is not as though he was already living in the cloister; he was in the land of Egypt, where murmuring rather than thanksgiving was wont to be heard, not the voice of the turtle-dove, but the noise of the hissing of serpents" (chap. 3, p. 7). He marvels at Ailred's reconciliation with his detractor: "Ecce novus Joseph in Egipto, alter Daniel in Babilone, Lot recens in Sodomis" (chap. 3, p. 8). Individual episodes from the Joseph story could be useful as well. Benno II of Osnabrück, having left the king's court temporarily to seek rest from its incessant turmoil and travail, drew on the episode of Potiphar's wife in a letter to Archbishop Sigwin of Cologne: "we have chosen rather to flee, leaving the pallium in the hands of Egypt's mistress than to serve her in bondage and shame" ("maluimus enim fugientes in manibus Egiptiae dominae relinquere pallium, quam emancipati eidem turpiter servire"—chap. 17, *LB*, p. 410). Petrus Cantor complains about unworthy clerics who seek promotion in the church by serving the king. They hope to gain honor, wealth, and a sweet life without toil; they want milk and honey, not the care of souls. They should consider that Joseph became lord over Egypt only after his wisdom was put to the test. Pharaoh made him lord of his household and prince of all his possessions, not so that he could see to the king's needs, not so that he could live and ride about in pompous clothing, or lie about and enjoy himself, but rather so that he could instruct the prince. Clerics should measure their qualifications for promotion by comparison with Joseph's wisdom.[6]

These are scattered *exempla* which show an occasional connection between the figure of Joseph and the court cleric. A work that makes significant use of the Joseph figure as a type of the court cleric is the *Morale somnium Pharaonis* by Johannes of Limoges, abbot of a Cistercian monastery in Zirc, Hungary from 1208 to 1218.[7] The work is dedicated to Count Theobald IV of Champagne. It consists of twenty letters which address the events following Pharaoh's dream of the fat and lean kine and the ears of corn (Gen. 41). Pharaoh writes to his magicians demanding an interpretation; the magicians reply that they cannot provide one; Pharaoh's chief butler writes commending the man who had interpreted his dream in prison. A number of letters are exchanged between Pharaoh and Joseph. The correspondence ends with an exchange between the flatterers and detractors of the court and Joseph. In his first letter, addressed by the abbot to Count Theobald, the author explains the frame of his fictional correspondence: Pharaoh represents the type of the *rex curiosus*, Joseph is the *consiliarius virtuosus*, Egypt represents "typum cuiuslibet regni studiosi" (Ep. 1, p. 72), a king given to investigation, a kingdom given to studies.

The work conveys an image of an ideal court minister which is worth observing. The king, writing to his magicians, says that both reason and the custom of antiquity prescribe that the king should surround himself with wise counselors:

cum regalis pondus regiminis giganteis etiam humeris formidandum singularis personae strenuitas portare non sufficeret, in susceptae partem sollicitudinis subministros convocare curaret, prudentes sicut serpentes, simplices ut columbas, prudentes in bono, simplices in malo, prudentes, ne fraudarentur, simplices, ne fraudarent, quos regalis prosequeretur benevolentia, specialis praerogativa favoris, tamquam egregia corporis sui membra, prudentiae claritate, justitiae agilitate, temperantiae subtilitate ac fortitudinis impassibilitate dotata.

since the assiduity of a single person is not sufficient to bear the burden of the king's rule—a formidable burden even for the shoulders of a giant—the king should take care to assemble ministers to share the cares of state, men wise as serpents but simple as doves [cf. Matt. 10:16]; wise in good things, innocent in evil; wise to avoid deception, innocent to avoid deceiving. These men the king should cultivate with benevolence, bestowing his particular favor on them as his own excellent members, empowered with clear seeing wisdom, a vigorous sense of justice, refined self-control, and unshakeable fortitude. (Ep. 4, p. 78)

The chief butler writes to Pharaoh commending Joseph. His description of Joseph:

recordatus sum excellentis interpretis, aetate juvenis, maturitate senis, conversatione coelestis, peregrinatione terrestris, intellectu fulgentis, affectu ferventis, affatu mulcebris et suavis, cuius innocentiam fraterna aemulatio non infecit, cuius modestiam blanda prosperitas non illexit.

[Your edict] . . . recalled to mind an excellent interpreter, a youth in age, a man in maturity, celestial in his bearing but wise to earthly ways, of swift mind and strong feelings, beguiling and charming in conversation. The envy of his brothers has not infected his innocence, nor has flattering good fortune spoiled his modesty. (Ep. 5, p. 80)

Pharaoh calls Joseph to his court in the diction of the Song of Songs: "Hasten my beloved: for our beloved, our elect, our dove, sweet Wisdom, has built its house here" (Ep. 6, p. 82). Joseph replies: he is reluctant to answer the call. Fear and trembling seize him; he senses the approach of tribulation and suffering. The dangers of power and friendship with the king are great; good fortune holds greater threats than the adversity he suffers in prison. His greatest fear is that at court he will be bound by conscience to speak the truth. But the truth will gain him enemies, while the distortion of it will set him at odds with God. Hence fears assail him from all sides. Pharaoh's other ministers have failed to interpret the dream. If he succeeds, he will open himself to their hate and machinations. And he ends by begging Pharaoh to consult another interpreter (see Ep. 7, p. 84 ff.). Pharaoh reassures him in the following letter. His hesitations are understandable, he writes, where so often virtue is drowned in a general flood of vice. But some good men are chosen to survive floods, and this kingdom is still guided by truth and justice. For even if I should leave the path of justice, is it not worse for you to fear the loss of life than to fear the extinction of justice and fairness in the kingdom? Is it not more glorious to die in the active struggle for justice than to wait passively for sickness and old age to produce the same effect? Is it not better to give your life over to virtue than to worms ("virtutibus quam vermibus")? Take courage, conquer fortune, and take this task upon you (see Ep. 8, p. 86 ff.).

Joseph's hesitations and initial refusal are consistent with the values of court critics. The dangers of the court should keep prudent men away. But Pharaoh's reply is a striking departure from these values. It is a stirring defense of court service, which even echoes (but not intentionally, of course) the decision of Achilles: better to die young in the service of honor and a good cause, than to live a long but undistinguished life.[8] True, the dangers are great, but courage, good judgment, and constant wisdom will prevail over them. This defense injects an element that is unique: the heroism of the courtier.

Joseph complies, "pierced by the sword" of the king's lively and persuasive speech, and enters "in obsequium vestrum, aut potius in divinum" (Ep. 9, p. 88). The next several letters are Joseph's instruction of the king, the curriculum of which is Pharaoh's dream and its interpretation. It has nothing to do with feast and famine, but rather with the dangers that beset a king and tend to distract him from the duties of a just and good ruler. Opposed to these are the *civiles virtutes*, which support the entire edifice of ruler's virtues through fear of God (Ep. 11, p. 97).

Johannes's conception of an ideal kingdom is rational rule under intellectual guidance, a king persistent and responsible in the execution of his duties, not distracted from them by sensual allurements, "curiosities" of speculation, or self-serving advisors. Joseph's teachings aim at shaping Pharaoh into a "rex rationabilis" (Ep. 11, p. 95). Whether this conception is in any way noteworthy or original in the early thirteenth century is beyond my capacity to judge. Wilhelm Berges has little to say that is complimentary about the work's teachings on the ideal prince, though he concedes the importance of its form.[9] But Berges placed the composition of the work wrongly at around 1255–60. Had he realized that it dated from the second decade of the century, his opinion might have been different. He detects a change in the political ethic of *Fürstenspiegel* in the early 1260s, the most important feature of which is *ratio* ("reason"), as the principle guiding the king's execution of his duties: "Die Verpflichtung des Fürsten der 'ratio' gegenüber—das ist überhaupt das zentrale Kapitel dieser neuen Fürstenethik" (p. 119). But *ratio* producing *regimen rationabile* is the guiding principle of Joseph's teachings in the *Somnium Pharaonis*.

But for our purposes it is the relationship of an idealized ruler to an idealized courtier that is important. The courtier is drawn into the king's service by the promise of a rule of reason and intellect, the king's reason, the courtier's intellect; and by the promise of an honorable struggle against the forces of disorder at court. The courtier instructs the king in virtue and just rule.

We also have a chance to observe Joseph's contention with the flatterers and detractors at court. They address a letter to him. They congratulate him on his rapid rise and ask him to use discretion in wielding his power. (They are vulnerable, having failed where Joseph succeeded, in interpreting the dream.) They also offer him advice on guiding the king and here we encounter ideas that are startlingly bold and original. Our king values true nobility, nobility of intellect over mere nobility of birth, they write, and he disdains to drape royal purple over a rustic mind. Hence he seeks occasion to study. He flees from the occupations of state. He retreats to meditation, putting aside all business and seeking stimulation of the mind in the repose of the body. He seeks our advice, wounded by the love of wisdom. We have been unstinting in our efforts, impressing on him the need to pursue the study of letters and the liberal arts. Of course, they continue, it is more fitting for a learned king to study the Scriptures, ponder questions of philosophy new and old, and penetrate the clouds with his prayers in private, than in the turbulence of the court. Who would be so foolish as to prefer involvement in secular affairs to leisurely study of things divine? "Quis enim sic desipiat, aut deliret, qui non sanctius sanciat militare divinis otiis, quam secularibus negotiis implicari?" (Ep. 17, p. 112). They accommodate him by relieving him as far as possible of the burdens of state.

If these sentiments were lifted out of their context, they would appear to most contemporaries, certainly to any tutored on court criticism, as sensible and salubrious, even pious. The king is young and requires instruction; he is the servant of the church and god-fearing. The counselors would make of him a *rex literatus et religiosus*. Well and good. The passage quoted has so much the greater power of persuasion for drawing on the vocabulary of court criticism: "damnnabile [est] . . . se curialibus aut saecularibus negotiis immiscere" (Peter of Blois, Ep. 14, PL 207: 43B). But whatever piety and sanctity may appear to reside in these sentiments is undercut by the fact that flatterers and detractors put them forward. And Joseph's vehement reply in Epistle 18 undercuts it further. The king, he writes, is a *rex curiosus*, given to excessive speculation, and the counselors are playing on this vice to insinuate themselves into his favor and into power. They usher him out of the center of power, cloaking the maneuver in pious claims that they are educating him. It is the situation that provides the plot for Shakespeare's *The Tempest*, if we substitute the king's brother for his counselors. Now Joseph scourges them for divorcing the king from his office. It may be good for an unmarried man to shun marriage, he writes, but it is evil for a married man to seek divorce. In the same way it is good for a private man to shun the cares of state, but evil when a king does it. Now you are seeking to put asunder what God has joined. If a king avoids his rule in order to pray, then prayer becomes a sin in his mouth. Woe to you who usher the minister of justice into a private place of meditation where the cries of the paupers and the laments of widows cannot penetrate. This is like giving your ear to the mute serpent and denying it to the clamor of the poor; like poring over dead parchment while ignoring one's fellow men who are yet alive (see Ep. 18, pp. 115–16).

Here we encounter the central idea of the tract: the king must remain at the helm of state, not give himself to pursuits, no matter how good, that distract him from it. Probably the rebuke of an overstudious prince was the actual occasion for writing the tract. Theobald IV of Champagne is known more for composing poetry and pursuing his amours than for rational rule. The work's dedication teems with oblique references to allurements faced by the Count of Champagne comparable to those faced by Pharaoh. He must not give in to bestial worldly wisdom, not be the plaything of every breath of wind, like a flute when the air plays through its vents and stops; he must persist in his course like the sun, not waver like the moon (Ep. 1,

p. 72). Both Joseph's interpretation of the dream and his letter to the flatterers reiterate this lesson. But apart from the real occasion, the work constitutes a powerful argument for the king himself and his ministers to serve the state. This point is made against the powerful opposition of various traditions. Johannes seems to confront court criticism directly. Some of its common sentiments are placed in the mouths of the foolish counselors of the king. And that proverb which dominated the genre, "exeat aula,/ qui vult esse pius," clearly has no place in the thought of Johannes of Limoges. Just the contrary: he pleads for virtuous administration of court and land which asserts itself in spite of an understandable fear of the task. In his work "leaving the court" can only be regarded in capable and courageous men as evil, as an abandoning of responsibility. In Joseph's letter to the flatterers, we also hear echoes of those major justifications of the cleric's court service: guidance of the state and aid for widows, orphans, and paupers. These are presented as duties of the king, but Joseph's next letter replying to the flatterers (Ep. 20) places these concerns in their jurisdiction as well (p. 124). Johannes of Limoges has a clear vision of the difficulties of court life for king and counselors, but also a conception of the importance of cultivating this life and the virtues that lend it dignity. Joseph pardons the detractors for their foolishness and inconstancy and tries to render them valuable members of the administration:

Nos . . . non immemores, quod virtutes civiles in vitiorum medio conversantur, quod facile sit deviari a medio, quod difficile medium invenire, vobis aequitatem zelantibus, licet zelum sine scientia, obsequium sine ratione . . . libenter ac liberaliter veniam indulgemus, humanius arbitrantes infirmari cum infirmantibus, quam insultare insultantibus et indignantibus indignari. (Ep. 20, p. 124)

Knowing that the civil virtues are constantly surrounded by vices, that it is easy to stray from the middle path and hard to find it, we pardon you freely and fully, seeing your zeal for fairness—albeit zeal without knowledge, service without reason—and feeling it more humane to share the infirmities of the infirm than to requite insult with insult, indignation with indignation.

This is a good example of Johannes's combination of high-mindedness with level-headed common sense. The person who possesses the civil virtues, Joseph, does not flee from the representatives of vice; these are in a sense the medium in which civil virtues grow. He maintains his position in the middle and tries to educate the others to virtue rather than fall to bickering with them. Here he is not far from Castiglione's notion that virtue arises as a counterbalance to vice; indeed we might see that as the principle which accounts for Joseph's rise at court. Again, Johannes is the opponent of court critics, who trade in indignation and seek to pull virtue from its moderating, educating position in the midst of turmoil and danger.

Perhaps more remarkable is Johannes's attempt to put prayer, contemplation, and the studious life "in their place." He issues a decisive reminder that praying is the business of men who have the leisure for it. In a king, prayer and the contemplative life are forms of vice, insofar as they distract him from public business. How remarkable these sentiments appear coming as they do from the pen of a Cistercian abbot, who had, moreover, at one time been prior of the monastery of Clairvaux! The figure of the great champion of the contemplative life, Saint Bernard of Clairvaux, looms over this work and influences its diction, its rhetorical patterns, and in part, even its form. But not its ideas. The imagery of the Song of Songs, which had supplied the allegorical language of contemplation in Cistercian mysticism, is here turned against its original object. The "secret chamber of the lord" is not for a king; repose there is a hindrance, not an aid, to the king's salvation.

The *Morale somnium Pharaonis* was influential and widely read during its own time, as Horvath has shown. In recent years it has suffered a fate worse than neglect: distortion and misunderstanding. No modern commentary that I know shows signs that its author has actually read the work. The author of the entry on Johannes of Limoges in the *Histoire littéraire de France* (18:393–95) finds in the entire work nothing but "stériles déclamations" (p. 395). Berges speaks of Johannes's "krause Art" of expression (*Fürstenspiegel*, p. 35), and sees in the work a "kurioser Versuch" at an imitation of Cicero's *Somnium Scipionis* (p. 51). But Berges includes Johannes among the writers who see in contemplation and visions the means to a king's political enlightenment (p. 56), and this cannot inspire confidence in his knowledge of the work. Contemplation in the king is *curiositas*; the tract opposes it. And Pharaoh's vision is a one-time, God-sent admonition to a king who has veered from the path of reason, not a normal means of political guidance in the way Berges suggests. Horvath's edition at least made the work available, though it did not counteract the general disregard in which it stands. It was based on a single manuscript and was not well circulated. It is not easy to find. I know of two copies in the United States. Here at least was a readable edition, a reliable biography, and some introduction to the works. But it has not brought scholars to the point where they read the text instead of fishing in it. Uhlig, in utter misunderstanding of the thrust of the work, took it as an example of the stereotyping of court criticism which occurred in the immediate wake of John of Salisbury (*Hofkritik*, p. 73). Just the contrary: the Middle Ages never came closer to producing a work of pro-court literature than in the *Somnium Pharaonis*. Of course it represents Pharaoh's court as teeming with flatterers and detractors, but they are there to show that the state falls into the hands of rabble when good men are lured from its service by such pious enticements as rest, study, and contemplation. It points up the absurdity of leaving the center of government in order to keep virtue alive; virtue lives and thrives in the center of vice. The work regards the urging "exeat aula" implicitly in the same light in which Lucan had originally placed it: as advice appropriate to an evil and unscrupulous counselor. And this we should read as a work of stereotypical court criticism! No: it is uniquely critical of those platitudes. It deserves a new critical edition and a serious and informed commentary.

Ulysses

In the mythographical and intellectual tradition of the schools in the Middle Ages, Ulysses was representative of the wise man.[10] In Benoît de St. Maure's *Roman de Troie* he becomes a wily trickster knight, more beautiful and eloquent than other men, given to mockery and derision.[11] But he also became a screen onto which the courtier, the clerical court advisor, could project his own values and ideals. The appeal of the figure for this group must have been great. Ulysses was the shrewd advisor of Agamemnon. He was eloquent and cunning and helped win by his advice a great war which ten years of exertion by less wise warriors had not brought to a conclusion. His destiny was passive suffering of the buffeting of fate, as opposed to that of Achilles, the man of warrior deeds. In a debate with the rash, hotheaded warrior Ajax he won by his eloquence the arms of Achilles that should by right have fallen to Ajax. He faced deadly allurements, actively exposing himself to them, but did not succumb. He showed patience and affability in enduring these trials.[12]

Two texts from the later twelfth century show us Ulysses transformed into a pattern of conduct for worldly clerics. In his *Ars versificatoria*, Matthew of Vendôme, a master of grammar and student of Bernardus Silvestris, included a series of portraits to serve as models for personal description. The first is a portrait of a pope, the second of a ruler under the name of Caesar, the third Ulysses.[13] The social order of the figures is evident, except in the case of Ulysses.[14] But our preceding discussion makes it possible to classify him. Matthew describes him as "adorned with eloquence, gladdened by good sense, invested with grace of manners (*morum gratia*), blessed by fame":

Purpurat eloquium, sensus festivat Ulixem,
Intitulat morum gratia, fama beat.

(1–2)

He is foresighted, incisively eloquent, and great in cunning. He is un-
surpassed in genius and a servant of the Good (*servitor honesti*). Some
twenty-five lines are devoted to the theme, "The wisdom of his words
procedes from the wisdom of his mind." Then the list of virtues continues: what he has received from nature he outstrips through acquired virtue, and this faithful master is "the intimate vassal of the
outer man" ("intimus est hominis exterioris homo"—ll. 31–32). He
weighs difficult cases in the balance, determining whether deeds are
good or evil. Age cannot impoverish his virtues, but rather it increases his wisdom. No arrogance defiles the flower of his mind.

The characterization is of an aged servant and counselor living in
the "world" (he has attained fame, l. 2; and honor, ll. 51–52). The
meaning of "intimate vassal of the outer man" is not immediately
clear.[15] But a ruler has vassals, and Ulysses is in the retinue of
Agamemnon. "Outer man" we can take to mean "men living in the
world" as opposed to spiritual men. The "intimacy" places Ulysses in
the *familia* of his feudal lord. The context and the framework of feudal
relations urge on us the rendering "favored servant of a ruler." He
combines wisdom with eloquence, the Ciceronian ideal of education
common in the humanist schools of the period and in portraits of
bishops. His manners are gracious, surpassing ordinary mortals
("moribus excedit hominem"—l. 33). The martial virtues are hardly
represented at all. Even *fortis* of lines 53 and 57 and *conflictu Caesar*
of line 61 most likely refer to strength of character, or fortitude in
the trials of public life. Moral and intellectual virtues far outstrip any
others in the passage. There is also a suggestion that Ulysses is of a
gentle and modest disposition, is a *vir mansuetus*, since he knows no
arrogance (l. 51). Had Matthew entitled this portrait according to social order, as he did that of the pope, he would undoubtedly have
used the words *curialis* or *consiliarius*.

The *curialis* defined his identity by social and intellectual talents
and by his relation to a ruler, certainly, but also by his opposition to
the knight. We have observed this opposition in the reality of court
life ("reality" as mediated by the biographer of course) for Ailred of
Rievaulx and the boorish knight, and for Adalbert of Bremen and the
Saxon dukes. We can observe the opposition in a fictionalized and
mythologized form in two debate poems pitting Ulysses against Ajax
in the contest for the weapons of Achilles.[16] Both poems are from the
second half of the twelfth century. Both are adaptations of Ovid, *Met-*

amorphoses books 12 and 13, and are preserved in two manuscripts.[17] The one includes, besides the two debate poems, four portraits from Matthew of Vendôme's *Ars versificatoria* (Pope, Caesar, Ulysses, and Davus); "Phyllis and Flora," a debate poem between two ladies on the relative merits of knight and cleric as lovers; and the "Miles gloriosus." The other has the same four portraits from Matthew of Vendôme and a debate between knight and cleric. Both manuscripts include a number of other poems, but it looks very much as if one object of the compilers was to collect a dossier on the theme, Knight versus Cleric. The two debates of Ulysses and Ajax fit this theme neatly.

Both debates hold closely to the text of Ovid's *Metamorphoses* over long stretches. "Causa II" is the more useful for our purpose. It is the more original, if—in Schmidt's judgment—less skillful of the two poems. It contains a number of interpolations that are the work of the twelfth-century poet. These stake out only a very modest claim on immortality for the poet, but they interest us for showing that he was projecting onto the Ovidian model the complex of concerns bound up with the opposition knight–cleric. Two of these insertions take the form of a simple piling up of antitheses. Ajax speaks:

> Audeo—formidas, fugo—cedis, milito—cessas,
>   Surgo—iaces, valeo—deficis, insto—lates,
> Effugis—accelero, torpes—precurro, quiescis—
>   Accedo, titubas—consto, rigesco—ruis,
> Arescis—vireo, marcescis—floreo, langues—
>   Prevaleo, resides—cursito, vinco—subis,
> Arceo—subcumbis, impugno—vinceris, alges—
>   Ferveo, desperas—spero, laboro—tepes,
> Ascendo—descendis, amor—contempneris, horres—
>   Aggredior, vigilo—stertis, anhelo—vacas.
>
> (53–62)

I show daring—you show fear; I give ground   you give up; while I wage war, you laze about; I arise—you stay in bed; in me there is strength—in you weakness; I go boldly about my business while you creep surreptitiously about yours; you slip into the shadows—I speed forward; your head is filled with fog—mine with strategy; you hold your peace—I give active assent; you waver—I am unshakeable; I am rigid—you fall apart; you are arid—I am verdant; you wither—I flourish; you languish—I prevail; you stay in one place—I hasten about everywhere; I conquer—you submit; I hold men at arm's length—you fall at their feet; I rush to battle—you to defeat; you are ice—I am flame; you despair—I have hope; I labor—you laze; I rise up—you sink; I am loved—you are despised; while you tremble, I step forward aggressively; while I wake, you snore; I am filled with enthusiasm—you are empty.

Even though this sort of accumulation builds a certain momentum and achieves a certain effect by sheer stubborn refusal to stop when the point is made, the passage would be none the poorer as poetry if it ended after two or three lines. Some of the opposing pairs apply at the most general level to the contrast of the man of deeds to the man of words. But many of them are based on a reproach that applies in the twelfth century specifically to the cleric: he is *otio deditus*, an epicure who spends much time in bed and grows fat and lazy.

> Tuus est in ocio
> Quasi brutum pecus . . .[18]

These lines from the love debate "Phyllis and Flora" wield one of the standard weapons in the arsenal of advocates of knighthood in the literature pitting knight against cleric.

More revealing is the corresponding answer of Ulysses:

> Consulo—nugaris, rapis—accipio, reprobaris—
>   Commendor, doceo—discis, honoro—noces,
> Advocor—excuteris, lucror—predaris, habundo—
>   Mendicas, peccas—corrigo, vendis—emo,
> Excruciaris—amor, sordescis—polleo, ledis—
>   Astruo, rixaris—placo, peroro—taces,
> Mando—venis, iubeo—pares, scio—desipis, intro—
>   Exis, dampnaris—iudico, ditor—eges,
> Blandior—insurgis, servo—consumis, acerbas—
>   Lenio, ieiunas—prandeo, poto—sitis.
>
> (233–42)

My counsel is serious—yours ridiculous; you snatch up gifts—I receive them graciously; blame is yours—praise mine; I teach—you learn; I do reverence—you do damage; I am summoned—you are snubbed; I earn wealth—you plunder it; I'm in the lap of luxury—you go begging; you commit sins—I correct them; you sell—I buy; harassment for you—affection for me; you get dirty—I grow powerful; you destroy—I build; you brawl—I win favor; I perorate—you are mute; I call—you come; I command—you obey; I have knowledge—you have ignorance; I enter—you exit; you receive condemnation—I render judgment; I grow rich—you grow poor; I am charming—you're a boor; I serve—you consume; you rub the wrong way—I smoothe out; you fast—I feast; I drink—you thirst.

Most of these pairs are *topoi* of the cleric's advocates in opposition to the knight. The cleric is the counselor, who serves at the side of the king, whereas the knight is an unruly element of court society, kicked about and at the beck and call of the king and his advisors. Flora's speech in stanza 38 is fully the counterpart of Ulysses' "Mando—venis, iubeo—pares":

> Universa clerico
> Constat esse prona,

> Et signum imperii
> Portat in corona.
> Imperat militibus
> Et largitur dona:
> Famulante maior est
> Imperans persona.

By custom all things favor the cleric, and he bears the sign of the empire in his crown. He commands the knights and he dispenses gifts. After all, he who commands is greater than he who serves.

The cleric has great wealth, while the knight is poor and gaunt. These are ideas reiterated in "Phyllis and Flora," stanzas 23, 24, 26, and 34. Likewise "doceo—discis" is echoed, here in the erotic context, in Flora's

> Quid Dione valeat
> Et amoris deus,
> Primus novit clericus
> Et instruxit meus;
> Factus est per clericum
> Miles Cithereus.
>
> (St. 41)

All that is in the realm of Venus and of the god of love the cleric knew first; my lover passed it on to yours through instruction. The knight was made into a lover by the cleric.

The cleric's obligation to "correct" the laity in its tendency to go astray ("peccas—corrigo") is a subject on which we will spend some time in a later chapter. I will just point out that the two activities "doceo, corrigo" constitute a justification of the court life put forward by court clerics themselves. They are sent to the king in order to instruct and correct men of the world. The speech is also useful for showing us that the clerical concerns here projected onto Ulysses have their context in the active life, in politics, the government of the kingdom and administration of the court, the giving of counsel and receiving of rewards in return. These are concerns of the worldly clergy serving at secular or ecclesiastical courts, not of monks devoted to contemplation or of priests devoted to pastoral care.

The author of "Causa II" was, if not Matthew of Vendôme himself, then surely a student of that master.[19] Hence the testimony for the identification between the courtier-cleric and Ulysses is limited to a single author and his influence. These at least are the only witnesses to this identification known to me. We are dealing, not with a tradition connecting Ulysses with the *curialis*, but with a single master's insight into the value of that figure as a pedagogic model for courtiers.

The aristocratic world generally took pleasure and pride in tracing their roots back to the Trojan War. Here was a figure who served a king with wise and cunning counsel, suffered the buffets of fortune to return safely to his homeland, and not least of all, sailed the dangerous waters of royal service without suffering shipwreck (or without succumbing to it). Ulrich von Hutten, in his anti-court tract, *Misaulus* (1518), still calls on the figure to provide a glimmer of hope for the courtier's survival:

ex aulicis quidam Ulyssem imitantur qui in turbulento hoc mari navigantes cera obthuratis auribus insidiosae Syrenum cantionis capaces non sunt et consilium habent praeternavigandae Scyllae vitandaeque Charybdis.[20]

certain courtiers who sail these turbulent waters imitate Ulysses. By stopping their ears with wax, they render themselves invulnerable to the insidious song of the sirens and find a way of circumnavigating Scylla and avoiding Charybdis.

Let Hutten's misrendering of the Homeric story serve as an indication of how improbable even this resourceful courtier/knight considered the possibility that any man could face those dangers with open ears and survive.

FROM COURT IDEAL TO LITERARY IDEAL: METAMORPHOSES OF THE COURTIER

T HE IDEALS that crystallized around the figure of the courtier bishop were not restricted to the royal chapel. Their diffusion among the worldly clergy was assured by the nature of their transmission: they were part of a program of education at the cathedral schools, preparation for state service, and if our sources seem to indicate that they were the private property of a small elite at court and in the episcopacy, this is because only the tip of that iceberg was visible; only the most distinguished were commemorated in biographies. But many others at all levels of the secular clergy cultivated the ideals of the courtier bishop. The requirements of the royal chapel provided the model on which lesser courts could pattern themselves, a development in the history of ethics with a clear counterpart in institutional history: the structure of the Carolingian court became the model for the courts of Europe generally. And the chapel of the Ottonian-Salian dynasties provided the model for this institution throughout Europe, including episcopal chapels and the chapel of the Roman curia.[1] It is easy to account for the influence of the royal chapel. It was cosmopolitan; its members were among the most gifted and talented men in Europe. The patterns of behavior that had accounted for their success at the highest level of European government were bound to shape the values of clerical administrators generally.[2]

A Christian-humanist ethic of worldly service arose from the model of the courtier bishop. The spread of this ethic is an essential factor in the civilizing of the European nobility from the tenth century on. It is visible wherever we encounter descriptions of clerics in court service.[3] It appears in its most elegant medieval transmutation in the knight and lover of courtly romance, and it is still detectable, if dramatically enriched, in the courtier of the Renaissance.

Ideals of courtier clerics were perhaps the most important factor that elevated the figure of the knight errant to his lofty position in the landscape of fiction and western ideals from the twelfth century on.

A major link joining the world of court clerics with that of the knight of romance is the romance of Tristan and Isolde by Gottfried von Strassburg. We have already drawn on it to show particular aspects of courtier values. But it deserves a more detailed treatment. I pointed out earlier that it is not a typical Arthurian romance. This genre in its classical formulation by Chrétien de Troyes places a civilized knight and lover in Celtic fairy tale landscapes, where by dint of chivalric prowess, by constancy of mind and affection, he overcomes fantastic barriers set in place especially to test him. He then wins his lady love and her lands and lives a life pleasing to God and the world ever after. *Tristan* is quite different. The main theater of action, the showplace and testing ground of human talents, is the court, not chivalric combat. The hero is disposed by nature and destiny to suffering and sorrow. His fate is a tragic love affair which sets him irreconcilably at odds with his lord and uncle, and which spells the destruction of both lovers.

In this romance clerical, courtier values provide the basis for the hero's character and destiny and far outweigh in their importance chivalric ones. The talents in the foreground are social, artistic, and intellectual. The hero makes his way in the early parts of the work by his eloquence, his learning, his skill in music, and his knowledge of languages, and hunting customs and the French terms for them. He impresses all who meet him by his *schoene site*, which is, we will see later, the MHG equivalent of the Latin *elegantia* and *venustas morum*. His charm, beauty, manners, and affability win him the love and favor of the court and the king. He puts forward his talents with the calculating modesty that Castiglione was to call *sprezzatura*, defusing envy and producing two-fold amazement in the court. He swiftly rises to become the favorite and, finally, the heir of the king. And all this is accomplished before a single tournament is held, before a single battle is fought. These are accomplishments of courtiership, not of knighthood. Gottfried refers to his young hero as "ein lieber hoveman" ("a beloved courtier"—3487).

Gottfried has adapted the iconography of the courtier cleric as it is also represented in the *vitae*. This becomes apparent in details of wording. Tristan repeatedly displays *elegantia morum, schoene site*. At court he makes himself "all things to all men": "er kunde und wolte in allen leben" ("he knew how to live for all men and did so willingly"— 3496). He was *omnibus carus* and *omnibus gratus*:

> swaz er getet, swaz er gesprach,
> daz duhte und waz ouch alse guot,

> daz ime diu werlt holden muot
> und inneclichez herze truoc.
> (3746–49)

Whatever he did, whatever he said, it all seemed so good—and was!—that everyone loved and held him in heartfelt affection.

He makes himself beloved of the entire court, *se toti curie gratum fecit*:

> sus was der ellende do
> da ze hove ein trut gesinde
> (3742–43)

And so this stranger became a beloved member of the retinue at court there.

But he was especially dear to the king, *regi, imperatori precipue carus*: "der sach in gerne und was sin vro" ("he delighted and joyed in the sight of him"—3396); and "er truoc im harte holden muot" ("he held him in deep affection"—3406). We are in the secularized and chivalrified atmosphere of the youth of a courtier bishop. The parallel becomes especially clear if we compare the court service of young Tristan with that of Otto of Bamberg. Both men traveled in their youth to foreign lands, learned the languages and customs so well that they could pass as natives:

Tristan 2133ff.:	*Vita Priefl.* chap. 2, pp. 6–7:
[The marshall, his foster father] . . . bade him travel about and familiarize himself with foreign countries and their peoples with an eye to learning their customs. This the young man did so laudably that at that time there was no child so virtuous and talented in the entire kingdom as Tristan.	Having awakened the full powers of his mind, he girded himself for the higher studies of virtue, and strove to speak and act as befits a man. . . . Leaving his fatherland for Poland, after a brief stay there he had mastered not only the customs but also the language so thoroughly that hearing him speak the foreign language you would not have taken him for a German.

Later Tristan has an opportunity to display his knowledge of languages and foreign customs to the members of Mark's court, and he handles himself like a native of the various countries whose languages he speaks (see 3690ff.).

Both Otto and Tristan impress all they meet through their eloquence, beauty, and elegance of bearing and manners. Both were court servants of a lady of high nobility, Otto the chaplain of Judith, Tristan the tutor of Princess Isolde. Both men proposed a bride to the prince, masterminded the wooing expedition, won the bride and brought her back to their lord.[4] Both were *viri expetibiles*, courted by the lord they served. Both rose swiftly in the favor of the lord and were invited to his private chamber to sing to him, Otto psalms and hymns, Tristan presumably Breton and Latin *lais*:

Tristan, 3648ff.:	Ebo 1.6, p. 15:
Mark spoke: "Come now, Tristan . . . I would like very much to hear your songs now and then at night when you cannot sleep. Do this, it will be for your good as well as mine." "Yes mylord, gladly."	The emperor Henry, recognizing Otto's reverent loyalty and wisdom, took him aside to a private place and asked whether he knew the psalter by heart and could sing it. On hearing him answer "yes," the emperor rejoiced and bade him come to his side when they were alone to sing and pray together.

In good courtier fashion both are constantly at the king's side, "ready at hand" to serve him:

Tristan 3399ff.:	Herbord 3.34, p. 201:
For at all times he was at his side, as it behooves a courtier, and offered him his service whenever it was called for. Wherever Mark was, wherever he went, Tristan was there like his second self.	when other chaplains were intent on other things, Otto was always at hand . . . morning and evening and at all times he stood at the emperor's side, psalter in hand, ready to serve.

And finally, both are placed in the role of "only son" of the king and take over the business of the court:

Tristan 4299ff.:	Ebo 1.3, pp. 12–13:
"Tristan, come and kiss me! I tell you, if you and I both live, I will be in the place of your father.	to such an extent had [Otto] won the affection of this most prudent of emperors that he embraced him as if he were his only son, . . . whatever was precious and valuable in the palace, he committed to his faithful keeping.
And 4460ff.	
"I have a further gift for you: my land, my people and all that I possess, let it all be in your keeping."	

These parallels are not accounted for by literary influence but by the common sociological ground from which the early careers of Tristan and Otto arose: the ideals, ambitions, and representative experiences of clerical court servants. This is the courtier in his rise to prominence: his virtues and talents find their place, become effective, and are recognized and rewarded.

But for Tristan the result is not only success but also envy, hate, suspicion, and the inevitable court intrigues against the king's favorite. There is one episode of intrigue in *Tristan* that permits us to identify with some exactness the sociological model that guided the poet's conception of character, motivation, and circumstance.

The episode (*Tristan* 8226 ff.) begins when Tristan returns to Cornwall cured of his poisoned wound. He is the darling of Mark's court, he has been named the king's sole heir and seems indestructible. This dizzying rise of an outsider inevitably arouses envy. His enemies, Mark's *lantbarune*, set to intriguing. They put out the rumor that Tristan is a magician who accomplishes all his ends by casting spells on those about him. His path to the succession must be cut off, the barons say, and to accomplish this they urge Mark to take a wife and provide the country with an heir. Mark refuses: Tristan is his heir. Now the nobles' hate of Tristan grows beyond all bounds, and they show him their feelings "in gestures and words" (8373). These strike such terror into Tristan that he goes about in constant fear of assassination. He seeks out Mark and begs him, in the name of God, to take pity on him and consider the danger and fear in which he lives. He knows he is to die, but not when. His fear is great enough to overcome any ambitions or claims he may have to the succession, since he urges Mark to appease the barons by taking a wife, and so remove the cause of hate and the motive for murder. Mark responds with his speech on the moral value of facing envy, which we analyzed earlier. The king ends by refusing a second time to take a wife. Tristan responds: "Then mylord, though I am at your command, I wish to leave the court. I am not equal to them. I can never maintain my position in the face of such hate. Rather than rule all the kingdoms of the world in such fear and uncertainty, I would remain landless all my life" (8424 ff.). The echoes in this speech and in the entire scene are very rich, and they become audible against the background of court criticism and of various other texts discussed earlier. "So wil ich von dem hove varn" (8425): it is the course of action urged incessantly by the court critics: "exeat aula." We recall the story Walter Map told of his steward, a good and God-fearing man, who came to him with tears in his eyes to complain of the harassments he suffered from other members of the household. His lord cannot console or hearten him, and he declares his intention to leave: "I alone cannot prevail against all of them. I prefer to give all things into your hands than to be tormented by these harassments. Farewell!" (*De nug. cur.* 1.10, p. 10) The formulation is strikingly similar to Tristan's ("Non possum ad omnes solus"; "ine mac mich vor in niht bewarn'') as are the logic of the speech in general and the sociology of the situation: a court servant comes in despair to his lord to complain of the torments he suffers at the hands of malicious enviers.

This constellation recalls the predicament of Adalbert of Bremen caught between the Saxon dukes and the emperor's court. The parallels are extensive and striking: the central figure in both cases is the gifted courtier with close ties to the ruler; in both, the feudal nobles conspire against the king's favorite. Adalbert's enemies sought to drive him from his position of favor using the same discrediting slander as Tristan's enemies: he is a magician who has seduced the king by spells. In both cases the ruler is the only counselor and protector of the embattled courtier. Here are independent responses to the same sociological phenomenon: the gifted courtier at the height of influence and power is persecuted by enviers at court. The sociological constellation is the same: the feudal nobility lines up against the king's favorite.

The way this scene represents the hero's fear tells a lot about the sociological factors that guided its conception. Recall that young Tristan had boldly avenged his father, and when still untested in battle, he had singlehandedly conquered the Irish champion Morolt when all others at court shrank from the task. Later he was to slay a dragon and a giant in desperate combat. In two of these encounters he reaches the extremity of danger, but is not touched by fear. And yet in the context of court intrigue this same hero is reduced to quailing by a few nasty words and gestures. When he goes to his lord for help and is denied the particular form of it he requests, he decides to leave the court, throwing his promised inheritance overboard. How can we explain this oddly timorous response to a fairly ordinary intrigue? It is not the response of a knight. It is unthinkable that a knight could come to his lord, confess his fear, and beg in the name of God that he be released from his service. At least it is unthinkable that the fear of a knight could be represented so openly.[5] For a chivalric audience, Tristan's fear could only appear as momentary cowardice. The hero of romance and epic is *unverzaget*. He knows no fear, certainly not when beset by ordinary dangers and threats. And even if he does, he does not admit it openly. The mask of idealizing, held tightly over the face of the hero in romance, drops momentarily in the episode from *Tristan*. That scene and the hero's behavior reflect social realities of court life, realities sufficiently unpleasant to fall far beneath the horizon of interests of the *romancier*.

The court critics regularly point to the anxiety and fears produced by court life with its snares and intrigues. Let us recall some of their words: "Anxiabar usque ad mortem"; "Exeat ergo aula necesse est qui hujus serpentis aulici virus metuit . . ."; "videtis, quia curia plena est laqueis mortis; mors autem inevitabilis et incerta . . ."; "Da [muoz man] lîbes und sêle angest haben!"[6] The court is viewed in the scene from *Tristan* through the eyes of a clerical courtier: the poet's language is tutored by the traditions of court criticism. But also the hero's response is the response of a courtier, not a knight, to court intrigue. Recall that Adalbert of Bremen's response to the hate and intriguing of the Saxon dukes was fear and anger: "ira et metu anxius moliri [coepit]," and anguish of soul: "dolor animi." Recall also that Thomas Becket often came to Theobald of Canterbury, tears streaming from his eyes, to complain of the harassments and torments to which his position as Henry's chancellor exposed him (see above, p. 60). Here is precisely the common ground in courtier experience from which the scene in *Tristan* arose; the tissue of social pressures and the feelings and responses they arouse are felt, perceived, and depicted, not by knights or lay nobility, but by court clerics. For this group, fear at court intrigue was an understandable and sane response to the snares and dangers, the inhumanity and moral perversion of the court. The urge to leave was not cowardice but a pious impulse.

This is not to say that Gottfried intended the scene to illustrate the dangers of the court and to urge courtiers to leave. On the contrary: he has Mark deliver his speech rousing Tristan to constancy and fortitude and showing him the value and dignity of facing and overcoming envy. And Tristan remains. He spins a counterintrigue. The barons have urged that Tristan lead the party to court Princess Isolde in the hope of sending him to his death among his mortal enemies (he has killed the uncle of Isolde, Morolt). But Tristan turns the tables on them. He agrees to captain the expedition under the condition that all the barons accompany him. They cannot refuse, and now it is their turn to taste "fear and torment" (8637). In short order their urge to kill him is transformed into an urge to preserve him; now their survival depends on his. In this light the scene can be read as urging the talented courtier: "remain at court," exercise wit and cunning to maintain your position. It is a lesson closely related to those of Johannes of Limoges: Joseph had suffered fear on receiving the summons to court, but, heartened by the king's urgings, he enters his service, asserts himself, and maintains his virtue in the midst of vice. In this scene as in many others Gottfried von Strassburg shows himself a *professor mundi*, a man "der zer werlt hat muot, swie so er si boese oder guot."

‹›

The comparison of *vitae*, court criticism, and courtly romance can lead us back into an entire complex of courtier values and courtier ex-

perience in the eleventh and twelfth centuries. These patterns of experience are, to some extent, sociological constants in the circumstances of courtier serving king. But from the tenth to the twelfth
centuries, they fell to the lot of the particular class, *curiales*, ambitious,
talented clerical administrators at secular and ecclesiastical courts in
Europe.

In our conventional understanding of the development of courtier
ideals, the phenomenon is associated with the Renaissance. The figure first gained a sharp profile through Castiglione's *Il Libro del Cortegiano*. A look at current and traditional views of the origins of the
courtier shows that the medieval foundations of the figure are imper-
fectly understood and in fact have escaped serious study. According
to the common formula, Castiglione drew on two main sources: classical antiquity and "medieval chivalry."[7] But Castiglione produced a
grand and exalted portrait of a figure that had been a social and political reality at European courts since the early Middle Ages. True, there
were constant fluctuations after the twelfth century in the stature of
the imperial courts. But the ensemble of characteristics that constituted the ideal clerical advisor lived on long after the conditions no
longer existed which had lent that figure the possibility of greatness.
From the thirteenth century on, direct representations of the *curiales*,
occur only from the negative perspective of court criticism. By the
early Renaissance this perspective is no longer predominant. In an
English *Fürstenspiegel* from 1445, one of many that went under the
title *Secretum Secretorum*, we find the following list of requirements
for a "trew counseiler or servaunt" of the king:[8] (1) "perfeccion of
lymmes"; (2) "godnes of lernyng and wille to understonde"; (3) a good
memory; (4) a clear and level head in difficult situations; (5) "courtly,
faire spekyng, of swete tonge . . . sped in eloquence"; (6) learned;
(7) "of good manners and complexion, softe, meke and tretable"
(here follows a list of vices to be avoided in a counselor); (14) composed and moderate in his manners, "yevying himself curiously to
men benyngly tretyng." Many tracts on the counselor, the legate and
ambassador from the Renaissance, could be cited here,[9] but this passage gives us a concise and remarkably comprehensive list of the chief
characteristics of our type. The Latin vocabulary for most of these is
readily at hand: *moderamen*, *eloquentia*, and *lineamentorum gratia*.
"Softe, meke and tretable" are the counterpart of *mansuetus*, *mitis et
tractabilis*; "men benyngly tretyng" is *benignitas* and *affabilitas*. The
tract predates Castiglione by more than half a century.

The *Libro del Cortegiano* is a complex work, a compilation of courtier ideals which is a veritable feast against the gaunt fare of the *Fürstenspiegel*. I do not intend to compare Castiglione's courtier to the

model of the courtier bishop in any detail. This model is to Castiglione's ideal figure what the partly erected frame is to the finished building. I can only suggest here that Castiglione did indeed build on a frame that had been established in the early Middle Ages.

Count Ludovico da Canossa formulates some of the basic qualities of the courtier:

> I would have our Courtier born of a noble and genteel family. [In the next chapter it is objected that he need not be of noble birth, so long as he possesses nobility of spirit.] . . . besides his noble birth, I would wish the Courtier . . . endowed by nature not only with talent and with beauty of countenance and person, but with that certain air of grace which shall make him at first sight pleasing and lovable to all who see him; and let this be an adornment informing and attending all his actions, giving the promise outwardly that such a one is worthy of the company and favor of every great lord. (1.17, trans. Singleton, pp. 28–30)

Some further qualities he must possess: he should be well built with finely proportioned members (1.20); highly talented, yet able to display his talents effortlessly and as though he himself placed no store by them (*sprezzatura*—1.26, 28); he must combine wisdom with eloquence (1.33), possess wide experience and sharp judgment (1.34), be learned in the sciences, the classical languages, and the "humanities" (1.42, 44). The pride to which such an array of talents might give rise must be tempered with modesty (2.7). His main and true calling is said to be fighting (1.17), but this occupation receives almost no discussion in the *Libro*, which is largely devoted to social graces and court pastimes. In book 3, the perfect court lady is described. The virtue she must possess above all others is "una certa affabilità piacevole," by which she will be able to entertain graciously every kind of man (3.5, ed. Maier, p. 343).

These few details represent a vast reduction of the *cortegiano*. But it establishes my point: that Castiglione did not create the courtier out of Cicero, chivalry, and Italian Renaissance court life. Some of the central ethical and social values of the figure described by Castiglione existed long before the Renaissance, even before the formation of a courtly chivalric code, as ideals that crystallized around the figure of the courtier bishop.

I do not want to suggest that the "origins" of the courtier and of courtiership lie in the Ottonian-Salian imperial courts. The courtier is a phenomenon of aristocratic society in general, and the social ideals of the figure are to some extent constants of that society. Charm, nobility, gentleness, affability, physical beauty, learning and judgment are qualities that inhere in the social situation of the advisor to an autocratic ruler. The court advisor at an Arabic or Chinese court will have embodied these same virtues, but with wide variation in detail. Here I have tried to show the forces that called forth this figure and nourished those ideals in a particular historical configuration. The peculiarity of the European courtier lies in the intersection of the position of courtier with the office of bishop. The strength of this connection and its close tie to the ideal courtier still in the Renaissance is evident in Castiglione's sketch, in book 4, of the careers of the participants in his dialogue. Of the seven men he mentions, four advanced from the court of Urbino to high ecclesiastical positions: Federico Fregoso became archbishop of Salerno, Count Ludovico da Canossa, bishop of Bayeaux; Bernardo Bibbiena, cardinal of Santa Maria in Portico; Pietro Bembo, secretary to Pope Leo X (4.2, ed. Maier, p. 447). Castiglione himself, during most of his life a courtier, then papal legate to Charles V, was offered the chair of bishop of Avila shortly before his death in 1529.

PART TWO

◇

COURTESY

ANCIENT URBANITY AND THE SPIRIT OF REVIVAL IN THE GERMAN EMPIRE

I N PART 1 we observed the institution of the royal court and studied the qualities that constituted *idoneitas* in the circle of the king's advisors. We focused on qualities that had, as it were, a political function; they gave assurance that the man who possessed them was suited to carry out the duties of king's counselor. But these qualities were part of a much broader set of social ideals that were at home in the royal court. This broader set of ideals constituted a code that regulated the whole economy of social interaction according to notions derived more from classical than from Christian ideals of the conduct of public life. This set of ideals has a direct, historical connection with the ethical and social code known in the vernacular as *cortezia, cortoisie,* and *hövescheit*. One might even say that it *is* that ethical code transferred from the courtiers of the ruler's court onto the lay nobility, enriched by the union with ideals native to that class, and finally apotheosized in the ideal realm of King Arthur's court in romance.

One of the greatest hindrances to seeing clearly the development of medieval courtesy is the fact that the main texts representing this code are vernacular courtly literature. In these works courtesy is generally subordinated to courtly love. But writers of romance were not speaking as scholars and historians of ideas when they said, "Love is the sole source of all courtesy and virtue." They were speaking as lovers or their advocates, and lovers tend to subordinate everything to the power in whose grip they are. The phenomenon known to the Middle Ages as courtesy was quite separable, however, from romantic love.[1] The original element in the amalgam of courtier, knight, and lover is a code of fine manners.

There is another misleading impression evoked by the one-sidedness of the sources. The courtly lover of romance and lyric was a knight, and this literature originated in France. It follows that the ideals of behavior represented in courtly literature were those of the French feudal nobility and that ideals of courtesy are in their origins "chivalric." This assumption is a distortion of very large proportions. It is as if we imagined that the values and ideals represented in western films must have originated with the cowboys onto whom they are projected and not with the authors and screenwriters who chose the cowboy as their embodiment.

The phenomenon of courtesy is represented in Latin texts, many of which predate the period of vernacular courtly literature. The history of courtesy looks quite different when approached via these texts. It looks much older, or to put it more accurately, its roots become visible. It will become evident in the following chapters that we misunderstand the nature and intellectual origins of medieval courtesy if we fail to see it as a survival or revival of ideals from classical antiquity.

There is an extensive and highly articulated Latin vocabulary of courtesy that appears in court literature from the early Middle Ages on. The sources are rich enough that it is possible to study this vocabulary in detail and to find its precedents in antiquity. It is curious that this vocabulary and the ideals it expresses have not been the basis and point of departure for discussions of the origins of courtesy and of the vernacular vocabulary.[2] Historians of literature would be very cautious about claiming that a literary form or convention arose spontaneously in the Middle Ages without looking for precedents and analogues in antiquity. Should it have been different with ethical-social concepts and terms? Gustav Ehrismann had a perfectly correct intuition that the ideals of the courtly chivalric ethic derived ultimately from classical antiquity.[3] But Ehrismann was ungently shouldered aside by E. R. Curtius, who forced the discussion onto the fruitful ground of history of literary forms, leaving uncultivated the equally fertile ground that had been the point of departure for their disagreement: the survival of an ethical code from antiquity.[4] Other scholars are certainly aware of the influence exercised by the ancients on the values represented in courtly literature. Edmond Faral and Jean Frappier stressed the classical education of the clerical authors of romance.[5] But the texts that would have allowed the connections to be demonstrated clearly were either not available or not recognized. To learn to recognize them and to investigate the classical roots of courtesy, it is necessary to begin with a brief overview of ancient urbanity and of the vocabulary in which Cicero articulated that ideal.

The circumstances of life in aristocratic society call forth codes of courtesy; this is a sociological constant. But the medieval West drew on a model to articulate its own notions of courtesy. This model derives ultimately from aristocratic ideals of ancient Greece. In Homer's epics we see an etiquette of politeness, largess, and hospitality governing the interaction of men at royal courts.[6] Athenian culture of the fifth and fourth centuries produced the ideal of the ἀστεῖος ἀνήρ. This ideal, in its origins that of a ruling aristocracy, is for Athenian culture the ideal of an urban elite, as the name indicates (ἀστεῖος, "town bred"; ἄστυ, "town"). It is a forerunner of Roman *urbanitas*. The city culture of Greece developed a high level of sophistication and articulated this through the contrast to country ways. The opposition of the ἀστεῖος to the ἄγροικος is a conventional pattern which we will of course encounter in the Middle Ages, where *rusticus* is opposed to *urbanus* or *curialis*; *vilein* to *courtois*;[7] and *dörperlich to hövesch*.

Lammermann gives a concise summary of qualities of the ἀστεῖος ἀνήρ. He is distinguished for his education. He brings to his dealing with other men a delicacy of feelings which seeks to avoid all embarrassment and boorish directness. The jailer of Socrates is a model of "urbane" tact and delicacy, of a refined sense of considerateness for the feelings of others. He brings Socrates the news of the death sentence with compassionate restraint.[8] To provoke ill-will unintentionally, to strew insults in polite conversation, is boorish; the opposite is urbane. In Athenian society, as in every context of urbanity we will observe, this ideal shows itself particularly in speech. Amiable and ingratiating speech is urbane, as is an elegant turn of phrase, a diction free of jargon and technical terms, and particularly a witty, ironic manner of speaking. Socrates, who struck the pose of ironic modesty before his fellow disputants, represents the epitome of urbane speech. He was never guilty of anger, dogmatism, or heated assertions. He remained superior to his fellow disputants; his positions prevailed, and yet he needed never to shed the pose of self-deprecating deference.

The Greek ideal of urbanity outlived Hellenic culture and the Greek city-state. Its literary expression reached a high point in the plays of Menander, which depict a full-blown ideal of the aristocratic, well-bred gentlemen. The ideal also informs the Hellenistic romance.[9]

Cicero plays a key role in the transmission of a vocabulary of urbanity to the Middle Ages. His *De officiis* summarized urbanity: it idealized a social code current among the aristocracy of Rome and subsumed this code among the ethical ideals appropriate to the Roman statesman. The significant stage at which urbanity was treated as an ethical ideal, a "duty," was apparently reached first by the Greek Stoics. The writer from whom Cicero adapted his *De officiis*, Panaitios, appears to have raised to a philosophic principle the Greek educational idea of *kalokagathia*, the notion that inner virtue, ἀρετή, expresses itself in elegance of bearing, physical beauty and prowess, and urbanity.[10] In Cicero's *De officiis* this ideal becomes projected onto the statesman. Public service is the theater in which virtuous men manifest greatness of soul (*De off.* 1.70–71). State service is the highest activity of mankind, certainly superior to that of the warrior. A single statesman can, through prudence and wisdom, avert wars that otherwise would consume thousands of men (*De off.* 1.79). This makes of statesmanship a form of heroism, ranked above the traditional form, warrior combat (cf. *De off.* 1.83).

Most relevant to our topic is Cicero's treatment of the fourth cardinal virtue, *temperantia*. This virtue includes modesty, restraint, considerateness (*verecundia*), moderation in all things, and the subjection of passion to reason. *Temperantia* is the Greek σωφροσύνη. This virtue "lends a certain polish to life" ("quasi quidam ornatus vitae"—1.93). Cicero dwells, within *temperantia*, above all on the quality *decorum*, propriety. He stresses that this quality is inseparable from virtue and moral perfection, that there is no decorum where *honestas* is absent, and in every exercise of *honestas* and *virtus* there will be an element of *decorum* (1.94, 95, 98). To strengthen this equation of moral goodness and external propriety of action, he calls on the comparison of healthfulness to physical beauty:

> Ut enim pulchritudo corporis apta compositione membrorum movet oculos et delectat hoc ipso, quod inter se omnes partes cum quodam lepore consentiunt, sic hoc decorum, quod elucet in vita, movet approbationem eorum, quibuscum vivitur, ordine et constantia et moderatione dictorum omnium atque factorum. (1.98)

> For as physical beauty with harmonious symmetry of the limbs engages the attention and delights the eye, for the very reason that all the parts combine in harmony and grace, so this propriety, which shines out in our conduct, engages the approbation of our fellow men by the order, consistency, and self-control it imposes upon every word and deed.[11]

Decorum requires, or brings with it, a certain reverence for men ("quaedam reverentia adversus homines"—1.99); it forbids us to wound the feelings of others. Qualities that will arouse friendship are also "decorous": *iocunditas*, *hilaritas*, and *affabilitas*. Ulysses is pressed into service, quite against the spirit of the Homeric poem, as an example of long-suffering affability. Returning home from his wandering, he bore himself with such affability that he even tolerated insults from his servants in order to accomplish his ends (1.113).

Decorous speech is treated at length. Charm and affability in conversation ("comitas affabilitasque sermonis"—2.48) win the affections of men to a degree that makes this kind of speech rank second only to oratory. Jesting (*jocus*) and wit (*facetia*) are important parts of decorous speech. When engaging in entertaining banter, the speaker must hold to a refined and witty style ("ingenuum et facetum"—

1.103), avoid all rudeness, loquacity, and coarseness, and cultivate speech that is "elegant, urbane, clever, and witty" ("elegans, urbanum, ingeniosum, facetum"—1.104). Wit is clearly a quality that Cicero prizes highly. He makes Socrates into the epitome of wit; he was "dulcis et facetus," striking attitudes in conversation which the Greeks call εἴρωνα (1.108). Indeed, in Cicero's usage, *facetia* and *urbanitas* can be synonomous with Greek εἰρωνεία.[12]

Decorum, finally, is a quality manifested in gesture and bearing, even in the tilt of the head and movement of the eyes (see 1.128), and this outer propriety is governed by the three principles, beauty (*formositas*), order, and "a grace which accompanies and suits each action" ("ornatus ad actionem aptus"—1.126). In dress and appearance, the ideal is a fastidious neatness (*munditia*) which holds the mean between rusticity and ostentation.

In summing up *decorum*, Cicero points to an equation that underlies much of his thinking on the subject and is evident in his vocabulary: the similitude of *decorum* in manners with propriety and elegance in speech. Just as an orator trims and shapes his oration into an ordered, balanced unity, so also the guidance of one's life and dealings with others can be shaped and ordered, structured aesthetically (see 1.144). *Decorum* requires in general that the *homo urbanus* subject his behavior to the rule of nature and the laws imposed on him by his own character. Both modes—the guidance of life and the structuring of an oration—presuppose an observing audience; both contain an element of *captatio benevolentiae*. *Decorum* and *honestas* aim at the harmonious regulation of one's dealings with other men, as the oration aims at winning men through persuasion, at creating a harmonious unity of sentiment.

Roman ideals of urbanity, linked to the ethics of state service, were kept alive in the Middle Ages through two channels. One was the actual practice of these ideals in government and court life. Counselors of the Merovingian kings were in part the direct heirs of the Roman statesman (the old Roman senatorial nobility); in part they were the indirect inheritors of the ancient Roman traditions through the survival of the Roman system of education. It is also evident from the epithets of rulers and bishops in panegyric and biographical writings that urbanity as an ethic of public life survived the end of the Roman empire. *Mansuetudo* and *affabilitas* were commonly applied to rulers and statesmen in late antiquity and Merovingian times; aristocratic restraint and graciousness could be cultivated in spite of the violence of the times, or perhaps even because of it.[13]

The second channel was ethical writings. The history of Cicero's influence on the Middle Ages is still to be written, alas.[14] His *De officiis* survived and was an important school text.[15] Along with Seneca, Cicero was the most influential of Roman ethical writers. Their influence was felt in a variety of imitations and adaptations by Christian writers. Saint Ambrose adapted the *De officiis*, taking over its form and altering its content to accord with the duties of a Christian "statesman" in his *De officiis ministrorum ecclesiae*.[16] The Spanish bishop, Martin of Bracara, in his tract on the four cardinal virtues, *Formula vitae honestae*,[17] produced a work that was to exercise an important influence in the Middle Ages, partly because it was ascribed early on to Seneca. The author opens with the forthright statement that he is writing for the simple guidance of life within the natural law of human affairs, not for that higher level of ethics and morality contained in Scripture:

non illa ardua et perfecta quae a paucis et egregiis deicolis patrantur instituit, sed ea magis commonet quae et sine divinarum scripturarum praeceptis naturali tantum humanae intellegentiae lege etiam a laicis recte honesteque viventibus valeant adimpleri.

[This book] does not instruct in those arduous and high goals achieved by the faithful few, but rather it urges the course of life which can be attained without the precepts of Scripture by laymen living an upright and moral life guided only by the natural law of human understanding. (Ed. Barlow, p. 237)

This influential tract, widely distributed in the eleventh century, gave legitimacy to a natural ethic.

The influence of ancient ideals of decorum on the eleventh century represents a peculiar blind spot in the study of medieval ethics. The venerable name of Hans Baron and the title of his article, "Cicero and the Roman Civic Spirit in the Middle Ages and the Early Renaissance," arouse high expectation, and the article is important for pointing to the survival of the Roman civic ideals.[18] But Baron badly underestimates the presence of this spirit and of Ciceronian ideals of statesmanship and decorum in the eleventh century. More disappointing is N. E. Nelson's study "Cicero's *De officiis* in Christian Thought: 300–1300."[19] For his treatment of the eleventh century Nelson was content to consult the indexes of Manitius' literary history, and this was bound to produce the conclusion: negligible influence.

Cicero's influence is most apparent in the epistolary and biographical literature from the cathedral schools of the period. If indexes be our guide, then those in Erdmann's edition of letters from the period of Henry IV will swell the tiny rivulet of Nelson and Manitius into a mighty tide.[20] The list of Ciceronian quotations occupies two columns in his index. In his studies of these letters Erdmann can refer to the

Bamberg schoolmaster Meinhard (mid-eleventh century) as "a true Ciceronian," who draws particularly on *De officiis* and the Tusculan Disputations, and whose style bears a clear "Ciceronian stamp."[21] Also telling is the collection that Erdmann calls the "Regensburg rhetorical letters." The author produced a rich assortment of citations from classical writers, above all Cicero. A scholarly work that studies the motifs of these letters as forerunners of the main themes at the French humanist schools in the earlier twelfth century is still to be written. It is a rich topic. The letter 10 of this collection (advice to a bishop-elect, ed. Erdmann, p. 320 ff.) makes particularly interesting reading. It is a cento of quotations from various works of Cicero and from Ambrose's *De officiis*.

Both Cicero's and Ambrose's *De officiis* were abundantly available in the cathedral and monastic libraries of the period.[22] The language of ethics and the representation of men in public life were saturated with the ideas and terminology from these works. The chapters that follow here will give abundant testimony to this influence. Let two examples of it serve for the moment. Anselm of Liège, writing around 1056, was guided by Cicero in depicting an incident in the life of Bishop Wazo. When Henry I of France threatened to invade Aix, Wazo prevented it by writing a letter dissuading him. Anselm's comment: thus undertakings that kings require great armies to prevent can be averted by the wisdom and eloquence of a single wise man.[23] Peter of Poitiers wrote some lines in praise of Peter the Venerable: "Sessio, vox, vultus, incessus, et actio tota, / In te lux hominum, plena decoris erant" (PL 189:51A). They are lifted with minor variations from *De officiis* 1.128: "Status incessus, sessio accubitio, vultus oculi manuum motus teneat illud decorum." The well-known tract ascribed to William of Conches, *Moralium dogma philosophorum*, was important for excerpting a number of ancient works on ethics (above all *De officiis*), but certainly not for introducing ancient ethical ideals to Europe.

The conditions that favored a revival of Roman senatorial ethical ideals were created in the Ottonian period. The influence of the three Ottos raised to the full light of consciousness the awareness that the guidance of the state and the conduct of public life had a powerful ideal model in the Roman senate. The Ottos styled themselves as revivers of empire, continuators of the emperors of ancient Rome and of the Carolingian empire. Some verses of Brun of Cologne in praise of his brother Otto the Great deserve our attention at this point. They are a dedication accompanying a copy of Frontinus' (first century) *Strategemata* presented by Brun to the emperor. The passage of interest to us hails Otto as a reviver of the "study and care for the ancients" after studies, suppressed by "savage barbarism," had lapsed into "dark ages":

> Gloria, pax, decus et requies
> Aurea te duce secla refert.
> Deciderat studium veterum
> Et vigilancia pene patrum,
> Cecaque secula barbaries
> Seva premebat et error iners.
> At tua dextra ubi sceptra tenet,
> Publica res sibi tuta placet;
> Exacuit calamos studium
> Fertque, quod apparat, ad solium.
> (MGH, Poet. Lat., V.ii.378, l. 19ff.)

The glory, peace, decorum and calm attained with you as our ruler call in a new golden age. The study and care for the ancients, our ancestors, had all but collapsed and left those dark ages oppressed by fierce barbarism and stagnant ignorance. But where your hand holds sway, the republic enjoys safety. Once more Study sharpens her pen and bears to the throne the fruits of her work.

Josef Fleckenstein and Hans Martin Klinkenberg have shown that the poem can be accepted with some certainty as a genuine work of Brun, not that of a follower of Gerbert writing to Otto III, as Carl Erdmann suggests.[24] Both Fleckenstein and Klinkenberg are persuaded that the "blind ages" are those that separate the reigns of Charlemagne and Otto; the revival is primarily that of Carolingian state and educational ideals. Fleckenstein interprets the "barbarism" as the invasions of foreigners, suppressed by Otto, whereas Klinkenberg interprets it as a reign of allegorical vices for which Brun's literary inspiration was Prudentius. Even though Brun may have had the thought of the Carolingians in the foreground, he surely was referring to the authors of classical antiquity when he used the words "ancients" and "fathers" or "ancestors." E. R. Curtius took these words to refer, however, to the church fathers.[25] While early Christian writers are not excluded by the general designation "ancient fathers," the main area of reference here is undoubtedly classical antiquity. After all, the emperor is addressed as "cesar" (l. 3) and "pater patriae" (11) and is lauded in epithets borrowed from Horace (14; cf. Horace, *Carm.* 1.1.2); the empire is called "res publica" (26). No matter how common these terms may have been in the Carolingian period, they evoked the aura of imperial Rome whenever they were applied. Modern commentaries on the poem have all but ignored the line, "Once more Study sharpens her pen and bears to the throne the fruits of her work." That describes precisely what Brun is doing by presenting a work of Frontinus to the emperor: he is bearing to the throne the fruits of his *studium veterum* and *vigilancia patrum*. The line restates allegorically the actual occasion for writing the dedicatory poem. And with this occasion in mind, the meaning of "ancients" and "ancestors" is clear: they are the contemporaries or near-contemporaries of Frontinus. Hence what is revived is the care for and study of the ancient Roman authors that had once been typical of the Carolingian age.

This poem calls our attention to the atmosphere that nurtured an interest in empire and to the writings celebrating and preserving the customs of empire. This atmosphere is detectable in many areas of Ottonian court life and culture.[26] In dress and ceremony, in the naming of offices, and in various aspects of imperial *representatio*, the Ottos surrounded themselves with the trappings of imperial Rome. At the same time they sought and established ties with the Byzantine court, their rival to the claim of continuing the Roman empire. Otto II married Theophanu, niece of the emperor Johannes Tzimiskes. She exercised an important influence on the German imperial court, importing new customs of dress and ceremony from the highly refined Byzantine court.[27] It is entirely possible that the refinement of manners which becomes such a prominent feature of imperial court life in the eleventh century owes much to fashions of conduct at the Byzantine court. We recall that Adalbert of Bremen considered himself a descendant of Otto II and Theophanu, and imitated the style of the Byzantines in manners and dress (see above, p. 70). But the Byzantine connection has left no impression on the vocabulary of refinement and sophistication in Europe. This is consistently borrowed from ancient Roman ideals of urbanity, as we shall see.

The role of tenth- and eleventh-century Italy in the formation of courtly ideals is an important question, but one on which I can shed very little light. It is apparent that ancient Roman ideals of urbanity had never died out altogether in Italy. Otto of Freising praises the Lombards for having maintained since antiquity and in spite of intermarriage with the pagan German tribes, the "urbanity of manners and speech" typical of ancient Rome (see below, p. 143). The attempt of the Ottos to integrate Italy into their empire regularly brought the less civilized Germans into contact with the last traces of a once great civilization. The Germans needed to appropriate the external signs of empire, and so it is logical to assume that whatever of these remained alive in contemporary Italy furnished a model to imitate. But the influence of Italy on courtly ideals is the subject for another study.

Otto III, the son of Theophanu, was an avid imitator of ancient Rome and contemporary Byzantium. Thietmar of Merseburg reports that Otto arranged seating at table in such a manner that he was placed at a raised dais "in the manner of Roman emperors," with the others grouped around him in semi-circles.[28] Otto was lauded in verses by Leo of Vercelli as the reviver of ancient Roman grandeur.[29] He also attracted some of the most gifted, learned, and illustrious men of Europe to his court. He admired the learning and urbanity of Gerbert d'Aurillac and invited him to his court to banish its "Saxon rusticity."[30] Gerbert, later Pope Sylvester II, so famous for his learning and statesmanship that a legend had it he had sold his soul to the devil, styled himself as "a faithful executor of the precepts of Tullius [i.e., Cicero], in both state affairs and in leisure."[31] By the end of Otto III's reign, the atmosphere of the imperial court is strongly colored by the idea of *renovatio imperii Romanorum*.

The idea began to articulate itself in a variety of ways in the reigns of Henry III (1039–56) and his son Henry IV (1056–1106). These rulers are of particular importance for the development of medieval courtesy. At the court of Henry III a code of court manners surfaced and was formulated for the first time, but this code presumably had existed in some prototypical form in Ottonian times. When Henry III married the daughter of Duke William V of Aquitaine, Agnes of Poitou, in 1043, opponents of the match claimed that it led to the importation into Germany of vain and frivolous customs from the courts of Provence. (We will look at the circumstances and the texts that report them later.) In this period we have the first occurrence of the phrase "elegance of manners" and of the word *curialitas* along with a description of the phenomenon. The milieu for both is the royal-imperial court chapel. In this period also the first romance-epic describing refined court manners and courtship customs involving deference to ladies was composed, the Latin *Ruodlieb*, probably by a monk of Tegernsee, dated as early as 1042 but as late as 1070. The distinct ties to the court of Henry III argue for a dating in his reign.[32] There is a confluence of this swell of courtly representation with a renewed spirit of classical revival under these two Henrys. In the reign of Henry III the emperor's court again is called *curia*. This word displaces the terms standard in Ottonian times, *aula* and *palatium*.[33] *Curia* designated the meeting place of the Roman senate in antiquity, and its revival is consistent with other classicizing tendencies of the mid-eleventh century.

These tendencies found expresson in a number of literary works, particularly from the milieu of the court chapel, notably the "Tetralogus" of the royal chaplain Wipo and the "Sermones" of Sextus Amarcius.[34] But we can best characterize these tendencies by reference to a peculiar and rich work, the panegyric *Ad Heinricum IV Imperatorem* of Bishop Benzo of Alba, who was probably an Italian, possibly a Greek, and who had served in the chapel of Henry III. The work is a collection of various writings by Benzo purportedly for the instruction of Henry IV. They were composed initially in the third quarter of the eleventh century and collected and copied as a single work between 1086 and 1090.[35] Much of the work consists of polemics favoring the party of Henry IV in his controversy with Gregory VII; many aim at stirring Henry's clerical supporters into action on the emperor's behalf. They show us a vivid picture of an idealized court chapel serving an idealized emperor. Over Henry's shoulders Benzo casts the mantle of the divine emperor, the successor of Julius Caesar and other noble Romans:

> Tantus es, o cesar quantus et orbis;
> Cis mare vel citra tu leo fortis,
> Presso namque tua calce dracone,
> Victor habes palmam cum Scipione.
> Ille quidem Penos exsuperavit,
> Sed tua Romuleos dextra fugavit;
> Ille palaciola fregit Elisse,
> Tu Romae muros Iulius ipse.
> Transcendens Fabios et Cicerones,
> Cunctos Fabricios atque Catones,
> Das populis iura cum Salomone, . . .
> Reges christicolas atque profanos, . . .
> Transilis hos sensu, viribus, armis,
> De coelo missus, non homo carnis.
>
> (6.7, pp. 668–69, ll.36–49)

You O Caesar are great as the orb itself. On both sides of the ocean you are known to possess the courage of a lion, for, having crushed the dragon under foot, you hold the palm of victory alongside Scipio. For if he conquered the Carthiginians, you set to flight the Romans with your right hand; he toppled the palaces of Dido, you, Julius Caesar embodied, the walls of Rome. Outstripping the Fabii and Ciceros, the Fabricii and Catos, you give the people laws with the wisdom of Solomon. . . . Outstripping them all, kings Christian and pagan, in mind, strength, prowess at arms, no man of flesh, but an emissary of the heavens.

Rome rejoices at the restoration of its desires, the uniting in one empire of all that Julius Caesar had conquered (see 6.6, p. 668, l. 27 ff.). The "Empire" in its wanderings has now come to rest perpetually among the Germans; they are the true heirs of the Greeks, Romans, and Lombards (see 3.1, p. 622, l. 15 ff.).

The works are replete with this sort of classical and mythological allusion. Particularly interesting is that Benzo depicts the king's counsel drawing on the model of the Roman senate. The gathering of the king's court is the *senatus* (p. 622, l. 7); its members are *senatores* (p. 616, l. 1), whom he addresses as *patres conscripti* (p. 622, l. 47; p. 631, l. 7; p. 671, l. 48). In his glorifying of the court counsel, Benzo gives us an important insight into the climate of the chapel:

Multi quidem nobiles et sapientes viri morantur in curia domini mei, qui Ciceronicis amministrationibus valuissent sedare commotiones imperii. (2.3, p. 614, l. 11 ff.)

Truly many wise and noble men reside at the court of my lord, who could with the administrative skill of a Cicero have calmed the turbulence in the empire.

He praises the Bishop of Turin: "You imitate Cicero, you follow Sallust, / Your name is recorded in the catalogue of illustrious men . . ." ("Imitaris Ciceronem, sequeris Salustium, / In kalatogo virorum es scriptus illustrium . . ."—4.4; p. 639, ll. 21–22). He compares the counselors of this age, not only with the senators and intellectuals of ancient Rome, but also with the great courtiers of the reign of Otto III. The Ottonian period was a kind of golden age, he says (p. 638, l. 29 ff.; p. 642, l. 23 ff.).[36] He admonishes Archbishop Theobald of Milan to come to the aid of Henry, citing the service of *barones episcopi* of Otto III, including Leo of Vercelli and Heribert of Cologne. As Hercules struck off the head of the Hydra, so Theobald should do battle with the king's enemies (see 4.1; pp. 634–35). And after the list of illustrious Ottonian *praesules*, he asks Theobald:

> Numquid patribus praemissis vos estis deterior?
> Omni genere virtutum apparetis melior,
> Natu, opibus, et sensu omnibus superior.

Are you less than these our ancestors from bygone days? No, in every sort of virtue you are clearly their superior, in nobility, wealth and intelligence. (P. 636, l. 5 ff.)

Benzo's vision of the return of a golden age is probably not entirely hortatory rhetoric. There was a feeling in the air that the men of this age could measure themselves against the greats of the past. Benzo himself possessed an ideal of the dignity of man and a keen sense of the abilities of some men to distinguish themselves by their natural human talents as opposed to the grace of God. On the question dear to the heart of a former chaplain, the selection of bishops, he opposes the notion that the king need only wait passively for some divine sign of election; rather the king selects men of distinction by exercising *specialis discretio* (1.25, 26; p. 609, l. 35). Benzo composed a praise of man which could have been the work of a Renaissance humanist:

In sanctis narratur aecclesiis, quod homo sit kyrrios bestiis,
Utens est quippe rationibus, quod denegatum est peccoribus.
Intellectus ei tribuitur, per quem flammis coeli coniungitur,
Erectus sursum habitudine, ornatur linguae pulchritudine.
(4.12, p. 645, ll. 33–36)

In holy churches it is told that man is lord over the beasts, since he possesses reason denied to animals. Divine understanding is said to be his lot, by which he is joined to heaven itself. Erect in stature, he is adorned by the beautiful gift of speech.

He unfolds his thoughts on virtue in an interesting allegory. Virtue is "dignity of mind, nobility of soul"; it makes man an object of wonder, even more, it deifies him:

Virtus est mentis dignitas, et animi nobilitas,
Quae homines mirificat, insuper et deificat.
(7.3, p. 673, ll. 20–21)

The path of virtue leads to God, and on it is erected the palace of virtue, radiant with topaze and constructed with twelve sorts of stone. Virtue and her helpers constructed the palace. *Fides* laid the foundation, *Spes* erected the walls, *Caritas* set the roof in place, and *Largitas* decorated the entire structure. Humility and Loftiness of sound intellect are the tower guards; Humility and her friend Purity keep watch at the windows; Chastity guards the gates; Compassion keeps the keys. Benzo continues in this vein and ends with praise of Friendship, who convokes the residents of the palace for the distribution of rewards (*munera*).[37]

The allegory has a distinct humanist cast to it and is a forerunner of a form popular in the renaissance of the twelfth century, the moralizing allegory of carts, temples, buildings, and so forth.[38] Benzo's work reflects a humanism and neoclassicism whose matrix is the royal chapel under Henry III and Henry IV. He was certainly not merely drawing on far-flung conceits and inflated sentiments that found no echo in his social milieu. Just the contrary; there was a widespread resonance. The glorification of the ancient and recent past was in the air.

C. H. Haskins observed that the "twelfth century renaissance" took place in France at a time when the investiture controversy in Germany paralyzed the forces that could have called forth a similar flowering there. The classical revival flourished in France in the intellectual and artistic realms: the Latin classics and Platonism became major literary influences, and the spirit of ancient Greece and Rome touched the forms of Gothic sculpture. Similar forces were alive and at work in the chapel of Henry III and Henry IV, it is evident. A "renaissance" that arose from these forces would have taken quite a different complexion from that which flourished at the French cathedral schools. At the imperial courts there was fertile soil for a revival of the classics and of humanist notions of the dignity of man, but the narrower context was state service. The main application of the classics was in the shaping of an ethic. The political and social climate, not only the literary scene, was pervaded by the notion of *renovatio*. Its implications were pursued into the conception of qualities appropriate to the king's counselors; his chaplains could envision no higher praise than that they were the imitators and heirs of Cicero and Sallust.

The forms of social intercourse are every bit as open to shaping and modeling as are the forms of poetry, painting, and sculpture, and in Germany the work of art that best expressed neoclassicism was the statesman. Alas, unlike his counterparts in the aesthetic and intellectual realm in France, he was mortal and had enemies who stymied his growth in the political realm. But his ideals of humanity and "elegant" comportment lived on, sublimated, in the ethical ideals of courtly romance.

Against this background, the rich vocabulary of *decorum* in Latin texts from the period becomes intelligible.

THE LANGUAGE OF COURTESY: LATIN TERMINOLOGY, VERNACULAR COUNTERPARTS

E MUST hold firm from the outset to a division in the medieval concepts of court behavior into two separable categories, the one ethical, the other social. There is a spectrum of attitudes among contemporaries about the degree to which these two should ideally be allied with each other. The rigorously orthodox position rejected any attempt to justify the cleric's life at court. The moderately conservative believed that court behavior was well governed by the ethical code, but that the ethical code was an emergency plan the cleric called on temporarily to help guide his behavior in court service until he could free himself from its snares and escape into the sanctified air of the monastic community; the courtly social code was to be shunned as sinful and "inordinate."[1] There was also a liberal humanist position. It is the one that interests us most, and it applied to the most distinguished men at court. This position attempted to reconcile the ethical with the social code, subordinating the latter to the former; the standard formulation for this position in our texts is "pleasing God and the world."[2] Finally, there was the purely worldly position of the *curialis* who did not hold to an ethical plan to guide his life in the world but took up court ways simply in the sense of fashions. Here courtesy degenerated into external show.

While these distinctions demonstrably existed throughout our period, the Latin vocabulary which bears them does not always maintain crisp distinctions. I will refer to the ethical code with the term *elegantia morum* and to the purely social code of court manners with *curialitas*. The latter usage however must be swathed in cautionings. The neologism appeared in the eleventh century applied with opprobium by conservative clerics to court manners in their lowest form, such as gluttony, lasciviousness, and luxurious clothes. But by the mid-twelfth century, *curialitas* has come to encompass the ethical code as well and to convey the liberal humanist position sketched out in the previous paragraph. It is therefore slightly arbitrary and perhaps unfair to the term to pin it to the worst phenomena to which it referred at an early stage in the emergence of court ideals. If the history of ideas had been accommodating enough to maintain a strict co-ordination of words and concepts over the period of time with which we are dealing, such qualifications and imprecise labelings would not be necessary. But alas the forces at work in the period did not have in mind the urge of scholars in the twentieth century to keep their concepts and the vocabulary that conveys them in tidy parcels.

I: Ethics: Elegantia Morum

An incident in Herbord's *Dialogue on the Life of Otto of Bamberg* gives us a full and remarkably lucid example of the ethical code and at the same time an example of what I have called the humanist position. The first part of this chapter takes the form of a commentary on this episode.

It occurred during Otto's first proselytizing mission to Pomerania. The narrator, Siegfried, describes Otto's preparations for baptizing the heathens. He begins by praising Otto's conscientiousness, fastidiousness, and sense of propriety (*diligencia, munditia, honestas*—2.16, p. 88). Otto scrupulously provided that nothing indecorous or unbecoming (*nichil indecorum, nichil pudendum*) might offend the converts during baptism. He had large basins sunk into the earth, their lips rising above the ground to the height of a man's knee. He ordered curtains spread, crownlike, around each tub. In addition, linen curtains were to surround and screen off the officiating priest, so that every possible precaution should be taken to respect the feelings of the converts ("quatenus verecundie undique provisum foret"—p. 89). The crowd of pagans gathered before these makeshift baptistries. They were led individually, the men segregated from the women, to the curtained fonts. Two priests stood within the surrounding curtain. One held the robe of the baptizand as he descended into the water, holding it before his own eyes until the ceremony was completed and the man robed again. The other, the ministering priest, diverted his eyes until he heard that the baptizand was immersed, then removed the curtain in front of him only long enough to administer the sacrament, and after replacing it bade the person leave the font. In the winter the water was warmed, and spice, incense, and scented oils added. At this point one of the participants in the dialogue interrupts to express his astonishment at the refinement and humane delicacy of these arrangements (*disciplinata et honesta baptizandi forma*—p. 90). The narrator replies:

"Nec mirum te ista mirari. Etenim, qui ea vidimus, mirabamur et ipsi tam hec quam alia complura morum eius atque virtutum insignia. Ipse namque in omni accione sua, . . . quandam a Spiritu sancto—hoc enim potissimum credo—cuiusdam singularis mundicie atque, ut ita dixerim, elegantis et urbane discipline prerogativam habebat, ita ut nichil unquam indecens aut ineptum inhonestumve quid in cibo aut potu, sermone, gestu vel habitu admitteret. Sed in omni officio exterioris hominis, quenam esset composicio interioris, ostendebat, bonitate, disciplina et prudencie cautela conspicuus." (Ibid.)

"It is small wonder that you are amazed. We who were present were amazed also, not only at this but at many other indications of his manners and his virtues. For in every one of his acts . . . he showed a special gift of singular fastidiousness and, if I may say so, of elegant and urbane breeding [*elegans et urbana disciplina*]. Never under any circumstances, in eating, drinking, in word, gesture, or dress, would he tolerate anything indecorous, inappropriate or unbecoming, but rather in every act of the outer man, he manifested the harmony that reigned within him, conspicuous as he was for his goodness, good breeding, and far-sighted wisdom."

This remarkable passage gives us a panorama of the qualities that comprise *elegantia morum*. This coincides significantly with an almost comprehensive listing of the virtues contained in the Ciceronian concept of *decorum*. The arrangements show Otto's refined and scrupulous sense of propriety and well-bred considerateness; the elegant and urbane breeding is the outer sign of inner virtue; the decorousness of the outer man reflects an inner harmony (*composicio*). It should also be noted that this elegant and urbane breeding is not at all restricted to the Christian context of the bishop converting and baptizing, but shows itself as well in the entirely worldly context of table manners, speech, gesture, and dress (*in cibo aut potu, sermone, gestu vel habitu*).[3]

DISCIPLINA

This is the overarching virtue of the above passage. The entire episode which calls forth the praise of Otto centers on his *disciplinata et honesta baptizandi forma*; the summation of Otto's *insignia morum* is his *elegans et urbana disciplina*; *disciplina* is one of the elements which comprise his inner *composicio*.

The word *disciplina* as it is used here and elsewhere in the context of court manners in the twelfth century has no counterpart in classical Latin. Its main area of reference in antiquity is school learning; it includes the particular objects of that learning ("the disciplines"), the process of learning itself, and the end product of that process. It retained this meaning in the Middle Ages.[4] But an area of reference at least as broad was monastic rule and the ordered religious life in general. It also meant chastisement, specifically flagellation. Probably both of these areas of reference, the schools and the monasteries, contributed to the meaning of the word as used in Herbord's *Dialogus*. But the originating context there is undoubtedly the court and behavior appropriate to the court. It is hardly likely that the "discipline" of the Christian life would be qualified with the terms "elegant and urbane"; these were qualities that Saint Augustine had rejected as the vanities of his youth.[5]

Disciplina in our period acquires the meaning of courteous, restrained good manners, the result of a courtly education. Hence the translation above with its suggestion of aristocratic breeding resulting in a polished gentleman. The earliest occurrences of the word in this context that I have found are in the *Ruodlieb*. The first occurs during Ruodlieb's embassy to the conquered *rex minor*. At the end of a scene which is a mirror of court ceremonial—table manners, etiquette of greeting and leave taking (4.120 ff.)—the legates are provided with a guide to lead them out of the kingdom; he is praised for his good services:

> "Disciplinate noster ductor vel honeste
> Servivit nobis in simplicitateque cordis,
> Huius dum regni confinia vidimus ampli."
> (4.170–72)

Disciplinate seems to be almost interchangeable with *honeste* in the poet's usage, joined as the two are by *vel*.[6] (They were also joined in the phrase *disciplinata et honesta baptizandi forma*.) Here the stress is on the guide's lack of guile and self-willedness; he guides them in good faith, and the suggestion of restraint must refer to the implied stifling of what might be an impulse to misguide and rob men at his mercy. Being legates of a hostile king, they offer their guide a real motive for guile. In general, the scenes depicting the court of the two kings in *Ruodlieb* stress the restraint and affection that governs human interactions: the atmosphere is free of anger, deceit, resentment, and boorish self-assertion; there is gaiety and amiability among members of the court, low and high. The restraint and good will implied in *disciplinate* is entirely at home in this atmosphere.

The second occurrence in *Ruodlieb* is quite different. The boorish *rufus* proposes an assignation with the young wife of an old peasant, while her husband is standing nearby. She accepts the proposal but must dissemble any joy or anticipation, lest her husband notice:

Disciplinate stans hoc audivit ut omne,
Interius gaudens tamen inquit ei quasi maerens:
"Cuncta libens facio. . . ."

(7.81–83)

Here *disciplina* is composure and self-restraint used to mask deceitful dealings, quite the opposite of the guilelessness of Ruodlieb's "disciplined" guide. But the common factor is apparent: reason is made the master of impulse; impulsive actions or feelings are subordinated to some more distant goal. The guide serves the "enemies" of his king with perfect good will, whereas he could easily mislead and rob them; the woman stifles her joy to put on a sad face, preventing detection and furthering her ultimate goal, the illicit liaison.

The social context of *disciplina* in this sense is undoubtedly the ruler's court. An incident in the *vita* of Paulina of Zell, written around 1135–50, urges this conclusion. The author, Sigebot of Paulinzell, praises Bishop Wernher of Merseburg (1059–93) for his "courtly disciplines" in a revealing context. There is a convening of the royal court (of Henry IV) at Goslar. In attendance are "princes of the realm,"

inter quos et aderat ipse Werenherus curialibus disciplinis et splendida quadam claritudine mentem adeo informans, ut inter aulicos et viros mundana gloria prefulgidos nichil rusticanae simplicitatis admitteret omnibusque gloriosus appareret.

among whom Wernher was present, and so replete was he with courtly disciplines and a certain brilliance of mind that among courtiers and men preeminent for worldly glory he appeared glorious indeed, banishing all trace of rustic simplicity.[7]

The passage is useful for juxtaposing rusticity and courtliness, as well as for placing *disciplinae* precisely in the context of the king's court. This quality is placed parallel to "brilliance" and both are qualities of the mind. We will meet comparable pairs of courtly qualities repeatedly, usually described by the formula, *litterae et mores*. Here the intellectual component of Wernher's excellence is *claritudo*, the ethical *disciplinae*. Another revealing text is from the *vita* of this same Bishop Wernher, a work derived in part from the *Vita Paulinae* and dating shortly after 1150. The wife of Wernher's brother, Ute, a prominent figure at the court of Henry IV, is praised as a woman, "in qua dignitas nobilitatis cum morum disciplina, divitiarum gloria cum forma speciosa concordabant" (MGH, SS 12:245, ll. 16–17). Here there is, as in Herbord's *Dialogus*, a suggestion of harmony linking inner and outer qualities: inner dignity appropriate to nobility has its counterpart in well-bred, acquired good manners; physical beauty finds its material counterpart and the means necessary to its proper adornment in "glorious riches."

The courtly ideal *disciplina* developed in secular courts between the mid-eleventh and mid-twelfth centuries. Its occurrence in *Ruodlieb* is sufficient to assure us that it had a part among the well-elaborated ideals of ceremony and etiquette at the court scene represented there, and this in turn is probably a mirror—naturally, an idealizing mirror—of the court of Henry III.

The concept had a glorious future in the vernacular. In MHG its counterpart, *zuht*, is, along with *hövescheit*, the central ideal of courtly manners as these are represented in lyric and romance. *Zuht* is undoubtedly a loan translation from the Latin *disciplina*. The courtly meaning of both has been transferred onto a word which earlier referred to chastisement, school-learning, and monastic discipline. Both have in common the interchangeability of singular and plural forms. The phrase we observed in Herbord's *Dialogus, elegans et urbana disciplina*, would have as its MHG counterpart *schöne und hövesche zuht*. Wernher of Merseburg's *curiales disciplinae* would translate into MHG as *hövesche zühte*, a term too common in romance to require the citing of examples here. *Zuht* in the courtly sense occurs in MHG literature as early as the *Rolandslied* of Pfaffe Konrad, written probably for Henry the Lion around 1171.[8] In German romance, from Heinrich von Veldeke's *Eneit* on, the term is literally ubiquitous. "Beautiful discipline" and "courtly disciplines" were high ideals preached by the romanciers and exemplified by the conduct of their heroes. Ehrismann discusses the concept, connecting it with Ciceronian *decorum*.[9] This clearly has validity in terms of history of ideas and manners, but not in word history. *Disciplina*—*zuht*, meaning courtly good breeding, is, in terms of word history, a medieval formulation.

ME takes up the Latin *disciplina* and, like MHG, makes the loan word into a central concept of courtesy. Its occurrence in this context however is remarkably late, if we can rely on the entries in the *Middle English Dictionary*. It occurs abundantly in the context of monastic discipline in the thirteenth century, but only in the mid-fourteenth does it take on the meaning of courtly good manners. The fifteenth century tract on the education of boys, *Stans puer ad mensam*, urges, "My dere child, first thiself enable / With all thin herte to vertuous disciplyne. . . ."[10] And Edmund Spenser still writes in the prefatory letter to his *Faerie Queen* that the intent of the work is "to fashion a gentleman or noble person in virtuous and gentle discipline."

Neither Provencal nor OF has a counterpart to ML *disciplina*, MHG *zuht*. That is, there is no word that the vernacular adapted directly from Latin. OF has the adjective *bien apris* to describe a courtly gentleman or lady,[11] and this has much in common with ML *disciplinat-*, and MHG *wolgezogen*, though the range of meanings is narrower in OF. The OF *bien apris* is coined for the specific purpose of comprehending a courtly ideal of education. Evidently the development of the vocabulary of courtesy took a different course in OF than in MHG. Another distinction is that *bien apris* is not particularly common in OF, whereas *zuht* occurs over 100 times in Hartmann's narrative works, about 120 times in Gottfried's *Tristan*, about 160 times in Wolfram's *Parzival*. *Bien apris* was an occcasional term of praise in OF, whereas *zuht* is the epitome of courtliness in Germany.

I hope that this observation will jar some of the traditional notions of the dependency of the MHG vocabulary of courtesy on OF. The few studies of these relationships (see chap. 7, n. 2) take as their point of departure the assumption of a total dependency of the German upon the French. Hence we are well informed on the provenance of the MHG terms for tents, lances, stirrups and other chivalric bric-a-brac. But the roots of the MHG courtly ethical vocabulary remain largely in the dark. There is a blind spot in our perception of the history of courtesy, one that has permitted an imperial tradition of court manners to go unobserved.[12] But the existence of such a tradition explains the fact that MHG authors could adapt the ethical language of the courtly romance in part from an *indigenous Latin vocabulary* of courtesy. That this was a tradition of the German royal courts explains why OF poets did not necessarily rely on it in forging their own vocabulary of courtesy, why, for instance, the OF *desceplin* remained restricted to the meanings of monastic order and chastisement.

One final point on the subject of "discipline." The two other collective nouns referring to the code of good manners at court, *urbanitas* and *curialitas*, indicate a place, a social setting as the originating factor in these codes: the city and the court. The native context of *disciplina* is the schools and the monasteries, education and restraint under a rule. This should not be taken as pointing to those social centers as originating factors, but rather to the contemporary perception of courtliness as an ideal of education. The word points to its intellectual, not its social origins.

ELEGANTIA MORUM

Otto's *insignia morum* were summed up in the phrase *elegans et urbana disciplina*. We will not go far astray if we assume that Herbord equated these qualities with the *elegantia morum* ascribed to Otto by both his other biographers (see above, p. 32). This is a rich and important concept. We want to study it in some detail along with its variants, *gratia*, *venustas*, *amoenitas*, or *suavitas morum*.

We have already observed that these qualities have a clearly determinable function in the career of a courtier. They were an important element of *idoneitas*; they attested to a man's suitability for service in the imperial chapel. By the end of the twelfth century they could be referred to as part of the *aulicorum ritus* that aimed at a swift rise to favor within the ruler's retinue.

The term *elegantia morum* derives from classical Latin. While it is not common, it occurs in contexts which make its meaning in antiquity evident. Seneca, in his letter-tract *Ad Marciam de consolatione*, traces various stages of Marcia's grief: at first she actively imposed it upon herself, now (at the time of writing) she is passively permitting it to continue. But soon, he urges her, she must put an end to it by an act of the will: "Quanto magis hoc morum tuorum elegantiae convenit, finem luctus potius facere, quam expectare" (8.3) ("How much more this will accord with your elegance of bearing, to put an end to mourning actively than to wait for it to present itself"). Quintilian praises Seneca's writing, in which there is "multa . . . morum gratia legenda" (*De inst. orat.* 10.1.129). Tacitus praises Pomponius in the *Annals* for his *morum elegantia*, "dum adversam fortunam aequus tolerat" (5.8). Evidently the phrase belongs to the vocabulary of Stoicism. Its infrequent occurrence and the fact that it never occurs in Cicero, however, indicate that it was not a central conception. It indicates a calm and graceful mastering of adversity, restraint of passion. It had not entirely lost this meaning in the Middle Ages. Thomasin von Zirclaere is evidently using the German equivalent when he writes, "swer in zorn hat schoene site, / dem volget guotiu zuht mite" (*Der Welsche Gast*, ll. 679–80). Here also the mastering of powerful and "negative" emotions constitutes "beatiful manners." However, I have not found a single occurrence of it in this context in the *vitae* or in any other Latin texts from the tenth to the twelfth centuries. Here it appears to be an ideal of decorum and courtliness. As I pointed out earlier, the terms are distinguished from other more common ethical terms (*probitas morum*, *boni mores*, etc.) by taking *mores* into the aesthetic sphere. We observed also that Cicero had compared decorous manners to physical beauty and harmony of parts, and that he called on the comparison of "composed" conduct to a literary composition to elucidate *decorum*. When an ideal of education results in the aestheticizing of manners and conduct, then an important stage in the process of civilizing is reached. Reason has so far subdued impulse and is to such an extent master of action, that the structuring of behavior becomes analogous to the structuring of a well-wrought work of art. Let us see what the sources on *elegantia morum* tell us about the stage of civilizing implied by the term.

Elegantia morum keeps close company with intellectual qualities, the products of education, and the well-disciplined religious life. These various connections, as well as the function of pleasing princes, were evident in the description of Hartmann, Abbot of Göttweig, the former royal chaplain, groomed for the bishopric of Salzburg:

Erat . . . summo religionis studio deditus, prudentia tam saeculari quam spi-rituali eximie praeditus, copiosa disertus eloquentia, morum exuberans elegantia.

He was . . . devoted to the supreme study of religion, highly endowed with both secular and spiritual wisdom, a font of copious eloquence, abounding in elegance of manners. (*Vita Altm.*, chap. 40, MGH, SS 12, p. 241, l. 31 f.)

Letters, religion, and beautiful manners are all linked in Orderic Vitalis' praise of Matilda, queen of England, wife of William the Conqueror:

Reginam hanc simul decoravere forma, genus, litterarum scientia, cuncta morum et virtutum pulchritudo, et quod his laude immortali dignius est firma fides et studiosus amor Christi.

The queen was endowed with beauty, noble birth, learning, all beauty of manners and virtues, and—what is and ever will be more worthy of praise—strong faith and fervent love of Christ.[13]

Clearly *elegantia* and *pulchritudo morum* have nothing to do with the frivolous vanities of worldly ways; they in no way exclude religious devotion. But they are evidently qualities appropriate to religious men and women living in the world: Matilda, queen of England; Hartmann the former royal chaplain who had been groomed for a bishop's seat. The configuration *litterarum scientia—morum pulchritudo* is a significant one. We recall that Marbod of Rennes had praised Saint Gualterius for "ingenii singularis vivacitas et elegans suavitas morum" (PL 171 : 1567B). These formulations call to mind the formula of education for an aspiring *curialis: litterae et mores*. The combination of genius and learning with elegance of manners constitutes the end point and ideal goal of such a two-fold education.

Elegantia morum is a central component of a "natural ethic" that crystallized in the milieu of the educated clergy at the ruler's court. This ethic was legitimate and thoroughly acceptable in medieval Christianity, though it is more closely related to ethical ideas of antiquity than to Pauline-Augustinian Christianity. Otto of Bamberg, in showing an "elegant and urbane discipline" of his *mores*, was practicing an ethical ideal whose native context is state service and the active life and which was transferred into the active life of the Christian bishop.

Any number of sources confirm that the terms in question refer to the urbanity and sophistication of court life. The medieval glosses on *elegantia* and *venustas* are somewhat instructive for determining the general ethical-social context of the vocabulary. The *Glossarium Ansileubi* from the mid-eighth century glosses *eliganter* with *urbane* and gives *elegans* as one of many glosses on *faceta, facetias*.[14] A ninth-century gloss gives *facetie* and *iucunditer* as glosses on *eliganter*.[15] The *Vocabulista* of Papias, mid-eleventh century, gives for *elegans*: *egregius, decens, nobilis*; for *eleganter, urbane*. Here *venustus* is glossed as *sapiens ornatus, decorus, modestus*, and *facetus*; *venustas* as *pulchritudo, urbanitas*, and *eloquentia*.[16] It is striking that the areas of reference of these words for beauty are ethical and social, with occasional forays into the intellectual. In this sense we must understand Papias' gloss on *venustus*: *sapiens ornatus* (intellectual, social?); *decorus, modestus* (ethical); *facetus* (social). *Venustas* and *elegantia* are seen, from the earliest Middle Ages on, as qualifiers of *mores*, ways of living and acting. These can be "beautiful" and "elegant," insofar as they are witty, urbane, and sophisticated (*facetia*), or even simply light-hearted and congenial. They are qualities once appropriate to the city aristocracy of Rome, now to secular and ecclesiastical courts.

John of Salisbury sheds some light on the worldly connotations of "beautiful manners." He devotes two chapters of his *Policraticus* to explaining the quality of *civilitas*. In this context he presents rules of banqueting laid down by Macrobius in his *Saturnalia* and praises the *venustas morum* displayed by the author in these prescriptions (8.10, ed. Webb, 2:284). Guido de Basochis (d. 1203), a cleric of Saint Stephens of Chalons, writes to Archbishop Henry of Rheims, praising him for preeminence in "imperiosa generis dignitate . . . et lucidiore morum . . . venustate." These two "crowns" (viz. high birth and *morum venustas*) are above all things necessary "ad elegantiorem persone dignioris ornatum."[17]

Saxo Grammaticus, from whom we learned that "charm of manners" constituted an element of "the rites of courtiers" (see above, p. 34), again comes to our aid in locating the social context of beauty of manners. In book X of the *Gesta Danorum* he gives an extensive summary of the *Lex castrensis sive curiae* which King Canute the Great imposed on the throngs of knights that crowded his household. Saxo compiled this description from oral court tradition, from a Latin redaction by Sven Aggesen dating from 1185, and possibly from a lost Danish original.[18] It is important to note that the vocabulary and con-

cepts of courtliness are entirely Saxo's contribution. At least there is
no trace of them in the text of Sven Aggesen. What was perceived by
the earlier writer as a simple imposition of *militaris disciplina* is transformed in Saxo's version into an education in courtly, civil behavior.
The passage is of particular importance, and so I quote it at length.

The knights who gather at Canute's court are "more weighty of
muscle than grave of manner," and they require schooling in court
manners. The king calls on his wise counselor, Opo of Seeland (whose
social class unfortunately is not revealed), to impose order. His program of courtly education is summed up in the sentence, "In order to
ally courteous affability with boldness, he imbued the most courageous knights with the most lovely manner of conduct" ("ut audaciae
comitatem adiceret, fortissimo militi speciosissimum moris habitum
ingeneravit"). Hence the details of this education stand under the general, collective virtue, beauty of conduct ("speciosus moris habitus"):

1. Plerisque enim amplior virium quam morum gravitas inerat, quique se
splendidius bello gesserant, obscurius pacis decora intuebantur, adeo ut, qui
foris insignes exstarent, domi ignobiles viderentur, vixque eadem et honesta
et acria ingenia reperiebantur. Igitur complures ad vim et rixam usque in aula
perniciosi esse consueverant.
2. Quos cum rex natione, linguis, ingeniis quam maxime dissidentes animad-
verteret (quippe variis ac perplexis invicem affectibus urgebantur; nam petulantia alios, alios invidia, quosdam etiam ira vexabat), quo minus seditiose se
gererent, saluberrimum castrensis disciplinae tenorem, qua tantae varietatis
discordiam rumperet debitamque militi maturitatem monstraret, exactissimis
edidit institutis.
3. Itaque circumspectissima eiusdem deliberatio, Oponis Sialandici, ceteros
prudentia atque auctoritate praestantis, monitis persuasa, ne externa forte
domestico crimine turbarentur, socialis odii tempestatem repressit legeque
severissime cavendo seditiosum militiae spiritum veluti fraterna quadam caritate coercuit. Atque ut audaciae comitatem adiceret, fortissimo militi speciosissimum moris habitum ingeneravit, clientelam suam effrenium ac litigioso-
rum convictu tamquam erubescenda aliqua sentina vacuefacere cupiens. . . .
6. . . . Adeo contumaciam contemptu multari placuit. Valuit enim apud regem spretae militaris dignitatis indignatio, eumque, qui parem venerari nes-
ciret, parum superiori delaturum esse existimatum est. Eodem poenae
genere in minutos quosque animadvertebatur excessus, ut si quis alium con-
vicio insecutus fuisset aut potione per contumeliam respersisset.
7. . . . Tanto enim studio rex verecundiam a suis servari voluit, ut etiam par-
vulo impudentiae excessu devios castigationis remedio coercendos putaret. . . . Ac ne quis socio flumen transequitanti ita equo concurreret, ut ad
ipsum turbulentior unda deflueret, pari industria cautum. Adeo scrupulosa
cura parvula quoque societatis officia pensabantur.

1. Many [of the knights who joined Canute] were more weighty of muscle
than grave of manner, and though they bore themselves gloriously in war,

they had only a dim perception of the ways appropriate to peace. The result was that those distinguished on the field were despised at court. It was rare indeed to find a man of ardent spirits who at the same time had some sense of the honorable conduct of life. Hence many of them, tied to pernicious habits, would bring violence and squabbling into the court itself.

2. Now when the king observed that these men formed a hodgepodge of different nationalities, languages, temperaments—some being the playthings of chaotic impulses, some driven by hot-headedness, others by envy, others yet by wrath—he started to inculcate, through a most exacting program of instruction, a most wholesome atmosphere of military discipline, in order to end the discord, provide a model of the maturity appropriate to a knight, and put a stop to their quarrelsomeness.

3. And so it was that at the king's urging, Opo of Seeland, a man distinguished for his prudence and authority, by his keen and circumspect planning stamped out this odious behavior, which otherwise may through domestic strife have thrown even foreign relations into confusion. This man set law and a spirit of brotherly love as a most severe guardian over the quarrelsome spirit of the knights. And in order to form an alliance between courteous affability and their boldness, he imbued the most courageous knights with the most lovely manner of conduct, with the hope of purging the retinue, like some disgusting cesspool, of the ways of unbridled and litigious riff-raff.

[In 4. and 5. Saxo describes at length an order of merit instituted to arrange the seating at meals, along with the punishments for offenses.]

6. . . . Furthermore he found it good to punish stubborn offenders through contempt. For the king's indignation at offenses against chivalric dignity was great, and it was assumed that the man who could show no respect to his equal would likewise not defer to his superior. The same kind of punishment [viz. exclusion] was observed for the minutest offenses, insult or abuse for example.

7. [If a knight charged with the care of horses used only that of his comrade in fetching water, he suffered the same punishment.] For the king was so eager for his retainers to practice a considerate respect, that he thought it fit for those guilty of only minor breaches and impudence to be subjected to correction by punishment. . . . Also if anyone in crossing a river should drive on his horse in such a way as to stir up waves in the path of a comrade, he imposed the same measures. And in this way even the minor duties of social life were enforced with scrupulous care. (*Gesta Danorum* X, xviii, 1–7, pp. 293–94)

If we are to take this passage as a paradigm for *speciositas morum*, then this concept would seem to consist in the imposition of government on impulses earlier unbridled and contentious; "beauty of conduct" is subjection of the "chaotic impulses" to the "duties of social life" (*officia societatis*), respect, considerateness, and sensitivity to the rights of others. Although far from the centers of European court life, Saxo is here a thoroughly reliable witness to the contemporary conception of these ethical notions. The above passage brings us very close to the definition of "beauty of conduct" put forward by Ambrose in his comments on Cicero's principle that *formositas* governs *decorum*:

Hoc est enim pulchritudinem vivendi tenere, convenientia cuique sexui et personae reddere. Hic ordo gestorum optimus, hic ornatus ad omnem actionem accommodus. (*De off. min.* 1.19.84, PL 16:49A)

For beauty of conduct consists in rendering to each sex and to each person the things appropriate to him. This is the highest rule of conduct, this the lustre appropriate to each action.

And Saxo's contemporary Gerald of Wales gave an explanation of *venustas morum* which accords neatly with the definition we have drawn from Saxo:

Cum autem morum venustas cuilibet ad se regendum apprime in vita sit utilis et accommoda, nulli tamen adeo ut illi qui multitudinem regit est necessaria. (*De princ. inst.* 1.1, RS 21:8:9)

Just as beauty of manners is the chief quality useful and appropriate to the individual's governing of his own life, so no one requires it more than he who governs the multitude.

From these texts we can define "beauty of manners" as harmonious self-government based on principles of respect for the social order and for the rights of other men.

But we should not leave this remarkable passage without noting its importance for our broader theme, the process of civilizing. The court discipline of King Canute is paradigmatic, not only for individual virtues, but for an entire wave of social change as well. A king finds an influx of unruly, warlike boors at his court. The disadvantages are not only social and aesthetic, but also political (the domestic turmoil endangers the conduct of foreign policy). The king chooses his wisest counselor and has him impose a strict discipline, "both of law and of a spirit of brotherly love." This consists in instruction in proper conduct and a system of punishment that brings social pressure to bear in enforcing rules: offenders are subjected to contempt, stripped of honor and prestige, and finally excluded. The episode reads in many ways like an illustration of Elias's "Entwurf zu einer Theorie der Zivilisation." The net of interdependencies at court tightens with an influx of soldiers; a rationalizing and "modeling of the economy of impulses" is made necessary by circumstances. The threat of punishment and exclusion arouses the fear of degradation. The result is the stifling of impulsiveness and the restraint of anger and passion. Ultimately a group of ruffian knights is transformed into a group of courtiers, the stage that Elias calls "Verhöflichung der Krieger." But the element of this process which has no place in Elias's theory is its origins: the king disapproves of domestic turmoil, and in order to create stability calls on a learned advisor to teach them manners. It is the constellation which was our point of departure, "Otto and Brun," the ruler and the educator/statesman. Here the process of civilizing has its origin: in a program of education imposed by "an especially wise and great man" on a class that threatens the order. Circumstances created and tailored by that man keep the process alive and nurture it. It begins in an act of imposing two rules: "law and brotherly love" ("lex et fraterna caritas"). These are the counterpart of the "law and respectfulness" imposed on mankind in its primal disorder in the myth by Castiglione discussed in the introduction. And so also the mythical diad Jove-Mercury has two striking historical counterparts: Otto and Brun; Canute and Opo of Seeland. In all three pairs the urge for order and stability sets a process of refinement and restraint into motion. The ruler calls upon an educator/statesman to administer a program of education. This man imposes strictures and social norms and enforces them, like any good educator, through a system of rewards and punishment.

But to return to the subject at hand, it should be evident how central the concept of "beauty of manners," "a most lovely mode of conduct," is to this process in its historical realization in the twelfth century. To define this rich concept I have drawn on a range of texts from two centuries, and this may arouse the impression that *elegantia morum* is a unified concept with no development from the tenth to the thirteenth century. Before going on to counterparts in the vernacular, I want to ask about the emergence of this ideal. Dating the evidence is a bit difficult. Current wisdom on the study of medieval biography and hagiography has it that the values expressed must be regarded as those of the author, not those of the subject. The greater the period of time separating the two, the more strictly this rule applies.[19] Notker of Liège (*morum elegantia insignitus*) was chaplain under Otto III. Anselm of Liège's description of him dates from about 1056. Bernward of Hildesheim (*morum gratia*) was the favorite of the Empress Theophanu and the tutor and chaplain of Otto III. This is an interesting constellation, since the Byzantine connection at the court of Otto II and Otto III, combined with the atmosphere of *renovatio imperii Romanorum*, would certainly have created an atmosphere in which an ethic of refined manners in state service with classical antecedents could have flourished. But unfortunately Bernward's *vita*, long dated around 1022 and ascribed to his teacher Thangmar, has recently been shown to contain later additions, and the description of his youth and court service appear to be among them.[20] These passages, and hence the epithet *gratia morum*, are tentatively dated mid-twelfth century. Meinwerk of Paderborn (*regio obsequio morum elegantia idoneus*) was chaplain under Otto III and Henry II. His *vita*, however, dates also from the mid-twelfth century. Otto of Bamberg is described as elegant, either in manners or appearance, in all three of his *vitae*. This could indicate a reliable testimony from his lifetime, but not necessarily. We are still in the middle of the twelfth century. The fact that these references are all to Ottonian courtier bishops, with the exception of Otto of Bamberg, is striking. But since the first reliably dated reference occurs half a century after the death of Otto III, there is no justification for placing the beginnings of an ideal of elegant manners among the Ottonian emperors, probable as this may be on the surface. It may also be that they have more to do with the glorification of the Ottonian period in the time of Henry III and beyond than with the actual held values of Ottonian chaplains. But the terms occur in clear profile as courtly virtues from the mid-eleventh century, and from this we can infer that *elegantia morum* was at home in the chapel since the reign of Henry III.

The spread of this ideal throughout Europe is evident from the number and variety of sources cited. It is now time to look for counterparts in the vernacular. One of the dominant trends of courtly literature is to aestheticize life and manners. This bodes well for the survival of an ideal of "elegant manners" in the chivalric culture represented in romance. Still, the terms have no direct counterpart in either Provençal or OF. Neither in Godefroy nor Tobler-Lommatzsch, nor in the abundant scholarship on the romance vocabulary of courtesy is a loan translation of *elegantia morum* to be found. We can be the more sure of this since Burgess has devoted a detailed chapter to the entire field of reference of the OF vocabulary of beauty (*Vocabulaire précourtois*, pp. 115–33). There is no OF counterpart; no form *beles manieres, meurs eleganles*. We find *bones mors* (Tobler and Lommatzsch 6.289.52), *bonnes meurs* (290.34), and this is clearly a loan translation of the Latin *boni mores*. There is also *de meurs bien ordinez* (291.29), obviously modeled on Latin, *mores bene compositi*. But these phrases are part of the general European ethical vocabulary; they lack any specific connection to the court and to *courtoisie*. There is a great difference between conduct that is good and conduct that is elegant. This is not to suggest that OF lacked the conception of "aesthetic culture of form."[21] The term *cointe* approximates the courtly meaning of *elegantia morum*.[22] The point is, while the courtly aesthetic of manners was international, the Latin terms expressing it were not adapted in OF and Provencal courtly literature, even though the Latin vocabulary predates the rise of courtly literature in France by half a century and more.

A clear counterpart of the Latin terms is abundant and central, however, in German courtly literature. The concept *schoene site* appears to have entered the MHG vocabulary of courtesy via Gottfried's *Tristan*, though Gottfried's predecessors, Heinrich von Veldeke and Hartmann von Aue, both use the term *schoene zühte*. *Schoene site*, a key ethical-social ideal in *Tristan*, can teach us much about the content of the Latin counterparts. Young Tristan is kidnapped by Norwegian merchants, who admire his *schoene site* and hope to turn a profit by selling this child prodigy (see 2240 ff.). Freed by the kidnappers in Cornwall, he meets two pilgrims and chats with them. Tristan, *der hovebaere*, speaks flowingly, answers their questions with such mastery of word and gesture (*rede und gelaze*—2740) that the two begin to marvel at his talents. They observe his bearing and his manners (*sine gebaerde und sine site*), and his handsome figure. They cannot take their eyes off his splendid clothing. Finally they exclaim: "Who is this child whose manners are so truly beautiful!" (*des site so rehte schoene sint*— 2754). Later there is a portrait of Tristan arriving at King Mark's court (3331 ff.). His gait was lovely, his body shaped according to the commands of the goddess of love. Then follows praise of his clothes. The summation of his "presence": "In his gestures, his bearing and his beautiful manners, nature had been so good to him that he was a delight to behold" ("an gebaerde unde an schoenen siten / was ime so rehte wol geschehen, / daz man in gerne mohte sehen"—3348–50). In these scenes the purely visual, sensual, and external predominates. *Schoene site* are refined, elegant appearance and bearing, suaveness in speech and gesture (in both scenes *gebaerde* and *schoene site* are linked). "Beautiful manners" are winning, charming, beguiling, and tinged with the erotic. But they also appear as an ethical ideal. Later in the romance Tristan becomes the tutor of Princess Isolde. She takes up many disciplines—languages, stringed instruments, "school subjects" (*schuollist*—7967). But she applies herself most diligently to the study of *moraliteit*, which, Gottfried tells us, teaches *schoene site*: ". . . moraliteit / diu kunst diu leret schoene site" (8004–5). This form of instruction makes common cause with God and the world ("ir lere hat gemeine / mit der werlde und mit gote"—8010–11); it teaches us to please both God and the world ("si leret uns in ir gebote / got unde der werlde gevallen"—8012–13). Isolde receives from her study of *moraliteit* "a beautiful and pure disposition, sweet and fine bearing" (8024–25). *Schoene site*, then, is also an object of moral instruction. Not only does it teach fine gestures and elegant bearing, but it also cultivates a "beautiful and pure" temperament ("schone unde reine gemuot"—8025). The concept in *Tristan* is, in short, an epitome of the various definitions of *elegantia morum* we have drawn from the Latin texts. It corresponds closely to Otto of Bamberg's *elegans et urbana disciplina*. In both concepts the quality shows itself in externals: in speech, gesture, and dress (*sermone, gestu vel habitu; rede, gebaerde, kleit*). Both *elegantia morum* and *schoene site* make a man admired and sought after at court. Both are external indications of an inner harmony or composed temperament. And finally, both are the results of a courtly, ethical education which reconciles its disciples with God and the world. In *Tristan*, the concept comprehends the "aesthetic form culture," the political aspects of the virtue (entry to court, favor), and the ethical (self government, inner harmony).

After Gottfried, *schoene site* is commonplace in MHG romance and didactic writings. Thomasin von Zirclaere is fond of linking it with *zuht*.

Schoene site stands in the same relation to the OF and ML vocabulary of courtesy as did *zuht*. There is no direct verbal equivalent of either one in OF; there is a full equivalent of both in Latin. Again we see that the German poets were able to draw on an indigenous Latin vocabulary of courtesy, the vocabulary forged within the imperial tradition of court manners.

URBANITAS

We have gained some understanding of Otto of Bamberg's *elegans disciplina*. Now let us look at his urbanity. The term *urbanitas* is hallowed by its reference to ancient Roman ideals of sophistication and aristocratic bearing, and these associations remain strong in our period. Otto of Freising praises the Lombards for having retained something of "Roman gentleness and sagacity," as well as the Romans' "elegance of Latin speech and urbanity of manners" ("Latini sermonis elegantiam morumque retinent urbanitatem"), in spite of their intermarriage with the barbarian invaders.[23] We can, again, form an idea of the word's range of reference by a look at the glosses. In Papias' Lexicon *urban-, urbanitas* gloss a number of words in the area of courtesy: *eleganter*: *urbane; faceta*: *urbana venusta iocosa, bene morigerata; facetiae*: *lepos, suavitas verborum, urbanitas; venustas*: *pulchritudo, urbanitas, eloquentia; iocus*: *lepos, urbanitas*. The twelfth-century *Glossarium Maii* gives as a gloss on *comis*: *facetus, urbanus, lepidus, curialis*. The eleventh-century glossator has hit the two essential meanings of *urbanus* (and *facetus*, as we will see) with the combination *iocosa, bene morigerata*: "jocund and witty in speech, possessing well-bred good manners." *Urbanitas* contains a double aspect present in so much of the vocabulary of courtesy: it is both an inner virtue and an external, social one, both sophisticated behavior and sophisticated speech. I will treat both aspects of urbanity in this section, even though I am dealing here with the ethical component of courtliness. Perhaps the best justification for doing so is that Herbord of Michelsberg applied the term *urbanus* to Otto of Bamberg referring to the delicacy of Otto's sensibility. Now let us try to form an idea of the word's range of meanings. First, urbanity in the sense of sophistication: Brun of Cologne is praised for the manner in which he transmitted his own excellent command of Latin to others at the court of Otto the Great: "Nullo autem hoc egit supercilio, sed cum domestico lepore tum urbana gravitate" (*Vita Brun.*, chap. 8, *LB*, p. 190). ("This he did with no arrogance, but with courtly[24] grace and urbane gravity.") John of Salisbury uses the term in an instructive context in the *Policraticus*. He is treating hospitality. This is a duty to be exercised with "omnis humanitas et sobria liberalitas" (7.13, ed. Webb, 2:325). One must not urge a guest to any action against propriety or his own will; the rules of charity and humanity apply to the exercise of hospitality, and this holds even when guest and host are separated by hostility or differences of religion. He tells a story (from Eusebius' *Church History*) of Bishop Gregory of Neocaesaria driven by a rainstorm to accept the hospitality of a pagan priest in a forest sacred to Apollo. The priest treats the bishop with the most kindly hospitality in spite of the bishop's reputation as a persecutor of Apollo. When the bishop is later reproached with ingratitude for forbidding the worship of Apollo, he composes a letter to the pagan god, inviting him to return from banishment and receive worship again. The priest, his former host, is so moved that he converts to Christianity. John summarizes by saying that *humanitas* in hospitality is not only a religious but also a social duty, one to be exercised with *urbanitas* and *comitas* ("non modo religiose sed etiam comiter et urbane"—ibid., p. 326). He takes the occasion to complain against the Cistercian customs, which eschew hospitality. Here John distinguishes strikingly between religion and courtesy. Their laws can coincide, but not necessarily. Bishop Gregory's kindness to a pagan god illustrates religion with humanity and urbanity; the Cistercian ordinances, religion without it. The passage is especially noteworthy for showing that the order of civility can take precedence over that of religion. Andreas Capellanus mentions *urbanitas* as a quality appropriate to a noble lover. In the dialogue between *nobilior* and *nobilis* (the woman), the latter says in deference to the man:

Vestra igitur nulla fas esset feminae recusare obsequia, quia, ut constare videtur, homo estis nimiae probitatis et multa urbanitate praeclarus ac generositate refulgens.[25]

It would not be proper for you to refuse your services to any woman, because, it seems clear, you are a man of excellent character, famous for your great urbanity and of most illustrious lineage.

Another woman turns down the request of a rejected suitor that she should not love any other man as "inurbanum satis . . . et a bonis moribus manifeste devi[ans]" (ed. Trojel, p. 122). Since women are the source of all good, we hear in a later dialogue, they should welcome those who approach them "hilari . . . facie et urbanitatis . . . receptu" (p. 159). Hence, suave, considerate, courtly good manners are contained in *urbanitas* in its first sense.

In reference to speech the word had two specific meanings: (1) a sophisticated and well-educated manner of speaking and pronouncing the Latin language, and (2) a witty, ironic manner of joking.

1. Baudri of Bourgeuil warns that any story, no matter how lofty its subject matter, becomes contemptible if not recited in an urbane manner: "quaelibet nobilis historia, nisi urbane recitetur, vilescit" (PL 166:1163B). William of Conches points to the gift of urbane and charming speech which certain men possess: "Quibusdam enim lepos inest, et fandi urbanitas" (PL 171:1035C). But repeatedly we find *urbanum eloquium* regarded with suspicion by conservative churchmen. It is an element of courtly frivolity and vanity, opposed to monastic simplicity. Saint Sacerdos is praised by his biographer for tempering his urbanity with modesty: "Astutiam ejus simplicitas commendebat, et urbanum eloquium modestia temperabat" (PL 163:985B). The list of miracles appended to the *vita* of Altmann of Passau gives us a charming example of orthodox suspicion directed at learned urbanity. It relates that a certain woman of the diocese was possessed by a demon whose name was *sciens*. This well-lettered devil compelled her to spew forth literature (or simply Latin utterances?) in learned and urbane recitations, "quasi eadem mulier litteraturae scientiam et modum urbanae pronuntiationis ab ipsis studiis consecuta fuisset" (MGH, SS 12:242, ll. 45–46). It may be that this backwoods compiler (certainly not the well-educated author of the *Vita Altmanni*) associated any learned talk with urbanity, but he shows us that this quality was regarded as a refinement of pronunciation.

2. Joking, urbane wit, biting sarcasm undoubtedly were favorite and much cultivated court pastimes. Petrus Damiani chides bishops, followers of the courts of kings, for their *verba otiosa, joci*, and *laetitia immoderata*: "Away with these puerile games! Away with this biting eloquence and urbane chit-chat!" ("Puerilis ludus abscedat, mordax eloquentia, urbana dicacitas evanescat"—PL 144:285C). Biting wit had been considered urbane in antiquity as well (cf. Cicero, *Pro Caelio* 3).

An anecdote related by Gerhoh of Reichersberg gives us a good example of sardonic urbanity taken to an extreme. It concerns Duke Frederick of Swabia, the father of Frederick Barbarossa. Gerhoh describes him as "a courtly man, altogether given to urbanity, not to say vanity" ("quem scimus esse hominem curialem totumque urbanitati, ne dicamus vanitati, deditum"). In his retinue was a man on good terms with various demons. Through one of them he learned the hidden sins of the men with whom he came in contact, and from this gift he and the duke drew many an occasion for "joking and deriding" at the expense of others. Two knights who sought out the duke armed themselves against this anticipated mockery by confessing prior to the audience. The duke's demoniacal companion is forced to admit that the secrets of these men, which he knew perfectly well, have been snatched from his memory as a result of their confession. In protesting the truth of this anecdote, Gerhoh appeals to the current gossip among the duke's knights and clerics, who tell this tale "along with other of his urbanities" ("inter ceteras urbanitates").[26] Urbanity had the power to cut deeply and humiliate, to cast a kind of spell over those who were its target, and in this capacity, and others, it may well have seemed to a rustic and monkish observer to be demoniacally inspired, a perversion of the inspired language that comes through the Holy Spirit.

Another type of urbanity in this sense is a form of joking known in American parlance as "putting someone on." It is more common under the name of *facetia*, as we will see, but a charming incident from the chronicle of the bishops of Eichstatt illustrates the urbane put on. Bishop Macelinus of Würzburg has a friendly joking relationship with the epicurean bishop Megingaud of Eichstatt. They regularly exchange gifts. One autumn Megingaud goes out to receive his friend's legate who, he believes, is bringing him a shipment of the fine wine of Würzburg. The bishop of Würzburg knows that his friend awaits the wine on pins and needles ("pendulus expectaret") and decides to play a joke on him: "iocari volens, . . . urbane illum prius elusit." He has his emissary unceremoniously throw down some wineskins of sour, new wine in front of the bishop, pretending that his lord was angered at the gifts he had received earlier. The disappointed bishop replies, "Foolish and ignorant was the king who placed such a man in so important a bishopric!" But then the good wine arrives, and the emissary presents it graciously. The bishop tastes the wine, finds it superb, and exclaims: "Blessed be my dear friend before God, and blessed be his gifts! A jewel among the prelates of Würzburg! Wise was the king, etc."[27] We have come a long way from the *urbana disciplina* of Otto of Bamberg.

Urbanus was not adapted directly to the courtly vocabulary of vernacular literature. Understandably so, since the literal rendering of the word results in a translation that in the twelfth century would have meant something quite different from the Latin word. Its meaning however was assumed under the words *curialis, courtois,* and *hövesch,* and so our discussion of urbanity in the vernacular can be postponed until a later section.

Otto shows "in every act of the outer man how great was the harmony which reigned within him." Outer refinements mirror inner virtue: this is a dominant conception in the passage, and in an ethic guiding the cleric's life in the world, it has an obvious role to play. If chaste and considerate behavior and an elegant and urbane breeding in dress, speech, gesture, and table manners manifest inner virtue and harmony, then the cultivation of these external refinements is not only legitimate, but it is also an obligation of the cleric living *honeste* in the world. Cicero had said that there could be no *honestas* if *decorum* was not present, and that every act of *decorum* manifested *honestas.* Ambrose summarized the idea, distinguishing *honestas* from *decorum* by using Cicero's comparison of health and beauty: just as there is no physical beauty without health, so also decorous acts are a necessary indication of inner virtue (*De off. min.* 1.45.218–19, PL 16:88–89). The idea survived in monastic communities as well, reinforced by related notions, for instance, the belief that the performing of miracles is *manifestatio virtutis.* A rich scene that brings together the two social contexts, monastic life and state service, is the visit of Abbot Hugh of Cluny to Cologne for the baptising of the infant Henry IV. It is related in the Life of Hugh by Hildebert of Lavardin and is a fine example of Hildebert's "courtly humanism." [28] Hugh comes to Cologne at the invitation of Henry III and leaves the Germans marveling at

the maturity of manners in this youth, the gentleness and ease of his comportment, the grace of his countenance, the mild flow of his speech. These being truly signs of his inner virtues, he won the affections of the king for himself and for the monastery of Cluny as if the king on his own had always embraced them in perpetual friendship.

Celebravit autem Pascha cum imperatore, in Agrippina Coloniae, Teutonicis mirantibus in juvenili adhuc aetate canitiem morum, conversationis mansuetudinem, vultus gratiam, verborum lenitatem. Quibus profecto virtutum indiciis, ita cum eo et cum Cluniacensi monasterio regis est anima colligata, ac si rex ipse perpetuam cum eis amicitiam pepigisset. (PL 159:864B–C)

Not only gentle restraint of manners but also physical beauty could be seen as testimony to virtue, though on this point Christian writers show some ambiguity. Ambrose had sought to put limits on Cicero's esteem for physical beauty ("Formositatem autem cur posuerit, non satis intelligo"—PL 16:48B). But he conceded that, while virtue is not necessarily immanent in physical beauty, still it confers gracefulness on its possessor; *verecundia* after all, he argues, has the power to suffuse the countenance with modesty and render it graceful and agreeable:

Ut enim artifex in materia commodiore melius operari solet, sic verecundia in ipso quoque corporis decore plus eminet. (*De off. min.* 1.19.83, PL 16:48B)

For just as a craftsman can work more skillfully in a more malleable material, so also *verecundia* shines forth from the very beauty of the body itself.

William of Malmesbury, commenting on the beauty of Saint Wulstan, echoes this position:

Cumulabat pectoris gratiam speciositas corporis; quam licet inter virtutes non numerem, non tamen omnino excludo, quia sicut ars opificis in commodiore materia elucet, ita virtus in pulchritudine formae splendidius eminet. (PL 179:1740D)

The beauty of his body crowned the grace residing in his bosom. This outer beauty I will neither number among the virtues, nor however will I exclude it from their number, for just as the skill of an artificer shines forth in a well wrought work, thus virtue radiates the more gloriously from beauty of form.

Gottfried von Strassburg is fond of the same image. He ends his portrait of the arming of Tristan by comparing the worksmanship of the armorer with the skill which created the man within:

> swie so der uzer waere,
> der inner bildaere
> der was baz betihtet, . . .
> daz werc daz was darinne
> an geschepfede unde an sinne
> vil lobelichen uf geleit.
> des wercmannes wisheit
> hi, wie wol diu dar an schein!
> (6643–50)

Artful as the exterior was, the inner work of art was more skillfully contrived. . . . both in cut of body and in mind the work within was wrought most admirably. Ah, how the skill of the artificer shone forth from it!

The notion that a courtly education tunes and harmonizes the inner world and that this inner harmony comes forth in graceful elegant manners is, we might say, the ethical foundation of courtly breeding, *zuht, cointe, elegantia morum*. This was apparent in Gottfried's exposition of *moraliteit* as instruction in *schoene site*. Isolde's diligent study of this discipline cultivated fine manners, a pure and good temperament, and graceful comportment:

> hie von so wart si wol gesit,
> schone unde reine gemuot,
> ir gebaerde süeze unde guot.
> (8024–26)

There is much to say on this important notion. If there is any scholarship on the subject in the Middle Ages, I have not found it.

‹›

It was somewhat artificial to restrict the commentary on *elegantia morum* to the scene in Herbord's *Dialogus*, rich though that scene was. Two important elements in this ensemble of virtues do not appear in the scene: *mansuetudo* and *affabilitas*. We have observed both of these as courtier virtues in their political context in an earlier chapter (above p. 36). Here I will only add a few observations on their tradition and role in the social life of the court.

Mansuetudo is a ruler's virtue in the classical laudation.[29] It is an ancillary virtue of *clementia*, and as such was formulated by Seneca in his *De clementia*, a work well known in our period. In Christianity the virtue is biblical, Pauline, patristic, indeed so common that an attempt to assign it to a particular social group is pointless. It is, however, connected with the office of bishop in late antiquity and in the early church.[30] As a ruler's virtue we encounter it in the *Via regia* of Smaragdus, a Carolingian *Fürstenspiegel*. He counsels the king to suppress anger: "mansuetus atque mitissimus esto; et si proruperit iracundia, restringe illam" (PL 102:963D). We have seen it at work in the *Ruodlieb* in the form of the "noble revenge" wrought by the king on his assailant. It occurs there also in a slightly ironic context, but one that allows us to glimpse this virtue working in the social life of the court. The conquered *rex minor* sends gifts to the *rex major*. Among them are two white dancing bears. They eat from dishes like men, they dance with the ladies, they twitter gently instead of roaring, and they do not get angry no matter how they are wronged ("Non irascantur quodcunque mali paterentur"—5.98; cf 5.84 ff.). This may be a gentle parody of the courtier's virtue, but just as likely is that the phenomenon of a civilized bear was meant to inspire awe and serve as a model to the human beings who had not yet reached the same level of civilization.

Von Moos has treated the role of *mansuetudo* in the milieu of the worldly clergy. It forms a part of Hildebert of Lavardin's ideal of *humanitas*:

Mit seiner Umgebung unbedingt in Frieden zu leben, überall seine Gemüts-
ruhe zu bewahren, das war ein grosses Anliegen des Bischofs. Er suchte es
durch eine gewisse stoische Gelassenheit zu verwirklichen. Weniger eine re-
ligiöse oder sittliche als eine politische Weisheit sah er darin, dass Schmä-
hungen hinzunehmen seien. (*Hildebert*, p. 172)

We noticed earlier that Otto of Freising distinguished between the
mansuetudo appropriate to the cleric and the *gladii severitas* of the lay
nobleman. But as the laity came to adopt courtly ways, this virtue also
migrated to the knightly sphere. Jean de Marmoutier praises Geoffrey
the Fair, count of Anjou, for his "gentle, gracious and mild spirit":
"He bore offenses and injuries patiently and clemently; upon hearing
abuse heaped on him he ignored it patiently. To all men alike he was
. . . amiable and jocund."[31]

The virtue had an obvious role to play in the cult of "courtly love."
It made possible the subjection of the man to the woman. Chrétien's
Chevalier de la charette is conceived to illustrate precisely Lancelot's
long-suffering endurance of disgrace and abuse. In the *Roman de la
rose*, the allegorical figure named *cortoisie* "never spoke ill of anyone,
nor did she bear resentment or rancor toward anyone" ("donc ne fu
hom par li desdiz, / ne ne porta autrui rancune"—1.39.1236–37). In
Germany the Minnesänger Reinmar der Alte gave drastic expression
to the virtue:

> Des einen und dekeines mê
>   wil ich ein meister sîn, al die wîle ich lebe:
> daz lop wil ich, daz mir bestê
>   und mir die kunst diu werlt gemeine gebe,
>   Daz niemen sîn leit alsô schône kan getragen.
>   dez begêt ein wîp an mir, daz ich naht noch
>   tac nicht kan gedagen.
>   nu hân eht ich sô senften muot
>   daz ich ir haz ze vröiden nime.
>   owê, wie rehte unsanfte daz mir doch tuot![32]

I wish to be known my entire life as a master of one thing and one thing only;
I seek the world's praise for this one skill, that no man can bear his suffering
as beautifully as I. If a woman causes me pain to such an extent that I cannot
remain silent night or day, I have so gentle a spirit that I'll accept her hate as a
source of joy. And yet, alas, how deeply that discomforts me!

Thomasin von Zirclaere gives a long dissertation on the courtly virtue
of *senfter muot*, referring to the examples of Moses, David, and Joseph
in Egypt (*Welscher Gast* 6859–60, 6971 ff.).

Affabilitas has no tradition in the Bible or in early Christianity. It is
a virtue of ancient Roman urbanity. It is a frequent term of praise for
rulers in late antiquity.[33] Cicero discusses it as a quality that a states-

man can cultivate in order to win the favor of the people (*De off.* 2.48), and Ambrose takes it over, warning against flattering affability (*De off. min.* 2.19.96, PL 16:129A). It characterizes courtiers since the early Middle Ages.[34] In late Roman times it was transferred onto the office of bishop; it becomes a frequent formula of praise.[35] It establishes itself firmly in Merovingian *vitae*. It is connected with the quality of a bishop which Heinzelmann calls "paternalism" ("Väterliche Herrschaft"—*Bischofsherrschaft*, p. 152 ff.). A bishop was father and mother to his flock, and his duty was to help and serve all men: *miseris et pauperibus affabilis* is a frequent formula of praise. In our period affability is, as Johnson observes, one of the most common epithets characterizing an imperial bishop (*Secular Activities*, p. 248). If frequency of occurrence is a measure, affability was the most important court virtue. Its importance is also indicated in its many variants: *gratus, benignus, amabilis, omnibus omnia factus*, and others. The king in *Ruodlieb* practices affability when he receives his master huntsman and allows him to address him "non ut domino sed amico" (1.131).[36] Oddly enough in view of the prevalence of this virtue, the vernacular does not take it over in the form of a loan word. In OF *affabilité* does not appear until the end of the thirteenth century (Krings, *Wortschatz*, p. 132 ff.). In MHG the rendering *liutsaelec* appears in Gottfried in a context clearly indicating what is conveyed in the Latin *affabilitas* (cf. *Tristan* 11088). But whatever name the virtue is called by, it is ubiquitous in romance, evident particularly in the elaborate ceremonies of greeting upon which vernacular poets lavish attention. In Chrétien's *Cligès* Alexander arrives at Arthur's court and

> N'an la cort n'a baron si haut,
> Qui bel ne l'apiaut et acuelle . . .
> Mont se feit amer a chascun. . . .
> (390–92)

There is no lord at the court and be he ever so noble who does not address him kindly and welcome him. . . . He gains the good graces of all.

‹›

Our discussion of the scene in Herbord's *Dialogus* leaves us with a picture of an ethical-social sensibility in Otto of Bamberg which was humane, delicate, and highly refined. It is a good illustration of *humanitas* as a held and practiced ideal at the turn of the eleventh to the twelfth century. It should be evident that the Christian life is not the native context of this ideal. It is not first and foremost a specifically Christian sense of shame, purity, and chastity which is expressed in Otto's fastidiousness. Ciceronian ethics were the main instrument in shaping these sensibilities, as they were the main provider of Herbord's ethical vocabulary. Clearly, an ethical code with classical models existed in the period; it was probably taught, or at least inculcated at the cathedral schools; it was cultivated by secular clergy and by clerical administrators at the ruler's court and in the bishop's office. The fact that the code derived much of its terminology from ideals of the Roman senatorial class will have added to its allure and legitimacy in the context of service to the emperor at court and in the imperial church. Of course, the code was nourished by Christian sensibilities and notions of the conduct of the active life. The dependency is evident in the relationship of Cicero to Ambrose writing on duties. Ambrose corrects Cicero and contradicts him, drawing the Christian superstructure over the pagan foundations, but over long stretches the Christian writer can accept and transmit largely unchanged stoic-Ciceronian ideas. How far Ambrose can depart from a rigorously Christian, theocentric morality is shown in his admonition (adapted from Cicero): "Let us follow nature [in arranging our dealings with other men]: its likeness is the pattern of discipline, the model of morality" ("Naturam imitemur: ejus effigies formula disciplinae, forma honestatis est"—De off. min. 1.19.84, PL 16:49A). Otto's baptizing of the pagans has the quality of illustrating this ideal scheme; it is best summed up in the phrase, speculum morum elegantiae.

II: Social Forms: Curialitas

At the beginning of this chapter I spoke of a division in the court values under discussion into an ethical and social category. In passing from the former to the latter we can focus more clearly on the distinction by regarding the court service of Ulrich of Zell (d. 1093) as represented in his two vitae (Vita prior, ca. 1095; Vita posterior, 1115–20). Born of high nobility and called to the court of Henry III, Ulrich served him so well that the emperor gave him first his friendship, then his love. Both the vitae stress that Ulrich cared nothing for the frivolous pastimes of the other chaplains ("levitas concapellanorum"—Vita prior, chap. 3, MGH, SS 12:251, ll. 29–30). He shunned inordinate behavior and had no affection for the court. The empress Agnes had a special love for him, and he became her personal chaplain.[37] She sought him out particularly for her service because she found in him "a suaveness of charming manners" ("delectabilium morum suavitas"—Vita poster., chap. 5, MGH, SS 12:254, l. 26). From his example and teaching she knew that she could find the "recte vivendi forma" (ibid., l. 29). He despised the "lewd excesses of courtly ways" ("cu-

rialis incontinentiae lasciviam"—ibid., l. 31). The passage gives us a
neat juxtaposition of virtues appropriate to a pious cleric at court and
the courtly frivolities to be shunned. Comprising his *suavitas delectabilium morum* are *religiosa gravitas, humilitas,* and *sanctarum virtutum
ornamenta.* Opposed to these are the components of *lascivia curialis incontinentiae*: *vana curiositas, superbia,* and *immoderatus pretiosarum vestium luxus.*[38] We have clearly not gone wide of the mark in seeing in
elegantia morum and its variants an ethic of worldly service legitimate
for the Christian. Even this rigorously anticurial author can see
suavitas morum as a legitimate and admirable guide to life in the world
for an ascetic like Ulrich of Zell: it aroused the love of the nobles and
endeared Ulrich to the king and queen. Distinguished from this is the
frivolous behavior of many less rigorous chaplains, which involves
luxury, excess, and sensuousness. The distinction to be made is not
between an ethic for clerics and an ethic for lay nobles, but between
an ethic for Christian courtiers that pleased God and the world on the
one hand, and the execrable practices, pastimes, and customs of
worldly men at court, lay or clerical, on the other. With a clear conscience a biographer can praise a bishop or saint for having possessed
the qualities discussed in the previous section; the same is not always
true of those courtly ways to which we now turn.

Here our point of departure is a text of particular importance in
the early history of medieval courtesy. A chronicler of the founding of
the church at Hildesheim, writing in 1080, describes the administration of Bishop Azelinus (1044–54), a former chaplain of Henry III who
was placed in the see by the emperor. During his administration a
spirit of "ambitious courtliness" crept into the diocese. Before Azelinus arrived, the chronicler tells us, strict monastic discipline had prevailed among the clergy. They had had no interest in splendid and
dainty clothing or in the delights of the palate which "are now the
rage among the clergy"; they preferred "rustic boorishness to courtly
wittiness and sophistication": "Delicatioris etiam vestitus tam nulla
illis erat cura, ut gulas, quibus nunc clerus ardet, nescirent. . . . Sic
ergo rusticalem stultitiam curiali facetiae pretulerant."[39] Earlier the
emperor Henry II had even preferred the claustral rigor of Hildesheim to his own foundation, Bamberg, since he knew that at Hildesheim the "perfect composure in the habits of the outer man" gave expression to the religiosity of the inner man. But under Azelinus all
this changed:

Eo enim presidente irrepsit ambitiosa curialitas, quae dum in vestitu mollior,
in victu lautior, in omni cultu accuratior[40] amari quam timeri maluit, disciplinae mollito rigore claustri claustra relaxavit.

During his rule there crept in an ambitious courtliness, which—being more gentle and effeminate in dress, more elegant and refined in manner of living, more scrupulous in every aspect of culture, seeking to inspire love rather than fear—led to the softening of monastic rigor. (Chap. 5, p. 945, l. 12 ff.)

Little is known about Azelinus. We learn from another Hildesheim chronicler that the church burned down during his administration, and he gained little praise for tearing down the remaining walls and rebuilding in a new location.[41] He was a chaplain at the court of Henry III and is praised for having attained honorably the apex "of worldly felicity" with the emperor and among men of distinction generally.[42] The fact that a contemporary writer found the matter for praise in his worldly success rather than in his sanctity accords well with the picture of a courtier bishop who imports the ways of the imperial court into his diocese.

The text from the *Fundatio* is important for several reasons: it represents the earliest known occurrence of the noun *curialitas* and contains a fairly detailed description of the phenomenon; it allows us to connect this phenomenon with the chapel of the imperial court, specifically the court of Henry III. "Courtliness," called by name, enters Europe introduced into an episcopal court by a courtier bishop. It is of course not an invention of Bishop Azelinus, but it represents the intrusion of court ways into the previously monastic atmosphere of Hildesheim. The origin of courtliness at the court is indicated not only in the word *curialitas* itself, but also in its slightly puzzling modifier, *ambitiosa*. It suggests that this code is at home in the vying for favor (for which Azelinus after all had made himself a name) among the ministers of the court.[43] The fact that it "creeps in" (*irrepsit*) indicates that the writer regards it as an ever present danger, held in check normally by rigorous discipline. Pomp, luxury, splendid dress, refinements and "novelties" of manners were commonplace at the imperial courts; they constituted an element of imperial *representatio*. The biographer of Brun of Cologne gives us a glimpse of courtier splendor under Otto I by the chance contrast it poses to Brun's rustic simplicity. Since Brun had passed his youth at the emperor's court, it is so much the more admirable that

Molles et delicatas vestes, in quibus nutritus et ad hominem usque perductus est, etiam in domibus regum multoties declinavit; inter purpuratos ministros et milites suos auroque nitidos vilem ipse tunicam et rusticanas ovium pelles induxit.

He frequently declined to wear the kinds of soft and fine clothing in which he had grown up and come to manhood, even when he visited the courts of kings. Amidst purple garbed courtiers and knights radiant in gold, he wore simple robes and rustic sheepskins. (*Vita Brun.*, chap. 30, *LB*, p. 222)

And Ruotger has his eye on manners and customs of the royal courts when he praises Brun for banishing from the church of Cologne "excesses of dress, objectionable mores and all that was effeminate and indecent" (chap. 21; *LB*, p. 210). But the chronicler of Hildesheim has a concept of court ways clearly profiled, and possesses a name for it, the meaning of which we will now examine.

CURIALIS—CURIALITAS

The noun form is an aggregate, the general designation of a code which subdivides into a number of specific qualities and customs. It has this in common with *urbanitas*. I pointed out earlier that the word *curia* as a designation for the king's court had fallen out of usage between Carolingian times and the reign of Henry III; its return represents a renewal of the classical Latin term. But at the same time as it came into common use as the designation of the king's court, *curia* and *curialis* took on a pejorative tone in the parlance of the church reformers. Petrus Damiani complains in his *Contra clericos aulicos* (ca. 1072) against clerics who desert the church to serve the court: "Fie on this prodigious madness! that a cleric in seeking to rise above clerics should become a courtier and make himself a slave of the world" ("Et, heu prodigiosa vesania! ut praeferatur clericis, qui de clerico efficitur curialis: factus est servus mundi"—PL 145:467C). The proverb, "curia curarum genetrix nutrixque malorum," stems from this period.[44] The earliest occurrence of the adjective in the sense of courtly sophistication is in Lanfranc's tract against Berengar of Tours, *De corpore et sanguine Domini* (ca. 1063). He distinguishes his own simple orthodoxy from the sophisticated evil of his opponent's thought: "mallem cum vulgo esse rusticus et idiota catholicus quam tecum existere curialis atque facetus haereticus" ("I would prefer to be, with the vulgar crowd, a rustic and unlearned catholic, than to be, with you, a courtly and sophisticated heretic"—PL 150:414C). Again, as in the *Fundatio*, *curialis facetia* is opposed to rustic simplicity to the advantage of the latter. "Courtly sophistication" is a wicked quality, part of that worldly wisdom which Christ has sent simple men to confound. Lanfranc casts himself in the role of the *sapienter indoctus*. This passage is quite instructive. It allows us to form an approximate idea of what the phrase *curialis atque facetus* refers to. Berengar had been a student of Fulbert at the cathedral school of Chartres. In 1040 he took up service as chaplain with the count of Anjou, Fulk Nerra, and continued in the service of Fulk's successor, Geoffrey Martel. As a teacher he gained a considerable following, not only for the originality of his ideas, but also for his theatrical and affected manner of lecturing. Guitmund of Aversa, one of his enemies in the Eucharist controversy, gave the following description:

cujusdam excellentiae gloriam venari, qualitercunque poterat, affectabat: factumque est ut pompatico incessu, sublimi prae caeteris suggestu, dignitatem magistri potius simulans quam rebus ostendens, profunda quodque inclusione inter cucullum, ac simulatione longae meditationis, et vix tandem satis desideratae diu vocis lentissimo quodam quasi plangore incautos decipiens, doctorem sese artium pene inscius profiteretur. (PL 149:1428B)

Whatever bespoke grandeur and distinction, he affected. This man, almost wholly ignorant, claimed to be a doctor of the arts, and persuaded people of it by virtue of his pompous posing, by elevating himself above others on a platform, by simulating the dignity of a teacher in his manner rather than by the substance of his teachings, by burying his head deeply in his cowl, pretending to be in profound meditation, then finally, when the expectations of the listeners had been whetted by his long hesitation, giving forth in an extremely soft and plangent tone, which was effective in deceiving those who did not know better.

This description, even if much of its tone can be put down to the author's enmity, gives us a very rich picture of affectations of speech: the theatrical hesitations, the soft and melancholy tone, the manipulation of the audience. Guitmund says later that it was the sweetness of his speech that corrupted his listeners ("per suos dulces sermones corruptos"—1429D). Probably these are qualities to which Lanfranc referred by calling Berengar "facetus." Perhaps also the affectation of dignity, the pursuit of "gloria excellentiae cujusdam," and the pompous bearing could be seen as negative representations of the qualities that make Berengar "curialis." In any case, Berengar's career led him between the schools and the courts of secular rulers, and it is most likely because of his attachment to worldly *curiae* that the term *curialis* became applied to him. The case of Berengar shows us, then, a cleric in the school/court milieu in France, affecting a refined manner of speech, gesture, and bearing and this just before the middle of the eleventh century; it shows us the vocabulary of courtesy applied to such mannerisms by 1063.

There is a steady increase in the stature and legitimacy of the qualities implied by the words *curialis* and *curialitas*. The noun appears first as a designation for worldly pomp—a sensuous, epicurean life—but by the mid-twelfth century it has assimilated to *elegantia morum* and indicates qualities perfectly consonant with the Christian's duties in the world. The author of the *Gesta Alberonis* (ca. 1150) praises Cardinal Bishop Guido of Cremona as "vir alti sanguinis, valdeque curialis et honestus dulcique eloquio" (chap. 23, *LB*, p. 596). A continuator of the *gesta* of the Bishops of Metz, writing around 1190, praises the blessed Stephen of Anereus, wracked by sickness and old age, for never losing his virile mind, his liberality, or the *curialitas* that had been his since youth (MGH, SS 10:545, l. 40 ff.). As early as 1114 the abbot of Oudenbourg in his Life of Bishop Arnulf of Soissons can praise the monks of Saint Medard at Soissons as "tam Dei quam mundi astutia callentes . . . nec enim esse poterant moribus inculti, qui totius Franciae et Romanae vel Remensis curialitatis erant frequentatione suffulti" (PL 174:1380D–81A). The passage points to very different circumstances in the monastic life of France than in Germany. French monasteries could be much closer to the atmosphere of life at the court of an imperial bishop in Germany than to that of the reform monasteries. Still, one wishes for more information on the exact nature of "the courtliness of all France, of Rome or (?) of Rheims." Thomas de Marleberge, the main author of the Evesham chronicle, writing around 1225, praises Pope Innocent III for his support of the downtrodden, "highly courtly man that he was" ("ut erat curialissimus, more suo liberalissimo oppressos consolans"[45]). The assimilation to *morum elegantia* is complete when *curialis* can refer to the humane execution of a clergyman's—here, a pope's—pastoral duties. The author of the *gesta* of the bishops of Halberstadt, writing in 1209, has lost sight of any distinction between the two concepts when he praises Bishop Gandolf as "morum . . . curialitate et tocius probitatis elegantia redimitus."[46]

It cannot be concluded from these citations that *curialitas* was necessarily restricted to the clergy or had originated in that estate. The *vitae* and *gesta* of the clergy are sources every bit as one-sided as the courtly romances. We should take the roots of the word seriously and accept that it refers to the qualities appropriate to ministers at the court of a ruler. By the later Middle Ages it has become canonical as a virtue of court servants.[47] The western consciousness of courtliness was shaped by educated aristocratic clerics, even if they were not its sole practitioners. The citations above at least place beyond doubt that the worldly clergy admired and practiced "courtliness" well before this became embodied in the knight and lover of courtly romance and lyric.

Until now we have managed to keep the phenomenon of courtliness quite separate from what is called "courtly love." The fact that the two were not inextricably bound to each other bears out Frappier's judgment (see chap. 7, n. 1). But there is much in the Latin sources that connects courtliness with love. Among the many complaints of Orderic Vitalis about the court of Fulk le Rechin, count of Anjou (d. 1109)—we will discuss the text in a later chapter—is the complaint that the various vain and novel customs of dress and personal culture aim at pleasing women: "Feminis viri curiales in omni lascivia summopere adulantur."[48] The "Love Council of Remiremont" is a satirical debate poem pitting two factions of nuns at Remiremont against each other to debate the relative merits of clerics and knights as lovers. The nun Elizabeth de Falcon sings the praises of clerics:

> Clericorum copula, hec est nostra regula . . .
> quos scimus affabiles gratos et amabiles.
> Inest curialitas clericis et probitas.[49]

> Union with clerics, this is our Rule . . .
> We know them to be affable, pleasing and lovable.
> In clerics there is courtliness and honesty.

The *curialitas* refers backward to the qualities *affabilis*, *gratus*, and *amabilis* (as *probitas* refers forward to their simplicity and guilelessness praised in the following lines). These were the same social graces that we have seen praised in court ministers from the earlier Middle Ages on.

To speak in a courtly way is appropriate to lovemaking. There is a very distasteful story told of the cleric Gervase of Tilbury that connects the two. Riding through the countryside with the archbishop of Rheims one day, he spied a beautiful woman working in a vineyard. He rides up, and after a closer look is smitten with desire. He begins to "speak to her in the courtly way of wanton love" ("de amore lascivo curialiter affatur").[50] Her stubborn defense of her chastity reveals her as a Cathar. Gervase reports the incident to the archbishop, and some days later she is burned at the stake. In the Evesham chronicle Thomas de Marleberge complains about Abbot Robert (d. 1195), "the most vinolent and luxurious monk in all England." He was appointed abbot by the king and brought courtly ways into the monastery: "Curialis etiam nimium extitit et dapsilis, et gloriosus in mensa, cibis et potibus abundantius affluens" (p. 104). He considered fornication not to be a mortal sin, and so he spared few women in his conquests, stopping short only of incest and adultery, though it was said that he did not shrink even from these crimes. Andreas Capellanus' use of *curialitas* is consistent with the citations given above. "Courtliness" appears as a summation of social qualities that make men and women agreeable, charming and lovable, gentle and well spoken (see *De amore*, pp. 159–62, 241). A man must possess these qualities in order to be a worthy lover, but they are not necessarily inseparable from love. One of the cases brought before the courts of love is instructive. A boorish knight is turned down as a lover by all ladies. Finally, through impetuous wooing, he wins a promise of love from one, who begins the process of educating him to courtly ways. Finally she makes a decent man out of him, renders him "in probitatis norma solide confirmat[um] et qualibet curialitatis decorat[um] virtute," only to see him fall in love with another woman. The court's decision calls for him to return to his original love, who had brought him "ad summum curialitatis ac probitatis culmen" (pp. 284–85). *Curialitas* here is the external culture, opposed to inner *probitas*. The former consists of deference, gentle speech, refined good manners, and restraint and modesty.

An anecdote told by William of Malmesbury draws together a number of concerns of this study and sets the love of a *curialis* in the social context that was our point of departure. William introduces the story to illustrate the good humor of Emperor Henry III. The emperor was very fond of his sister, a nun. They were inseparable friends. Once when Henry is kept from court by a severe snowfall, "a certain court(ly) cleric" ("clericus quidam curialis") falls in love with her and passes long vigils in her room at night. At length they become lovers. The news spreads, and soon everyone but the emperor knows of the affair. One night the two lovers are together until early morning. The cleric fears that his footprints will betray him, and he persuades his mistress to carry him on her back to his own quarters through the snow. The emperor catches sight of the cleric mounted on his sister and begins to ponder a suitable punishment. When a bishopric becomes vacant, he calls the cleric and offers him the position, but admonishes him to give up riding horseback on women henceforth. At the same time he makes his sister abbess of a monastery, but whispers to her the admonition that she should no longer permit clerics to ride her (*Gesta reg. angl.* 2:190, RS 90:1:231–32). This slightly frivolous story (which was not original with William) at least shows us that a fairly severe and sober writer like William of Malmesbury could regard with humor a situation where a courtly cleric/lover becomes a bishop. Whether there is any connection between the attribute *curialis* and the amorousness of the man thus described we cannot learn from this story. The adjective may well refer only to his station as a cleric of the court.

Let us review briefly the dating of these terms before turning to their counterparts in the vernacular. The noun *curialitas* does not occur before 1080. The *Fundatio* refers to the rule of Bishop Azelinus between 1044 and 1054, but, lacking other evidence, we have no reason to place the origin of this collective noun in the reign of Henry III. The

Ruodlieb poet does not use the term or any variant. Probably we are correct in saying that a collection of qualities that were common ideals of court behavior had not yet crystallized into a code and been given a name outside the court. However, the Hildesheim chronicler speaks of a change from *rusticalis stultitia* to *curialis facetia*, and Lanfranc of Bec, writing around 1063, speaks accusingly of Berengar as *curialis et facetus*. Both attacks presuppose an earlier dating of the social phenomena described, since the existence of a practice must precede the opposition it provokes. We can confirm through one of the *Visiones* of Otloh of Saint Emmeram, written around 1062, that Hildesheim had been touched by tastes for luxurious clothing and "frivolities of conduct" (I will discuss Otloh's testimony later), and this lends weight to the possibility that the author of the *Fundatio* was transmitting accurate information about Bishop Azelinus and perhaps using terms current in the mid-eleventh century. But our only firm dates are: *curialis* meaning "courtly," ca. 1063; and *curialitas* meaning "courtliness," 1080.

If available sources accurately reflect the historical relationships, then the corresponding vernacular terms trail along behind the Latin. The development in France diverges slightly from that in Germany. OF *curteis, corteis* develops from the Latin *cohors, cortis*, and hence belongs to a different word family from ML *curia, curialis, curialitas*. Krings points to the occurrence in 1088 of the phrase *male curtensis* in a Latin text, referring to a man who performs a thoughtless, willful act of violence (*Wortschatz*, pp. 30–31). The association of the court with restrained, humane behavior here is significant. It is significant also, that in the competition for dominance between these two groups of Latin words, the victor was the one with distinct classical overtones, the one that appears first associated with the imperial tradition. This is not to construct a dichotomy between Latin usage in Germany and in France; for this the use of *curia, curialis, curialitas* is much too widespread. But it is interesting to note that this sidetrack in the Latin vocabulary of courtesy generated the Romance vernacular terms *cortes* and *curteis*.

Cortes appears in Provençal around 1100 in William IX's poem to joy.[51] The earliest occurrences in OF are from the *Chanson de Roland*, notoriously hard to date.[52] The epithet *li proz et li curteis* is twice applied to Olivier (576 and 3755). Krings connects this with the description, "Olivier est sage" (1093) and sees in the pair *curteis-sage* "eine Sinneinheit" (*Wortschatz*, p. 32). There is abundant support in Latin sources for this interpretation; I will discuss it later. Burgess doubts that *curteis* had the full meaning of well-bred restraint and fine manners of speech and bearing which it acquired in later works, since "la cour à l'époque de la *Chanson de Roland* n'était qu'un quartier général; la vie de cour était en effet essentiellement militaire" (*Vocabulaire précourtois*, p. 22). As we have seen, however, the court was a great deal more than a military camp well before the composition of the *Song of Roland*. It is much more likely that the slightly ill-defined concept *curteis* in this work shows us a very early transition in the application of the word from men of the court, mainly clerics, to the warrior class. Applied to Olivier, *curteis* is an appropriation from the domestic sphere; but Olivier acts in the epic as a warrior. This displacement accounts for the paleness of the epithet. *Curteis* also makes its appearance in the vernacular in *Chanson de Roland* in the sense of a polite, affable, and moderated way of speaking (see 1162–64, 3823).

The earliest preserved occurrence of MHG *höfscheit* is in the work *Priesterleben*, which is ascribed to "the so-called Heinrich von Melk" and has been dated, at the earliest, around 1150. He attacks priests who live with women and says that they have about as much courtliness as an ass has brains.[53] It is significant that the first known occurrence of *höfscheit* in the vernacular in Germany is in the context of the virtues appropriate to a priest. For this writer it is a sign of *höfscheit* for priests to preserve their chastity. In MHG epic the first occurrence is in the "Strassburger Alexander," dated around 1160. By 1174, in the earlier sections of Veldeke's *Eneit*, the word has become entirely commonplace.

"Courtliness" was articulated in Latin first, then in the vernacular. The vernacular had to adapt a primitive ethical vocabulary to a highly sophisticated, differentiated Latin vocabulary. The language of ethics had no tradition in the vernacular; it had a tradition of over a thousand years in Latin. I have avoided discussing particular areas of reference of *curialis, curialitas* in the previous section, because it is a composite virtue: "curialitas est quodammodo omnis virtus qua nobilitatem morum quasi omnis virtus concomitari debet" (Aegidius Columna, *De reg. princ.* 2.3.18); "reht tuon, daz ist hüffscheit" (*Welscher Gast* 3920). The elements of courtliness can best be discussed individually.

FACETIA

The clergy of Hildesheim came to prefer *curialis facetia* to their rustic simplicity; Lanfranc accused Berengar of being *curialis atque facetus haereticus*. In these earliest references to courtliness in Latin the two qualities *facetus* and *curialis* are joined, and the connection remains common in Latin usage into the thirteenth century and beyond. The glosses cited in earlier sections show how central *facetia* is to the vocabulary of courtesy. *Facetia* and *facetus* have specific and general areas of reference: *facetia* is an agglomerate of courtly virtues, like *curialitas*, and it is a way of speaking and jesting.

FACETIA AS WITTY SPEECH. We observed that the form of jesting of which Cicero approved was *ingenuum et facetum*. He praised Socrates' way of speaking as *dulcis et facetus*, because he simulated ignorance in relation to his fellow disputants, and this stance allowed his actual superiority to assert itself in a much more effective way than through undisguised thrusts of genius. Quintilian has a long dissertation on humor (*De inst. orat.* 6.3.1 ff.), including observations on *facetia* ("decoris . . . et excultae cuiusdam elegantiae appellationem puto"— 6.3.20). Isidor gives a rough definition in the *Etymologiae*: "Facetus [dictus est] qui iocos et lusus gestis et factis conmendat, a faciendo dictus."[54] The terms are very common in our period. They never occur, however, in the catalogue of virtues of a bishop. Many a bishop may have been a *vir facetus*, but the virtue was not in the canon even of worldly episcopal qualities. *Facetia* was worldly and in a cleric, frivolous. It was appropriate only to the secular courts. William of Malmesbury, having described the warrior ways of William Rufus, praises him for his gentleness and wit when at court:

Intus et in triclinio cum privatis, omni lenitate accommodus, multa joco transigebat; facetissimus quoque de aliquo suo perperam facto cavillator, ut invidiam facti dilueret et ad sales transferret.[55]

At home and around the dining table in the company of his friends, he softened his harshness with abundant mildness and gave forth with many a jest. In a most witty and urbane manner he made light of some praiseworthy deed he had done, and in this way he warded off any possible envy, making a witty joke out of his action.

Urbane and witty jesting found disapproval in the monastic community.[56] Ambrose had proscribed jokes and witticisms for men of the church: "Nam licet interdum honesta joca ac suavia sint, tamen ab ecclesiastica abhorrent regula" (*De off. min.* 1.23.102, PL 16:54B). But even he is of two minds on the subject:

Non solum profusos, sed omnes etiam jocos declinandos arbitror; nisi forte plenum suavitatis et gratiae sermonem esse non indecorum est.

(ibid., 54C–55A)

Not only fulsome jokes, but all alike are in my opinion to be rejected, unless perhaps it is not indecorous for speech to be informed by charm and grace.

Martin of Braga echoes this ambiguity: "Sermones utiles magis quam facetos et affabiles ama." Jokes should be made with the dignity of the wise man: "Non erit tibi scurrilitas sed grata urbanitas" (*Formula vitae hon.* 4, ed. Barlow, p. 243). Bernard of Clairvaux forbids priests to use "verbum scurrile, quod faceti urbanive nomine colorant," and this refers to the reciting of *nugas vel fabulas* as opposed to the Scriptures.[57]

Speaking *facete* appears frequently as a means at a courtier's disposal for disguising a reproach to the ruler. The biographer of Godfrey of Cappenberg tells of a great convocation of Frederick Barbarossa's court at Utrecht. In the presence of the emperor a certain Swabian prince, pretending not to know Barbarossa, proceded, *facetissima urbanitate*, to hold a long speech criticizing him as if he were absent (MGH, SS 12:522, l. 9 ff.). Saxo Grammaticus gives an interesting instance of the same brand of wit. The duty of avenging the murder of King Canute falls on his successor, Sueno. But Sueno allows himself to be dissuaded from a campaign against the assassins by the danger involved. He is treated to a witty raking by Bishop Absalon of Roskyld (later archbishop of Lund, one of Saxo's patrons): "desidiam eius eludens facetissime cavillatus est." To Absalon's question why the expedition was canceled, the king answers that he is reluctant to expose such courageous men to such danger. "Well then," replies Absalon, "carry out the expedition with cowards and villains! No need to postpone the slaughter of base men!" Saxo's comment:

Ita lepidi ingenii adolescens indignationem suam ad inertiae exprobrationem sub ioci specie convertit. Quae tam faceta eius urbanitas tacitum regis convicium fuit. (*Gesta Danorum* XIV, xx, 2, p. 412)

In this way the quick-witted youth charmingly concealed his actual indignation, transforming the reproach of slothfulness into a jest. And thus with his witty urbanity he managed to issue a subtle rebuke to the king.

These citations make the social function of *facetia* in this sense quite evident. Jesting was one form of legitimized criticism, of telling the truth to the ruler without offending him.

To speak *facete* was at the same time to issue sharp, witty replies. An anecdote of Gerald of Wales gives a fine example of the combining of this with the license to speak *facete* before the ruler. Charlemagne, the story runs, sat at the dinner table with his learned tutor, the Scotsman Alcuin, across from him. The monarch posed the provoking question: "What separates a Scot from a sot?" To which Alcuin replied *tale facetum*: "Only this table."[58]

The residents of medieval courts were no less fond of wit, of the biting reply, the quick and cutting rebuke or the masked rebuke, and the ironic pretense of false motives, than were their counterparts at the courts of Europe in the Renaissance.[59] All these forms of "facetiousness" are illustrated in abundance in the chronicles and romances, and a history of *facetia* from antiquity to the Renaissance would be a rewarding task. A particularly subtle and charming scene, one rich with courtly coloring, occurs in the *vita* of Archbishop Conrad of Salzburg (1106–47). The biographer describes the entry of Conrad's father into the court of Henry IV. Conrad's grandfather, Count Babo, had sired thirty sons and eight daughters. When the sons were all of age (a strict sense of time would blunt the point of the story), Babo decided to place them in the service of the emperor. One day he received a summons to meet with the emperor during a hunt. The summons enjoined him to bring only a small escort. He seized the opportunity to present his sons. He provided each of them with one armed knight and one squire, and all set off on horseback to keep the appointment. The emperor was taken aback on seeing this crowd of armed men approaching with Count Babo in apparent defiance of his command. And here is the source of dramatic tension in the scene. The emperor's summons represented a veiled threat.[60] But Babo answered with another ambiguous and threatening gesture. To approach with 93 armed men is to place the unarmed emperor—who may have known tales of assassinations that took place on the hunt[61]— in acute danger. Henry asks reproachfully, yet with modesty and restraint ("modeste tamen"), why, when ordered to come with few men, he comes surrounded by such a throng. Babo responds that he has come with only one knight and one squire. The emperor asks with a charming expression and perfect calm ("blanda facie et verbis placidis"): "and the others?" "The others are your servants, my lord," he replies, "my sons whom I offer for your approval and commend to your favor." The emperor embraces and kisses each of the sons graciously and with bright good humor ("gratanter atque hilariter"—MGH, SS 11:63, l. 29 ff.). Count Babo was "just kidding," just "putting the emperor on." What appeared to be a hostile reaction to the emperor's ambiguous summons reveals itself as an affable and charming gesture of devotion. The count's skill shows itself in his husbanding the dramatic tensions and not relieving the emperor's apprehension until asked directly. This is *urbanissima facetia*, even though the author does not call it so by name.

In Chrétien's *Yvain* (1905 ff.), Hartmann's *Iwein* (2216 ff.), there is a scene that mirrors very clearly the structure of humor in the episode just discussed. Lunete has just persuaded her mistress, Laudine, to take Yvain, the slayer of her former husband, as her bridegroom. After waiting long enough to maintain the fiction that Yvain, hidden in the castle, is being summoned from Arthur's court, she approaches to give him the good news, but puts on a grave face. She tells him that her mistress is furious with her for concealing her husband's murderer and has ordered him brought before her. This sounds like Yvain's death sentence. He follows her to Laudine and waits in fear and apprehension. But then all is cleared up: "just kidding." The knight who thought he was a dead man finds himself a bridegroom; fear turns into joy. Chrétien unfortunately has or uses no word to describe this impish trick played on his hero's expectations. Hartmann, who takes over the episode virtually unchanged, says that Lunete was speaking "durch ir gemelîche," "for the sake of jesting" (*Iwein* 2217). The word *gemelich*, cognate with Engl. "game," has precisely the meaning of *facetia, facete* in the sense of humorously masked motives. It also can mean out and out "irony." In Konrad von Würzburg's *Trojan War*, Paris and Helen reminisce about her abduction from Menelaus. Unsuspecting Menelaus had commended Helen to the care of her would-be abductor. Paris chuckles: "How I wanted to laugh at his words, and it was only with the greatest effort that I restrained myself. It seemed to me so ironic ["ez duhte mich so gemellich"] that he placed you in my care."[62]

The Latin *facetia* did not provide the vernacular with a loan word for wit and irony in our period. The French *facet, facetement* appears in the fourteenth century.[63] MHG *gemelich* takes over meanings encompassed by *facetus* without being related to it in terms of word history. It has been suggested that the irony in courtly romance may be connected with the clerical background of the poets. The clerical courtly poet is displaced socially; the educated man whose roots are in the church stands at a distance from the world he describes, that of knights and chivalric combat. His relation to this world is ambivalent—now envious, now critical.[64] Such a consideration may well explain an occasional ironic jibe, wry characterization, or even the predominant attitude of an individual cleric/poet who feels isolated in his sense of superiority to the world of knights. But wit, irony, jibes, and jests were so much the accepted atmosphere of banter at court, urbane and "facetious" chit-chat so admired and cultivated by lay nobles and clerics alike, that the notion of a specific class distinction could only explain individual cases. Irony and wit were the rule at court, not the response of an outsider to a somewhat foreign sphere on which he looks with ironic disdain.

FACETIA AS COURTLY REFINEMENT OF MANNERS.   The noun form, *facetia*, competed with *curialitas* to express the entire code of refinement and sophistication that developed at European courts in our period. Geoffrey of Monmouth describes the high courtly culture attained at the court of King Arthur during a long period of peace. The king gathered together the best men in the land and assembled an illustrious retinue. He became the envy of Europe: "coepit . . . tantam facetiam in domo sua habere" that he was copied everywhere:[65]

Ad tantum etenim statum dignitatis Britannia tunc reducta erat, quod copia divitiarum, luxu ornamentorum, facetia incolarum cetera regna excellebat (Chap. 157, p. 246)

England at that time enjoyed so high a reputation because in wealth, luxurious display, and the refinement of its inhabitants it excelled all other lands.

A passage that has been of some interest to historians of courtly love is Geoffrey's observation in the same context that at Arthur's court there were *facetae mulieres* who refused the love of any man who had not proved himself three times in battle. The love of such women ennobles men (ibid.). "Courtly ladies" would seem to be the appropriate translation, or "women skilled in courtly ways." It is a clear indication that the cult of love, at least one aspect of it, was present in the mind of Geoffrey, writing around 1135, that is, two decades before the first romances were composed.[66]

Around the middle of the twelfth century an anonymous cleric composed a didactic poem of some five hundred lines which came to be known as *Facetus de moribus et vita*, or simply *Facetus*, from its first lines:

> Moribus et vita quisquis vult esse facetus
> Me legat et discat quod mea musa notat.[67]

It is an important poem for various reasons. For one, it is not dependent on models in ethical writings. It simply brings together a series of observations on the skilled conduct of a good and proper life, loosely organized according to classes and ages of men. The release from the framework of the four cardinal virtues made for a certain freshness of observation and vividness. For another, it engendered a whole series of didactic poems which go under the name *Facetus*, a word that became something like a genre designation.[68] In the original poem from the mid-twelfth century the word *facetus* does not indicate specifically court manners. It refers to a life guided by wisdom, good manners, and decorum:

> Expedit inprimis cupientes esse facetos
> Mente, fide, verbo, nobilitate frui.
> (5–6)

Fides and *mens* are dealt with in short order; then the poet turns to speech, beginning with the startling advice:

> Esto verecundus falsum quandoque loquaris,
>   Nam semper verum dicere crede nephas.
> Crimina multociens laus est celare faceto,
>   Maxima rusticitas turpia verba loqui.
>
> (9–12)

> Retain your modest restraint even when speaking falsehoods.
> For, always to speak the truth you may take to be wrong.
> For the skilled man, it is often praiseworthy to conceal wrongdoings.
> The greatest villainy is to use foul speech.

The *urbanus* speaks little and only after careful thought. He avoids pride, maintains a placid expression and meek though refined bearing (15 ff.). The approval of a certain slyness and worldly-wise shrewdness is a consistent feature of this poem, and it may be implied in the word *facetus* itself. We have already seen that as a form of joking *facetia* can involve the skillful creation of an unpleasant illusion which is then broken with theatrical effect to reveal a courtly and agreeable state of affairs. *Facetia* involves a certain magicianship with words, and this brings us into the area of deception and sleight of hand. The *vir facetus* should be eloquent, but also learned and diligent, liberal, well-dressed in a manner proper to his estate, and scrupulous in his table manners (see 20 ff.). After these general comments the poet turns to particular groups of men: a young cleric (33 ff.), a young layman (63 ff.), merchants (73 ff.). Most of the poem is devoted to the art of loving, with model speeches, and specific instructions on kissing and embracing (131 ff.). The lover must speak in a charming and ingratiating way to his beloved ("blandus sermo"—207), greet her with a face radiant with joy ("facie gaudente salutans"—269), and adhere to the golden mean in courtship and lovemaking: "Nam sine mensura nil valet esse bonum" (278). He ends with praise of friendship and admonitions to judges, knights, and old men.

This writer shows no interest in the court life and gives no indication that his lessons are appropriate to the court. His ethical vocabulary is distinctly Ciceronian (*officia, decorum, verecundia, urbanus, facetus, ingeniosus*, etc.), though it may be rash to suppose that its Ciceronian provenance was distinct in the mind of the poet, diffused as this vocabulary was throughout the ethical writings of the Middle Ages. Probably he is summarizing the sort of moral instruction available to noble families through private tutors (whom he commends to the parents of noble children—64); the poem is too informal, too light on learned citation and traditional form to be considered a reflection of instruction in *mores* at a cathedral school.

Two final points are important for our purposes. The shaping of life through art and skill, and the reasoned guidance of life are ideals of this poet. Let each man learn the skills and develop the gifts that nature has given him, he urges; for a man without any art is no better than brute cattle: "Ars hominem format" (86), and though the gifts of nature are variously distributed, every man has the raw material by which he can shape and form himself: "Sic habet omnis homo quo se possit fabricare" (93). Here the skills of the handcraftsman or sculptor ("fabriles artes"—79) become a metaphor for the guidance of life. Again we find ourselves at that high stage of the civilizing process at which life itself is regarded as a work of art, and the untrained, undisciplined man is marble and raw material. But our author seems to place so high a value on this aesthetic of ethics that he makes it into the measure of humanity: "Art makes the man"! It is our ethical duty to be our own author, to sculpt and mold ourselves, perceiving like the inspired artist the particular design of nature implanted in us. The second point is that this process is a process of education: "Ut per doctrinam vivere discat homo" (32), "Let man learn through instruction how to live well." This poem sets forth an entire plan of civilizing: education transforms life into a work of art; elegance of manners and of speech are closely related; the artistically shaped life develops forms of deportment that are close to literary forms.

In this survey of the poem *Facetus* we have as sharp a commentary as we could hope for on the statement of the Hildesheim chronicler that *curialitas* is "in victu lautior, in omni cultu accuratior" ("more refined in way of life, more scrupulous in every aspect of culture"). It is precisely scrupulousness in dress, table manners, learning, the guidance of life, gesture and speech, and lovemaking which is demanded of the *vir facetus*. Slovenliness or indifference in words and action is *rusticitas*. When cultivated elegance of word and deed are the result of a conscious choice and decision, when each passes the rules of tact, taste, and decorum, then *facetia* is attained.

HILARITAS-IUCUNDITAS

The Hildesheim chronicler said that "courtliness" sought to inspire love rather than fear: "amari quam timeri maluit." This aspect of a code he was attacking was listed along with other execrable features opposed to monastic simplicity. This is odd coming from a cleric who clearly favors rigorous monastic discipline. The Benedictine Rule stipulates that the abbot should seek rather to be loved than feared:[69]

"Studeat plus amari quam timeri." Why then should a cleric opposing "irregular" behavior on the part of a bishop deplore the cultivating of an atmosphere of love? Probably because by the mid-eleventh century this atmosphere was associated much more closely with the life of the court than with that of the monastery. Cicero had commended the advantages of love over fear in the public man's guidance of the state (*De off.* 2.23). Ambrose took over Cicero's thought on the subject with little change:

Ac primum noverimus nihil tam utile, quam diligi: nihil tam inutile, quam non amari. . . . Popularis enim et grata est omnibus bonitas, nihilque quod tam facile illabatur humanis sensibus. Ea si mansuetudine morum ac facilitate, tum moderatione praecepti, et affabilitate sermonis, verborum honore, patienti quoque sermonum vice, modestiaeque adjuvetur gratia, incredibile quantum procedit ad cumulum dilectionis. (*De off. min.* 2.7.29, PL 16: 111B–C)

First we should know that there is nothing so useful as to be loved, nothing as inexpedient as the opposite. . . . Goodness is popular and agreeable to all men, and nothing impresses itself with such ease on humane sensibilities. And if we bring this goodness to fruition through a gentle and polite manner, moderation in commands and affability of speech, respectful choice of words and unassuming form of address, and a graceful modesty, it will bring us amazed to the pinnacle of affection.

The passage is quoted in Gerald of Wales *De principis instructione* (1.2, p. 11), and this shows us the social context in which the precept was most at home in the Middle Ages: the ruler and his relations to his household and subjects. Helena Gamer, in her study of the ethical vocabulary of *Ruodlieb*,[70] pointed out the persistence of the "virtue" *amor*, in reference to the ideal climate not only of personal but also of public, state relationships. The court of the vanquished *rex minor* is delighted to receive from their conqueror an offer first of service, then heartfelt love ("Primo servimen post fidi cordis amorem"—4.92). They hear that their own captives were treated "like friends" of the king in whose custody they were (4.106). On the departure of the emissaries, the *vicedomnus* embraces and kisses them, taking leave "in profound love" ("grandi amore"—4.167). When the kings meet for peace negotiations no word is spoken until the ritual of mutual kissing, a ceremony referred to as *amor* (5.31), has come to an end. These are just a few examples of a virtue that is ubiquitous in the poem. This is the more noteworthy, since, as Gamer points out, the author never refers either to the four cardinal virtues or to the Christian virtue of *caritas*. Is there any connection between *amor* in the *Ruodlieb* and the rule of love that Azelinus instituted at Hildesheim? The common factor would perhaps be the court of Henry III, or the continuing influence of ideals of that court, if the *Ruodlieb* was composed in the reign of Henry IV. Does the *curialitas* of Azelinus confirm the historical reality of the *amor* that received a fictional representation in *Ruodlieb*? Probably the connection is less specific. From the early Middle Ages on we find that happiness, joy, and good fellowship (*laetitia, hilaritas, amicitia*) constitute an ideal court amosphere; amiability and good fellowship create it; anger and resentment, openly expressed, destroy it. The king and his court were bright spirited, maintained gaiety and jocundity as the ground tone of social intercourse, even when plotting murder, or rather especially then. An aphorism of Thomasin is paradigmatic (*Welscher Gast* 5056–57):

> Swer zu hove wesen sol
> dem zimet vreude wol.

The social virtue had a function in the power relations at court. Any surliness, unruliness, resentment, and open anger at court could be taken to diminish the authority of the ruler. It was in his interest to maintain an atmosphere of modest restraint and bright good cheer among his retinue. This atmosphere is the palpable assurance that he is in command and in control. To violate it is to break an unspoken law and potentially to issue an insult and challenge to the prince himself. To laugh and joke in a restrained and amiable manner is to give proof of one's acquiescence to the ruler's will, to show that one walks at ease before the unseen curtain of his authority.

A bright and cheery countenance appears in idealized portraits of men in antiquity.[71] It is doubtful if there is any time or culture in which this did not appear as an agreeable quality. Joy was cultivated at the ruler's court as early as Carolingian times. Smaragd says of the virtue *clementia* in his *Via regia*: this virtue "brightens the king's countenance to its most jocund. . . . It administers jocundity and happiness to all members of the royal palace" ("ipsa est quae iucundissime regis facit hilarescere vultum, sicut Salomon ait: 'In hilaritate vultus regis, vita. . . .' [Prov. 16:15] Ipsa est quae omnibus in palatio regis jucunditatem ministrat atque laetitiam" (PL 102.958D).[72] This atmosphere was apparent at the court of the *rex major* in *Ruodlieb*. He speaks to his retainers as to friends and maintains a jocund atmosphere at table:

> Ad mensam comites superexaltans locupletes,
> Dum convivatur, nobiscum fando iocatur.
> (1.104–5)

At table in the midst of banqueting, he chats and jokes with us [his servants and retainers], while rich counts sit there ignored.

Emperor Henry III, who may well have been the model for the *rex major*, is described by William of Malmesbury as "joci plenus" when relieved of the tumult of reign and "cum se communioni et hilaritati dedisset" (*Gesta reg. angl.* 2.190, RS 90:1:231). Benzo of Alba says that the king should love the ministers who love him and by his love stir them to more fervent service (MGH, SS 11:600, ll. 31–32). In his allegorical "palace of virtue" the very sun in the firmament of worldly life is *amicicia*: "Huius virtutis gratia sol est in mundi patria" (p. 674, l. 13).[73] A cheery face and friendly speech could be seen as an element of *humanitas*. A passage in Saxo's *Gesta Danorum* shows this in the context of pardoning a vanquished enemy: "Quem [i.e., Gelderus surrendering] Høtherus amicissimo vultu, benignissimoque sermone exceptum non minus humanitate quam arte perdomuit" (3.2.7, p. 65). It was also an essential quality of courtly lovers. Women receive their lovers with joy: "hilari receptione suscipitis et curialitatis verba secum adinvicem confertis et amoris eis opera suadetis" (*De Amore*, p. 162); and joy is itself the quality of love: "Amor enim est, qui dolorum claustra disrumpit et laeta solus meruit gaudia subrogare et suavia delectationis solatia ministrare" (ibid., p. 173). The celebration of joy and gaiety among the troubadours and in romance is far too common to require discussion here,[74] but I will just point to the convention of lavish descriptions of court festivals at which joy is the predominant tone of the event.[75]

It is hard to find praise of these qualities in the monastic communities in the twelfth century. Here we find grave warnings against excessive *hilaritas* and *iocunditas*. (Cf. Petrus Damiani, PL 144:259B.) Bernard of Clairvaux places the pursuit of *laetitia* among the sins of pride: "Proprium est superborum, laeta semper appetere et tristitia devitare, iuxta illud: 'Cor stultorum, ubi laetitia'" (Eccles. 7.5).[76]

At the end of this section I will quote at length a series of idealized portraits of the members of Frederick Barbarossa's court, which were composed by the Italian Acerbus Morena around 1164. These portraits give us an extensive list of the virtues and qualities which, in the mind of this author at least, constituted a courtly nobleman and lady:[77]

Imperator igitur de nobilissima prosapie ortus fuit et mediocriter longus erat, pulcre stature, recta et bene composita membra habens, alba facie rubeo colore suffusa, capillis quasi flavis et crispis; hilari vultu, ut semper ridere velle putaretur; dentibus candidis, pulcherrimis manibus, ore venusto . . . velocis ingenii, in sapientia multum abundans; amicis ac bonis dulcis et benignus, malis vero terribilis et quasi inexorabilis . . . ab omnibus fere dilectus, et in quo rerum natura nihil deerraverat, preter quod eum mortalem finxerat, cuique a longevis retro nullus fuit imperator equiperandus.

Beatrix vero coniunx ipsius imperatoris fuit, et ipsa de nobili genere orta de provincia Burgundie, mediocris stature, capillis [. . . .], facie pulcherrima . . . vultu modesto, oculis claris; suavibus et blandis sermonibus pudica; pulcherrimis manibus, gracilis corpore. . . .

Rainaldus electus archiepiscopus Colonie, . . . erat . . . disertus et optime litteratus, facundus, providus et sagacissimus, . . . erat quoque largus, hilaris, affabilis, alti cordis. . . .

Hermanus Verdensis episcopus de Saxonia erat non multum longe stature; benignus, misericors et pius, sapientia imbutus, dulcis et affabilis, hilari corde, amator iusticie, timens Deum et mandata eius observans. . . .

Fredericus dux de Rottemburgo . . . erat magnus, pro etate fortis, virtutis cupidus, bene compositus, grossus, spissus, albus, pulcer atque formosus, hilaris, iocundus, capillis quasi albis et mollibus. . . .

Comes Redulfus de Lindo erat magne ac spisse stature, formosissimis et rectis membris, venustam et pulcherrimam ac hilarem faciem habens. . . .

Comes Gabardus de [. . . .] erat . . . in bello fortissimus, honoris avidus, largus, dapsilis, hilaris atque iocundus. . . .

Marchio vero Gulielmus de Monferato . . . fuit mediocris stature, bene compositus . . . maxime loquax, virtuosus et sapiens, hilaris atque iocundus, munificus, non prodigus. . . .

Comes Conradus de Ballanuce erat stature non magne, albus, facie formosa, capillis albis; litteratus et sapiens, dulcis et affabilis, providus et in bello strenuus, tam lingua Teutonica quam Ytalica doctus, et in consiliis imperatoris maxime potens.

The emperor, then, born of the highest nobility, was fairly tall, of handsome posture, his limbs straight and well shaped, his complexion light with a flush of red, his hair blond and curled; his countenance was so joyous that it seemed as if he were constantly about to break into laughter; his teeth were white, his hands most lovely, his mouth beautiful . . . quick minded and abounding in wisdom; gentle and courteous to his friends, but terrible and nearly inexorable to evil men . . . loved by all and in all things so perfect that since time immemorial there has been no emperor who could reasonably be compared to him.

His wife the empress Beatrix was also born of noble stock from the province of Burgundy. Of medium height, her hair shone like gold, her face, most beautiful . . . of modest aspect, her eyes, bright, gentle and friendly; her speech was chaste, her hands exquisite, her shape slender. . . .

Rainald, archbishop elect of Cologne . . . was well-spoken, and most literate, eloquent, foresighted and extremely wise. . . . He was also generous, gay, affable, high spirited. . . .

Herman of Saxony, Bishop of Verdun, was of medium height, gentle, compassionate and pious, suffused with wisdom, gentle and affable, gay of heart, a lover of justice, fearing God and keeping His commandments. . . .

Duke Friedrich of Rotenburg . . . was large for his age, possessing strength and a zeal for justice, well shaped, stout and heavy-set, fair and handsome, gay, jocund, with light colored and soft hair. . . .

Count Redulf of Lind [Rudolf von Pfullendorf] was tall and heavy set, with very handsome and well-composed limbs, his face beautiful, lovely and gay. . . .

Count Gebhard of [. . . .] was most powerful in war, ambitious for honor, generous, wealthy, gay and jocund. . . .

Margrave William of Montferrat . . . was of medium height, of handsome figure . . . virtuous and wise, gay and jocund, liberal but not prodigal.

Count Conrad of Ballhausen was below medium height, light of complexion, handsome of face with light blond hair, lettered and wise, gentle and affable, foresighted and severe in war, learned in both the German and the Italian tongue.

The predominant qualities are physical beauty and cheerfulness; the latter occurring in each of the portraits. Moral virtues receive little attention. What matters is effectiveness in court society and the practical affairs of the empire: war, politics, and social intercourse. Frederick as the emperor "so cheerful of countenance that he seemed always about to break into laughter" was the embodiment of a virtue that gained a high profile in the twelfth century, but which had been cultivated by kings and their courts since the early Middle Ages.

‹›

There are many other ideals, values, and qualities that deserve detailed discussion, but which I will only mention at this point: *comitas*, courtly, affable, amiable behavior; *civilitas*, well-bred, affable, courtly ways, the social qualities appropriate to skilled statesmanship;[78] *verecundia*, the quality that Cicero described as the essence of *decorum*, the delicacy of feeling which avoids whatever could offend other men, a chaste sense of propriety and regard for others shown for instance by Otto of Bamberg in the baptizing arrangements described by Herbord.[79] There is an entire aspect of *ambitiosa curialitas* which I have not touched on, the purely material side of it: sumptuous clothing, refinement of personal grooming, dainty foods and fine drink. This is the subject of the next chapter.[80]

‹›

To sum up, a tradition of courtliness existed well before this phenomenon came to expression in the courtly literature of the twelfth and thirteenth centuries. This tradition represents a social and ethical phenomenon rooted in the particular social context: court service. The study of its history through its representation in imaginative literature is doomed to be one-sided; courtly literature is the cresting of a wave of civilizing that began to swell in the mid-eleventh century. Courtliness does not represent "indissolublement liés, un fait social et un fait littéraire."[81]

We have dealt with a set of values that divides into two separable, if not always clearly distinct, codes: the one ethical, the other social;

the one at least acceptable to orthodox Christianity as a guide to the public life of the Christian, the other damnable. What we have observed of the former justifies our speaking of "an imperial tradition of courtliness," designated by terms like *disciplina* and *elegantia morum*, and embodied by courtier bishops like Otto of Bamberg. The *suavitas delectabilium morum* which endeared the ascetic Ulrich of Zell to the Empress Agnes and to Henry III form a crisp contrast to the levity of external show and frivolous manners practiced by Ulrich's fellow chaplains. The assimilation of *curialitas* to *elegantia morum* was, from the perspective of the history of ideas, made possible across the bridge of *kalokagathia*; external refinements and scrupulousness of manners are *insignia virtutum*; the refinement of the outer man mirrors the well-ordered inner life. At the imperial court under Henry III this assimilation took place on a large scale and raised a new ethical-social code into popular consciousness among worldly clergy and lay nobility. The spirit of renewal of empire and the neoclassicism of that court set the intellectual climate that favored the rise and spread of this ethic.

The transmission of courtly ethics to Germany has caused much agony, chronicled in the collection of essays entitled *Ritterliches Tugendsystem* in the series *Wege der Forschung*. The connection between "chivalric" ethics and the transmission of Cicero has caused considerable disagreement. Curtius maintains that Ehrismann vastly overrates and simplifies the influence of Cicero on this code. Our treatment of the Latin vocabulary of courtesy suggests perhaps a more fruitful line of criticism. Certainly an argument is to be made that Curtius underestimates the importance of Cicero, while Ehrismann overestimates the role of William of Conches' *Moralium dogma philosophorum* in Germany. The adaptation by Werner von Elmendorf of this work ascribed to William of Conches permitted scholarship to tie the spread of ethical ideas to the conventional notions about the spread of *courtoisie*. It was assumed that this sprang up spontaneously in France and was transmitted thence to Germany. Therefore the adaptation by a German of a French work modeled on Cicero gave Ehrismann all he could wish for in the way of apparent historical correctness. But the appearance deceived; the model for the origins and spread of courtesy was incomplete. With some knowledge of the imperial tradition we can suggest quite a different model.

A "courtly ethic" developed at the European cathedral schools, at the German probably earlier than the French, since these were intimately tied to the preparation for state service in the imperial church. In its earliest form this was an ethic of state service based on classical models, intended for the instruction of aspiring *curiales* in *mores*. These values, still largely in the province of the educated secular clergy, spread outward through the ranks of the worldly clergy in Germany, France, and England. *Curiales* and rulers alike urged this code upon the chivalric class, and at some point this class eagerly accepted it (this process is the subject of a later chapter). This acceptance occurred first in France; the knighthood here first was instructed in—sought instruction in—courtliness. At this point "courtly" ideals became transformed into "chivalric" ideals. This development occurred in Germany only when the German lay nobility saw their French counterparts behaving themselves like modest, urbane, and elegant gentlemen. Then they wanted nothing more than to be like them, suave in speech and manner, courtly in lovemaking. But in taking up courtliness, the German laity were adopting patterns of behavior that had been in their own back yard—or rather front yard—for generations, practiced at the royal courts by the educated aristocracy. As long as courtiers and bishops—who were after all the allies of the emperor and the traditional political rivals of the feudal nobility—behaved in softer, more civilized ways, these patterns of conduct were merely *pfafflich*. But if the French lay aristocracy began to behave in the same way, that was a different matter. Now the German nobility required enlightenment, instruction, and guidance in courtly ways and found it in the form of clerical tutors and the courtly romance. These teachers of courtesy in Germany could draw, in part, on the preformed ethical vocabulary of the imperial tradition. Hence *disciplina* became *zuht*; *elegantia morum* became *schoene site*. In this way the imperial tradition made its way in significant trickles into German romance, while the main flood of "chivalric" and courtly vocabulary entered through France.

It does not require a William of Conches or Werner of Elmendorf to explain this transmission of ethical ideals. On the contrary, against the background of the imperial tradition, they appear not as innovators but as compilers and summarizers.

◇ 9 ◇

THE CLERICAL REBELLION AGAINST COURTLINESS

T HE COURT life was suspect to conservative clergy. By its very nature it was "inordinate"; the classifications of the divine hierarchy became blurred here. The court was *mundus* and *saeculum*, its ruler Pharaoh and Nebuchadnezzar, its location Egypt and Babylon. Service there was a hateful form of servitude to which pious men went only like Joseph into Egypt. A place where luxury and refined tastes were sanctioned, where sophisticated fashions of conduct and dress were cultivated could only appear to the orthodox Christian in the Middle Ages as a breeding ground of corruption. We observed the case formulated against the court and courtiers in an earlier chapter. But conservative clergy, specifically the church reformers, mounted an attack on precisely the code named by the Hildesheim chronicler *curialitas*, and in following the protests against this code we will be able to see the issues of that text against the background of a much broader swell of resistance. The target of these protesters is the corruption of clerics and lay nobles through court manners and fashions. An overview of this anti-courtly position and its spread across Europe will tell us much about courtliness itself—viewed at its most shallow and materialistic—and about its development in Europe.

We have seen that the biographer of Brun of Cologne, writing in the 960s, contrasted the sumptuous ways of imperial courtiers with the rustic simplicity of Brun and praised the archbishop for banishing "excesses of dress, objectionable mores and all that was effeminate and indecent" from the church of Cologne (*Vita Brun.*, chap. 21, LB, p. 210). But this does not constitute a clearly highlighted attack on court ways; only praise of Brun, whose stance toward worldly ways was correct and orthodox.

Protests against court ways as such are brought into focus by a particular historical configuration: the confrontation of the monastic reform movement with the spread of courtly ways in Provence. There is clearly a powerful cultural ferment in Southern France at the end of the tenth and the beginning of the eleventh centuries. The area enjoyed a long period of peace and prosperity during the eleventh century,[1] one which no doubt accounts for the birth of "courtly love" celebrated among the troubadours.[2] Peace leads to *curialitas*. This formula, which we find in a number of texts, had an ominous ring to the ears of conservative clergy. Since the earliest Middle Ages writers had regarded peace as a potential threat to the morality of the European nobles, whose duty was to fight.[3] During long periods of peace the knights grew lazy, flabby, and dissolute. The very words "court," *cour, hof,* and their derivatives, *cortois* and *hövesch,* rang with an antithesis to warrior ways, to combat and the field. These two formed a contrasting pair with ethical overtones as distinct as those in the pair *êre* and *gemach,* "honor" and "comfort." Placed in opposition to combat and the field of battle, "the court" had a ring of turpitude and degeneracy. This tone of contempt for courts in peacetime still sounds clearly in the opening monologue of *Richard III,* where the "weak piping time of peace" and its "idle pleasures" oppose the "stern alarums" and "dreadful marches" of "grim-visaged war," and the king, to his shame, "capers nimbly in a lady's chamber to the lascivious pleasings of a lute." A scene in Geoffrey's *Historia regum Britanniae* is paradigmatic for this feeling that court life with its sensual allurements corrupts the fighting spirit. It follows the passage in which Geoffrey has described the high courtly culture developed at King Arthur's court during a long period of peace. Arthur receives a letter from "Lucius, procurator of Rome," challenging him to battle. The Britons decide to go to war. Duke Cador of Cornwall is delighted and gives the following speech:

"Hucusque in timore fueram ne Britones longa pace quietos otium quod ducunt ignavos faceret famamque militiae, qua ceteris gentibus clariores censentur, in eis omnino deleret. Quippe, ubi usus armorum videtur abesse, alearum vero et mulierum inflammationes ceteraque oblectamenta adesse, dubitandum non est ne id quod erat virtutis, quod honoris, quod audaciae, quod famae ignavia commaculet. . . . Deus igitur, ut nos liberaret segnitia, Romanos in hunc affectum induxit, ut ad pristinum statum nostram probitatem reducerent." (Chap. 158, ed. Faral, p. 248)

"Up to now I have been in fear lest the leisure which the Britons have enjoyed because of the long peace should render them listless and cowardly, destroying the fame of their deeds of war in which they are deemed greater than other nations. Indeed, where the exercise of arms is seen to make way for the allurements of dicing and women, and other pleasures, it is inevitable that the reputation for strength, honor and daring is tainted by the reproach of cowardice. . . . For the sole reason of freeing us from this sloth, God has stirred up the Romans against us, so that they may restore our prowess to what it was in the old days."

There are two important witnesses to this softening at the courts of Provence in the first half of the eleventh century. Radulfus Glaber complains in his *Historiae* (1046–49) about the corruption of the French through contact with Provence. As a result of the marriage of Constance of Arles with Robert the Pious in 1003, France experienced a flood of

homines omni levitate vanissimi, moribus et veste distorti, armis et equorum faleris incompositi, a medio capitis comis nudati, histrionum more barbis rasi, caligis et ocreis turpissimi.[4]

men puffed up with every sort of levity, corrupt in manners and in dress, dissolute in their use of arms and the embellishments on their horses, cutting their hair as far back as the middle of the head, shaving their beards like actors, utterly obscene in their style of hose and leggings.

Radulfus composed some verses condemning these customs with motifs which we will encounter frequently in clerical protests: the men of the past strove for a restrained, composed way of life and opposed vain novelties; the past would laugh at the present; shortened, tight dress renders men *ineptos*, womanish ways weaken the empire (*Historiae* 3.9.40). Abbot William of St. Bénigne at Dijon[5] went to the king and queen, Ralph continues, and complained bitterly that they permitted the land, "nuper omnium honestissima," to be thus corrupted.

Here the clerical protest against courtliness takes forms which will recur in similar complaints throughout Europe in the next two centuries: foreign customs and inane novelties are corrupting the moral strength of the land; the example of great men of the ancient past is spurned, and all cleave to softened, effeminizing vanities. The obligation of the clergy to "correct" the profligate ways of laymen is invoked in the example of the courageous abbot complaining to the monarch and his wife.

In Germany the alarm was raised by the abbot Siegfried of Gorze. Writing a few years before Radulfus Glaber, he inveighs against the importation of fashions from Provence. In 1043 he wrote to his fellow abbot Poppo of Stablo, complaining of Henry III's marriage to Agnes of Poitou. Besides the marriage itself Siegfried is troubled by many things stirring in the empire, things he hesitates to mention for fear of arousing the emperor's wrath. But about one thing he cannot remain silent:

honestas regni, quae temporibus priorum imperatorum veste et habitu nec non in armis et equitatione decentissime viguerat, nostris diebus postponitur, et ignominiosa Franciscarum ineptiarum consuetudo introducitur, scilicet in tonsione barbarum, in turpissima et pudicis obtutibus execranda decurtatione ac deformitate vestium multisque aliis novitatibus, quas enumerare longum est quasque temporibus Ottonum ac Heinricorum introducere nulli fuit licitum. At nunc plurimi patrios et honestos mores parvipendunt et exterorum hominum vestes simulque mox perversitates appetunt ac per omnia his etiam similes esse cupiunt, quos hostes et insidiatores suos esse sciunt, et quod magis dolendum est, hi tales non modo non corriguntur, verum etiam apud regem et quosdam alios principes familiariores habentur. . . . Hoc vero alii videntes eorum similes fieri non verecundantur et, quia eos impune ferre simul et munerari considerant, maiores novitatum insanias excogitare festinant.[6]

The honor of the kingdom, which in the reigns of previous emperors flourished most decently, not only in respect to clothes and custom, but also feats of arms and chivalry, in our days is brushed aside, and the scandalous rule of French frivolities displaces it. Men cut their beards, for instance, and—shameful to behold!—they shorten and deform their garments in a way most vile and execrable. They indulge in many other novelties which no one would have dreamed of in the days of the Ottos and Henrys. But now many despise the honorable customs of their own lands and seek out the ways of dress of foreigners, and their perversities cannot be far behind. They are striving in all ways to be like their enemies, men plotting against them, and, more lamentable yet, such men not only avoid correction, but are taken into the close favor of the king and of certain other princes. . . . Others, putting aside all shame, then strive to do likewise, seeing their fellows rewarded and unpunished; they even strive to think up mad novelties on a still greater scale.

This letter is often cited as evidence of the early importation of French refinement and courtliness into comparatively backwoods Germany.[7] It is clear that luxurious dress and stylish ways were cultivated in the courts of Provence from whence they spread. But court style was international; the testimony of Ralph Glaber and Siegfried of Gorze to its emergence in Provence do not prove that the French nobility invented it. It is an unhappy conspiring of one-sided sources and nationalism that has granted such longevity to that idea. Brun of Cologne had grown up among courtier splendor, and the objectionable customs he refused to take into the church of Cologne were not occasional aberrations at the imperial court but rather the norm. What we learn from the letter of the abbot of Gorze is that the courts of Midi begin to outbid the imperial courts; the French were ingenious and imaginative in their shaping of style. The "novelties" wrought there went beyond common practice at the imperial courts and so captured the imagination in Germany and the North.

Ordericus Vitalis gives us a vivid description of the inventiveness of the French and of their success in shaping court fashions. In his *Historia ecclesiastica*, completed in 1142, he attacks ways at the court of Foulk le Rechin, count of Anjou (d. 1109). Orderic accuses this lord—in his opinion vice-ridden and degenerate—of shaping a new style of shoe with pointed, turned-up toes in order to conceal the deformity of his own feet. The fashion catches on and spreads "through the entire west," an example of the "perverse mores" among laymen. The more honorable men of an earlier age would have judged them utterly obscene, Orderic tells us. But nowadays men find such ways "sweet as honey, and they flaunt them as if it were some special distinction."[8] The "pulley shoes" are a *frivola adinventio* foisted on the world by *effeminati* who now set the fashions among the nobility:

sodomiticis . . . spurciciis foedi catamitae flammis urendi turpiter abutebantur. Ritus heroum abiciebant, hortamenta sacerdotum deridebant, barbaricumque morem in habitu et vita tenebant. (8.10, ed. Chibnall, 4:188).

foul catamites, doomed to eternal fire, unrestrainedly pursued their revels and shamelessly gave themselves up to the filth of sodomy. They rejected the traditions of great and illustrious men, ridiculed the counsels of priests, and persisted in their barbarous way of life and style of dress.

These customs include growing their hair long,[9] parting it in the middle, curling it with hot irons, and wearing long, tight-fitting shirts and tunics. At night there are feasts and drinking bouts, idle chatter, dice and other games. Part of the purpose of these fashions was to please women: "Femineam mollitiem petulans iuuentus amplectitur, feminisque viri curiales in omni lascivia summopere adulantur"— ibid. ("Our wanton youth is sunk in effeminacy, and fawning courtiers seek the favours of women with every kind of lewdness.") A persistent theme in the entire passage is the virtue and strength of the men of bygone days, which are now being sapped by the new-fangled courtly ways: gone or going are the ways of "men of honor from earlier days" ("olim honorabiles viri"—4.186); the ways of heroes ("ritus heroum") are put aside; the "customs of our ancestors" are ignored ("mos patrum"—4.188), as are the "upright ways of our ancient ancestors" ("honestus patrum mos antiquorum"—ibid.); the new ways have driven out the times when "our ancestors—skilled horsemen and swift runners—used to wear decent clothes, well-adapted to the shape of their bodies" (4.189); now however, the "veterum ritus" is being distorted beyond recognition (4.188). This becomes a standard formula for castigating courtly fashions: oppose them to the sterner more upright ways of men of old.

William of Malmesbury observed and attacked many of the customs reported by Orderic when they made their way into England. In his *Gesta regum anglorum* there is a lengthy attack on the court of William Rufus. Here also the king is accused of importing the fashion of shoes with curved toes. His courtiers live outside of "militaris disciplina," feeding themselves fat on the possessions of the *rustici* and cultivating effeminate ways:

Tunc fluxus crinium, tunc luxus vestium, tunc usus calceorum cum arcuatis aculeis inventus: mollitie corporis certare cum foeminis, gressum frangere gestu soluto, et latere nudo incedere adolescentium specimen erat.[10]

Then arose the fashions of long, flowing hair, luxurious clothes, [and] shoes with curved tips. To compete with women for softness of body, to break stride with a cultivated negligence of gait, and to walk with the hips thrust forward: this was the epitome of style for youth.

In his continuation of the *Gesta*, the *Historia novella*, William attacks customs at the court of King Henry I, who brought back from Normandy the custom of long hair. Now the men of the court, he laments, are all eager to make women of themselves in their ways of dress. One of the knights dreamed that he was strangled with his own locks. Shaken by this warning, he and the others cut off their superfluous hair. But within a year "all who fancied themselves courtly" ("cuncti qui sibi curiales esse videbantur") had relapsed into this vice.[11] William also praises King David of Scotland, who had vigorously opposed the incursion of courtly ways into his country. He was a "juvenis ceteris curialior," who through association with the English, says the Englishman William, had lost his "Scottish rust" and gained a certain polish. He levied a three-year tribute on all his countrymen "who wished to live in the more refined way, dress more elegantly and eat more daintily" (*Gesta reg. Angl.* 5.400, ed. Stubbs, 2:476–77). The ambiguity of the word *curialis* is evident in the fact that William can castigate "those who fancy themselves *curiales*" for their corrupt customs, but praise King David as *"ceteris curialior."* Evidently courtliness as a code of ethics and manners was acceptable to this writer, while "novelties" of dress and personal grooming, which he calls by the same name, are not. In any event, David of Scotland can be *curialis* and at the same time gain praise for punishing others for qualities called by the same name. He is, to my knowledge, alone among contemporary monarchs to be lauded for having resisted courtly luxury.

   In Germany we have seen that tensions between court manners and the life of episcopal clergy existed at least since the reign of Otto the Great. The political and social circumstances in the empire sketched out earlier encouraged the spread of court ways precisely into episcopal courts. When a chaplain was placed by the emperor into a bishop's seat, he left a center of power and urbanity to take up the administration of rustics and clergy who were anything but well-bred, sophisticated gentlemen. The impulse of a courtier bishop to surround himself with the atmosphere of the court is understandable, if not praiseworthy. When the transformation of a courtier into a pastor was slow or did not occur, the diocese could find courtly ways thrust upon it. The protest against these circumstances is far more common in Germany than are complaints about the courtliness of lay nobility. Thietmar of Merseburg, writing between 1012 and 1018, gives us a significant bit of testimony to an early "outbreak" of courtliness in a German diocese. He points more with regret and misgiving than with outrage to the excesses of Gebhard, bishop of Regensburg, formerly a chaplain of Otto III, who was placed by the emperor into the see against the express wishes of clergy and populace and against those of his saintly predecessor, Wolfgang of Regensburg.[12] Gebhard's episcopacy was an honorable one, he allows, even if troubled by *inaequalitas morum* among the clergy.[13] This phrase points to an often lamented feature of life among episcopal clergy. There was no generally accepted rule that standardized dress and manners, regulated possessions, and provided a uniform way of life. The result was that some canons lived as paupers, others as feudal lords. Gebhard of Regensburg seems to have outdone himself in respect to luxury. He was much criticized by the populace of Regensburg for his extravagant ways, and though Thietmar is reluctant to take sides in judging the bishop,

Hoc solum scio, quod moribus et raris apparatibus huic similem numquam vidi neque de antiquioribus audivi. Si interiora exterioribus concordant, aut melior est caeteris aut longe inferior. Optime prius culta diruens, novis insudat maximis laboribus. Patriam cum commissis deserit, aliena, et quamvis longe sunt, supervacuis cultibus colit. (6.41, ed. Holtzmann, pp. 324–26)

This I do know, that as far as manner of life and rare pomp and magnificence are concerned, I have never seen the like of this man, nor have I heard anything similar reported from antiquity. If inner things harmonize with externals, then he was either better or far worse than other men. Trampling on the wise practices of earlier generations, he spared no efforts in panting after novelties. He abandoned the ways of his fatherland and all that goes with it, cultivating superfluous foreign refinements, and be they ever so exotic.

This passage should put to rest the notion that Germany had not known courtly refinement before the importation of French novelties in the reign of Henry III. Thietmar's testimony makes it difficult to maintain the French origins of *curialitas*. Here we have in full blossom the themes and motifs of the clerical protest against courtliness: foreign customs are cultivated; the ways of our ancestors are spurned; refinements of manner and luxury in dress drive out honorable and wise customs. Lacking is only the vehemence of the monastic reformers. Unfortunately Thietmar does not elaborate on these foreign refinements. Gebhard was in the chapel of Otto III. The mother of this emperor, Theophanu, had imported Byzantine customs and manners of dress into the German court, and it may be that Thietmar's awe at Gebhard's exotic tastes is directed at these ways, which by all accounts must have been awe-inspiring. But Thietmar compares him for extravagant luxury with the ancients, and he would seem to have the model of the Roman emperors in mind. Or is it simply that the formula, "foreign customs are corrupting our good old ways" may be nothing more than a *topos*, empty of any real content, politely evading the admission that the "corruption" comes from within.

In this early text, we encounter a constellation typical for Germany: a courtier bishop brings the ways of the court into the comparatively rustic diocese and provokes complaints about the importation of foreign customs. This is precisely the constellation we encounter in the complaint about Azelinus of Hildesheim: a former royal chaplain, more renowned for worldly success than for religion, imports courtly ways—here called by name, *curialitas*—into his rustic diocese. The letter of Siegfried of Gorze warning of French novelties at the court of Henry III tempts us to interpret the influence of Azelinus as the continuing diffusion of Provençal fashion throughout the empire. But the evidence of "vain frivolities" and foreign customs at the imperial courts prior to Henry III warns against overestimating the importance of Provence.

It is probably the influence of Azelinus that is commemorated in one of the *Visiones* of Otloh of St. Emmeram, written about 1062–66. While he was a young man at Hersfeld, he met a cleric of Hildesheim who told him of an odd incident in that diocese. An angel appeared repeatedly to one of the priests and warned him against the "pretiosissima vestimenta" worn by the clergy. The cleric places the blame on the bishop each time the remonstrating angel appears to him. He tries to pluck up his courage and "correct" the bishop's ways, but, apparently fearing episcopal wrath more than angelic, he hesitates. Finally he warns the bishop and clergy, telling them of the apparition. Still they refuse to give up their "noxia voluptuosi ornatus blandimenta." But when lightning strikes and destroys the church they finally abandon "non solum superflua vestimentorum ornamenta, sed etiam inutilia morum fastigia."[14] Although Otloh was in Hersfeld in the 1020s, it seems most likely that this anecdote refers to the same phenomenon castigated by the Hildesheim chronicler. It could hardly refer either to the revered Bernward of Hildesheim (993–1022) or his saintly successor, Godehard (1022–38). It incorporates two of the few known accomplishments of Azelinus' reign, the burning of the church and the importing of courtliness. Probably Otloh is projecting these wrongs into the past to deflect blame from any individual. Regardless of what the anecdote refers to, however, by the mid-1060s Hildesheim had a reputation for once having "gone courtly." In this anecdote and elsewhere a certain form of behavior accompanies rich clothing and fine food, the material signs of courtly luxury: the useless frivolities of manners given up by the clergy would probably, in the setting of the king's court, have been called *facetia, urbanitas* or—with positive accents—*curialitas*.

For conditions in Germany in the twelfth century I will point briefly to a chapter in ecclesiastical history: the attempts of church reformers like Gerhoh of Reichersberg to regularize the life of episcopal clergy.[15] The time came when conservative churchmen no longer passed over *inaequalitas morum* among cathedral clergy without criticism. The attempts to subject the clergy to monastic discipline under the rule of Saint Augustine were particularly intense in Bavaria and Austria. Bishop Altmann of Passau (1065–91) instituted the rule in his foundation churches. A few excerpts from his biography, written between 1130 and 1140, will give an idea of the conditions he sought to root out. At St. Florian the clerics were "coniugiis et lucris saecularibus intenti, negligentes servitium Dei" (*Vita Altmanni,* chap. 9, MGH, SS 12:231). At St. Hippolytus they were "ebrietati, voracitati, libidini et usuris impliciti" (ibid.). Kremsmünster was "magna infamia respersum." Its residents threw off monastic rule, "longe prae saecularibus saeculariter viventes . . . ventri et luxui . . . dediti . . . praelati erant voluptatum amatores" (chap. 10, p. 232). Altmann's prohibition of concubinage and marriage in Passau itself was greeted with open rebellion. Confronting the angry clerics publicly, Altmann would have been torn limb from limb "had God not interceded." The rebels expel their bishop and turn Passau into a "brothel for whoremasters" ("prostibulum scortatorum"—chap. 11, p. 232–33). Throughout the century the rule found stiff opposition in monasteries and cathedral churches, where bishops and clergy were often landed aristocracy, reluctant to give up their privileges and possessions to live according to ideals of the common, apostolic life.

Gerhoh of Reichersberg is a militant opponent of regal splendor at episcopal courts. He cites Gregory the Great as authority, warning bishops not to keep "knights among their retinue in the manner of kings, whose courts are full of men dressed in fine, soft garments" ("milites ministros ad similitudinem regum, in quorum domibus hi sunt, qui mollibus vestiuntur"—PL 194:1205B–C). This is interesting for showing that soft and sumptuous clothing, and presumably other refinements of life cultivated at episcopal courts, are not without a specific quasilegitimate social context: they belong at the king's court. Gerhoh's attack continues: the bishop's knights swear homage to him, but then through their sumptuous way of life waste the goods of the church (cf. 1215B). What has a bishop to do with precious clothes and armies of knights? (1219B).

A somewhat more detailed look at anti-courtly sentiments in the same geographical area is provided by the "so called Heinrich von Melk." In his rhymed tract, *Das Priesterleben*, he paints a picture of clerics living in the lap of luxury: "Wine and mead are brought, the goblets are passed around as they lie on soft cushions, many a sport and jest is played. After this they speak of love, about which they read a great deal. [Their sentiment is]: 'No one but clerics should sport with beautiful ladies; let us go about our pastimes, and all laymen be-gone!'"[16] In his work, *Von dem gemeinem lebene*, he speaks of knights and noble ladies. They expend much ingenuity, he laments, on think-ing up "new fangled ways" ("niwe site"); this is pride, the devil's own work. Such vices drive out "geistlich zuht." In view of all this novelty, he asks, "where is the wisdom of the ancients, about whom no one speaks in this entire generation?" All who live nowadays prac-tice only deceit; youth is corrupted and possesses neither honor, breeding, nor virtue (cf. 10.1–12.25, ed. Maurer, 3:319 ff.).

The most vehement and prolix of the critics of courtliness in Eu-rope lived on its northern fringe. We have often cited Saxo Gram-maticus in earlier chapters as a witness to the Latin vocabulary of courtesy, without indicating that he was one of the critics of the phe-nomenon. He wrote his *Gesta Danorum* between 1186 and approxi-mately 1218 for two patrons, Archbishop Absalon of Lund and his successor Andreas.[17] An important distinction between Saxo's work and all the forms of protest observed until now is that Saxo wrote pseudo-history, "ancient tales" of the ancestors and heroes of bygone days,[18] gathered, he claims, from records chiseled into the stones and cliffs of his fatherland. Here the tales of the ancient ancestors become an instrument to castigate the wrongs of the present generation. In his prologue he sets forth the purpose of his work in terms with which we are by now familiar. He paints a picture of his countrymen sunk in listlessness and ignorance. He praises Archbishop Absalon (the same who had stung King Sueno with his witty reply), whose example re-calls men prone to a loose life ("lascivioris vitae studiosos") "from weak flabbiness to a manlier frame of mind" ("ad honestiorem mentis habitum ab enervi mollitudine"). To this softened, sensual life of his contemporaries Saxo wishes to oppose the example of the Danes of bygone days. Throughout the *Gesta* we encounter attacks on courtli-ness which speak the language of the continental polemics. It would not be exaggerated to say that one of Saxo's main ethical purposes in writing the work was to scourge the infusion of dainty "Saxon" cus-toms into Denmark, which were sapping the strength of the Danes and corrupting their ancient and traditional heroic ideals.[19] Of the many attacks on "Teutonic" customs in the work, the central episode is the visit of the hero Starcatherus to the court of the Danish king Ingellus. Ingellus' noble father Frothi has been killed by the Saxons, and now, instead of seeking revenge, the dissolute son marries the daughter of Frothi's murderer, invites his bride's brothers to his court, and imports the customs of cuisine, dress, and lovemaking hatched in German lands.[20] I can only refer to a small sampling of the lengthy and biting polemics against Ingellus and his court. Saxo's moral ferocity exceeds all measure and would do justice to a Savanarola. But in his vehemence he tends to long-windedness and repetition.

Ingellus threw over the pattern of his ancestors, Saxo tells us, and gave himself wholly to the "allurements of extravagant riotousness" ("petulantissimi luxus illecebris"—VI, vi, 1, p. 157). He assembled a variety of cooks, a host of kitchen staff, pots and pans, and numerous "factories of gluttony" (ovens presumably). With these came dainty spices. His idea of greatness was confined to the kitchen; he let warfare fall by the wayside, and, "abiecto virili studio, femineum aemulatus est" (ibid.). Not only did he adapt "mores Theutoniae" but also submitted to their "effeminata lascivia" (VI, viii, 7, p. 167). Now follows a heated attack on Germany, which I quote in Oliver Elton's superb translation:

Ex cuius sentina in patriae nostrae fauces haud parva luxuriae nutrimenta fluxerunt. Inde enim splendidiores mensae, lautiores culinae, sordida coquorum ministeria variaeque farciminum sordes manavere; inde licentioris cultus usurpatio a ritu patrio peregrinata est. (VI, viii, 7, p. 167)

No slight incentives to debauchery have flowed down our country's throat from that sink of a land. Hence came magnificent dishes, sumptuous kitchens, the base service of cooks, and all sorts of abominable sausages. Hence came our adoption, wandering from the ways of our fathers, of a more dissolute dress.[21]

Why did Saxo place the blame for this corruption so squarely and so persistently on the shoulders of the Saxons and the Germans in general?[22] If we had only his account to rely on, we might infer that Germans were the only nation to cultivate sumptuous dress and refinements of grooming, speech, cuisine, and love. The Danish kings in the twelfth century had close ties with France and dynastic ties with the Normans. But these nations bear none of the brunt of Saxo's outrage. It seems unlikely that the learned chaplain was ignorant of the fact that other critics of court ways were pointing the finger at the French. But he pointed exclusively at the Saxons as corrupters of the Danes. There may be some personal, local, or national resentments and rivalries at work here (though they were evidently not at work in the mind of Saxo's parents when they gave their son his name). What we can learn from his attacks on the Germans for our purpose is that by the turn of the twelfth to the thirteenth century a conservative cleric in Denmark could consider the Germans as the bearers and transmitters of "corrupt" courtly ways, without giving any indication that that nation itself had only recently been corrupted by the French. But there is little historical value in this: it shows us only that the conservative clergy of each nation pointed to a near neighbor as its corrupter. But Saxo would not have done so unless he regarded courtly ways as thoroughly entrenched and at home in Germany by the end of the twelfth century.

Opposing the scene of Teutonic corruption at Ingellus' court is Saxo's greatest hero, Starcatherus. He is the antithesis of the effeminate, debonair Ingellus; he embodies the homespun, pagan virtues of the ancient heroes of Denmark. He dresses in rags, is old, ugly, treacherous, and murderous, and he is satisfied with crusts of bread and rancid, charred bits of meat. But he is unbending in his obligation to warrior prowess and to the ethic of revenge. Various layers comprise the character of this remarkable figure.[23] But, pagan, Germanic elements aside, he also represents a position taken on a contemporary social issue.

Starcatherus seeks out Ingellus to set things right at his court. He has served in Frothi's army and is appalled to hear of the degeneracy of Frothi's son. When he enters the royal hall, the king's wife takes him for a beggar and contemptuously seats him at the far end of the table; the courtiers greet him with scorn and ridicule.[24] But Ingellus recognizes the old warrior and upbraids his wife. She is then at pains to appease him. She offers him a gold bracelet, which he flings back in her face. A flutist plays to soften his anger, but he hurls a bone at him. The queen offers him a hair band, which he also flings into her face. Invited to table, he rejects the dainty dishes and gnaws on some smoky, rancid meat, since "he had no desire to weaken the sinews of true manliness by contamination with the synthetic sweetness of foreign rarities" ("ne verae virtutis nervos externarum deliciarum contagione tamquam adulterino quodam dulcore remitteret"—VI, viii, 6, p. 167). Finally he spontaneously composes and sings a long poem bitterly chiding Ingellus for his effeminacy. The king, stung to shame, takes up his sword and on the spot slaughters all of his Saxon guests.

What Starcatherus accomplishes in this scene reiterates Saxo's ethical plan in the work as a whole: he recalls to valor and warrior ways a Dane sunk in courtly wantonness. The society represented is in a twilight area between two stages of civilizing: courtly ways and the an-

cient warrior ideals. Starcatherus (and through him, Saxo) resists the
"Verhöflichung der Krieger"; the hero is a fictionalized realization of
a value high in the consciousness of anti-courtly polemicists: the
mores antiquorum patrum. His actions represent the *ritus heroum.* It is a
peculiar feature of Saxo's conservative Christian reforming zeal that it
can make common cause with a fierce, pagan ethic of self-assertion
and revenge.

In most of the texts from the continent attacking courtliness we
noticed that love—or to put it from the point of view of our infor-
mants, fornication and lasciviousness—was seen as a component of
this code. It appears as such in the *Gesta Danorum* as well. Again the
antagonist of courtly ways is Starcatherus. The protagonist is a goldsmith who has married the sister of Ingellus. "Glib in blandishments"
("blanditiis compositus"), the low-born smith had turned the head of
this girl of the royal family through "a lover's courtesies" ("amatoria
comitate"—VI, vi, 2 [p. 157]). Starcatherus catches wind of the situation and decides to punish the smith's arrogance. Wearing a cheap
and tattered cloak, he sits down at the threshold of their house. He
watches as the smith enters in an amorous mood and approaches his
wife. The scene is commemorated in a poem which Starcatherus composes afterward:

> . . . faber ille procax lascivis gressibus intrat
> hac illacque agitans instructo femina gestu
> nec minus ad varios intendens lumina nutus;
> castorio cui tegmen erat chlamys obsita limbo,
> instratae gemmis crepidae, toga cultior auro.
> Splendida nexuerant tortum redimicula crinem,
> et variata vagum stringebat vitta capillum.
>
> (VI, vi, 8, p. 159)

in came that bold artificer with wanton steps, swaying his thighs this way and
that with supple motion, throwing glances with each different nod; his
mantle was edged with beaver's fur, his sandals dotted with gems, his cloak
threaded smartly with gold. Bright ribbons bound his twirling locks, a rain-
bow headband held his straying hair. (Trans. Fisher, p. 177)

The smith's wife warns him of Starcatherus, but he ignores him, thinking that no one dressed in rags could be a great warrior. Starcatherus
throws back his cape and bares his sword. The smith, "qui nil nisi
lascivium noverat", panics and runs. Starcatherus deals him a blow in
the buttocks, which leaves him half-dead. Here the wrath of the hero
is directed as much against the smith's effeminized courting as against
the perversion of the social order. The seduction scene is an over-
wrought parody of fashionable amatory behavior:[25] the sidling, hip-

swinging gait, also described by William of Malmesbury, the erotic message sent through the eyes, and the splendid clothing and colored ribbons in the man's hair. It is a portrait of an *effeminatus* practicing a "courtly" love stripped of all loftiness.

Clearly Saxo attacks the same *curialitas* opposed by Orderic Vitalis, William of Malmesbury, Radulfus Glaber, and others. All these opponents of courtliness see this code as shallow and materialistic. It is evident that anti-courtly sentiments developed a set of *topoi*, some of them no doubt with parallels in antiquity: *laudatio temporis acti* and the motif of *antiqui* against *moderni*. But the conventionality of some formulations in these texts should not obscure the fact that from the early eleventh down to the late twelfth century an epidemic of *curialitas* swept through Europe, bringing with it affected ways of dressing and walking and refinements of speech, eating habits, and customs of courtship. Wherever these fashions appeared they were opposed by conservative clerics often touched by the ideals of the monastic reform movement. (That it was the abbot of Gorze who raised the hue and cry in Germany is no accident.) Saxo is an especially valuable witness to this whole shift in *mores* and the conservative reaction to it. Writing later than the others, he speaks the language of courtliness, uses the Latin vocabulary that we studied in the previous chapter, and so allows us to test our analysis of those conceptions showing them to us through the eyes of a harsh critic. His account of the reforms of King Sueno in book 14 is instructive:

Igitur Sueno, perinde ac bellorum metu solutus, in superbiam lapsus, patrios mores, quod parum sibi viderentur exculti, tamquam agrestes et inconditos, petita a finitimis urbanitate, mutavit, spretoque Danico ritu, Germanicum aemulatus est. Nam et cultum Saxonicum sumpsit et, ne eo invidiosius uteretur, militum studia ad similem vestis usum adduxit, rustici moris taedio comptioris famulitii grege palatium instruens. Quin etiam, epulandi rusticitate depulsa, externas mensis comitates ascivit comissationumque ritus cultiore ministerio gerendos instituit. Nec solum cultum novavit, sed etiam edendi bibendique facetias tradidit. (XIV, ix, 1, p. 387)

And so Sueno, relieved thus of the fear of war and lapsing into pride, reformed the customs of his ancestors, which to his mind were far too unrefined, and, despising Danish traditions, he took up German ones. For he too adopted Saxon ways, and to avoid resentments he persuaded his knights to cultivate a similar style of dress, providing, out of annoyance with rustic ways, the palace with a flock of elegant followers. Furthermore, throwing over provincial table manners, he opened the doors to foreign courtesies of feasting and instituted the rites of revels performed with high refinement. He not only reformed manners, but he also brought in sophistications of eating and drinking.

Here the entire complex of motives that inspired anti-courtly polemics is clearly laid out: peacetime turns a ruler's thoughts to luxury and refinement; he brings in foreign customs and spurns the ways of his ancestors. But we see as well that the protest is directed against the components of *curialitas* studied in the last chapter: *urbanitas, facetia, comitas,* and *exculti mores* in general. Saxo also helps us to strengthen a distinction on which we have repeatedly insisted between the two aspects of *curialitas*: it is an ethical code and a social code, and the two were evaluated quite differently by orthodox Christianity. Saxo has no objections to courtly refinements as long as they guide the conduct of men at court along ethical paths. Jermenrik, described in book VIII of the *Gesta* (see above, p. 34), rises to the highest prominence at court by distinguishing himself through "egregia morum amoenitate," and this is the common practice of courtiers ("iuxta aulicorum ritum"— VIII, x, 1, p. 230). Clearly the social order is not disturbed when a courtier behaves according to this code; on the contrary, it is admirable behavior. We recall also that Saxo had only praise for that counselor of Canute the Great, Opo of Seeland, who administered a program of education aimed at civilizing the unruly pack of knights at court. Saxo has no reproach to make against the humane refinements of manners and sensibilities implied in *amoenitas morum* and *disciplina*; he objects to the civilizing of a warrior class only when it makes women of them.

The MHG epic poem *Nibelungenlied* has much in common with Saxo's *Gesta Danorum*. Both works revive the ancient tales of national heroes from bygone days. Both arose in lands on the fringes of European society, regions where courtly ideals were a recent import. In both works these ideals are represented as a gloss over a heroic, warrior culture. Saxo was a cleric writing for an episcopal court. The most probable conjecture concerning the poet of *Nibelungenlied* places him in the same class and social setting.[26] Most likely he was a chaplain of the bishop of Passau, Wolfger of Erla. The poem in the form in which we now have it was composed around 1203–5. Another common feature is that both poets have an antiquarian bent; they glorify the pagan past. Saxo was an unashamed adherent of a fierce ethic of revenge. While the *Nibelungenlied* is based on the theme of revenge exacted cruelly and on a grand scale, the poet does not make his feelings on the subject unambiguously clear.

The same is true of his attitudes toward courtliness. There is a clear courtly overlay to the poem, and this often makes for a certain incongruity. The Germanic hero Siegfried courts Kriemhild in the courtly way. He moons and pines for her; he despairs that he will ever be able to win her love; he flushes and turns pale. Their whole courtship is decked out in the trappings of courtly love, described with the formulae of the *Minnesang*.[27] To evaluate the courtly elements of the poem is a real problem. The poet himself is little help; he is annoyingly sparing in rendering judgments on his characters' values and conduct. But the historical background of the clerical protest against courtliness can throw some light on the question.

The Nibelungen poet distinctly speaks the language of the rebellion against courtesy. A good example is an incident late in the epic, the murder of the courtly Hun in Aventiure 31.[28] The Burgundians have come to visit their sister Kriemhild, now married to King Etzel. She is plotting revenge against Hagen, the murderer of Siegfried, her former husband. In the brief period when the appearance of a jolly visit and good relationships is maintained, the Burgundians and the Huns participate in a *buhurt*, knightly sport. Volker and Hagen observe one of the Huns prating about like a man in love, dressed "like the bride of some noble knight" (st. 1885). The mere sight of the man makes Volker livid with rage. He itches to give this *trût der vrouwen* ("darling of the ladies") a good knock, and against the warning of his king, Gunther, he rides into the fray and spits the man on his blunted lance, a shocking breech of etiquette. Here the poet is translating into bloody deeds sentiments which he shares with anti-courtesy polemicists: the Hun prates about like a dandy ("weigerlîchen rîten"), wears fine clothes ("wol gekleidet") and is "effeminized" ("sam eines edeln ritters brût"). The parallel to Starcatherus and the amorous goldsmith is evident: in both cases the flaunting of dainty and refined lovers' ways releases aggression in hardened warriors. But the mixture of motives present in the scene in Saxo (the smith married above his station) is not present in the scene from *Nibelungenlied*. Here it is the man's foppishness and nothing else that outrages Volker and spells his doom. He is guilty in Volker's eyes of a betrayal of a warrior code. To what sensibilities could the poet have been speaking here, if not to anti-courtly ones?

Likewise the advice given to the Burgundians by the kitchen master Rumold as they depart for Etzel's land resonates distinctly with anti-courtly sentiments. He advises them to choose the comfort of home above the dangers and uncertainties of their visit to Kriemhild:

ir sult mit guoten kleidern   zieren wol den lîp:
trinket wîn den besten   unt minnet waetlîchiu wîp.

Dar zuo gît man iu spîse,   die besten die ie gewan
in der werlte künec deheiner . . .

(sts. 1467–68)

Here you can deck yourselves out with fine clothes, drink the best wine and make love with beautiful damsels. Even more: here you'll have meals the like of which no king has ever seen before.

The nature of these allurements is evident: they are the material and sensual trappings of *curialitas*. Rumold is clearly the advocate of the soft, gentle, refined, and sensuous life at court, and in this context he is a negative figure, set in place rather clumsily in order to give voice to an antiheroic bit of advice. We recall also that among the sources of annoyance to Saxo were the peculiar Teutonic rituals of the kitchen, involving all sorts of pots and pans. Rumold is the kitchen master of the court of Burgundy, and earlier in the poem, the poet pointed ironically to his overlordship over an army of pots, pans, and cauldrons (see st. 777).

In short, the poet was capable of directing barbs at courtly ways; the object of these barbs becomes quite clear against the background of the clerical protest against courtliness. The poet shares with anti-courtly polemicists a materialistic conception of this phenomenon. It is represented as a shallow etiquette which regulates dress, speech, gesture, table manners, and courtship customs. It is inseparable from sloth and lasciviousness. An advocate of court manners would have represented these externals as the visible signs of inner virtue. How far the Nibelungen poet is from that loftier conception of courtesy we learn from the description of Dancwart arriving in Island on the courtship expedition to win Brunhild:

> Swie blîde er pflege der zühte,   und swie schoene sî sîn lîp,
> er möhte wol erweinen   vil waetlîchiu wîp,
> swenn' er begonde zürnen. . . .
>
> (st. 415)

However blithe he is in his practice of courtesies, however elegant his appearance, he could well cause the suffering of many a fair damsel if he got angry.

The poet sees Dancwart's *zühte* as a cloak thrown over his shoulders which he can cast off when serious matters force him to act like a man.

There is a great deal that argues for an anti-courtly bias of the Nibelungen poet.[29] The difficulty in interpreting the poem as an instrument of anti-courtly sentiments is that the poet himself does not openly condemn the courtliness of his main characters. He depicts Siegfried the courtly lover without comment and without calling on any of the anti-courtly formulae which were abundantly at his disposal. This clearly separates the poet from Saxo, whose condemnation is shrill and long. (I have tried to explain this restraint of the poet elsewhere—see n. 29.) In *Nibelungenlied* the two codes, courtesy and warrior valor, are not harmonized; they stand one next to the other in ethical parataxis. It was the great accomplishment of the courtly romance that it resolved the differences between the two, subordinating the warrior to the lover and courtier and producing a heroic type that could inspire admiration in more liberal and refined factions of the lay nobility. But in *Nibelungenlied* courtly ways still form a contrast to warrior ways and stand out clearly as "new-fangled ways" (*niwe site*). As such they will have appeared offensive to the more conservative faction of the audience, as they did in Geoffrey's *Historia* to the duke of Cornwall. The poem arose in its classic form in the Bavarian-Austrian region, probably in Passau. But we have seen that precisely this region was polarized by the movement to reform secular clergy. A clerical poet in this diocese writing for the courtly bishop Wolfger of Erla may well have been prudent to let the events speak for themselves, to depict Siegfried, without open criticism, as a man brought low by his flirtation with new-fangled ways. After all, Bishop Altmann of Passau in the previous century had been nearly torn limb from limb because of his insistence that the clergy of Passau give up their wives and concubines! In any case, the *Nibelungenlied* depicts the destruction of a warrior culture touched superficially by courtly ways. This situation in itself cannot fail to have resonated clearly with anti-courtly sentiments that were in the air. There was a widespread feeling among the clergy that the lay nobility, the inheritors of a once glorious heroic tradition, were in danger of being corrupted by a frivolous, effete courtly culture. It is against this background also that we can understand the motives that drew a clerical poet to the "pagan" contents and ethos of the poem. He, like Saxo, wanted to represent and glorify the *ritus heroum* and to place it in contrast to the corrupting influence of courtliness.

‹›

The clerical opponents of courtliness were in an odd position. When they mounted their protest against listless and unwarriorlike ways among the laity, the church was working at the same time to institute the "peace of God." This aimed of course at restraining the lay nobility and limiting the bad results of their fierce warrior ways. The opponents of courtliness urged them in the opposite direction. They sought to arouse their fighting spirit when it had gone slack, to provoke "useful anger"[30] in the knighthood and to sting them out of torpor and into action—as Starcatherus stung Ingellus—by showing them the shallowness of courtesy and the greatness of ancient, heroic ways. "Correction" of the laity by the clergy has these two faces. Orderic Vitalis expressed this two-fold task in the lucid metaphor of the rider who guides the horse with both spurs and reins:

The rider uses sharp spurs on the stubborn steed only
And with many strokes of the whip urges him on to gallop.
Such is the law of the Church in the hands of loving teachers,
For with their admonishings they goad on the idle and rein in the
    most eager.

(Hist. eccl. 11, prol., ed. Chibnall, 6:11)

COURTLINESS IN THE CHRONICLES

HE CRITICS of courtliness were reactionaries. They had no eyes for the civilizing value of the new mood that had come over the European nobility. The ultra-conservative mentality always equates restraint with cowardice and sees heroism and manhood threatened by the advance of civilization. It was this clash of new civilizing forces with ancient warrior values in German lands in the eleventh and twelfth century which first gave shape and definition to sentiments which were to play a dubious role in the later history of Germany, and which called forth a great epic poem as the bearer of those sentiments, *Nibelungenlied*. Nietzsche wrote some mortal and forgettable verses which reformulate them:

> Denn der Mensch verkümmert im Frieden
> Müssige Ruh ist das Grab des Muts.
> Das Gesetz ist der Freund des Schwachen
> Alles will es nur eben machen
> Möchte gern die Welt verflachen
> Aber der Krieg lässt die Kraft erscheinen
> Alles erhebt er zum Ungemeinen. . . .

Saxo Grammaticus would have found little to quarrel with in these lines; perhaps he could even have been won for the idea that law is the shelter of weaklings. In any case this mentality has a store of *topoi* which are effective in stirring up primitive aggression and making hatred and violence appear as noble instincts, and revenge as a heroic act. It is the propaganda of the reactionary to which *Nibelungenlied* was to lend itself on more than one historic occasion.

There is, it is true, a distinction in modes of existence between the warrior type and the cultivated, educated statesman or man of the court. Cicero himself pointed to the distinction, giving the statesman the greater credit. Testimony to this dichotomy is preserved in the conventional topic, the contest of weapons and learning.[1] The resolution of these two basically opposed modes is no simple matter. The notion that growing refinement of the mind and of manners, and growing sensitivity to humanity gradually erode the aggressive warrior impulses of man is not easily opposed on either historical or psychological grounds. Shakespeare's Hamlet is the epitome of the civilized man paralyzed through his advance beyond warrior spontaneity. Wit, charm, learning, and a fierce and biting eloquence are gifts that do not serve a man in wreaking revenge. Just the opposite: they create a rift between thought and deed which he can no longer cross. Insight does not generate the spark of action; it only produces an urge to search for ever further confirmations of the need to act. How far he is from the crafty and utterly effective avenger, Amlethus, whose story Shakespeare borrowed from Saxo Grammaticus!

The rebellion against courtesy sought to pull the warrior class back into the primitive ethical atmosphere of the heroic epic at a time when that ethic had shot its bolt. Hagen and Starcatherus prevailed against the mocking laughter of courtiers in *Nibelungenlied* and Saxo, but the rough and ready arm breakers and head splitters who were stirred by the tales of these heroes in the thirteenth century and beyond were enmeshed in a net of idealism in which they necessarily appeared as dolts and rustic villains.

One great accomplishment of courtly romance is that it achieved a synthesis of the warrior and the statesman, the knight and the courtly cleric. From the second half of the twelfth century, we encounter a literary hero who represents the harmonizing of those two codes seen as so crassly at odds in the writings of the conservative clerics: warrior valor and courtliness. This new hero magnanimously pardons vanquished enemies. He speaks flowingly as he greets fellow knights and particularly ladies in elaborate formulas. His manners are modest, decorous, polished, and restrained. He is in control of himself and knows, or learns, compassion and regard for other human beings. He courts damsels in flowery speeches filled with high sentiments. He washes meticulously after removing his armor, puts on soft and tight-fitting clothing, shaves, attaches puffy sleeves to his shirt, and cleans his fingernails.[2] A man who would not shrink from savage acts on the battlefield is overcome by tender emotions when he catches sight of his lady; he is transported aloft by her smile, reduced to tears by her frown, and receives angry words from her with patience and humility. The knight remains an efficient engine of death and destruction in combat, but at court and in the presence of ladies his soul is strung as finely as a harp.

Does this reorientation toward civilized manners in romance reflect an actual, historical softening and civilizing among the lay nobility of Europe in the twelfth century, or is it a literary fiction?

An earlier generation was persuaded that courtly ideals had their origin among the class that embodied them in romance, the knighthood. The idea had the support of such great scholars as Sidney Painter and Marc Bloch,[3] and textbook treatments of chivalry regularly pass on the idea as a historical truth. But it is difficult to support with sources other than imaginative literature. Some knowledge of the Latin vocabulary of courtliness opens to us an entirely new set of sources: chronicles and biographical writings from the period preceding the flowering of courtly literature. Here we find in abundance stylized and idealized portraits of feudal nobles reflecting the values of that class. When did ideals of courtliness enter them?

Here we must confront a problem: the value of our sources. Chroniclers and biographers regularly ascribe all sorts of qualities to their subjects which have little to do with the actual personality and character of the man described or with the values he actually held. Whose values are reflected in the portraits of medieval historical texts? The question is complicated, but we can make some rough distinctions according to genre. A common type of biographical writing is the form which Hans Patze has called "Stifterchronik."[4] It commemorates the patron and founder of a monastery; it tends to make the patron into a saintly, virtuous layman suffering against his will the burden of life in the world.[5] In a variety of chronicles the description of lay nobility becomes a pedagogic instrument in the hands of the clergy for the correction and instruction of the laity. The author praises the values in his subjects that he wants the laity to cultivate: he was a great warrior, a friend to all good men, an enemy to all evil men, and a great protector of the church, to which he gave lavish gifts; he respected priests and their commands, and so forth. Orderic Vitalis and William of Malmesbury tend to this sort of description and are not useful for the present purpose. The form that serves the purpose best is the family or dynastic chronicle. The form begins with the *Gesta* of the Norman and Angevin dynasties.[6] One of its purposes is *representatio*, the projection of the values of the dynasty contemporary with the writer. Those values come first; the author's own or those of his social order come second. These texts are also important for the purpose of this study, because they give us a corrective to the clerical polemics against courtliness. Anti-courtly texts saw in that code only sloth, degeneracy, frivolity, and voluptuousness. If there was an ethical component to the new customs observed among the laity since 1043, its critics closed their eyes to it. But the authors of the family chronicles are advocates of the feudal nobility and proclaimers of their values. They represent these values in the best light. Therefore if *elegantia morum* was a component of *curialitas*, suppressed by its clerical critics, this will become visible in the texts before us now.

We find throughout our period a distinct difference between the descriptions of kings and emperors and lesser nobles. Adalbold of Utrecht, writing around 1026, ascribes to Otto III qualities appropriate to the courtly gentleman:

corporis speciositate floridus, morum probitate modestus, aetate quidem iuvenis, sed ingenua capacitate senilis, benignitate mirabilis[,] . . . omnibus placebat, nemini displicebat. (MGH, SS 4:684, ll. 2–3)

a flower of physical beauty, modest in his probity, a youth in age, a man in mental capacity, marvelous for his goodness[,] . . . he pleased all, displeased none.

The German emperor Henry II was, in the words of a twelfth-century biographer, "tam bonitate quam nobilitate regia conspicuus et universa morum honestate praeclarus," steeped in the study of letters, orthodox in faith and deeds (MGH, SS 4:792, ll. 8–9). Helgaud of Fleury (mid-eleventh century) describes Robert the Pious as follows:

Numquam injuria accepta ad ulciscendum ductus, amabat simplicitatem: communi se affatu et convivio et incessu prebebat. . . . Exstitit mitis, gratus, civilis animi et lepidi, magis beneficus quam blandus.[7]

No insult could provoke him to revenge[;] he loved simplicity and behaved in an affable, convivial, welcoming manner to all alike. . . . He was gentle, agreeable, of a civil and elegant bent of mind, generous more in action than in words.

Radulfus Glaber praises an elected king of the Hungarians as, "affabilitate gratissimus, ac liberalitate perspicuus atque humilitatis gratia preditus . . . universis circumcirca existebat amabilis" (*Hist.* 5.1.17, ed. Prou, p. 127) ("most agreeable in his affability, distinguished for liberality, and endowed with the gift of humility[;] . . . to one and all alike he was amiable"). Kings and emperors will certainly also be praised for their martial qualities, but their catalogues of virtues are quite different from those of lesser nobility.

Dudo of St. Quentin's description of the first Norman Duke, Richard I, in his *Deeds of the Dukes of Normandy* (ca. 1017), gives us an extensive catalogue of the epithets which the writer considered appropriate to a Norman duke at this earliest terminus of our period:

> Hic nam vir fortis, constans robustus in armis.
> Pacificus, bonus, atque probus, pius, ipse modestus.
> Magnificus, meritus, praecelsus, nobilis, almus.
> Inclytus, egregius, mirabilis, atque decorus.
> Maximus, eximius, praecellens, magnanimusque.
> Praecipuus, justus, sanctus, humilisque, venustus.
> Propitius, lenis, mansuetus, mitis, acerbus.

> Longanimis, celebris, solemnis, amabilis, atque
> Clemens, indulgens, miserens, scelerum puniensque.
> Protector, censor, tutor, largitor honorum.
> Prudens et sapiens, industris, gnarus, enormis.
> Linguarum, diversarumque sciens regionum.
> Attentus, docilis, cupidus, sitiensque bonorum.
> Mirificus, stabilis, suavis, fidusque, fidelis.
> Tranquillus, placidus, laetus, sine nube, serenus.
> Jocundus, dulcis, blandusque, affabilis omni
> Facetus, felix, frugalis, juridicusque.
>
> (PL 141:740A–C)

It continues at some length. I have omitted physical qualities and epithets that show him as a benefactor of the poor and downtrodden. The passage concludes, "Dum mundo viguit, sic omnibus omnia factus . . ." and it seems as if Dudo had taken *omnibus omnia* as the principle of selection in this grabbag of often contradictory qualities: "meek, gentle, and harsh"! (*mitis, mansuetus, acerbus*). He has not even spared the books of rhetoric in his ransacking (*attentus, docilis*). Encyclopedic as the poem is, it is important for showing us that the vocabulary of courtly, civil virtues (*laetus, jocundus, affabilis, facetus,* etc.) was at the disposal of a dynastic chronicler in this early period. Dudo provided the foundation for the later Norman chroniclers, and if the authors did not describe the Norman nobles as courtly, it was only because they chose not to.

William of Jumièges wrote his *Gesta Normannorum ducum* in about 1070.[8] The first four books are adapted from Dudo. The next three are laced with interpolations, and the eighth book was composed around 1149 by Robert of Torigni, prior of Bec, later abbot of Mt. St. Michel. Threading our way through the interpolations, we find in the very sketchy descriptions of the nobles a fairly primitive picture. The following is a standard portrait:

Richardus . . . militaribus triumphis oppido conspicuus . . . in armis admodum strenuus, ubique armatas militum legiones nobiliter rexit, de inimicis victoriam semper capere assuetus. Et quamvis saeculari actui foret deditus, totus tamen fuit fide catholicus et erga Dei cultores benevolus ac devotus. (5.1, PL 149:823C)

Richard . . . renowned in the environs for his triumphs in war . . . was highly skilled in combat, nobly commanding legions of knights wherever he went, accustomed to conquest of his enemies. And yet, though devoted to worldly deeds, he was through and through catholic in his faith, benevolent and reverent to the faithful.

This description is entirely typical for William's image of the Norman noble: a bold and successful warrior; a good Christian. But significantly, that of his continuator in the mid-twelfth century differs not at all from William's.[9]

Writing a few years later, Guillaume de Poitiers gives us a much more vivid picture of the Norman duke. Here is his stirring portrait of William the Conqueror as a young man:

Dux noster, plus intelligentia rerum honestarum et vi corporis quam aetate adultus, arma militaria sumit; qui rumor metum Franciae detulit omni. Alium non habuit Gallia qui talis praedicaretur "eques et armatus." Spectaculum erat delectabile simul ac terribile, eum cernere fraena moderantem, ense decorum, clypeo fulgentem, et galea teloque minitantem. Nam uti pulchritudine praestabat cum indumenta principis gestaret aut pacis, ita ornatus qui contra hostem sumitur eum singulariter decebat. Hinc virilis in eo animus et virtus enitescebat egregia claritudine.[10]

Our duke, an adult more in his straightforward understanding of honor and in strength of body than in years, took up the arms of a knight; the news of it struck terror into all of France. All Gaul had none to compare with this man when armed and mounted. The spectacle was at once delightful and terrifying, to see him drawing in the reins, decorated with his sword, resplendent with his shield and gesticulating threateningly with helmet and lance. For just as he was preeminent in beauty when he donned the robes of a prince in peacetime, so also the garb of warfare became him singularly well. From this picture there shows forth the virile spirit and the strength within him with admirable clarity.

One seeks in vain in this portrait and elsewhere in Guillaume's work for traces of gaiety, affability, compassion, moderation, and willing acceptance of insults. The description seeks to inspire fear rather than love, in contrast to the *curialitas* which the courtier-bishop Azelinus had introduced into Hildesheim at nearly the same time as William was first striking terror into the hearts of the French. This is a useful text for my purposes, since it was written (ca. 1073) by a Norman educated in Provence about a nobleman whose career took him across France and England. It sweeps the lands traditionally associated with the beginnings of courtesy, and yet is innocent of any traces of this code. But after all, the work concerns a man more famous for slaughtering and conquering than for winning the love of his contemporaries.

Gaufred of Malaterra, a monk of Norman descent, wrote shortly after 1099 a history of the winning of Sicily by Robert Guiscard. It was written on commission from Count Roger of Sicily, the brother of Robert.[11] His image of the feudal noble differs little from that of William of Jumièges, but there are some interesting departures from the typical formulae. Here is his description of Normans in general:

Est quippe gens astutissima, injuriarum ultrix spe alias plus lucrandi, patrios agros vilipendens, quaestus et dominationis avida, cujuslibet rei simulatrix, inter largitatem et avaritiam quoddam medium habens. Principes vero delectatione bonae famae largissimi; gens adulari sciens, eloquentiis [var.: eloquentiae] in studiis inserviens in tantum ut etiam ipsos pueros quasi rhetores attendas. . . . Equorum caeterorumque militiae instrumentorum et vestium luxuria delectatur. (PL 149:1102B–C)

This is a most astute folk, given to increasing its possessions by the revenging of wrongs, holding its native soil in small regard, avid for profit and domination, skilled at deception, holding the mean between prodigality and avarice. Their princes however spare no expense in cultivating fame and good report. This people knows the art of flattery, practicing the study of eloquence to such a degree that even their young boys appear rhetors. . . . They delight in rich clothing, horses and other instruments of warfare.

We need not necessarily see this as eulogy, though highly ambiguous qualities appear in a positive light; the writer appears to take their skill in flattery as a result of their rhetorical studies. He describes Robert Guiscard as "vir magni consilii, ingenii, largitatis et audaciae" (PL 149:1103C). The education of him and his brothers: "coeperunt militaribus disciplinis adhaerere, equorum et armorum studia frequentare, discentes seipsos tueri et hostem impugnare" (1103D) ("they took up their military training, the study of the use of weapons and horses, learning thus to defend themselves and attack their enemies"). Later he describes Duke Roger of Sicily as

sua sapienter disponens, in omnibus strenue et provide agebat [though a youth in age, he was a man in his behavior]. Militiae assiduus, frequentiam militum amans, colloquio affabilis, muneribus largus, labori vigiliisque indeficiens, Ecclesiarum defensor. (4.4, PL 149:1186A)

With the exception of the isolated courtly quality, *colloquio affabilis*, the values of the Norman dukes in this author's presentation are exhausted in military prowess, wealth, shrewdness, energetic and dogged defense of possessions and prerogatives, boldness and liberality.[12]

The chronicles of William of Malmesbury and Orderic Vitalis are, as I mentioned earlier, not very useful for my purpose at present. Far more instructive in the twelfth century are the chronicles of the counts of Anjou and the lords of Amboise in the convenient edition by Louis Halphen and René Poupardin.[13] The Angevin dynasty is of particular interest in the context of the beginnings of courtesy, since works on the subject have pointed to the Angevin count Foulk le Réchin (d. 1109),[14] the lord on whom Orderic Vitalis heaped abuse for his scandalous innovations and vice-ridden ways. The customs at his court, Jeanroy and Bezzola suggest, mark the stirrings of *courtoisie* as an actual code of manners in France. In this dynasty therefore we want to look carefully for the intersection of the vilifying and the glorifying of courtesy.

These chronicles, which cut across the twelfth century and were written by a series of authors, allow us to observe the emergence of courtly vocabulary.

The earliest chronicler is Thomas de Loches. He wrote between 1135 and 1151. Here are some of his descriptions of Angevin counts: Ingelger of Anjou:

Qui juvenis alacer, miles optimus, patris virtutem non solum equiparans, sed etiam superans, beneficia ampliora adquisivit, facta fortiora et audaciora manu sua gessit. (P. 29)

This energetic youth, best of knights, not only equalled but even surpassed the strength of his father; he also performed deeds greater and bolder [than his father's], acquired a more bountiful harvest of benefices, and single-handedly performed deeds greater and more daring.

Herbert of Anjou: "miles acerrimus" (p. 52). Geoffrey Martell: "Martellus, pre omnibus generis sui animosior" (p. 55).
Vilermus of Poitiers:

vir equidem bellicosus, nulli audacia secundus, prudentia preditus, divitiis copiosus, militaribus auxiliis constipatus, cupidus laudis, inflatus supercilio jactantie, magni nominis homo. (P. 59)

a truly warlike man, second to none for boldness, gifted with wisdom, abundant wealth, and large crowds of men at arms, puffed up with pride and arrogance, a truly distinguished human being.

The *Gesta Ambaziensium dominorum*, written in about 1155, shows us virtually the same picture of the lords of Amboise. Some examples:
Lisoi of Bazougers:

Erat . . . vir illustrissimus, genere clarissimus, moribus conspicuus, armis strenuus; cujus corporis vigor animique ferocitas et virtutis prestantia etiam in remotis regionibus, fama predicante, insignis habebatur. (P. 77)

He was . . . a most illustrious man, of the most renowned lineage, outstanding in character, tireless in combat. For physical strength, fierceness of mind, and preeminence in virtue [strength?] he was deemed distinguished even in distant lands, his reputation spreading far and wide.

Count Fulk: "sagacissimus et bellator fortissimus" (p. 78). Lisoi of Amboise: "vir animosus" (p. 86). Gosfried of Montcalv (Gosfridus de monte calvo): "vir mirande pulchritudinis, stature congruentis, summe prudentie, mire facundie, ingentis eloquentie, armis strenuus, providus in consilio, in omnibus morigeratus" (p. 88).

Apart from a brief detour into intellectual and social virtues in the last citation, the qualities given in these earlier sections of the chron-

icle show us a picture of a warrior caste whose values are as yet un-
softened by the notions of courtesy common at the imperial and royal
courts. The highest values are good lineage, good judgment, military
prowess, high spiritedness, strength of body, and wealth or the knack
of acquiring it. These values differ in no way from those that Karl Bosl
assigns to the "archaic" period of the feudal nobility; they go back to
the eighth century at least.[15] It is the archaic social picture of a heroic
society depicted for instance—in antiquarian reconstruction—in the
Nibelungenlied. Compare this description of the Burgundian nobles:

> Die herren wâren milte, von arde hôh erborn,
> mit kraft unmâzen küene, die recken ûz erkorn . . .
> in diente von ir landen vil stolziu ritterscaft . . .
> (sts. 5–6)

These lords were generous, of high lineage, bold and powerful beyond all
measure, these excellent warriors. . . . Armies of proud knights from their
lands served them.

Mitis, *mansuetus*, and *affabilis* are qualities that have no place in this
picture; the counts of Anjou and Amboise in this period, far from suffering abuse patiently, were probably provoked by small wrongs to
great revenge and were pleased to have this penchant recorded.

The first continuator of the Angevin chronicles was Breton d'Amboise. He wrote between 1155 and 1173. In his work we find a minor
infusion of courtly vocabulary. But it occurs only in two portraits and
still is overshadowed by martial virtues and praise of sheer strength
and bellicosity. In his section we find a portrait of Geoffrey the Fair,
father of Henry II of England and the man who fused the Angevin
with the Norman dynasty. Geoffrey was,

probitate admirabilis, justitie insignis, militie actibus deditus, optime litteratus, inter clericos et laicos facundissimus, fere omnibus bonis moribus re-
pletus, et . . . ab omnibus dilectus. (P. 71)

of admirable probity, distinguished for his sense of justice, devoted to acts of
warfare, most highly lettered, commanding eloquence which set him far
above both clerics and laymen, replete with nearly all good manners, and . . .
beloved of all.

This description is balanced between the "archaic" warrior values
and courtly ones. The threshold nature of the passage is apparent in
the phrase "militie actibus deditus." I have rendered it "devoted to
acts of warfare," giving the weight to the archaic. It could with equal
justice be translated, "devoted to deeds of chivalry." Most striking is
the stress on Geoffrey's education. He is a highly lettered warrior. It is

a neat illustration of a progression taking place on a very broad scale that we can observe in the descriptions of Geoffrey the Fair the transition in distinct phases from warrior values, through education, finally to courtly ideals.

The final stage is represented in the portrait of Geoffrey in his biography by Jean de Marmoutier, the third continuator of the Angevin chronicles who wrote between 1170 and 1180:[16]

> Supreme in military glory, his fortune was equal to his industry; he was devoted to chivalric, courteous combat and to liberal studies; the provider of a just love, excellent to his friends. . . . His speech was jocund, his precepts admirable and amiable. . . . This man was quite adept in arms, and, so to speak, most wise in his simplicity; generous to all, noble of build, with a beautiful and ruddy face, lean and sinewy body, flashing eyes.

Here Jean inserts the description by Breton d'Amboise quoted above, then continues:

> He was therefore gentle, gracious, of a most mild spirit; he bore offenses and injuries patiently and clemently; upon hearing abuse heaped upon him, he ignored it patiently. He was amiable and jocund to all men alike, but especially to knights; and there was so much goodness and kindness in him that those whom he subjected by arms he conquered even more through clemency.

> militari gloria summus, fortuna par et industria, civilibus armis et studiis liberalibus deditus; affectator justi amoris, in amicos egregius . . . Sermo illius jocundus preceptaque admirabilia et amabilia. . . . Hic vir armis quidem strenuus et, ut ita dicam, simplicitate protendendo sagacissimus, optime litteratus, liberalis omnibus, corpore procerus, pulcher aspectu et rufus, macer ac nervosus, oculis fulmineus. . . . Fuit igitur mitis, gratus, benignissimi animi; in cives clemens, offensarum et injuriarum indultor fuit. Convicia sibi a multis illata audiens, patienter dissimulavit; omnibus universaliter, militibus maxime, amabilis et jocundus exstitit; tante etiam bonitatis et benignitatis fuit ut, quos armis subegerat, clementia magis vicerit, ut sermo subsequens declarabit. (Pp. 176–77)

Like Dudo of St. Quentin a century and a half before, Jean jumbles together warrior and courtier qualities, but it is not the crude ethical parataxis which can tolerate unsynthesized contradictions ("gentle and harsh"; "puffed up with pride and arrogance, a truly distinguished man"). Jean understands the principle that harmonizes the warrior with the courtier to produce the statesman: the ruler who possesses warrior prowess shows greatness of soul by tempering his *ferocitas* with *clementia*. There is no softening of his *strenuitas*, no sapping of warrior strength through the exercise of gentleness and clemency, but rather his strength shines so much the more brightly for being tempered with restraint. This is evident in the observation that his conquests were achieved as much by clemency as by warfare. Conquest and the strength and spirit it requires are intact as warrior values, but the exercise of clemency bespeaks an even greater human spirit; he is beyond vengefulness and squat, stupid exercises of brute strength. Gone however is any praise of wily cunning. True wisdom for Geoffrey is simplicity. The syncretism of the passage is perhaps most evident in the observation that Geoffrey was "devoted to civil warfare," or "courteous combat" ("civilibus armis deditus"). The phrase places us squarely in the ideology of what we now know as "chivalry." When combat is "civil" then it becomes a theater for magnanimity, no longer merely for the exertion of physical strength and warrior prowess. Here the transition from knight as warrior to knight as courtly gentleman is complete. A comparable phrase is "affectator justi amoris." As a point of contrast we can take the portrait of William the Conqueror by Guillaume de Poitiers. That noble spread fear throughout the land, fear which Guillaume regarded as laudable and admirable. In that archaic ethical atmosphere, love as the dominant climate of one's public life could only be seen as resulting in a flabby tolerance: justice is unserved, wrongs are overlooked, insults tolerated, crimes go unpunished, and the fighting spirit slackens where love is preferred to fear. I take the phrase *justus amor* to address precisely that point of view: when Geoffrey carries on his public dealings in an atmosphere of gaiety, affability, and tolerance, he maintains the affection of all while still effecting justice. We notice also in this description that the ideal of the lettered ruler is present, underscored by Jean's taking over the passage from his predecessor and setting Geoffrey above clerics and laymen for his learning.

Hence in Jean de Marmoutier's portrait of Geoffrey the Fair, three human types are resolved into a single figure: the warrior, the learned man, and the courtly gentleman. This is the chivalric knight in full flower, or nearly full.

But now we should bring these findings into focus with what we know of the history of courtesy and the literary climate of the times.

This reading of the Norman and Angevin chronicles in the period prior to the beginnings of courtly literature tells us that courtliness has no tradition in these families. The presence of this code occasionally makes itself felt in isolated terms of praise (*colloquio affabilis*), but these are decidedly on the periphery of the clearly defined set of warrior values that forms the dominant in the representation of these nobles. A real swell of courtly terminology enters in the last third of the twelfth century, not before. This is heralded by praise of learning in certain of the princes. In the *vitae* of German and French bishops and in other writings from the milieu of the worldly clergy, however, the vocabulary of courtesy had a tradition that went back at least to the reign of Henry III, perhaps even to Ottonian times. The years 1120–70 marked the flowering of the episcopal *vita*, with a high-point being reached between 1145 and 1160 (the three *vitae* of Otto of Bamberg, and the *vitae* of Meinwerk of Paderborn, Bernward of Hildesheim, Norbert of Xanten, and Conrad of Salzburg, to name a few). And far from being restricted to this genre, ideals of courtesy were widely diffused through the entire milieu of the worldly clergy.

Jean de Marmoutier wrote between 1170 and 1180. His audience was the royal court of England, with Henry II and Eleanor of Aquitaine at its head. By this time the major romances of antiquity had been composed: *Roman de Thèbes* (ca. 1157), *Roman d'Enéas* (ca. 1160), and Benoît de St. Maure's *Roman de Troie* (before 1173, most likely ca. 1165). The Norman Wace had already composed his romanticising version of Geoffrey's *Historia regum Britanniae* (1155). The work was dedicated, if we are to believe the statement of Wace's later adapter, Layamon, to Queen Eleanor, though nothing in the work indicates that it was commissioned. *Thèbes* and *Enéas* likewise may well have arisen at that court. On the continent, it is very likely that Chrétien had finished his first romance, *Erec et Enite*, and, if we can accept his own statement in the prologue to *Cligès*, a version of the story of Isolde and King Mark. The dating of Chrétien's works is very uncertain. If we follow the traditional chronology, given for instance by U. T. Holmes,[17] then Chrétien had completed all his works except the fragment of *Perceval* by 1169. But recent research argues for placing his major works in the 1180s.[18] We do know, however, that the fifteen years before Jean de Marmoutier began his biography had seen the blossoming of the early romances. His conception of Geoffrey the Fair as a courtly knight is formed at least contemporaneously with the rise of that figure in romance; most likely the historian lags behind the romancier. This suggests to us that Jean based his representation of Geoffrey on the model of the hero of romance. Henry and his court patronized precisely the literature that brought this figure into prominence, and having encountered the courtly knight in fiction, they wanted to see their forebears cast in this mold in the family chronicles. The most compelling argument for this idea is that in 1160 Henry commissioned Wace, author of the *Brut*, to write a chronicle of the family, the *Roman de Rou*, which was begun in 1160 and broken off in 1174. In that year or the previous one the same task was given to Benoît de St. Maure (perhaps taken out of the hands of Wace), who proceded to compose his mammoth *Chronique des ducs de Normandie*.[19] In short, Henry sought out men who had distinguished themselves in the writing of romance to compose the family chronicles.

All this suggests strongly that the figure of the courtly knight did not originate in the real social-political circumstances of life of the lay nobility but that this class of rough-cut and boorish warriors[20] embraced the model of the courtly knight only after they had encountered him in fiction.

We can strengthen this thesis by reference to one further chronicle. Lambert of Ardres wrote his *Historia comitum Ghisnensium* at the turn of the twelfth century, 1194–1206. He makes Arnold of Guines, his patron, still living at the time of completion of the work, into the epitome of the courtly knight. Here is Arnold's catalogue of virtues:

in armis strenuus, moribus et probitate prospicuus, in omni curiali facecia preclarus . . . vultu hilaris, facie super omnes in curia coevos decorus, mitis erga omnes et affabilis, per omnia et in omnibus ab omnibus dicebatur et erat gratiosus.[21]

courageous in combat, outstanding in manners and moral uprightness, distinguished in every aspect of courtly sophistication, . . . of a happy countenance, handsome far beyond all of his comrades at court, gentle and affable to all men, and in all things he was said to be, and was indeed, gracious.

By now we are able to judge how conventional and derivative the above description is. *Curialis facetia* is the quality that had troubled the Hildesheim chronicler well over a century before. *Gratiosus* and *gratia* were the qualities that had made Bernward of Hildesheim sought after by various lords. *Mitis et affabilis omnibus* are qualities so common among courtiers that we need not point to a particular predecessor. Likewise gaiety and handsomeness of countenance were qualities praised in all of the members of Barbarossa's court by Acerbus Morena. Clearly the picture of Arnold as a courtly gentleman is wholly conventional. But it was anything but outmoded; just the contrary. The feudal nobility has at long last discovered the qualities of the courtier, adapted them, and integrated them into the life of the nobility, encouraged to do so no doubt by the example of the knight of romance.

In Lambert's account of Arnold's youth and maturing this dependency of biography on romance becomes quite evident. Arnold was sent to the court of Philip of Flanders "to have his manners polished and to be introduced to and imbued with the duties of a knight" ("moribus erudiendus et militaribus officiis diligenter imbuendus et introducendus"). After several years he returned to Guines, having been heaped with honor and wealth by Philip. At Pentecost, 1181, Arnold was knighted during a great festival. There was a lavish celebration with sumptuous dishes, abundant drink, and crowds of minstrels. At its conclusion Arnold set out with his comrade Eustace of Salperwick for a two-year stint of knight errantry. He became a hero (*heros*) and his fame, having spread abroad through all lands, eventually came to the ears of Countess Ida of Boulogne. Ida was a widow who, having seen two husbands to the grave, turned her thoughts to the pleasures of the flesh and the delights of a worldly life. She conceived a powerful passion for Arnold ("venereo amore dilexit") and did what she could to allure him "with feminine levity." Messages were exchanged, then "secret signs of a certain love," and with these Arnold was brought to the point where either he loved her as she did him, or "with manly prudence pretended to do so." But now Raynald of Dammartin comes on the scene to play the role of envious villain and abductor. He is so taken with Ida that he sheds his wife and pursues the countess. Ida "turns"; she has a brief fling with Raynald, then turns again to Arnold. She sends for Arnold frequently, and "in the hidden chambers of secret places in the countryside of Boulogne," as Lambert discreetly puts it, they "hold close counsel on the secrets they share" ("in cameris et in locis abditis secretum de secretis habuerunt consilium"—chap. 94, MGH, SS 24:605, ll. 30–31). Finally Raynald, jealous and frustrated, abducts Ida and makes off with her for his estate in Lorraine. Ida sends a secret messenger to Arnold and begs him to deliver her, assuring him of her love and loyalty. Arnold at once gathers a band of men and sets off to the rescue. But he falls into a trap set by Raynald and oddly enough Ida herself, and spends some time in prison. Here the romancier in Lambert yields to the monk. A chastened and wiser Arnold eventually returned to his home, his eyes opened to feminine wiles. He is a reformed man. He retains only the vices of tourneying, hearing fabulous histories, and banqueting with his companions. To while away the winter evenings, he hears the stories of the Roman emperors, of Charlemagne, Roland and Olivier, of King Arthur of Britain, and of Tristan and Isold. And this, it is fairly apparent, is also the cloth from which the narrative of Arnold's own youth is cut. This "historical" narrative is unthinkable without two models: the etiquette of courtesy and the courtly romance.

These observations about the spread of courtly values to the laity are confirmed by Joachim Bumke's important study on the concept of the knight. Bumke finds no traces of the noble, courtly knight in the realities of the life of the nobility in the twelfth century. His conclusion is worth quoting at length:

The chivalric knight of courtly literature is not explainable in terms of shifts in the class structure. It is an educational ideal of great significance, and a phenomenon of intellectual rather than of social history. The reality of the nobility around 1200 clearly looked quite different. . . . Poets set the ideal of chivalric virtue against this harsh reality, the dream of the gentleman who has tempered his nobility with humility, and who strives to fulfill his worldly duties and to serve God at the same time.[22]

In short, romance does not mirror the chivalric values of the feudal nobility; it creates them. This bears out a much earlier judgment of Edmond Faral: "Le chevalier amoureux est une invention littéraire du clerc."[23] But it should also be evident that the ideal of the chivalric knight was not fabricated from thin air. The ethical elements of that ideal were adapted from a code that long since was a social reality in the lives of courtiers. The chivalric ideal represents an assimilation of the imperial tradition of courtesy to archaic values of the feudal nobility.

We can draw one further conclusion from this evidence. We asked earlier whether that sensual, materialistic code that the critics of courtesy attacked contained the ethical component of *elegantia morum* with its ideals of humanity, restraint, "discipline," and gentleness; whether this ethical aspect was purposely suppressed in the polemics as a positive and justifying element in a fashion they sought to eradicate. Apparently not. Those fashions attacked by conservative clerics appear in France by the early eleventh century. But we have seen that the ethic of courtliness does not appear in the dynastic chronicles until the late twelfth. It may be nevertheless that the phenomena observed by Radulfus Glaber, Orderic Vitalis, and others brought with them a refining of sensibilities—table manners, delicate tastes in food and dress, and a cultivated form of love—but we have found no evidence that this coincided with the lay nobility's adopting the ethic of courtesy.

What then can be rescued of the idea that this class in France had an important role to play in the creation of the values of courtesy? The answer is that while the French chivalric class had nothing to do with the "creation" of courtliness, with the formation of those sublime qualities ascribed to Geoffrey the Fair by Jean de Marmoutier, they were the first among the European feudal nobility to adopt these values and effect their integration into the values of the warrior class. This process is the subject of our next chapter. Another contribution of the French lay nobles is the cult of courtly love and the lyric that gave expression to it. This aspect of courtesy has so far overshadowed the importance of the ethical code that it has given us quite a skewed picture of its importance in the reality of social life in the twelfth century. Courtly love was most prominent—at least is most visible to us now—as a literary phenomenon. Its existence—in approximately the form given it in troubadour lyric and the romance of Lancelot—as an actual practice of the nobility is not so easy to demonstrate.[24] In any case, romantic love was the main theme of courtly literature, largely because of the tastes of the French nobility, and this certainly accounts in part for the attractiveness of that ethical and social code that became so firmly attached to it.

◇ 11 ◇
INSTRUCTING THE LAITY
IN COURTESY

E BEGAN this study with a look at the type of the courtier bishop; this chapter discusses some of the factors that produced the metamorphosis of this figure into the courtly chivalric knight. There are some important differences between the two ideal types, apart from the obvious ones. The ideal of the courtier bishop was a projection of the qualities best suited to the offices of royal chaplain and imperial bishop. The ideals of the office were shaped by the real conditions—social and political—of the office as these were embodied in the most distinguished holders of it. The cultivation of those qualities was a practical necessity to the *curialis*; hence the ideals of the royal chapel filtered down among the ranks of *curiales* and worldly clergy elsewhere to shape their values into an ethic of worldly service. How different the ideal of the chivalric knight. Courtesy is not naturally suited to the office of the warrior. Its adoption therefore required the thorough reshaping and reeducating of what Elias calls knighthood's "economy of impulses" ("Triebhaushalt"). The warrior had to restrain his natural urges within the confines of the court. Even on the field, the splitting of skulls and the breaking of arms was a pleasure that was left to him only under strictly demarcated circumstances, only when the urge to indulge in it survived a sifting through ideals like humanity, compassion, gentleness, the renunciation of revenge, and the service of justice, fair ladies, and God. The values of the court cleric had a real social context; the ideal of the courtly knight was quixotic from its inception. Its "reality" was the fairy tale landscape of adventure in romance. In the realities of court life there were social advantages to the adopting of courtesy for the unfree knights, the lower levels of the chivalric orders. We have seen those advantages for the boorish knight in the Life of Ailred and the unruly knights at the court of Canute the Great. But the higher nobles, the counts and dukes, were not subject to those social forces.

The enthusiasm of the lay nobility at all levels for the figure of the courtly knight, however, was real. Henry II clearly was far from objecting to Jean de Marmoutier's depiction of his father as a man who bore abuse meekly, won over vanquished enemies by his clemency, and humbly struck up jovial conversations with forest boors.[1] This is not to say that Henry himself and his knights put those ideals into practice. But he evidently recognized in some sense their superiority to violence, arrogance, vengefulness, and impulsiveness. Chivalry and chivalric behavior became a held and practiced ideal in the course of the high and later Middle Ages.[2]

What accounts for the shaping of this new sensibility and for the passage of this ideal from *curiales* to knights? Elias' *Prozess der Zivilisation* is the most serious and detailed study of the social circumstances that produced or encouraged the laity's adopting of courtliness. He points to such factors as growth in the population, transformation of a rural barter economy into a monetary economy, the tightening network of interdependencies in court life, and the consequent obligation to restrain impulses, to subject actions to reason and foresight. Elias is a sociologist, and his task was to analyze the structures of feudal court society that led to civilizing. His entire analysis is based on an *evolutionary* model of development and "civilizing": changes in circumstances trigger psychological mechanisms in the human being, which impose adaptation to a changed environment; the "superego," the internal regulator of restraint, is formed when external prohibitions become internalized. Was the adoption of courtesy among the knighthood a response to a changed environment? No one who has read Painter's study of French chivalry or observed the sublime and ridiculous forms of behavior inspired by the courtly model can be fully persuaded by an approach that does not take into account the knighthood's ability to be inspired by an ideal. The nobility's enthusiasm for courtliness was no more a broad-scale adaptation to circumstances than was its enthusiasm for crusades. True, the court had its own laws and rules, starkly opposed in the "archaic period" to those that governed the social life of the warrior class. True, the knights bound to the ruler and retained at his court were forced to conform their behavior to court rules by a tightening network of interdependencies. The failure to conform brought to bear on the offender the enforcing mechanism of shame, exclusion, and inferiority.[3] But another factor is that the passage from a social sphere that tends to coarsen and harden the individual to one that forbids coarse and harsh behavior has a civilizing effect in itself. The outsider observes the operation of rules that he recognizes as loftier and more humane. This factor in part accounts for the adoption of courtliness by the higher nobility. It was won for courtly ways by the lucid insight into the superiority of these customs, not by the dully sensed advantage or the gradual perception that it served their interests to adopt them.

The chivalric knight was, as Bumke maintains, "ein Erziehungs- und Bildungsgedanke . . . ein Phänomen der Geistesgeschichte." The architects of chivalry were clerics functioning in their capacity as educators; their most effective pedagogic instrument was the courtly romance. The worldly clergy had to justify a life caught up in secular business. Peter of Blois accuses them of glossing over their true motive— ambition—with the claim of "correcting and instructing kings": "Ad correctionem et eruditionem regum, inquiunt, missi sunt" (PL 207: 46C). This statement for all its sarcasm undoubtedly transmits a real justification and perception of the purpose and usefulness of court life. Both of these tasks were important civilizing influences, important impulses in the transmission of courtly ideals of education. We want to learn what we can of their execution.

Eruditio

The *curiales* who advanced to bishoprics not only had excelled in their studies but had also been school teachers: Brun and Anno of Cologne, Altmann of Passau, Benno of Osnabrück, and Otto of Bamberg. The profession of headmaster, *magister scholarium*, appears almost as an obligatory or at least a perfectly normal stage in the preparation of a courtier bishop. Many courtier bishops had exercised teaching duties while they were chaplains at the king's court by tutoring the sons of the king. Pedagogy was related to state service as the practice of law is to government service today.

The German cathedral schools prepared young men for state service. The main subjects and disciplines that led to this goal are indicated in the phrase *litterae et mores*. Burchard of Worms studied under Willigis of Mainz, learning *salutaris sapientia* and *nobiles mores* (MGH, SS, 4:832, ll. 47–48). Anno of Cologne applied himself at school to all things that would "sharpen his mind and ennoble his manners" ("Quicquid ad exercendum ingenium, quicquid ad nobilitandos mores"—*Vita Anno.*, chap. 1 [MGH, SS, 11:468, ll. 8–9]). The two remain linked into the Renaissance and beyond, generalized to the education of a gentleman. Castiglione writes: "good masters teach children not only letters, but also good and seemly manners in eating, drinking, speaking and walking, with appropriate gestures" (*Libro del Cortegiano* 4.12, trans. Singleton, p. 297).

The mastery of *litterae et mores* constituted *idoneitas*. Bishop Eberhard of Bamberg is praised by Wipo as "vir ingenio et moribus rei publicae valde necessarius" ("a man in mind and manners highly necessary to the republic").[4] Probably the specific demands of service in the chapel lie more in the area of *mores* than *litterae*. The latter could be taught adequately at monasteries; but these schools gave way to the cathedral schools in the preparation of men for imperial service. We hear much more about young men called to the king's court or rising in favor there for their personal qualities, *elegantia morum, suavitas morum*, and *nobilitas morum*, than for literacy and knowledge.

We formed some idea of the contents of these phrases in earlier chapters. What were the subjects and disciplines, however, that produced *nobilitas morum*? The answer to this is largely lost to historical recovery. We know that there was a subject called *ethica doctrina* or *moralis philosophia*.[5] This formed part of a program of studies: "Prius est homo instruendus in moribus per ethicam" ("Man is first to be instructed in manners through ethics").[6] This was linked to the trivium: "Grammaticus . . . viam grammaticae recte ingreditur et per eam graditur, quando post rectam locutionem vitae et morum sequitur aequitatem" ("The grammarian enters onto the path of grammar in the right way, and advances on this path until, after proper locution, he pursues equity of conduct and character").[7] The reading of the "authors" provided texts from which ethical lessons could be drawn. But a large part of the ethical instruction in the setting of court and cathedral school is lost to recovery for the simple reason that the teacher himself constituted it. Books were important; men were more important, or just as important. The men who possessed *elegantia morum* taught by precept and example. The Empress Agnes retained Ulrich of Zell as her private chaplain, "quoniam eum honestius ceteris conspexit vivere." She profited greatly from *familiaritas* with Ulrich, because in his manner of life and his promptings she was able to find the exemplar of proper conduct: "in cuius vita et admonitione recte vivendi formam poterat invenire" (MGH, SS 12:254, l. 29). It is as much *vita et admonitio* as *lectio* that form the subject of *mores*.

It is an odd fact in the history of education that the schoolmasters of the tenth and eleventh centuries did not write books. Much was written for and around the court by men educated at the schools, but one is hard put to name more than a handful of works that arose as a product of scholarship and teaching at the cathedral schools of Italy, France, and Germany in these two centuries. Gerbert of Aurillac has left us some mathematical treatises. From his illustrious opponent in the debates at Ravenna in 980, the Magdeburg Master Ohtricus, nothing has survived. Fulbert of Chartres has left some puny monuments in the form of a few poems of scholastic content. And yet the schools presided over by these men and—what is more significant—by others

of far lesser stature, are regularly praised by contemporaries as blossoming, becoming a second Athens under the guidance of a second
Plato. For those who measure the success and quality of schools by
the productivity of their masters, the tenth and eleventh centuries are
bound to appear a wasteland, and the fulsome praise of contemporaries empty rhetoric. But I believe that Margaret Gibson has seen
very clearly the reason for the dearth of texts and has given an important insight into the nature of instruction at the early schools in some
comments on Fulbert of Chartres:

preeminently he was a man who understood the art of government, in which
their own careers [i.e., those of Fulbert's pupils] were made. His school was a
centre of administrative expertise rather than original thought, and it was the
gateway to promotion: these are more convincing reasons for its fame in the
world than a breakthrough in pure scholarship.[8]

Philosophy was important as a means to ethical perfection, not to
some abstract Truth that demanded formulation in scholarly treatises.

The curriculum was comprised in part by the person of the master
with all his personal and intellectual attainments. Ease and grace of
manners, gravity and urbanity can be imparted much more effec-
tively through the presence of a man who embodies them than through
the comparatively dry and lifeless form of written precepts. The text
for the subject of *mores*, apart from the traditional *auctores*, were the
men who taught it. The position of teacher necessarily precedes that
of chaplain-courtier partly because the teacher must embody the qualities that qualify men for imperial service.

Were there schools within the imperial courts? There was something like a formal "palace school" under Charlemagne, which educated the children of the nobles, the *discipuli* mentioned by Hincmar.[9]
Charles the Bald appears to have continued the tradition to some
extent. There is some debate about whether the courts of the Ottos ac-
commodated a formal school.[10] But whatever the institutional arrange-
ment, there can be no doubt that the conception of a "court education" existed and that this form of education was highly valued.
Eudes de St. Maure, biographer of Count Burchard of Vendôme, writing in 1058, indicates that it was customary for the high nobility of
France to send their children to the king for their education:

curie regali, more francorum procerum, a parentibus traditus est. [he distinguished himself in Christian works, was prudent and honest] . . . in aula
regis, cunctis tam celestibus quam militaribus imbuebatur institutis.[11]

He was sent by his parents to the royal court according to the custom of the
French nobility. . . . At the king's court he was steeped in all the subjects of
learning, religious as well as military.

Since the nonmilitary instruction is said to be *celestibus institutis*, the passage gives us no indication of instruction in behavior appropriate to the court. Conrad of Pfullingen, murdered in 1066 before he could take up the archbishopric of Trier, had been sent to his uncle Anno of Cologne for his education, because Anno was a "vir tocius prudentiae et aulicae nutriturae" (*Vita Conradi*, chap. 2, MGH, SS 8:214, l. 39). In Herbord's *Dialogus* the task of narrating Otto's life at court is given to the monk Sefridus, because he is a "homo curialis et in curia enutritus" (1, Proem, p. 7). Henry of Huntingdon praises Simon, son of the king's chancellor as "regaliter nutritus" (PL 195:983B). The best evidence I have found for the actual contents of "royal" or "courtly" nurturing is from the *vita* of Bishop Wernher of Merseburg (who had distinguished himself at the court of Henry IV for his *curiales disciplinae*). Writing shortly before 1150, the author describes the brother of Wernher, the knight Moricho, father of Paulina of Zell:

in primaevo pubertatis flore in curia Heinrici IV imperatoris enutritus, multam fiduciam, multam familiaritatis gratiam, utpote liber et splendidae administrationis homo, apud imperatorem obtinuit. . . . Erat enim optimus moribus, iusticiae tenax, providus consilio, fidus auxilio, liberalis admodum et integerrimae famae, civilis in moribus, florentis adhuc aetatis, regalis mensae dapifer et cunctis in ministerialibus acceptissimus. (MGH, SS 12:245, ll. 9 ff.)

nurtured in the flower of youth at the court of emperor Henry IV, he rose to a position of high trust and intimate favor with the emperor as a man of nobility and a splendid administrator. . . . For he was impeccable in his conduct, firm in respect to justice, foresighted in counsel, faithful in rendering aid, most liberal and of immaculate repute, courtly in manners. While still in the flower of manhood he was steward of the royal table and most suited to all administrative tasks.

This list of virtues can be taken to enumerate the results of *curialis nutritura*; all the qualities have to do with his rendering administrative service to the ruler, with the creation of a *splendidae administrationis homo*. And his *civiles mores* are intimately connected both with his suitability for high court office and with his favored stature. There is interestingly no mention of his literacy, and this is perhaps more consistent with the lower level of learning among the German than among the French lay aristocracy. At this point we should note, however, that a man who was *illiteratus* was not necessarily *ineducatus*, a fact largely overlooked by students of lay literacy in the Middle Ages.[12] Sichard of Cremona can praise Frederick Barbarossa as "illiteratus, sed morali experientia doctus" (MGH, SS 31:165, ll. 17–18). For laymen at least, *mores* were separable from the mastery of *litterae*. Very likely a fair number of the high nobility was in this situation, certainly those who had received *aulica nutritura*: not uneducated, merely illiterate.[13] Even for a gifted cleric it was possible to gain praise for his study and mastery of *mores* above his grasp of letters. William Fitzstephen writes of Thomas Becket, in service at the court of Archbishop Theobald of Canterbury along with many men distinguished for their learning:

> Thomas minus litteratus erat; sed longe quidem altior est ratio morum quam litterarum, et ipse sluduit moralitati et prudentiae intendere, ut inter eos, litteris adhuc inferior, moribus conspectior et acceptior appareret. (*Vita Thom.* chap. 5, RS 67:3:16)

Thomas was less proficient in the study of letters; but the practice of moral conduct is far superior to that of letters, and Thomas applied himself to the attainment of moral perfection and wisdom, so that among men to whom he was inferior in letters his superiority in judgment and graciousness would be evident.

The study of *mores* in the context of state service must have aimed at the "courtier's art," the pleasing of princes. There is confirmation of this in a well-known passage from Wipo's *Tetralogus*. He urges Henry to reinstate the custom of educating the lay nobles, not just clerics:

> Tunc fac edictum per terram Teutonicorum,
> Quilibet ut dives sibi natos instruat omnes
> Litterulis legemque suam persuadeat illis,
> Ut, cum principibus placitandi venerit usus,
> Quisquis suis libris exemplum proferat illis.[14]

Then send an edict through all German lands that the wealthy should have all their children instructed in letters, and let it urge upon them the emperor's law, so that when it should come time for them to exercise the custom of pleasing princes, anyone at all can profer to them an example in his books.

The line "cum principibus placitandi venerit uses" is crucial, but alas difficult to understand. I take it to mean that those who surround the king or other princes must be able to instruct him by pointing to examples in books of good conduct and proper running of the state. This is one aspect of the art of pleasing princes. But apart from the difficulties of understanding the above passage, two things are clear: Wipo has a conception of the art of pleasing princes, and lay education is important to this art.

Courtliness is undoubtedly connected in its earliest medieval formation with this same art. We observed that the gentle, affable, and well-spoken man of elegant manners rose quickly to the pinnacle of favor, borne upward by these qualities. Siegfried of Gorze lamented that precisely the cultivators of new and foreign fashions were taken into the king's closest favor; the Hildesheim chronicler called the *curia-*

litas of Bishop Azelinus *ambitiosa*, and this must mean: practiced by those who strive for the favor of princes. At some point this code becomes part of the curriculum in *mores*, bound up with *aulica nutritura*. Henry II of England sends his son to Thomas Becket for this sort of instruction: "rex filium suum . . . beato Thomae cancellario commisit alendum et moribus et curialitatibus informandum" [15] ("the king . . . committed his son to the care of Thomas his chancellor to be nurtured and instructed both in *mores* and in courtly ways"). And the close connection between instruction and courtliness is apparent in much of the vocabulary: *disciplina, bien apris, zuht, wol gezogen*. It is transferred from the realm of the school into that of the court.

We have seen repeatedly that whereas courtliness seemed to apply alike to lay and clergy in France, in Germany it was almost exclusively the clergy in the eleventh and twelfth centuries who were credited or blamed with practicing this code. There is an intriguing bit of evidence linking Benno of Osnabrück to the dual instruction of letters and courtesy. As a young man Benno came to the attention of the *optimates* of Saxony for his distinguished service to the king. They competed for his services, and the victor in this competition was none other than Bishop Azelinus, who, having recently been set by Henry III into the see of Hildesheim, was on the lookout for gifted men to bolster his administration. Benno became *scholarium magister* in Hildesheim, whither he was lured by the grand promises of Azelinus ("magnis . . . promissionibus . . . abductum"). But he found that the clergy of Hildesheim was hopelessly backward in learning: "rusticano quodam more educati, pene sine litteris ac idiotae." Benno set about seriously educating them. The result was that he transformed Hildesheim into a center of learning second to none in the region and rendered the clergy distinguished "cum claustralis honestate disciplinae, tum litterarum scientiam ardore discendi" (*Vita Benn.*, chap. 5, *LB*, p. 380). We must bring this report of Benno's activities into focus with the statement of the Hildesheim chronicler about the *ambitiosa curialitas* imported by Azelinus. In one important point they disagree: Benno's biographer, Norbert, claims that Benno's efforts produced "honestas claustralis disciplinae," whereas the author of the *Fundatio* claims that those of Azelinus destroyed that very discipline. While we can appreciate that Norbert sought to put the best face on Benno's efforts, we cannot stretch the imagination enough to argue that he seriously equated *curialitas* with *claustralis disciplina*. On the other hand, the points of agreement between the two reports of the reforms at Hildesheim are striking. The clergy prior to Azelinus, both agree, were rustics ("rusticalis stultitia"; "more rusticano educati"). For the chronicler this is praise, for Norbert blame. Both agree that the clergy experienced a transformation that eliminated their rusticity. In the *Fundatio* it gives way to *curialis facetia*; in the *vita* it yields to "ardor litterarum scientiam discendi." There is common ground between these two qualities. Both imply refinements of speech, or heightened eloquence. *Facetia* invariably contains or implies this aspect, even when it conveys a much broader refinement, as in the *Fundatio*. Hence we have a picture of Benno implanting in these rustics a "zeal for the study of letters," while Azelinus urged on them courtly refinements of manners: Benno, *litterae*; Azelinus, *mores et curialitas*. If we had a less biased witness to the reforms of Azelinus, I believe that this combination of texts would give us a very clear picture of a program of education in "letters and manners," the latter wholly in the context of ways appropriate to the court. Certainly the *Vita Bennonis* provides a corrective to the criticism of Azelinus in the *Fundatio*. The *Fundatio* pictures him as an epicure, determined to enjoy his office now that the king has given it to him. The *Vita Bennonis* suggests that he came to this backwoods diocese with a serious program of reform in mind. What need for a bishop whose highest design was self-indulgent luxuriousness to court a highly talented (and expensive) young cleric with "grand promises"; and conversely, what incentive for a sought after young man like Benno to leave the royal court at Goslar to follow an inordinate and Epicurean bishop into the backwoods? Clearly the *Fundatio* has given a distorted picture of Azelinus. He was a serious reformer, whose reforms aimed at instituting a program of court education, one that had perhaps the active encouragement, at least the tacit approval, of the king.

Instruction in courtesy was by and large in the province of clerics, not laymen. Thomasin von Zirclaere urges all lords and nobles to educate their children. Just as they give them nursemaids as infants, so also they should nurse their minds (*nutritura* in the vernacular). They should keep at their courts "meister wol gelert" who will teach their children "zuht und hüffscheit" ("discipline and courtesy") and give them the best of all gifts, "wol gelerter muot." From this gift one acquires the art of pleasing God and of living well in the world at the same time (*Der Welsche Gast* 9251 ff.). In the later thirteenth century the poet Frauenlob enumerates the roles of the three orders of society. Of clerics he says,

> . . . wie stêt der pfaffen sin?
> si lêrent wol gebaren,
> kunst, wisheit, aller tugende kraft,
> vride, scham und dar zuo vorhte.[16]

> To what do the clerics incline?
> they teach good manners,
> skill, wisdom and the meaning of all the virtues,
> peacefulness, modesty and respect.

Here again the instruction in good manners is subordinated to general instruction in ethics, *morales disciplinae*, and the discipline is placed squarely in the province of clerics.

There are a number of episodes in romance describing the educating of nobles which corroborate this. The OF *Roman d'Alexandre* (composed shortly before 1177) describes the education of Alexander the Great as follows:

> Li reis Felips quist a son fil doctors:
> De tote Grece eslist les .vii. mellors.
> Cil li aprenent des esteles les cors,
> Del firmament les soveirains trestors,
> Les .vii. planetes e les signes auçors
> E les .vii. arz e toz les granz autors,
> D'eschas, de tables, d'esparvers e d'ostors,
> Parler ot dames corteisament d'amors. . . .[17]

> King Philip sought out teachers for his son,
> choosing the seven best from all of Greece.
> These men teach him the paths of the stars
> and the distant meanderings of the firmament,
> the seven planets and the higher signs
> and the seven arts and all the great authors,
> chess, backgammon, sparrow hawks and other hunting hawks,
> to speak to ladies courteously of love. . . .

The last line reminds us of the comment in the love debate of Phyllis and Flora that the cleric knows the rules of love and teaches them to the knight,[18] a passage which Hennig Brinkmann took as the motto of his *Entstehungsgeschichte des Minnesangs*. But in the above text eloquence in courtly lovemaking is integrated into a program of studies which includes the seven liberal arts and the "great authors."

In Gottfried's *Tristan* we encounter an interesting minor figure who has received little attention, but who probably comes close to representing the station and office of the poet himself. When Tristan arrives in Ireland poisoned from the wound received in battle with the Irish champion Morolt, he is introduced to the queen by a courtly cleric, a *pfaffe*, who is *meister unde gesinde* to the queen, and who had exercised her "in many a good discipline" since childhood. He is drawn to Tristan's singing because he himself is a skilled musician. Also he knows a good many foreign languages and has devoted great effort all his days to acquiring "skill and courtesy" ("vuoge unde höfscheit"). He is tutor to the Princess Isolde, a position which he later yields to Tristan (cf. 7696 ff.). In the MHG *Prose Lancelot*, the hero is educated by the Lady of the Lake. No sooner has he left his nursemaid than he is given to a monk for "disciplining" and for instruction in courtesy:

Und da er der ammen nit me bedorfft, da gab man im ein mönch der ynn zuchtiget und yn wysste hubscheit.[19]

When he no longer required the care of a nursemaid, he was given into the care of a monk who disciplined him and taught him courtesy.

We have in an ambling way been pursuing various metamorphoses of the program of education designated by the phrase *litterae et mores*. It is at home in the cathedral schools. We can observe its implementation at court, integrated into *aulica nutritura*. We see *mores* expanded by the element of *curialitas*. We see these subjects taught, ordinarily by clerics who themselves practice what they preach, both to clergy and to laymen. We see the transposition of this program into romance. The testimony of historical, biographical, and didactic writings, and imaginative literature confirm that clerics at school and at court were the transmitters of courtliness. The only instance known to me of a lay nobleman teaching courtesy to a knight occurs in romance. In Wolfram's *Parzival* Gurnemanz tutors Parzival in courtly behavior.

These observations and much in the preceding chapters give us some basis for judging the program of education mapped out by Gottfried under the name *moraliteit*. Let us recall: this was one among various disciplines in which the young Tristan tutored the Princess Isolde. It was the most important and the one that she studied most diligently. It teaches *schoene site* (8005), "beautiful manners." The commandments of this discipline teach us to please God and the world (8012–13). It is given as a "nursemaid" to all noble hearts to seek nourishment and life in its instruction (8014 ff.). From her application to this art, the princess becomes "well-mannered, of a beautiful and pure temperament, of sweet and good bearing" (". . . wol gesite, / schone unde reine gemuot, / ir gebaerde süeze unde guot"—8024–26). It is evident from our preceding discussions that Gottfried is using terms and ethical ideals that were current in the instruction and practice of ethics in the twelfth century. We can translate the main concepts of the passage into the Latin terms with which by now we are quite familiar: *moraliteit = moralitas;*[20] *schoene site = elegantia morum;* "nourishment" = *nutritura; wol gesite = bene morigeratus;* and for *schone unde reine gemuot*, compare *compositio interioris hominis*, which is indicated outwardly in *gebaerde süeze unde guot, (dulcis) gestus et habitus*. Given Gottfried's penchant to borrow forms of expression and ideas from the Latin learned tradition, we have good reason to believe that the ethical vocabulary of this passage derives from ethical instruction as actually practiced in the twelfth century. At least the shared ethical vocabulary makes it unlikely that there is a high degree of fictionalizing in Gottfried's exposition of *moraliteit*. But if Gottfried did not invent this program, but assembled it from current notions and ideals, then the passage on *moraliteit* should receive the credit due it: it is the most lucid, detailed exposition of a program of courtly ethical education produced in the twelfth and early thirteenth centuries, one with a strong claim on the attention of historians of medieval ethics. The passage quoted above (p. 219) from Thomasin's *Welscher Gast* has some striking parallels to Gottfried's *moraliteit*, but it is slightly suspect as a second witness to the historicity of the program mapped out by Gottfried, since Thomasin may have adapted his notions of courtly education from *Tristan*.

Courtliness was originally in the province of *curiales*, and they transmitted this code by education and example to the laity, that is, the knighthood. A lucid illustration of the transition is provided in a passage from Alexander Neckham's *De naturis rerum* condemning *milites* who ape the ways of *curiales*:

Quid quod multi [milites] operibus inhonestis vitam commaculant, ut curialium damnabilem curialitatem, immo foedam scurrilitatem, imitentur?[21]

What shall we say to the fact that many knights besmirch their lives by imitating the damnable courtliness—or should I say putrid scurrility—of courtiers?

This shows us at least that a foe of courtliness still in the first decades of the thirteenth century regarded *curialitas* as the province of *curiales*, to which knights were outsiders. It also shows us the passage of this code into the realm of knights. Our informant takes a dim view of the blurring of distinctions between the orders of society.

Romance and history around 1200 show us a picture of the knighthood seeking to soften its warrior harshness with the lessons of courtesy. We want to have a closer look at the motives for this transformation of manners. The network of social pressures we observed at work in Ailred's taming of the boorish knight at the court of King David and in Opo of Seeland's disciplining of the unruly knights at the court of Canute the Great was one of these motives. But this fairly primitive motivation applied to unfree knights, those bound in service to a ruler or prince and residing at his court. The land-owning aristocracy was not susceptible to such pressures, or at least was free to ignore them.

But without compulsion they gave in to them. An interesting example is Gottfried's representation of the youth of Tristan's father. He is excessively rash, proud, arrogant, and impulsive. He trusts entirely in his physical strength and is incapable of conciliatory behavior, which, Gottfried tells us with distinct Ciceronian overtones, is precisely what the most powerful of men cultivate (cf. 269–70). Rivalin had to return every wrong in kind. But it was his youth, we are told, not a fixed trait of character that drove him to live blindly and shortsightedly, guided only by impulse. But then after waging an unjust war against his liege lord, he takes advantage of the ensuing peace to journey to the court of King Mark of Cornwall, the font of honor and courtesy (421), there to learn virtue and chivalry and to "smoothe down his manners":

> [er dahte] . . . ein jar mit ime vertriben
> und von im werden tugenthaft
> und lernen niuwan ritterschaft
> und ebenen sine site baz.
>
> (456–59)

This turn in his way of life is not motivated; Rivalin is simply taken suddenly by the wish to polish his warrior ways. It is represented as a step in a process of maturing, as if the young man arrives at this stage as naturally as he arrives at manhood.

Around 1170–80 a German cleric wrote a brief and badly transmitted tract instructing knights in the art of love, the so-called *Heimlicher Bote*.[22] The author refers to a source that he calls *phaset*. Ehrismann identified the cryptic word with the poem *Facetus* discussed earlier.[23] Women, he teaches, praise the man who can love them well, who can keep their love secret. But many mistake the qualities that win a woman's love. Some think winning a woman requires only a strong body; others trust in their manliness, handsome hair, physical beauty, knightly prowess, or boldness of spirit. But these qualities are often only a source of annoyance to women; they do not bestow their love "on this sort of courtesy" ("unbe sogetane hobeschet"—l. 14). What pleases women is the "wol minnende[r] man," about whom the author has instructions from his authority, *Phaset*. "Good love" is service rendered with humility ("denen mit demute"); the good lover avoids evil ways and practices virtue, elegant responses, and "wise and sweet greetings." He acts sensibly, in such a way that all men will love him and speak well of him. This lesson in courtesy, then, is above all a lesson in love, to which humble, amiable service is subordinated. Important for our purposes is the specific sociological constellation: the educated cleric (he cites a Latin poem on the subject he is teaching) attempts the transformation of the rough-cut, unpolished, boasting knight into the gentle and amiable lover. The lessons in love in *Facetus* did not have a specifically detectable social context. In *Heimlicher Bote* we encounter the situation comparable to the civilizing of Rivalin in *Tristan*: the courtly lessons are a preparation for love. We can take it that a new attitude toward romantic love is an important impulse to the blossoming of courtesy in the twelfth century and its spread to lay nobility.

But the underlying causes of this civilizing are more complex. Certainly another major factor in the spread of courtesy, as separable from courtly love, was the growth of lay literacy. The laity's adoption of courtesy is as closely tied to its literacy as *mores* are to *litterae* in a program of court education. Here we can point to a decisive difference between France and Germany, one which either is itself the cause or is at least a major symptom of the German laity's lagging behind the French in the adoption of courtesy and the creation of a vernacular courtly literature. In France the nobles traditionally sent their children to school or to court to receive an education. The custom had flagged in the tenth century, but was revived in the eleventh.[24] For Marbod of Rennes, the schooling of a noble is an obvious step in his preparation for life: "Cum ergo ad pueritiam pervenisset, qua primum aetate, mos est nobilium liberos in disciplinam dare, traditus est litterarum magistro" (*Vita Magn.*, PL 171:1549A).[25] One searches in vain for indications in Germany that it was customary for the sons of nobles to receive an education in letters. Here the opposite is true: an education can be regarded with a certain contempt.[26]

In both France and England the educated knight had become an ideal, and the German laity had fallen out of step. For France we have two interesting letters of Philip of Harvengt, abbot of Bonne-Esperance, which attest to this ideal. He wrote in about 1168 to the young Philip of Flanders,[27] who had recently succeeded his father as count. I will pick out some of the central ideas of the letter and give a running commentary on them. The layman who has acquired Latin letters, he writes, should absent himself from crowds and business to read in the tracts, letters, and commentaries of pagans and Christians. Here he will find much that can "ornament his dignity, explain warfare, enspirit youth. These works build upright behavior ['aedificant mores'], sharpen the mind, and promote virtue." Thus far we have an enumeration of the elements in a curriculum of *litterae et mores*: knowledge, sharpness of mind, and virtuous good behavior are its results. What follows is different: these writings also argue against slothfulness and spur zeal, he writes. They delineate justice, moderate anger, and urge clemency and gentleness. Here we have a list of vices corrected. Hence the abbot's commendation of reading and learning aims at instruction and correction, the two duties of clerics instructing laymen. A prince of noble mind, he continues, does not disdain to read this sort of work. But he refuses to lend his ear to foolish tales (*fabulae*) or to lend his hand to the shaking of dice. Two types of literature are available to noblemen, we see. The one educates in virtue, wisdom, and manners; the other is foolish and vain. Philip then praises a certain Count Ayulf as a most valiant and learned knight. So accomplished was he in Latin that he was taken for a cleric. At the same time he was a worthy knight, as he proved by giving his life in a crusade. But learning and knighthood, he argues, do not exclude each other, and here he puts forward the ideal of the lettered knight:

Non enim scientiae fortis militia vel militiae praejudicat honesta scientia litterarum, imo in principe copula tam utilis, tam conveniens est duarum ut . . . princeps quem non nobilitat scientia litteralis, non parum degenerans sit quasi rusticanus et quodammodo bestialis (Ep. 16, PL 203:149B–C).

For manly chivalry does not preclude learning, nor does knowledge of letters in a moral cause preclude chivalry. But in a prince the combination of both is so useful, so fitting . . . that a prince whose mind is not ennobled by the knowledge of letters degenerates in no small degree from his proper state and becomes like a rustic boor or even a beast.

This passage represents more than a simple admonition from a cleric to a layman to cultivate the study of letters—Philip of Flanders is already lettered. It is an argument for the harmonizing of learning and chivalry. It posits an ideal prince mighty in arms and ennobled by study; it shows contempt for the divorcing of these two realms. The contempt is expressed in a term that in philosophical parlance ordinarily is opposed to the rational man: *bestialis*; and with a term ordinarily opposed in courtly parlance to the gentleman: *rusticanus*.

Philip's second letter was addressed to Henry the Liberal, count of Champagne, husband of Marie de Champagne.[28] He reiterates the same arguments in the same phrases, and holds up to this lord, whose court rivaled that of Philip of Flanders for patronage of courtly literature, the same ideal of the lettered knight. Philip wrote these two letters to men who had attained this ideal; he urges them to "become the men they are." It is hard to escape the conclusion that this chivalric ideal was closely connected with the chivalric ideal propounded in romance: literacy and courtliness in the laity went hand in hand in this period, and literate knights patronized courtly literature. Their literacy was one factor which accounted for the existence of a literature idealizing chivalry.

Writing somewhat later, Gerald of Wales held up the ideal of the lettered knight in ringing terms. Great princes of the past, he writes, were great both in combat and in learning. Their success in war in fact stood in direct proportion to the extent of their literacy; the more lettered, the greater the warrior: "quanto litteratiores erant et eruditiores, tanto in rebus bellicis animosiores . . . et strenuiores" (*De princ. instr.* 1, praef, RS 21:8:7). A prince who strives for both qualities gains lasting praise; a kingdom whose knights are clad in both the toga and in armor excels others. Philosophy and knighthood are wont always to make common cause, at least, he implies, in the greatest of kingdoms: in Greece under Philip, in Rome under the Caesars, in France under Pipin and Charles (ibid., p. 8). We can take Gerald's impressive image—the knight clad in toga and armor—as an emblem of the civilizing process in question here. It conveys a reminiscence of the historical origins of courtesy—the Roman senator—and makes the chivalric knight into the inheritor of that tradition.

The ideal of the lettered knight was in the air. This was something different from the ideal of the learned king. The learned king went back much further. Here it is knights in general, not only princes, who are urged to this ideal.

Correctio

"Correction" of the laity was also a pastoral duty of the clergy.[29] Since we have seen abundant examples in previous chapters of clerics attending to "correction," I will add here only a few observations and some reminders of points made earlier.

The popular idea that a bishop could not enter heaven had partly to do with the worldliness of the office and the temptations it held for its occupant, but it also was connected with the belief that uncorrected vices and unpunished sins in the diocese became the property of the bishop. He was called to account for them by God as strictly as were those who had originally committed them. This was a strong incentive for the bishop to urge vigilance on his clergy in keeping watch over the lives of the laity. Kings and nobles were constantly receiving unsolicited letters from clerics informing them of their vices and urging the correction of them; they regularly found uninvited visitors at their gate come to restore order at their courts, or at least to preach its restoration. *Curialitas*, as we have seen, was high on the list of provocations to correction in the eleventh and twelfth centuries. Abbot William of St. Bénigne at Dijon went to King Robert the Pious and Queen Constance to complain about the ways of Constance's Provencal retainers. Siegfried of Gorze roused Poppo of Stablo to the same task with his letter against the incursion of French novelties at the court of Henry III. Peter of Blois' dialogue between Henry II and the Abbot of Bonneval also shows us a cleric correcting the vices of the ruler.[30] It opens with the king in a high rage over the betrayal he has experienced at the hands of his sons. He calls for revenge from the *Deus ultionum*. The abbot calms him, argues against the natural impulses of wrathfulness and vengeance, and urges patience, humility, clemency, and love of enemies. In the end the king confesses his sinfulness and asks the abbot to impose an appropriate penance.

<>

Various activities at court and in the service of princes justified the court life of clerics. Most important for the spread of courtliness are the two just sketched out, instruction and correction. The duller witted of the correcters and instructors at court will have preached, ranted, and thrown the Bible and the writings of the fathers at the profligate nobility. But some much more clever teachers observed the nobility's appetite for ancient tales of the heroes and kings of bygone days, and they allied their pedagogic impulses to court narrative. I believe that in following the stages of this alliance we lay bare some of the basic impulses that led to the creation of the courtly romance. Kings, princes, and nobles were instructed by examples held up to them in books, books written by the "grand authors," examples collected by contemporary authors, or books written by contemporaries which claimed the authority of antiquity. It stands to reason that the clerical urge to instruct the laity and present it with compelling examples of ideal behavior should have sought forms of expression appropriate to the contemporary scene. We want to follow the path by which these new forms arose. A book that claimed to formulate the honorable and admirable customs of the ancients held a powerful appeal for the courtly audience; these customs were perceived as the very core of ethical instruction for the knighthood.

The Customs of the Ancient Ancestors

We observed earlier in passing that the complaints against courtliness were regularly couched in a conventional opposition of the "ways of our ancient ancestors" to the vain frivolities of a dissolute modern generation (above p. 180). The importance and weight of the appeal to *patres nostri, mos antecessorum, usus olim virorum honorabilium, ritus heroum*, and so forth, is hard to overestimate. There is an interesting work to be written on the subject. Here I can only offer a few notes.

In our period these formulae had a quasilegalistic power. They occur commonly in official documents to legitimize the transaction recorded.[31] To follow the "examples of our ancestors" is to act in an ordained, legal way. Therefore, the study of the examples of past generations constitutes a part of instruction in morals, even apart from the school tradition of ethical instruction through reading the *auctores*. It forms part of the instruction of kings throughout the period. Benzo of Alba urges Henry IV:

[rex] . . . legat quantulumcunque de historiis patrum praecedentum, ut inde sibi assumat bonae imitationis emolumentum. Legere enim aliorum annales plurimum valet ad instruendos ritus imperiales. (*Ad Heinricum* 1.1, MGH, SS 11:600, ll. 35–36)

[The king] . . . should read whenever possible in the histories of past ancestors, and draw thence the profit of a good example. For to read the annals of other rulers is most useful instruction in the customs of empire.

And it becomes a commonplace in the prologues to historical works.[32] William of Jumièges writes his *Gesta Normannorum ducum* for William the Conqueror, "ob recolenda priscorum patrum . . . piissimorum actuum exempla" (PL 149:779A), and in the hope that the virtues of the most distinguished men will live and bear fruit in the consciousness of men of the present ("ut virtutes optimorum virorum . . . utiliter et in hominum notitia vivant"—780A). Jean de Marmoutier relates that the ancient ancestors strove to record the deeds of distinguished men to serve as a spur to religion and the spread of virtue and as an incentive to fortitude; such records raised later generations up to the level of these greats and encouraged the swift stifling of any dishonorable behavior.[33] Hence the "ancient tales" combine the two functions of instructing and correcting. If we are to accept the testimony of medieval historians, we must recognize that kings and rulers had a keen interest in this form of edification: *historia patrum antecessorum*. Henry the Lion is said to have commissioned a collection of ancient chronicles, which he had read to him through entire nights, and is praised for his knowledge of the "lives of the ancients."[34] In his continuation of Otto of Freising's *Gesta Friderici*, Rahewin praises Barbarossa for his diligent study of the scriptures and the deeds of ancient kings.[35] Baldwin III, king of Jerusalem, likewise was "historiarum precipue auditor; antiquorum regum et optimorum principum gesta moresque diligenter investigabat."[36]

In the sociology of literary life at court we can distinguish two basic types of narrative poet: the professional singer of tales, and the cleric in possession of the deeds of the ancients preserved by written record. A keen battle was fought at court between these two types for the attention of princes and their retinue. The clerics argue against the *fabulae* and commend the salutary effects of their own "truthful" historical material. Philip of Harvengt's letter to Philip of Flanders discussed above opposes the writings of the ancients to the foolish tales (*fabulae*) that offer no moral instruction, and since both this and his letter to Henry the Liberal are partly in praise of lettered clerics at court, this also might be seen in light of a competition for the attentions of the court audience. Gottfried of Viterbo dedicates his *Speculum regum* to Henry VI, urging him to put the book to use in schools, "since it is more honorable to impress on the mind of a reading child the histories and characters of kings and emperors, by whose example the world is instructed and ornamented, than the fables of Choridon and Melibeus."[37] The clerics, then, possessed a powerful argument for the superiority of their works: they brought useful moral instruction; the fables merely filled the heads of the listeners with foolish lies. But what commended the fables was that they contained the element of the marvelous or miraculous, and the appeal of this for a lay audience in the twelfth century was very great indeed.

The victory of clerics in this contest was inevitable. It was possible for them to co-opt and "improve" fables, the material of "cil qui de conter vivre vuelent," as Chrétien claimed to do at the beginning of his *Erec*. But the archaic singer of tales, operating in an oral tradition, had only limited access to the histories; for him to attempt to throw a cloak of learning and historical truthfulness over his tales could only have appeared as affected and inappropriate. On the other hand, in the early twelfth century we see clerics producing a new type of history in which *fabulae* become assimilated to *Gesta regum* and *Historiae principum*.[38] The earliest successful and influential amalgamation of the two was Geoffrey's *Historia regum Britanniae*. This work marks a major transition in the development of medieval narrative and of the romance. A cleric discovers the entertainment value of the fables and combines these with the informing, edifying, correcting function of the *Historiae regum*. This discovery sealed the doom of the oral tradition of narrative. It may not have made the singer of tales completely superfluous from then on, but the purpose he served would henceforth be performed better by the clerical poet. Given the weakness of the lay nobility for fashion, given their interest in courtly ways, the cleric who taught courtly ways through quasihistorical fables was destined to outstrip the competition.

This shift from oral to literary tradition is also closely linked to the

growing literacy of the laity, the rise of romance, and the civilizing of
the class to which that form spoke most directly. Hence the conventional motif in the prologues to history and romance—"we record the
deeds of the ancients for instruction and so that they will not perish
from memory"[39]—is no empty *topos*, but a symptom of an important
moment in intellectual history: the shift from reliance on oral transmission to reliance on the written word. An interesting confirmation
of this is the fact that the same formulae served the writer of histories
and the writer of official documents. A deed of inheritance from
Bishop Theobald of Passau begins,

Ne res gesta vertatur in fabulam nec per oblivionem aut incuriam, vel etiam
per industriam fallendi tam exquisitam . . . acte rei fiat alteracio, litterarum
beneficio solet precaveri. Littere namque sunt iudices rerum, note verborum
quibus tanta vis est ut absentibus sine voce loquantur et unica memorie cus-
tos est scriptura. Necessario igitur et utili litterarum freti ministerio scriptis
mandari precepimus, quod . . . etc. (ca. 1187, *Mon. Boica*, 28:2, p. 258, no. 37)

Lest deeds should be distorted into fables, and lest there should be an altera-
tion of performed acts through forgetfulness or neglect or the active will to de-
ceive, men have become accustomed to prevent this by the exercise of writing.
For letters are witnesses of things, the characters of words, in which resides
such power that voiceless they speak in things absent, and writing is a unique
custodian of memory. Therefore, supported by this necessary and useful service of writing, we have ordered it mandated in writing that . . . etc.

Compare the opening lines of Wace's *Roman de Rou*:

> . . . grant pris durent cil avaor
> qui escristrent premierement,
> et li auctor planierement
> qui firent livres et escriz
> des nobles fez et des bons diz
> que li baron et li seignor
> feirent de temps ancianor.
> Tornez fussent en oubliance
> se ne fust tant de remembrance
> que li escriture nos fait,
> qui li estoires nos retrait.[40]

Those who first wrote and the authors who composed the books and writings
of the noble deeds and wise sayings of barons and lords from ancient times
deserve great praise. All these would have fallen into oblivion if writing did
not keep their memory alive and history did not preserve them for us.

Here we see the common ground between history/romance and official documents: both kinds of texts keep alive the memory of the
deeds and thoughts of the ancients, the one by recording them di-

rectly in narrative, the other by showing their reenactment in the de-
cisions of moderns; both tutor men of the present and regulate their
dealings with one another; the high value of both is a strong commendation of literacy.

This reminds us that the transition from "memory to written record" was a broad movement that had implications in all areas touched
by literacy.[41] The common ground of these formulations is the education of a worldly cleric and its application in the court chapel and
chancery on the one hand, and in the literature of the court on the
other.

Ancient Tales in the Literary Life of the Court

There is clearly a large constellation of concerns bound up with this
wave of educating and civilizing the laity: the activity of the learned
cleric in correcting and instructing, the recording of the deeds of the
ancients for the sake of moral instruction, the translation of a program of court education into the idiom of the chivalric class, and the
aesthetic realization of an entire courtly world view transposed from
the milieu in which it arose onto the world of the warrior class.

We want to look now at two descriptions of literary life at court
which epitomize this constellation.

The first is from the earlier part of the twelfth century. Orderic Vitalis tells that at the court of Hugh of Avranches, a lover of the world
with a bustling and rich court, there lived a chaplain, Gerold of Avranches, a man of piety, learning, and character. He strove to convert
the *viri curiales* to a better life by holding up to them the example of
the knights of bygone days: "ad emendationem vitae propositis antecessorum exemplis invitabat" (*Hist. eccl.* 6.2, ed. Chibnall, 3·216). He
made a great collection (now lost) of tales of the combats of holy
knights ("sanctorum militum tirocinia"). He included tales from the
Old Testament, saints' lives, and more recent *Gesta*, among which he
mentions the story of Guillaume d'Orange, hero of a cycle of *Chansons
de geste*.[42] The purpose of this collection of tales is to combat the *car-
nalis petulantia* of men living in the world and to convert them to a life
of monastic discipline. This reveals one motive for the writing or col-
lecting of literature at court: it is an instrument of correction. True, the
activities of Gerold are recorded by an avid adherent of the rebellion
against courtesy, Orderic. But whatever Gerold of Avranches actually
did and whatever his motives actually were, at least we know that Orderic Vitalis himself was capable of conceiving of *Chanson de geste* as
an instrument in a program of correction. In Gerold's collection, fic-

tion borders closely on history; the stories are not vain fables, but tales of ancient ancestors aimed at provoking the listener or reader to a better life.

The urge to make the ancient tales into instruments of correction was an important element in the intellectual history of the twelfth century. We can confirm this by reference to Saxo Grammaticus. We have seen that at least one purpose of his *Gesta Danorum* was precisely to castigate the corrupt ways of his contemporaries by opposing to them the upright warrior ways of the ancient ancestors. Likewise it is probable that the anonymous clerical poet of *Nibelungenlied* regarded this as one of the ethical purposes of his work, even if he did not refer to it directly.

What these examples suggest is that the urge to correct the laity on the part of conservative clerics could express itself in the form of "heroic" literature, *Gesta*, *Historiae*, literature perceived by its clerical authors and compilers as holding up ancient heroic ideals, embodying the grand customs of *patres nostri*, and expressing the *ritus heroum* in *exempla antecessorum*. This is not to say that what is traditionally called heroic literature, "Heldendichtung," in general had this function of admonishing a "corrupt" younger generation against the evils of courtliness. The case of Bishop Gunther of Bamberg (1057–65) shows us that this is not so. The master of the Bamberg cathedral school, Meinhard, boldly and wittily exercising the duty of correction, took his bishop to task for preferring tales of Etzel and Amelung (i.e., Attila and Dietrich of Bern) to the word of God.[43] The bishop paid excessive attention to these *fabulae curiales*, and this provoked correction. There is a clear-cut progression in the function of these tales from the vain fables castigated by Meinhard in the mid-eleventh century to the *Historiae*, *Gesta*, and *altiu maere* of the twelfth, which serve as instruments of correction; the subject matter is not decisively different; but the function has changed from entertainment to moral edification.

Our second example of literature functioning at court within the framework of instruction and correction is from the end of the twelfth or the beginning of the thirteenth century. In Lambert of Ardres' *Historia comitum Ghisnensium* there is a chapter describing the literary activity at the court of Guines. It occurs after Arnold of Guines' chastening experience with Ida of Boulogne. With his knights and his close friends he often indulged in jests, sports, and tournaments "as youth is wont to." But he also retained revered older men at his court,

eo quod veterum eventuras et fabulas et historias ei narrarent et moralitatis seria narrationi sue continuarent et annecterent. (Chap. 96, MGH, SS 24:607, ll. 13–14)

because they recited the deeds of the ancients to him, both fables and histories, adding to their narration the serious observations of moral instruction.

There was, for instance, a veteran knight called Robert of Coutances, who both instructed him and delighted his ears with the tales of the Roman emperors, of Charlemagne, Roland and Oliver, and of Arthur of Britain. Another knew the stories of the crusaders; still another "diligently instructed him" in the "deeds and fables" of the English, among others the story of Tristan and Isolde.

It would be wrong to take Lambert's description as an objective rendering of unvarnished reality (whatever that is); we need not necessarily imagine groups of hardy young knights engaging in serious discussions with wise veterans about the moral profit contained in the story of Tristan and Isolde. Lambert, a conservative mind given to moralizing, idealized the situation, but in doing so has given us what we are looking for: the testimony of a contemporary to the ideal function of courtly narrative. The Arthurian material was supposed in the minds of its clerical authors to operate in the framework of moral instruction, whatever the actual practice may have been. Most illuminating in this passage is the phrase, "they recited both fables and histories, adding to their narration the serious observations of moral instruction" ("moralitatis seria"). In short, both fabulous narrative (the stories of Arthur) and history (the Roman emperors, Charlemagne) can serve as the subject matter of *moralitas*.

‹›

It is a peculiar fact, one not explainable within the traditional notions of the chivalric origins of courtly narrative, that courtly romance is the creation exclusively of clerical authors: Geoffrey of Monmouth, Wace, the author of the *Roman d'Énéas* and the *Roman de Thèbes*, Benoît de St. Maure, probably Chrétien de Troyes,[44] and in Germany, Ulrich von Zatzikhoven, Albrecht von Halberstadt, Herbort von Fritzlar, and Gottfried von Strassburg certainly were clerics; the poet of the *Nibelungenlied* and Heinrich von Veldeke probably were. Indeed, in the classical period of German romance, only three poets are known to have been knights: Hartmann von Aue, Wolfram von Eschenbach, and Wirnt von Gravenberg.[45] This fact has not escaped the notice of scholars, and Jean Frappier showed a keen instinct for the overriding importance of the cleric in the conception and literary formulation of *courtoisie*:

Les auteurs des romans courtois sont des "clercs" pourvus d'une culture acquise a l'école des Anciens. La peinture de l'amour, comme l'art d'aimer enseigné a la dame et au chevalier, relève d'une tradition humaniste et d'une certaine "clergie", dont il importe de preciser dans la mésure du possible la condition sociale et le tour d'esprit.[46]

But in general scholars have been slow to focus on the really decisive role of clerics not only in the composition of romance but also in the forging of the ethical ideals on which those works are based. It was imagined that while the clerics, being literate, were necessarily the authors, they recorded values and an idealized world appropriate to knighthood; they were the more or less passive embroiderers of a natively chivalric idealism, serving the lay nobility as the scribe serves the lords for whom he prepares documents. Another misleading model is the relationship of patron to artist. A patron conceives a program of painting, sculpture, or literature, and commissions a skilled artist, craftsman, or poet, to execute his ideas and to express his values. It is easy to imagine a clerical poet receiving the material of a story and simply executing the tale or translation according to the tastes and values of the patron. Chrétien tells us that his *Chevalier de la charette* was composed in this manner under the patronage of Marie de Champagne. But the work falls in his middle period. He had already produced an impressive body of works—*Erec, Cligés*, possibly *Yvain*. This brought him a reputation and patronage. The originating factor in twelfth-century narrative was almost never patronage. We know of no patron of Wace's *Brut*, though it may have been dedicated to Eleanor; we know of no patron of Benoît's *Roman de Troie*. But we do know that the success of these works attracted patronage. Their chronicle works were written on commission after the success of their romance-histories. In Bumke's studies of patronage in MHG literature, it becomes apparent that this factor played next to no role in the originating of narrative works. Of twelve epics that he treats from the twelfth century, the patronage is clear in only one case, the *Rolandslied* of Pfaffe Konrad, written on commission for Henry the Lion (see *Mäzene*, p. 85 ff.). Heinrich von Veldeke mentions Hermann von Thüringen in his epilogue as the patron of the *Eneit*, but the Landgrave, we learn from the same passage, formed an interest in the work after it was largely finished. Likewise the patronage of the major works of MHG romance remains a mystery: Hartmann's epics, Wolfram's *Parzival*, and Gottfried's *Tristan*.[47]

A much more compelling model for the impulses that produced romance is the framework of correction and instruction. Just as clerics wrote unsolicited letters urging noblemen to behave themselves or to continue to be the ideal gentlemen they are, so also clerics wrote romances. Just as Philip of Harvengt put forward the ideal of the *miles litteratus* to Philip of Flanders and Henry the Liberal of Champagne, so also the writers of romance put forward the ideal of the *miles bene morigeratus* in romance.

I am not suggesting that all these writers were high-minded moralists who had in mind only the ethical improvement of the laity. They knocked on the patron's gate with finished manuscript in hand just as modern authors starting out knock on the doors of publishing houses (or at least send letters or agents to plead for them). Ambition and the desire for fame and fortune usually keep close company with the urge to improve the world and to vent one's own creative impulses. But the clerical poets who created the romances of antiquity and the Arthurian romances did not appear before great lords as petitioners or as hired scribes, but as teachers. They rode a large wave, a wave pushed up by the urge to educate the laity, suffusing traditional warrior values with the courtly ideals of the learned clergy. The lay nobles—first in France, then in Germany—were willing students. They eagerly accepted the lessons of romance, not out of self-interest or social pressure, but because they admired and were inspired by the rule of life they dictated.[48] Probably in terms of *Realpolitik* it was then and always will be practical for a warrior to put his vanquished enemies to death, to inspire fear rather than love, to return every insult in kind and with interest. But it is not noble, not sublime, not magnanimous, qualities which now stood high in the chivalric hierarchy of values. The enlightened among the feudal nobility showed themselves capable of being inspired by courtly ideals, and this capability above all accounts for the civilizing of the chivalric class in Europe.

COURTLINESS IN THE ROMANCE

E CAN distinguish two narrative structures in romance and epic that present us with two very different views of courtliness. The first we will call courtier narrative, the second chivalric narrative. In both the hero is a knight. The terms specify the social role within which the essential struggle of the hero with his destiny takes place.

Courtier Narrative

To gain a general impression of the characteristics of the courtier narrative we can start with a few examples:

1. Walter Map's tale of the king of Portugal:[1] A certain king of Portugal, under attack, is saved by an unknown youth, "superior of body and handsome of appearance." Taking up residence at the king's court, the young hero shows such courage that it seems impossible one man could possess it all. He becomes the king's favorite and is honored and rewarded above all the other courtiers. But the members of the court feel that the honor done to the newcomer depletes the finite store of royal affection and deprives them of their due share. "Thrown into a frenzy of envy, they strove to bring him low with a malice the equal in evil of the supreme virtue which had brought the youth to favor." They can not attack him openly, and so, knowing that the king's great weakness is jealousy, they put out rumors that the knight is engaged in a secret love affair with the king's wife. In a rage, the king orders the intriguers to kill his former favorite in secret. They ingratiate themselves with the youth by speaking kindly to him and serving him in many ways. Finally they lure him to a hunt and slit his throat in a grove. The king, receiving this news, rushes to the chamber of his pregnant wife and attacks and kills both her and the unborn child with his blows. Map's comment: "These are the pleasant pastimes of the court; these are the snares of the demons there."

2. The first half of *Nibelungenlied*: A young hero, Siegfried, enters the court of Worms as a stranger to woo the sister of the king. He appropriates a high position at court for himself by the threat of force—

unlike the knight in Map's tale, who earned it. He serves King Gunther well but is driven by a heedless urge to be first in everything. He is incautious in dealings with the king's wife, which allow of a nasty construction and open her to a fatal insult. This ultimately spells his ruin. The members of Gunther's court lure Siegfried onto a hunt, dissembling friendship and good fellowship, and the chief intriguer, Hagen, spears him in the back while he drinks at a brook.

3. Gottfried's *Tristan*[2]: A genial prodigy appears as a stranger at the court of King Mark of Cornwall. He rises swiftly to the highest position of favor at court through a display of personal virtues, intellectual talents, and courtier skills. But he arouses the envy of the court and is the victim of slander and persecution. He wins a wife for the king, but falls in love with her himself. The situation exposes the lovers to constant dangers at court. It brings about Tristan's banishment and eventually their death.

I have sifted out many elements of the last two epics, extracting what I take to be the central core of a courtier narrative. But the structure occurs in a pure form in Map's anecdote with striking similarities to the other two, richer and lengthier narratives, and this gives us some assurance that we are dealing with an actual narrative structure, not just random common elements. They are based on a representative courtier experience, one which was in the air at this time, sought expression and found it in various works. One is tempted to create a medieval genre to encompass this form, and call it *De casibus curialium*, "On the Fall of Courtiers." But it is not a specifically medieval form. It occurs in a good many historical settings. Its roots are in the realities of court life, the real circumstances in the life of the gifted courtier and favorite at a ruler's court, and the perils that attend on them. The social setting of the form is invariably the court of an autocratic ruler. The Old Testament gives us several examples: Genesis 39–41, Joseph in Egypt; and Daniel 1–6, Daniel at the courts of Nebuchadnezzar, Belshazzar, and Darius. From the post-Renaissance period we have J. M. von Loen's *Der redliche Mann am Hofe*; parts of Voltaire's *Zadig*; Wieland's *Agathon*, bks. 10–12, Agathon at the court of Dionysius of Syracuse; Stendhal's *Charterhouse of Parma*, a work that still preserves, in addition to the form of courtier narrative, the historical circumstances that account for the rise of the courtier figure in the West: a talented and ambitious young man serves a prince in order to attain a bishopric.

The common features of the form are: a stranger appears at court, dazzles the king and his court with his charm and talents, rises swiftly to favor and power, inspires envy, and becomes entangled in romantic complications with a woman close to the ruler, and these lead to his eventual fall. This form operates in the mode of tragedy, and it is, in the western tradition, a vehicle for court criticism. The prince is portrayed as weak and sensual, petty and arbitrary; the court consists of flatterers and detractors, ambitious and unscrupulous intriguers.

The role that courtliness has to play in courtier narrative is not a glorious or ideal one. The argument of this book has been that in its origin courtliness has a social and political function in court life. As such it certainly has an ideal aspect: it draws on the ethical writings of ancient Rome for its articulation. But we have also seen that this code originated as a response to disorder. It helps to maintain the obligatory atmosphere of calm and good fellowship at court. The result is that all conflict submerges and is carried on beneath the surface order and elegance of court life in the form of intrigue. Under these circumstances restraint, moderation, and self-control become requisite qualities for entry into court service. We recall that Meinwerk of Paderborn was "judged suitable for royal service because of the elegance of his manners," and that meant self-control, a foresighted channeling and governing of impulse. It is in these two contexts that courtliness has a specific role and function in courtier narrative. By lavish displays of courtliness and talent the courtier lays down his credentials and his qualifications for court service. We recall the observations of court critics that ambitious *curiales* stage displays of modesty, affability, restraint, and gentleness, in order to insinuate themselves cunningly into the favor of princes. This is the perspective from which courtier narratives ordinarily view courtly attainments: as means of entré, as instruments of ambition. The calculation behind courtly performances need not even be concealed, and both the performance and the calculation can be perceived as objective testimony to the courtier's merit, much the way our students' grades are accepted by potential employers who do not sniff dubious motives behind a young man's urge to excel. In Tristan's displays of courtly attainments before the court of Cornwall, the element of calculation is evident and does not even escape King Mark. He strikes a modest pose and underplays his talents, thus putting his *modestia*, or, to apply the term anachronistically, *sprezzatura* on display. He is the stager and director of his own performance and is admired both for his work on stage and, as it were, behind the scenes. Mark marvels at his abilities to underplay his talents, and calls this skill *kündekeit*, that is, "cunning" or "craft":

Now Mark sat nearby the whole time taking all of this in, observing his friend Tristan closely. And he marveled very much at Tristan's ability to conceal such courtly attainments and such impressive skills of which he himself [i.e., Tristan] was perfectly aware. (3576–83)

His motives are penetrated. But far from arousing disapproval, this show of modesty, this conscious and calculating refusal to share in the enthusiasm that he has provoked, in itself becomes an object of admiration. And no sooner has he finished his performance, than Mark invites him to become his private musician and takes him into the close circle of his favorites. This is a moment familiar to us from the Latin texts: "ad summum familiaritatis gradum mox provehitur." Here courtliness functions to catch the eye of the king and insinuate the courtier into his favor. It is a learned and cultivated form of behavior, but it works like an intellectual juggler's trick.

The main role of courtliness is different. It is a commonplace of court life that all faces viewed in open encounter are masks. No courtier who wears his heart on his sleeve can survive in the conflict with which that institution teems. The first rule of survival is that the courtier composes a mask, a surrogate character, that puts forward a personality and a set of motives conventionally acceptable to the court and the king. It may be that the result is hollow show, empty adherence to the expectations of society; it may be that—in exceptional cases—the outward show is a true mirror of the inner man. In either case, the life of the court divides human beings into outer mask and inner man. This is very much the situation Alan of Lille had in mind when he had the virtue of *Honestas* equip the New Man in the *Anticlaudianus* with the following "moral" quality:

[Honestas advises him] . . . to have an interior life of his own which few have and an exterior life which many have, living his interior life for himself and his exterior life for the many; to . . . show himself all things to all men.[3]

Clearly Alan of Lille is far from being deterred by moral scruples from commending a stance that must appear to people not living and working in the setting of the court as dishonest. He places this advice in the mouth of *Honestas*, which might be translated "moral perfection," or simply "virtue." But the division into ingratiating, bright-spirited mask, and inner, unique man is simply an obvious necessity and a sensible form of self-preservation in a social and political setting where the will of the prince has the force of law. Assertions of one's own opinions against the will of the prince can constitute insult of majesty; to insist with conviction on an opinion contrary to the ruler's can be a request for martyrdom—as it was for Thomas More. For the most part this division did not confront courtiers with a serious moral dilemma. They solved the problem as Thomas Becket, the "two-fold man," *vir geminus*, is said to have solved it, by serving the will of the king openly and accomplishing his own ends by cunning, intrigue, or artfulness, or merely by cultivating the inner life while paying outward observance to duty. The authors of courtier narrative seem impelled to put to the test the conviction with which their heroes maintain a mask, to show the lengths to which they will go to conceal the inner self. A classic scene making a courtier's hypocrisy into a virtue is the debut of Fabrizio del Dongo at the court of the prince of Parma in Stendhal's *Charterhouse of Parma*. Fabrizio is an ardent Bonapartist who feels only contempt for the petty tyrants ruling in Italy, the prince of Parma among them. And yet when he is introduced to the prince, he holds a speech praising monarchy, asserting that the sole duty of a subject is blind obedience to the will of the prince, that the words "liberty, justice, the good of the greatest number" are infamous and criminal. The prince sees through this staged performance but is forced against his better judgment to admire Fabrizio for pulling it off so coolly. The bourgeois reader may be shocked by such calculation, but by and large the members of court society will have taken it, as King Mark and the prince of Parma do, as a sign that the man who practices it well has what it takes to survive in court life.

We can take a scene in Tristan as paradigmatic for the function of courtliness within this division of inner and outer man. In Ireland the two Isoldes have discovered that the dragonslayer they took to be the minstrel Tantris is really their deadly enemy, Tristan, the slayer of their kinsman Morold. Tristan is at their mercy, and they try to decide how to procede. The lady-in-waiting Brangaene advises them first to look to their advantage in his presence (he did after all kill the dragon), and to "turn their coats in the direction the wind blows" (10426–27). Whatever their real feelings toward him may be, their bearing toward him must be courtly: "swie iu daz herze hin zim si, / sit im doch höfschliche bi" (10453–54). The exchange to some extent characterizes Brangaene, but it also characterizes the life of the court in general. Courtliness is the disguise that puts forward the claim: all relations are calm, normal, and friendly. Behavior that is *höfschlich* creates a certain freedom for its wearer, freedom to maneuver, to seek advantage, and to ward off the attempts of others to penetrate the mask and uncover the real motivations it conceals.

One of the ethical problems raised in the mind of the modern reader by the phenomenon of courtliness is the connection between this pattern of behavior and inner virtue. Ideally the gentleman is considerate because he is compassionate, because he loves and respects his fellow men; he is modest and restrained because he possesses greatness of soul; he is witty, affable, and of good humor because he has an honest mind at peace with itself; he is on sovereign good terms with all the world because he is the master of himself.

These are the kinds of bridges that ideally connect outer forms of behavior to internal dispositions, "Sitten" to "Sittlichkeit." It is ironic
that the very social setting that called forth courtliness, and within
which this entire economy of virtue ought to function, is regularly
seen as destroying the connections between social form and inner virtue. This is not to say that at court all are unprincipled rascals and
humanity has no chance to survive. But humanity is measured by the
courtier's *negative response to the life of the court*, by the kind of inner life
he cultivates and manages to preserve from the corrosive influences
surrounding him. Oddly enough, in courtier narratives the most
common form in which humanity is preserved is the clandestine love
affair. The lovers come to form a spiritual elite set against the shallow
materiality of the court. The logic that connects the cruelty and inhumanity of the court with love is not easy to perceive. Again, Stendhal,
a keen observer of court life, gives us a good commentary. In his
treatise on love, he describes how court ladies exploit fashion to display their bodies with the aim of catching and manipulating men; that
is, the outer object of passion is prostituted. He sums up: "Here is a
whole society acting without morality and above all without passion.
All this [i.e., viciousness, self-interest and material pleasure] . . .
drives away any considerations of virtue and inner satisfaction of a
heart living at peace with itself. I have noticed that a feeling of isolation in the midst of all this predisposes sensitive hearts to love" (Fragment 79). And so "sensitive hearts" are drawn together precisely by
their common loathing of the life around them. They are people capable of maintaining inwardly the integrity of the emotions, the ability to love. The turning inward of humanity that occurs at court is indicated in the vocabulary that frequently attaches to the lovers: they
form an elite of heart and soul. In *Tristan* the lovers and the like-
minded among the readers are "edele herzen," "noble hearts"; in
Wieland's *Agathon* the lovers are "edele Seelen," as are the lovers in
Loen's *Der redliche Mann am Hof*. And Stendhal's lovers in *Charterhouse*
are called "âmes généreuses," noble souls. Gottfried tells his readers
at the beginning of *Tristan* that the work will endear virtue and loyalty
to them. Those words, applied to an adulterous love affair, become
meaningful within the social context of the court.

Courtliness functions within this complex of the divided self as a
screen set before the inner man. It creates for him a form of freedom
and an atmosphere in which he can pursue private obligations. In this
sense it provides a shelter for the individual in the perilous circumstances of court life, a shelter that accommodates both villainy and
humanity.

Chivalric Narrative

Chivalric narrative represents courtliness as a sublime ethical code. This lofty vision of courtesy is closely connected with one purpose of the chivalric romance, the civilizing of the knightly class. William of Malmesbury and a host of historians and didactic writers were persuaded that in reading the deeds of the ancients, men of the present day learn *mores*, upright behavior. The authors of romance carried this pedagogic intention further than was possible for the historian. They represented the deeds of heroes of bygone days as beginning with—or entirely comprised of—a process of education. Not only was the hero's mature conduct of life an example for the reader, but also the steps by which he arrived at maturity.[4] Chrétien de Troyes gave the Arthurian romance its classic form. That form has been described by the convenient German term *doppelter Kursus*. A knight of great promise and potential worth sets out in search of adventure, wins by his prowess honor, a place in society, a wife, and lands. But what was won by raw ability and unshaped, unformed virtue, is lost again because of the sins, errors, and atrocities the knight commits for want of some inner ethical sense and human respect. In the earliest of Chrétien's preserved works, *Erec et Enide*, this form is present, though it is not yet the vehicle of a high vision of the ethical duties of knighthood.

The two later romances, *Yvain* and the fragment of a Perceval romance, convey an ideal of courtly humanity. Here I want to limit my discussion to the German adaptations of these two works, Hartmann von Aue's *Iwein* and Wolfram von Eschenbach's *Parzival*. These take up the essential action and thought of Chrétien's works, and Wolfram succeeds in developing the central ideal of the work he adapted beyond Chrétien's conception.

The social standing of the poets is of interest for our theme. Chrétien, there can be little doubt, was a cleric. His romances put forward a model of behavior to the laity, not a mirror of practiced chivalric ideals. This is entirely in keeping with the duty of the cleric to instruct and correct the laity, entirely in keeping with the purpose of *Gesta* and *Historiae* to provide a pattern of *mores*. But in Germany, where the barbarianism of the warrior class was more recalcitrant than in France, these two works, the high point of courtly humanity, are taken up by poets who belong to the warrior class. The literary vehicle conveying ideals of civilized and refined social life has passed from the jurisdiction of its clerical originators to the class of men for whom it is intended, knights. Hartmann and Wolfram are far from rejecting the ideals of humanity, restraint, and respectfulness put forward by Chrétien. They do not insist, as members of the warrior class, on the good old archaic values of unrestrained manhood, violence, vengefulness, and self-assertiveness. This is the attitude of reactionary clerics, like the author of *Nibelungenlied*. The civilizing of the knighthood found resistance at this level of society, not, for the most part, among knights, and certainly not among those knights who wrote lyric and narrative poetry. On the contrary, Hartmann and Wolfram—as knights—had a profound understanding of the value and necessity of this new ideal; perhaps—as knights—their understanding of it was even clearer than Chrétien's. This passing of the courtly romance from a cleric to knights is understandable within Elias' framework of "Verhöflichung der Krieger." The essential moment in this process occurs, he argues, when the set of prohibitions and taboos imposed on the warrior class from without becomes internalized. For the knighthood this means that the laws of conduct and humanity enjoined on it by court legislators, whoever they may be, gain the force of an inner law imposed on each knight by himself. The instruments of enforcement come to reside in the individual psyche, not outside it in the form of threatened punishment. Each individual holds himself to the ethical laws because to break them would violate his own values and call down psychological punishment, loss of self-respect. In the transition from Chrétien to Hartmann-Wolfram, we see precisely this moment in the process of civilizing occur at the level of class. A code of behavior urged on the knightly class by a cleric is taken up and urged on that same class by its own members; the lawgiver is now "internal" to the class.[5]

Hartmann appears to have come to an acceptance of the terms *hövesch*, *hövescheit*, late in his career as a writer.[6] His use of them is sparing in his early work *Erec*; *hövesch* occurs once in the *Klagebüchlein* and *Der arme Heinrich*, not at all in *Gregorius*. But it is common in his last narrative work, *Iwein*.[7] *Höveschcit* and its variants have a wide range of meaning in this romance. The first husband of Laudine, Ascalon, is praised for always having a plentiful store of fine clothes in the castle, "courtly gentleman that he was" ("als ein hövesch man"— 2195). On the other hand, it can mean compassion and refined and humane sense of respect for the feelings of others. The countess of Naribon with two of her ladies come upon Iwein sleeping in the forest in the state to which his rejection at the hands of his wife has reduced him—namely naked and insane. One of the ladies is moved to tears by her "courtliness and goodness":

> ir höfscheit unde ir güete
> beswârten ir gemüete,

> daz sî von grôzer riuwe
> und durch ir reine triuwe
> vil sêre weinen began,
> das einem alsô vrumen man
> diu swacheit solde geschehen
> daz er in den schanden wart gesehen.
>
> (3387–94)

The sight of a man of such valor suffering such wretchedness and disgrace so weighed down her courtly and compassionate nature that out of profound sorrow and innocent tenderness she burst into tears.

The passage brings *höfscheit* into close proximity with a central theme of the story, *güete*. Hartmann's prologue opened with the announcement that *rehtiu güete* is the prerequisite for an honorable and happy life. In fact courtliness here is in company with virtues at the top of Hartmann's hierarchy of values. *Reiniu triuwe* was the quality shown by the young girl in *Der arme Heinrich* in offering her life's blood as a cure for her master's leprosy. *Hövescheit* as sympathy and compassion occurs again in *Iwein* to characterize Gawein. He and Arthur had so intimate a friendship,

> . . . daz ir ietweder truoc
> des andern liep unde leit.
> hie erzeicte sîne hövescheit
> her Gâwein der bescheiden man . . .
>
> (2712–15)

. . . that each rejoiced when the other felt joy, each suffered when the other felt pain. This showed the courtliness in that prudent man, Gawein.

We have seen that this sensibility was pronounced among the ethical virtues of courtliness: a sensitive awareness of the feelings of other men, a humane regard for them. *Hövescheit* can bear a meaning close to the Latin *verecundia*. In the scene where the countess's lady revives Iwein, then steps behind cover lest her presence should embarrass him, this meaning is especially clear:

> vil drâte sî von im entweich,
> wand sî daz wol erkande
> daz schämelîchiu schande
> dem vrumen manne wê tuot,
> und barc sich durch ir höfschen muot . . .
>
> (3488–92)

At once she slipped away, for she knew quite well how painful a disgraceful state is to a man of valor, and, courtly spirit that she was, she hid herself.

This brings us very close to the sensibility shown by Otto of Bamberg in the elaborate preparations for baptizing the heathens, the care taken to avoid embarrassing men and women naked before their converters. The Latin writer had called this sensibility *verecundia*; for Hartmann it is *höfscher muot*.

It is evident that Hartmann does not distinguish sharply between the context of shallow fashion and that of ethical sensibility, humanity, in his use of the word *hövescheit*. But in his concepts he does. Here we can come to an understanding of his ideal of chivalric courtliness by a comparison of two figures, Kalogreant and Iwein.

I know of no portraits of a shallow, hollow courtier in medieval literature that can rival Hartmann's Kalogreant. He might be compared with Osric in *Hamlet*, had Shakespeare not treated this figure with such bitter scorn. Hartmann depicted Kalogreant with such a delicate irony that the satiric edge could escape even very distinguished modern readers.[8] *Iwein* begins with Kalogreant's narrative of a shameful event that had befallen him some ten years before. Members of Arthur's court are gathered together telling stories, when the queen joins them inconspicuously. Of the group, only Kalogreant sees her coming. He springs up at once, bows down, and receives her graciously. Now this gesture bears a fixed meaning for court society. It is the gesture of a polite, perhaps sycophantic courtier. Recall that Innocent III had said that the ambitious man is always anxious not to displease; he puts on a show of modesty and affability, he "bows to all, frequents courts, visits potentates, rises up and embraces them, praises and flatters them" ("universis inclinat, frequentat curias, visitat optimates, assurgit et amplexatur"—*De cont. mundi* 2.26; see above, p. 57). This describes Kalogreant's gesture exactly, and it is interpreted in just this way, as "courtly" behavior. The chider Sir Kay berates Kalogreant for his dainty and sycophantic regard:

> "uns was ouch ê daz wol erkant
> daz under uns niemen waere
> sô höfsch und als êrbaere
> als ir waenet daz ir sît."
> (114–17)

"It didn't take this incident to show us that there's no one among us who is as courtly and deserving of favor as you fancy yourself."

This is the event which frames Kalogreant's narrative of his failure at the adventure of the fountain. In the course of the narrative itself Kalogreant reveals himself as timorous, even cowardly. He trembles at the sight of a forest monster and the strange animals raging around him. He undertakes the adventure, not out of surging knightly spirit, but only on the consideration that he is out questing for adventure, here it is, and he might as well forge on in spite of his misgivings about the promptings of his own "foolishness" ("mîn unwîser muot"). He tries to appease the defender of the fountain rather than fight with him: he had meant no harm in issuing the challenge. And, defeated, he sits on the grass filled with self-pity and consoling thoughts of his good intentions.

From the beginning, Hartmann establishes Kalogreant's identity as a courtier-knight. In what follows he exposes the emptiness of the figure. Like Osric he has "only got the tune of the time and the outward habit of encounter; a kind of yeasty collection, . . . and do but blow them to the trial, the bubbles are out." This describes the role of Kalogreant rather well: his courtliness does not bespeak virtue, strength and magnanimity, but is merely "the outward habit of encounter." His knighthood, including his famous definition of adventure, is empty show. Put to the test, he fails.

This might suggest that Hartmann speaks here as a critic of courtliness: Kalogreant is a shallow weakling, an effeminized, fawning courtier, and this is the fate that the clerical polemics against courtliness foresaw for a knighthood contaminated by courtly ideals. But neither Hartmann nor Chrétien is a critic in this sense. In this scene they put forward their rejection, not of courtliness itself, but of this code in its lowest form: aristocratic deference is empty without the strength of character from which it ideally derives.

Iwein attempts the adventure of the fountain and conquers its defender. He deals Ascalon a mortal blow. The wounded man heads for his castle, but Iwein, rather than letting him go, pursues him to end the combat, moved by the thought that if he has no token of his victory to take back to Arthur's court with him, no one will believe him. On this consideration he chases a wounded man, presumably to deal him the final blow. It is a crass violation of humanity, and Hartmann says as much: "her Iwein jaget in âne zuht" (1056). It is precisely *zuht*, courtly restraint, humane good sense, that is lacking in Iwein.[9] He shows it again in a seemingly trivial context, the failure to return to his wife on the day arranged. It is at least a much lesser crime than the reckless, unchivalrous pursuit of a half-dead opponent in combat. But as it can happen that a man's worst faults escape punishment when they cause grievous damage to others, only to find it when they cause none, Iwein is rejected by his wife for this small lack of regard. He falls into dishonor and madness, the self-imposed punishment for violation of the code.

The second part of the romance, after his revival by the magic salve, shows Iwein engaged in knightly adventure, to be sure, but it is adventure of a wholly different kind. A sequence of encounters and combats allows him to act as the selfless helper of the oppressed, to show his sense of justice, humanity, compassion, loyalty and love, and in the end he is reconciled with his wife and returns to a life pleasing to God and man. The theme of *Iwein*, then, is the development, the education of a knight to these values, the tempering of a reckless, heedless war-like spirit through ideals of regard, humanity, and compassion. By juxtaposing the courtier manners of Kalogreant to the acquired humanity of Iwein, Hartmann opposes the empty sociability of the courtier to a much higher form of courtesy. This higher form is embodied by Gawein and other figures on the periphery and ultimately by Iwein himself. If it is not said explicitly that the *rehtiu güete* to which Iwein attains also includes this higher form of *hövescheit*, we can infer it from Hartmann's use of the term and from the proximity in which the two stand to each other.

In Wolfram's *Parzival*, on the other hand, courtliness, called by name—here ordinarily *zuht*—looms large in the development of the hero and is central to the theme of this, perhaps the greatest of medieval romances. Parzival enters the world of chivalry bursting with vitality and ambition and riding roughshod over anyone in his path. His mother brings him up isolated from society. She purposely deprives him of all knowledge of chivalry and social forms because she is embittered over the death in combat of her husband. But he once encounters three knights, whom he takes for gods. The mistake places his early errings under the sign of idolatry: he makes knighthood into his God. He charges off to become a knight, heedless of his mother's wishes. Shortly after she dies, and her death is later reckoned as one of his two "great sins" (499,20).[10] The nature of this and other of his "sins" is a central problem in interpreting the romance. Of course much can be said to mitigate his responsibility for the death of his mother: he had no idea of the effect his departure would produce; young men must leave home, and it would be a milque-toast who would stay at home to please his mother; sin is defined as conscious consent to the will to do wrong, and so forth. But within the ethical values of courtliness it is perfectly possible to come to an understanding of this "sin." His mother's worst fear was that he would become a knight; this much he learned from her. She had suffered deeply from the death of his father. The fear and love that induced her to bring up her son in this way may have been misguided, but they were deeply felt and deserved respect. But Parzival's blind urge to become a knight dims his vision for any other considerations, and he crassly ignores his mother's feelings. This shows a lack of the sensitivity called in

Latin *verecundia*, ascribed by Hartmann to Gawein and the countess's lady and called *hövescheit*: the sympathetic, sensitive awareness of the feelings of others. Gawein suffered everything his friend Arthur suffered and presumably would have taken pains not to wound or injure him; in Parzival there is a great void where this sensibility ought to be, and so he does not even suspect what act of his will kill his own mother. This may not be a "sin" but it is a grievous violation of a widely accepted and admired virtue of civil life.

But where should he have gained this sense? He is uneducated, deprived of all *zuht*, and the last stratagem of his mother to frustrate his ambitions is to send him into the world a fool in inner and outer habit. His headlong ways plunge him into further misdeeds. He meets a beautiful woman asleep in a tent and takes a kiss and ring from her by force, in accord, he is content to believe, with the instruction in the ways of the world he received from his mother. The woman, Jeschute, is disgraced in the eyes of her husband, and for Parzival's rashness she begins a life of suffering and deprivation that ends only when Parzival frees her from it and clears her name some time hence. In order to become a knight, he kills another knight in an unchivalric way and strips him of his armor, acts tantamount to murder and corpse robbing. His victim, a renowned and honored knight, Ither, is a relative of Parzival, as it turns out. And so his path to knighthood is strewn with acts of inhumanity and violence. Parzival's "courtship" of Jeschute is a violation of courtliness and of humanity at the same time. Or rather the lack of courtliness leads to a violation of humanity. He is to win the kiss and ring of fair ladies, as his mother told him. But given the realities of human social life, this cannot be done without carrying out elaborate wooing ceremonies that stretch over a long period of time. In a courtly society these ceremonies, surrounded by all sorts of taboos, carried out only with great skill slowly acquired, are so much the more demanding. His courtship borders on the burlesque for a modern audience. To thirteenth-century court society it will have appeared so much the more a violation of social custom and humanity, which are mutually reinforcing.

For the theme of courtesy the most important station in his development is his visit to the aged and learned gentleman knight, Gurnemanz, "the captain of true courtesy" ("houbetman der wâren zuht"— 162,23). His mother had told him to seek education in manners from a gray-haired wiseman (127,21), and so Gurnemanz's lessons are welcome to him. The elements of his ethical teaching[11] are for the most part well known to us by now. Parzival should always retain his sense of shame, a quality Wolfram had described in his prologue as the keystone of all virtues (3,5). He should be a protector of all the oppressed.

He should be generous and practice moderation in all things. He must learn to restrain his habit of chattering nonsense and not ask too many questions, but respond to questions put to him with well-considered replies appropriate to the tone of the question. In battle he should show mercy to those he conquers, combining boldness with compassion. At court he should be manly and of good cheer ("manlîch und wol gemuot"). This phrase registers an important concern of Wolfram, namely, that courtly ways should not deprive a knight of his manliness. It is a concern he shares with the clerical critics of courtesy, and these critics were giving voice to what must have been a widespread suspicion of gentle, refined, and softened manners in the warrior class. But Wolfram's phrase, while putting the two qualities into opposition to one another, also shows the possibility of a reconciliation and balance struck among them, something not envisioned by critics of courtliness. The phrase implies, Be of bright good cheer without losing your manliness. It should be read as parallel to another common formula in Wolfram's vocabulary of courtesy: he calls Gawein "ein manlîch hövesch man" (430,20), which is not ill rendered as "a man who is courtly but manly at the same time," or "courtly without sacrificing his manliness." Of Parzival and his brother Feirefiz he says later in the narrative, "manheit bî zuht an beiden was" (745,10), that is, both of them combined courtly breeding with manhood, no small accomplishment, he implies. Wolfram's formulations contain a warning and a promise at the same time: courtly ways can be reconciled with chivalry, but the courtly knight must be on his guard to keep both in proper relationship with each other. The implied turn of thought reminds us of Philip of Harvengt's assurances to Philip of Flanders and Henry the Liberal that book learning need not exclude *fortis militia*, manly chivalry (see above, p. 225).

Gurnemanz's lessons continue with instructions on relations to women and end with practical training in combat. Parzival's foolishness falls from him like a veil; knightly deportment and courtesy (179,14–15) have washed over him like a wave in the form of Gurnemanz's words, and he adopts them with the same facility as earlier his mother's lessons. Of course it is Gurnemanz's advice that is to prove his downfall later: he fails to ask the redeeming question at the Grail castle, and the fault is assigned to his courtesy: "durch zuht in vrâgens doch verdrôz" (239,10). It was the very courtesy he learned from Gurnemanz that restrained him from asking the question, "Uncle, why do you suffer so?" But it would be mistaken to see in this code in itself a shallow, false rule that misleads men and diverts them from their human duty of compassion and mercy. No sooner has Gurnemanz given him the fatal advice to avoid questions than he adds: "You can hear and see, taste and smell. Let these senses bring you wisdom" (171,22 ff.). When he later confesses his failure to the Hermit Trevrizent, it is not for following the rule of *zuht* the hermit reproaches him, but for his failure to use his five senses:

> dô dir got vünf sinne lêch
> (die hânt ir rât dir vor bespart),
> wie was dîn triuwe von in bewart
> an den selben stunden
> bî Anfortases wunden?
>
> (488,26–30)

God gave you five senses, but since they denied you their aid, what hope was there for you to show charity in the moment when you saw the wounds of Anfortas?

Not the code called *zuht* is responsible for Parzival's great failure to show compassion, but rather Parzival himself. He knows how to fight and how to behave; he possesses *manheit bî zuht*, but has not the wisdom and human feeling to interpret the messages of his senses. Therefore the love, loyalty, and compassion—all of these suggested in the word *triuwe*—of which he is capable fail to assert themselves at the critical moment. In short, it is not doctrine, learning, and education that make the man, but the human feeling that first gives doctrine meaning. Courtliness without humanity is an empty code; the two joined produce a life pleasing to God and the world. This implies that even Christian doctrine empty of understanding and human feeling, without love, loyalty, and compassion, becomes a senseless code. And here is the core of Wolfram's humanism, a humanism of a wholly different sort from that of the humanist-poet Gottfried von Strassburg. The highest ethical duties of a man are shame and compassion; these are mediated by manly courtesy.

One learns these more from suffering than from instruction. Parzival is denounced before Arthur's court by Kundrie, outwardly monstrous, inwardly pleasing to God—just the opposite of Parzival, who bears the outward signs of knighthood (315,10), but whose heart is empty of compassion and of what she calls "rehte sinne" (cf. 316,3 ff.), perhaps "reasoned judgment," or "common sense." In this context it also implies the human decency to wish to help a suffering man. Neither his bold heart nor his manly courtesy were any use to him in facing this duty:

> waz half in küenes herzen rat
> und wâriu zuht bî manheit?
>
> (319, 4–5)

Far from seeing the cause of his failure, Parzival makes Gurnemanz and his lessons in courtesy responsible for it:

> sol ich durch mîner zuht gebot
> hoeren nû der werlde spot,
> sô mac sîn râten niht sîn ganz:
> mir riet der werde Gurnemanz
> daz ich vrevellîche vrage mite
> und immer gein unvuoge strite.
> (330,1–6)

If now I must suffer the scorn of the world for following the commandments of courtesy, then perhaps something was lacking in the counsel of worthy Gurnemanz when he urged me to avoid foolish questions and strive ever against boorishness.

But this can no more be taken to represent the author's sentiment than can Parzival's rejection of God a few lines later. He accuses God for not having warded off the shame and disgrace he now suffers. Both the captain of courtesy and the God of Christianity have let him down, have failed to pay him the service they owe him, and so he renounces both of them. It is self-pity and self-excusing worthy of a Kalogreant, and Wolfram, who knew Hartmann's *Iwein* very well, was certainly aware that his hero was in the grips of a test of humanity, of his sense of self and personal responsibility, that Hartmann's hero had taken and passed. No sooner is Iwein denounced in circumstances parallel to Parzival's, than he takes all the blame upon himself:

> er verlôs sîn selbes hulde:
> wan ern mohte die schulde
> ûf niemen anders gesagen . . .
> (*Iwein* 3221–23)

He fell out of favor with himself, since he was not capable of blaming anyone else for his own guilt.

The burden of guilt he takes on himself drives him mad. Parzival, in pointed and probably intentional contrast to Iwein, rides about the countryside stewing in his own juices, fighting, thinking of his wife and the Grail, and in his long period of *goteshaz* it gradually becomes clear to him that neither God nor Gurnemanz have led him astray, but only his own profound foolishness.

Neither warrior ways nor courtliness nor piety are questioned values in Wolfram's work, but any one of them becomes dangerous and a source of a man's moral destruction when they are practiced without the core of human feeling which gives them substance and validity.

Parzival develops a new sensibility in his years of wandering, and this incorporates courtly good manners with that fine sense of humanity and compassion that is the essence of courtesy at its best. The events on Good Friday that lead him to Trevrizent begin in an encounter with his cousin Sigune, now a hermitess living a life of penitence, mourning over the corpse of her dead lover. He approaches her cell on horseback, but when he sees a woman through the window, he at once regrets his lack of courtesy in riding so close; he hears her voice, wheels his horse around, and trots off at a distance. He feels "shame" ("diu selbe schame tet im wê"—437,8), but this is that shame that directs the fear of offense in both directions: outward toward the person to be shielded and inward to one's own conscience, that is, *verecundia*. Here it is the fear of being thought eavesdropping, of giving offense or causing embarrassment to an unprotected woman. His bearing is the "taking back" of the rape of Jeschute. He ties his horse to a tree and lays aside his shield and sword "durch zuht," out of courtesy. This sensitivity of feeling is symptomatic for a new composition of the inner man. Now his "manly courtesy" is nourished by true human feeling. And it is precisely this quality that in part leads to the *metanoia*, the inner reversal that changes the course of his fate. He leaves the Grey Knight Kahenîs and his daughters, and is overcome by a feeling of remorse and sorrow, a longing for innocence and reconciliation with God:

> hin ritet Herzeloide vruht.
> dem riet sîn manlîchiu zuht
> kiusche und erbarmunge:
> sît Herzeloide diu junge
> in hete ûf gerbet triuwe,
> sich huop sîns herzen riuwe.
> (451,3–8)

Away rides the son of Herzeloyde. His manly courtesy urged innocence and compassion on him: and since young Herzeloyde had bequeathed to him a loving and merciful nature, remorse swelled up in his heart.

It is difficult to reconcile a negative interpretation of Gurnemanz's lessons with the lines "dem riet sîn manlîchiu zuht / kiusche und erbarmunge," since they show that two of the highest values of Wolfram's work, *kiusche*[12] and *erbarmunge*, are called forth at a critical moment by *manlîchiu zuht*. His return to God required this quality. What occurs in the above passage is something like an internal healing, a psychological cure, and this takes the form of a knitting of ideologies that have been in a state of schism. Courtliness and humanity now work in concert with his inherited *triuwe*.

The scene that follows, Parzival's time spent in lament and confession with Trevrizent, is a mirror of true courtesy. The two men converse long and intimately. The air is free of anger and resentment, even when the older man chides the younger harshly. The two forage together for food; they become comrades ("gesellen"—486,1). Trevrizent is an embodiment of *triuwe* and *erbermde*, charity and mercy. He has renounced knighthood and the service of ladies in order to do penance, not for himself, but for his brother, Anfortas, so that God would ease Anfortas' suffering. It is Christ-like self-sacrifice, vicarious suffering, and it is consistent with this stance that at the end of the scene he takes Parzival's sins upon himself. The atmosphere of the entire episode is set in direct contrast to the customs and pastimes of the court: their kitchen was bare, there was no baking and roasting there, and yet no host had ever treated him better, neither Gurnemanz nor the entire host at the Grail castle (cf. 486,10 ff.); there is no laughing and joking; Parzival, the sad one, not the merry one (491,18), is weighed down by the burden of remorse.

Werner Schrader sensed in Wolfram's use of the concept *hövescheit* something like a protest against courtly culture.[13] If such a mute protest is present at all, then it is directed against the life of the court, not against the ideals of courtliness and humanity that arose in that culture. At the end of *Parzival* Wolfram gives us a description of the hero's son Loherangrîn, which I would take as a close approximation to Wolfram's notions of the ideal man:

> er kunde wol gebaren.
> man muoste in vür den klaren
> und vür den manlîchen
> haben in al den rîchen,
> swâ man sin künde gewan.
> hövesch, mit zühten wîs ein man,
> mit triuwen milde, âne aderstôz
> was sîn lîp missewende blôz.
>
> (825,3–10)

He knew how to bear himself well. In all lands to which his reputation spread he was known as beautiful and manly, courtly, and wise in his courtesies, generous in his compassion; he led a life free of vacillation and wrong-doing.

Here again we have the combination of manliness with courtesy, and again the purely external ("wol gebaren") is accompanied by that inner quality highest in Wolfram's hierarchy of virtues, *triuwe*.

‹›

To the many antitheses that distinguish Gottfried von Strassburg from Wolfram von Eschenbach we can add one more: these two poets show us in as distinct a polarity as we could hope for two aspects of courtliness inherent in that concept. In Gottfried's *Tristan* it is a code of refined behavior which maintains order and regulates the interactions of men at court, court manners. But here it invariably becomes a network of stratagems, a set of acquired skills aimed at pleasing princes, capturing favor, warding off envy and intrigue, and advancing the man who masters them in a career. It is a screen that masks off the inner world of noble hearts and souls from the civilized jungle without. In Wolfram's *Parzival* courtliness is an ideal code which permits humanity and compassion to express themselves in the composition of a man's outward bearing and in the orchestration of his dealings with others. The field of combat, the forest, the unknown, and even occasionally the court, become the school of magnanimity and the theater of compassion.

It is an odd paradox that the court and court society call forth a code of virtuous and humane behavior, which in its real application is invariably contaminated to some extent by its very practicality, by its usefulness in the life of the court. It is at the same time an ethical code, an instrument of ambition, and a mask for self-interest, always practiced with an element of dissimulation. But the air that the chivalric courtly knight breathes is pure and uncontaminated. This is yet another factor that commended the figure of the knight to the clerical authors of romance. Their own world was the dispiriting realm of intrigue and self-seeking, tinselled with external pomp and gaiety, the court. It must have been like a return to innocence to escape to the pure realm of Celtic fairy tale and amorous adventure where courtliness could be practiced with only the highest of motives.

Conclusion

I N THE course of the late twelfth and early thirteenth centuries the church reform gradually destroyed the institutional basis of this wave of civilizing. The bishopric no longer was a political instrument in the hands of the king; the art of the courtier no longer was a means of attaining it. A broad, humanistic education lost its value as a preparation for state service, and young men sought specialized training in the law. The episcopacy no longer required a great, commanding, and exceptionally gifted human being. The administration of dioceses was carried out by administrative machinery set in place and operated by the papacy, and the person of the bishop, as long as he was loyal to papal political interests, made little difference.[1] The episcopacy sank back into mediocrity, and if an occasional man of brilliance rose above that level, it was due more to chance than institutional design.

The vanishing of a period of greatness was not lost on contemporaries. Toward the end of the thirteenth century, a Bamberg schoolmaster, Hugo of Trimberg, lamented the decline of the episcopacy, evoking the great figures of the past:

> Sant Otten, sant Annen, sant Gothart
> Und sant Thomas von Kandelberc
> Brâhte ir zuht und reiniu werc
> Ze hofe an hôhe wirdikeit.
> *(Renner* 782–85)

Saint Otto, Saint Anno, Saint Godehard, and Saint Thomas of Canterbury, attained high honor at court by their courtesy and their good works.

The greatness of these clerical courtiers from the past, he continues, has its cause in the fact that good and honored princes were once able to choose men of upright and honest disposition as their servants. Now, however, the choice of bishops has fallen into the hands of the clergy, and the result is that there are no more "heilige bischöfe" to be found on earth (786 ff.). Hugo's observations are in harmony with those of modern historians. The investiture controversy had set limits on the participation of the secular ruler in the selection and installation of bishops. The figure of the mighty imperial bishop, whom Hugo calls "pfaffenfürsten" (825), therefore disappeared from the scene. It is remarkable that a canon of the Bamberg cathedral and head of the school could place the blame for this decline on a return to canonical procedure in the selection of bishops! We can take it as a testimony to the strength of the imperial tradition in Bamberg that this schoolmaster could glorify the days when the emperor still controlled episcopal elections.

By the middle of the thirteenth century there was a widespread awareness that a great age had passed and a period of decline had set in. The heirs of the great tradition of romance in Germany sensed that their own works stood in the shadow of those of their predecessors. Rudolf von Ems laments that he and his contemporaries are mere workmen who paste together words and rhymes, but the substance and the high ethical ideals of past poets elude them. Konrad von Würzburg complains about the proliferation of poetry and the corresponding decline in its quality. The heart and soul seem gone out of narrative. Alas, these are not just humility formulae put to the lie by the great works they introduce. The endlessly long and endlessly tedious epics produced by writers like Rudolf and Konrad more than bear out their authors' feeling that only the outward form of the classical romance remains; the sublime vision of the courtly-chivalric knight whose character develops in his encounter with destiny has lost its roots in reality.

The mournful atmosphere of a work like the Old French *La Mort le Roi Artu* reveals a great deal about the climate of the times. The title announces the theme: Arthur's death and the collapse of the civilization whose highest representative he was. When the romance opens the main characters, Arthur, Gawain, and Lancelot, are old men. Twenty years have passed, we are told at the beginning, since any *aventure* has occurred in the entire realm of Logres. These tired and sapped has-been warriors have no hope of reviving the vitality of bygone days. Disillusioned and gloomy, they face enemies who are their match; they suffer wounds that cause real physical agony; they go relentlessly toward their destruction, having lost that magic cloak of invulnerability they had worn in the works of earlier writers. Thomasin von Zirclaere had lamented as early as 1216 that in his times there are no more Gawains, Parzivals, and Lancelots, that virtue is passing from the world, and the courts are peopled by coarse, ruthless, and grasping scoundrels.

There is certainly an element in all this of *laudatio temporis acti*, golden age thinking, and it is tempting to believe that in the real circumstances of chivalric life, little had changed from the middle of the twelfth to the middle of the thirteenth century. But no, the *topos* is not empty, but an observation of contemporary reality. There had been real changes in the economy of Germany. The weakening of the emperor had begun that was to continue in a more or less straight line until the unglorious end of the Holy Roman Empire. The impoverishment of the German nobility had begun, a development that found effective resistance only in the Lutheran reformation.

At the same time the humanist schools were in a period of decline. Scholasticism guided thought and inquiry into the rigid strictures of its method. Poetry fell into discredit as a means of conveying truth, and while great works of humanistic poetic philosophy like Alain of Lille's *Anticlaudianus* may still have aroused admiration, they no longer inspired imitation. Young poets did not conceive works as poetic replies to Claudian aimed at outbidding antiquity in the level of truth and of poetic accomplishment. By and large they did not even read the ancient authors anymore, let alone pit themselves against that age in grand poetic replies. They conceived disputations and filed away at sentences and syllogisms, and if anyone from antiquity commanded their attention, it was Aristotle.

One bequest from the twelfth century that did remain vital in the midst of this transformation of intellectual and social life was the veil of idealizing the writers of romance cast over the life of the knight. Courtly ideals maintained themselves in romance like a cocoon that has given up the life in it and waits for a new occupant, an event that occurs in the life of ideas and literary forms, if not in that of butterflies. The revitalizing of courtliness that occurred in the Renaissance of the fifteenth and sixteenth centuries nourished and expressed itself regularly in the idiom of courtly romance.

‹›

Now it is time to look back and summarize the developments we observed earlier.

I do not think it would overstate the case too badly if we say that courtliness is medieval Europe's memory of the Roman statesman, of his humanity and urbane skillfulness in guiding the state and in facing the trials of public life. It overstates it only to the extent of putting the intellectual history of courtliness in the foreground. In its social history it first emerges attached to that institution which was and saw itself as the continuator of the Roman empire: the German imperial courts. Otto of Freising, we recall, admired the Lombards particularly because, in spite of the mixing of Roman with German blood, they retained the urbanity of the Latin language and the refined elegance of Roman manners, and they continued to imitate the ways of ancient Rome in the governing of their cities. (Cf. *Gesta Frid.* 2.13, p. 116; see above, p. 143.) These are indeed the things an intellectual and statesman with close ties to the emperor in the twelfth century is bound to admire: elegance of manners and speech combined with statesmanship in imitation of ancient Roman ways. Among the men in imperial service the memory of ancient Rome and its ruling aristocracy never faded altogether. That memory, preserved in the form of imperial tradition and school curriculum, was a shaping and articulating force upon which any emperor with a sufficiently broad vision or a sufficiently sharp historical sense could call to lend style and the aura of antiquity to his administration and to the activities of the men who surrounded him. The counselors of a king are always gentle, modest, and restrained. The power relationships in force at court impose this kind of behavior on that group of men. The same is true in any situation where authority is concentrated in a single person. The children of an authoritarian father or the pupils of an authoritarian teacher will feel what force it is that imposes restraint and good manners on them, even if they have never been taught manners by a humanistically educated pedagogue. But the forces that commend orderly behavior at a ruler's court or at any center of government are far more complex than the mere concentration of authority. The two main complicating factors are policy and competition for favor. These two make of speech and action something quite different from what they are in everyday life. Words, gestures, intonation, and facial expression all bear meaning, express policy—no act or gesture is random. The elements of favor and standing in a hierarchy become so much a part of behavior at Japanese and Chinese courts that they are expressed in depth of bow, tone of voice, and a wide spectrum of forms of address. Circumstances in court society subject action to etiquette, prescribe a stylized speech and posture, force character itself into preformed molds, order human beings into typical constellations, and guide them along typical chains of events. Conduct becomes so highly structured that life approaches art: the courtier is himself a work of art, his appearance a portrait, his experience a narrative. It is more than just a whimsical metaphor to say that court life is literature operating in the medium of reality rather than the written word. Court life acquires its own style, its aesthetic of behavior, its cast of characters. But at the beginning of this process of aestheticising is the decision of a ruler and the shaping and articulating imposed on conduct by some "genial and especially clever individual." If, as I said earlier, the forms of behavior are as open to shaping and modeling as the forms of sculpture, then both arts must also have their artist and his style. The style of European courtliness was neoclassical; the artists and architects of that code shaped the style and aesthetic of court life according to the memory of the Roman statesman, and we can still see Gerald of Wales at work sculpting the values of lay nobility according to this model when he says that the ideal country is that whose knights are clad both in the toga and in armor.

The imperial church under the Ottonian emperors was the matrix for courtliness in medieval Europe. From the narrower context of the court it spread into the empire, and an essential factor in this spread was the cathedral schools and their role of preparing men for service to the state. The innovations of Otto the Great and Brun of Cologne insured the continuity of court ideals by making them part of a program of education. Elias' conception of the process of civilizing credits education with only a peripheral role. He sees its origins and continuity rooted in factors built into a feudal-courtly society enjoying a growing population and economy. We can say decidedly that this model by itself cannot explain the civilizing trends among laity and clergy in our period. This development is inseparable from instruction, from a system of education institutionalized in the cathedral schools, a program of educating which became practical because it was linked to the governing of the state. No courtier from the tenth century on would have sensed any misunderstanding if he were asked whether courtliness were not the result of an education in court manners and ways, *curialis nutritura* or *regalis nutritura* or *höveschiu zuht*. Courtliness is learned from a teacher especially qualified by his *suavitas delectabilium morum* to transmit the *forma recte vivendi*.

I stress again that court manners did not originate in the reign of Otto the Great. The innovation of Otto and his brother Brun was to create an institutional basis for the widespread teaching of an ideal of court manners based on a Roman model. To locate the exact beginnings of this ideal in earlier medieval Europe has not proven possible here. We observed the spread of court manners, as part of a program of education, in particularly clear focus in the reforms of Bishop Azelinus at Hildesheim. He came to this once illustrious, now rustic diocese from the court of Henry III, a court that represented a highpoint of imperial neoclassicism. It was a court populated by men like Wipo, Anno of Cologne, Anselm of Besate, and Adalbert of Bremen. Azelinus set about imposing the ways of the court on the local clergy. He taught them refinement, scrupulousness, and sophistication in manner of living and dress; he ruled in such a way as to be loved rather than feared; he no doubt strove to create an atmosphere of joy, affability, and good humor, such as the one that prevailed at the court of Henry III and which also found expression in the *Ruodlieb*. He enjoined on them table manners and refined good taste in the choice of foods. But the other half of this education was instruction in Latin letters, and he was so intent on furnishing a "literary" education of high quality, that he engaged one of the most talented and sought after young men in the empire, Benno, later bishop of Osnabrück, luring him away from the emperor's service with "grand promises."

This model is paradigmatic for the spread of courtesy, in its earliest recognizable form, from the court outward into the empire. It shows us the importance of the courtier bishop and of the cathedral school as transmitters.

We gained some insight into the content of an education in ways appropriate to the court. A central ideal was "beauty of manners" or "elegance of manners." This is restrained self-government or self-control, and it implies that actions are subjected to ideals of delicacy, humanity, considerateness, and respect for the feelings of other men. It is a high ideal, cultivated by orthodox and worldly clergy at court, as well as by laymen. The mastery of this virtue produces a life in harmony with the demands of God and the world. In our discussion we were able to confirm that Gottfried von Strassburg's observations on *moraliteit* in *Tristan* represent an important text in intellectual history and the history of education. The lines run,

> under aller dirre lere
> gab er ir eine unmüezekeit,
> die heizen wir moraliteit.
> diu kunst diu leret schoene site:
> da solten alle vrouwen mite
> in ir jugent unmüezic wesen.
> moraliteit daz süeze lesen
> deist saelic unde reine.
> ir lere hat gemeine
> mit der werlde und mit gote.
> si leret uns in ir gebote
> got unde der werlde gevallen:
> sist edelen herzen allen
> zeiner ammen gegeben,
> daz si ir lipnar unde ir leben
> suochen in ir lere;
> wan sin hant guot noch ere,
> ezn lere si moraliteit.
>   (8002–19)

Amidst all these forms of learning he imposed on her one discipline that we call "moral instruction." This is the art that teaches beauty of manners. All women should occupy themselves with this in their youth. Moral instruction, this sweet art, bestows a blessed life and renders its devotee above reproach. Its teaching makes common cause with the world and with God. Its rule teaches us to please God and the world. It is given to all noble hearts as a nursemaid, in whose doctrine they can seek nourishment and life; for without the guidance of moral instruction they will attain neither wealth nor honor.

Other elements of "beauty of manners" are *urbanitas, disciplina, mansuetudo, verecundia,* and *affabilitas.*

But accompanying this doctrine, and in varying degrees legitimately attached to it, is a social code of elegance, urbanity, and refinement. It is expressed in scrupulousness of dress and table manners, refinement in eating and drinking, in speech and gesture. Indeed, the mastery of external refinements of life is seen as an outward sign of that inner control, harmony, and composition that is the essence of *elegantia morum.* A man who masters all aspects of this ideal is suited for service in the royal chapel, as we learned from the description of Meinwerk of Paderborn: "Meinwerk . . . born of the royal family, was judged suited for royal service because of his elegance of manners, and, called to the palace, he became a royal chaplain."

I began this book with a look at popular views of the Middle Ages as a period brutal and coarse but capable of high flights of fancy and airy ideals. I would like to place the complex of court virtues grouped under *elegantia morum,* and the whole social scene in which these virtues came into effect, against those popular views. A more balanced picture would show the Middle Ages as the first period in the modern West when ideas of polite civil life arose and spread on a broad scale, when knights first took it upon themselves to mitigate the violence typical in any warrior class with ideals of restraint and mercy. The cruelty and inhumanity of the age can justly be seen as departures from a powerful, effective, and widely held ideal of delicacy and respect for life and the feelings of others.

Courtliness and courtly humanity were, next to Christian ideals, the most powerful civilizing forces in the West since ancient Rome. If the perception of this role has been dim in modern times, it is partly because court bishops and worldly clergy lacked historians who observed their civilizing role directly. Their biographers observed it only indirectly. Courtly romance gave eloquent testimony to the effects of this civilizing force, but its roots and motives were obscured by the displacement from educated aristocracy to the knight, from court to the field and forest, from love and respect for humanity to love and respect for women. Now we see that the ideal of courtly humanity in *Parzival* had roots and a real social context in court life more or less contemporary with Wolfram. It was not merely some high-flung dream-vision masking a crude, brutal reality.

This brings us to the role of conservative clerics and the monastic world in the formation of courtly ideals. It is evident that the clergy were largely the bearers and transmitters of these ideals. But this is the worldly clergy, the high aristocracy in state service, members of the imperial church and those who strove for that position. The court was the nurturing institution. In respect to the monasteries, the religious movements tossed up by the church reform, Cluniacs, Carthusians, Premonstratensians, Augustinian canons, we can say decidedly that these were by and large a retarding force in the spread of court manners, not a cultivator, certainly not an originator of them. Conservative clergy resisted courtliness vehemently, not only in members of the clerical order, but particularly in lay nobility. How should this have been otherwise? The practice that was at the root of this entire wave of civilizing was lay investiture, the emperor's granting of bishoprics to his favorite courtiers. But this practice was one of the main targets of church reformers, the one that gave its name to the entire conflict. The conservative clergy and adherents of the reform movement saw in courtliness by and large only its negative aspects: splendid clothing, materialism and sensuality, love of wealth, pursuit of vainglory and foolish worldly wisdom. They saw courtliness as a blight on the lay nobility, numbing its warrior spirits, holding it enchained in sloth, luxury, and lustfulness. They regarded it as a real political danger, a threat to the divine order, since it is the god-given task of the warrior to fight. These sentiments were completely reconcilable with the church's concern to maintain peace among the laity, with the movement for the "peace of God." It was necessary to stop senseless slaughter by pacifying the warriors; it was necessary at the same time to check depradations against individuals, the church and the order of the state, and this required a warrior class willing to fight. General peace and war in the name of justice were entirely reconcilable goals. The dual task of the clergy to attain them was neatly expressed in the metaphor of Orderic Vitalis: the cleric exercising correction on the laity is like a rider guiding his horse with both reins and spurs.

The ideal of a civilized knight apparently had little meaning for this level of the clergy. This is not to say that individual abbots and monasteries were not susceptible to court ideals. Just the contrary, these had a powerful appeal at all levels of educated society. But a courtly monastery was an anomaly and a potential object of attack for conservative churchmen. Courtliness can by no stretch of the imagination be seen as having arisen in the monastic life, whatever inroads it may have made there. The influence of conservative, orthodox

Christian thought on the figure of the chivalric knight of romance is quite a different question. Here the crusading ideal and the notion of the *miles christianus* certainly had a part to play. But that question is outside the scope of this study.

The advisors to the German kings, impelled by the nature and requirements of their office and inspired by the intellectual heritage of classical antiquity, fashioned medieval courtesy in its earliest formation. Under the Ottonian and Salian emperors it gradually developed into a code. Its practitioners were depicted as urbane, splendid, handsome, and skillful courtiers, highly learned, highly articulate—marvels and paragons in every regard. It was probably not only the most frivolous among them who had sharp eyes for fashion and style. We hear of a courtier bishop like Gebhard of Regensburg who struck amazement into Thietmar of Merseburg through the exotic foreign customs and manners he adopted. We hear of the eager acceptance of new fashions from Provence in the mid-eleventh century at the court of Henry III. We hear of Adalbert of Bremen claiming with dubious justification to be a descendant of Otto II and Theophanu and cultivating Byzantine dress and manners to display the fact. Should these be taken to show how threadbare and rustic the Germans were, since they repeatedly have to appropriate customs from foreigners? Probably they show us how open to style and fashion the imperial courts were. Had the German courtiers been backward and rustic in comparison to the French, the resistance to French customs would surely have been more widespread than it was. Siegfried of Gorze in his protest against French frivolities at the German courts was stopping one minor hole in a dike long since riddled with other, bigger holes. The German imperial courts surpassed in stature those of the French king and of the French feudal nobility. This was known and accepted by contemporaries. Chrétien de Troyes takes as the heroine of his *Cligès* the daughter of the German emperor. She comes onto the scene because the wifeless Byzantine emperor, seeking an appropriate match, is urged to court the charming, gentle, beautiful daughter of this rich and powerful monarch (*Cligès* 2619ff.). He could hardly have depicted Fenice this way and assigned her that station if the German courts were perceived in France as comparatively backward. Nor is it conceivable that Chrétien might have conceded superiority in power and wealth to the empire while holding a low opinion of the emperor's court on the score of manners and customs. Chrétien knew perfectly well—and it was common knowledge among the educated generally—that while superiority in learning and chivalry had passed from Rome to France, Germany had inherited empire, and that meant the traditions of Roman rule and Roman statesmanship. The awe in which the French lay nobility stood before that bequest and those traditions is best depicted in Jean de Renart's *Roman de Guillaume de Dole*.

Courtliness went hand in hand with empire. Konrad von Megenberg states this principle outright, and while a statement from an emperor's household book from the mid-fourteenth century cannot be expected to shed much light on relationships two centuries earlier, it is not unlikely that there is a strong imperial tradition preserved in his comment:

Congruit igitur ministros Cesaris tanto curialiores esse, id est bonis moribus splendidiores, quanto curia eius sublimior est curiis omnium secularium miliciarum.

It behoves the ministers of the emperor, then, to be all the more courtly—that is, resplendent with good manners—in the same degree that the emperor's court is exalted above the courts of all secular powers. (*Yconomica* 2.4, chap. 12, p. 199)

But whatever memory of past tradition is present in Konrad's words, it is a virtual certainty that standards of behavior, ethical and social ideals modeled on antiquity, guided the life and action of the imperial ministers, probably since late antiquity, and that these tended to spread among worldly clergy with the advent of the Ottonian imperial church.

At the same time that courtly epithets become attached to court clergy, they appear in the descriptions of kings and emperors. The qualities that applied to the advisor also were seen as appropriate and the matter of praise in the monarch: modesty, clemency, gentleness, and affability. In descriptions of lesser feudal nobility, however, we do not encounter courtly epithets until the second half of the twelfth century. The portraits of nobles that have come down to us portray them prior to this date within the archaic value system of a warrior class. The ideal duke or count is shrewd, wealthy, generous, and powerful. He inspires fear in his enemies and has great armies of loyal followers. He may also be described as a good Christian, friendly and generous to priests and monks, a benefactor and protector of churches and monasteries. The urge of the lay nobility to appear in their portraits as courtly gentlemen makes itself felt only after the idealized knight of romance has captivated the interest of this class, molded its values and sensibilities.

In discussing the influences that commended an ideal of courtesy to the knighthood, we found it useful to distinguish between unfree and free knights. The military retainers attached to a ruler's court lived under circumstances very different from those that obtained in the life of the land-owning nobleman. Elias' model of the beginnings of the civilizing process applies very well to the former. When a warrior class collects at court, tensions arise which make the taming and *Verhöflichung* of this group a social and political necessity. We had a marvelous illustration of this in Saxo's description of the discipline imposed at the court of Canute the Great. At the end of a campaign, a great crowd of knights collects at the court, and the resulting disorder makes discipline imperative. Canute calls upon his wise counselor, Opo of Seeland, to institute such an order. He does so, polishing their boorish, ruffian manners, and imbuing even the boldest of them with a "beautiful habit of conduct." They learn respectful civil conduct, down to the minor duties of social life. The punishments for abusers of the code are severe: debasement and exclusion. What we can add to Elias' model from the lessons of this example is the element of instruction, the imposition of a program of discipline on an unruly warrior class by an educator and royal advisor acting at the command of the king. Again we see that the beginnings of courtliness are inseparable from the influence and active volition of a ruler, working together with an educated minister of the court. Court life by its very nature rewards wit, cunning, eloquence, and a restrained and modest bearing; it punishes boorishness, open conflict. But this "nature" is not some blind and elemental law of aristocratic society, but rather a potential inherent in the structure of power relationships at the center of government, called to life by the conscious volition of a ruler, transmitted and held in force by instruction.

What influences and considerations commended courtliness to the higher lay nobility is a much more complex question. I can only suggest an indirect answer to it. We know that this level of the nobility was very open to fashion. Long hair, curly-topped shoes, and tight-fitting dress swept like wild-fire through the European aristocracy at the end of the eleventh and beginning of the twelfth century. "All those who fancied themselves courtly" embraced these customs, even at the peril of their souls. But this rash and impulsive eagerness for fashion is only the materialistic and outward expression of a spiritual penchant endemic to the class: its susceptibility to ideals. This penchant is at work in inspiring armies of noblemen to join the crusades. Alongside the crusading ideal, that of the courtly gentleman and the educated knight was in the air.

But whatever influences were in the air, the inspiration that remains for us most visible was the courtly romance and the character it had invented, the chivalric knight. The worldly clergy had obligations to the laity, to instruct and correct their ways. A common instrument of instruction at court was the history, *Gesta antiquorum principum*, *Historia regum*. These gradually assimilated to the *fabulae* which competed with them for the attention of court audiences, and the assimilation is strikingly realized in Geoffrey of Monmouth's *Historia regum Britanniae*. Two decades after the appearance of Geoffrey's work the vernacular romance in rhymed verse, retelling the fabulous or historical deeds of ancient kings and knights, was wildly popular.

The romance is the invention of clerical authors. Their motives were various. The poets of romance could become famous and wealthy. They could obtain a place in the favor of worldly lords by the writing of narrative, just as an earlier generation could gain or retain favor by writing panegyrics to the ruler or by dedicating learned works of rhetoric or history to him. But this is to see their motives at their lowest. They also were exercising the clerical duty of correction and instruction. The romance instructed in courtesy. Hence the knights at the court of Arnold of Guines could spend winter nights hearing the tales of Arthur and Guinevere or of Tristan and Isolde, to which the learned narrators added the "serious observations of moral instruction." Thomasin von Zirclaere attacks the romances because of the lies and fables they contain, but does not condemn them altogether, because they also contain lessons in courtesy which urge that code on the listener as a model to imitate:

> wan si bezeichenunge hât
> der zuht unde der wârheit:
> daz wâr man mit lüge kleit.
> (*Welscher Gast* 1124–26)

[Romances] contain representations of courtesy and of truth: they use the lies of the literal meaning to clothe a higher truth.

In creating the figure of the chivalric knight, the poet-cleric amalgamated ideals at home in the milieu of the court clergy with those of the warrior class. In doing so the poets of romance will have felt urged on not only by a pedagogic impulse and a sense that they, the courtly clerics, are the possessors and administrators of a higher code of civilized life, but also by envy for the life of the knight. Whatever their feeling of superiority on grounds of learning and manners, they knew that their form of life denied to them the heroism of the knight's. We recall the cleric-lover of Andreas' *De amore* who, rebuffed by the lady to whom he pays court because of his effeminate robes and his sedentary, studious way of life, replies that he would like nothing better than to show boldness of heart and chivalric courage, but is restrained from doing so by custom and law. Thomasin also points out that clerics, for all their sense of superiority, envied knights their way of life (*Welscher Gast* 2642 ff., 2669). And so it may be that the cleric-poets of romance were not only creating an educational model for knights and laymen to imitate, but were indulging in their own wish-dreams of a form of life that combines the freedom, heroism and amorous license of the knight with the civilized ideals of the courtly cleric.

The earliest romances, the romances of antiquity, have two themes: love and chivalric combat. But a quite different theme enters romance in the works of Chrétien: the education or the moral formation of the knight. Mere chivalric activity without some higher motive brings a knight to ruin. Only the gradual acquisition of the values of human-ity, respect for human life and for the feelings of other human beings, can reconcile Yvain and Perceval with God and the world. In these two works and their German translations the moral element of medi-eval courtesy finds its most sublime expression.

In the course of my reading for this book, my eyes were open from the outset for any traces of what has come to be called "courtly love." But I found nothing that would confirm a cult of "courtly love" as it is represented in, say, the poems of the troubadours, in Chrétien's *Lan-celot*, in the Tristan romance, or in the first two books of Andreas' *De amore*. True, the biographer of Conrad of Salzburg accuses Henry IV of awarding abbacies and bishoprics solely upon the advice of beau-tiful women of high nobility, whose voices carry great weight at court. But this is more a discrediting slander than a revelation of a cult of the woman at that court. The reproach of uxuriousness touched a fair number of courtier bishops and courtly clerics, but this also says nothing about a cult of courtly love. But we have also seen, on the periphery of our theme, indications of a cult of refined love. It may be that its essential nature is distorted in *Lancelot* and *De amore*, but it existed nonetheless. The author of *Facetus* was writing a practical guide to life for young gentlemen. He certainly would not have de-voted the majority of his work to instructions on refined and sophisti-cated conduct of love if he were speaking to a sensibility that did not exist. Let us say that the sources treated here simply do not shed much light on notions of romantic love current in the twelfth century. These notions were connected with the ideal of courtliness and could form an amalgamation with that code. We cannot penetrate further into the nature of courtly love on the basis of what we have learned here. But this after all is not particularly surprising. The best sources on this cult of love are lyric and romance, not Latin historiography or biography. The twelfth century discovered, perhaps it would not be an exaggeration to say—with C. S. Lewis—it invented the notion of romantic love. The silence of historical sources on the subject is no argument against its existence. I wonder what the results might be if we searched in historical writings from the eighteenth century and in the writings of clerical authors for traces of the kind of romantic sensibilities expressed in Goethe's *Die Leiden des jungen Werther*. These sensibilities were or became widespread. If pastors, historians, and court favor-seekers saw this brand of emotion as sinful, ludicrous, or if they merely ignored it, this would tell us nothing about its ability to shape and give expression to the sentiments of Goethe's readers. Imaginative literature is the best source for history of sensibilities. The courtly literature of the twelfth century shows us the emergence in that age of a new mode of feeling, a new cult of emotion. The uncertain state of scholarship on the subject of courtly love shows us only that it is an area much-studied but ill-understood.

But I do find it surprising that in the many texts giving us vivid glimpses into the life of the medieval court in the eleventh and twelfth centuries, there is no trace of the exaltation of women, so prominent a feature of courtly literature. My subject was the civilizing of Europe, and not only traditional scholarship but common sense lead us to believe that women had a role to play in this process. The presence of women exercises a moderating, restraining influence on male society. And in the setting of a ruler's court, where restraint, friendliness, and respectfulness are inalienable rules of conduct, it stands to reason that these modes of behavior came to apply to the treatment of women. But what of the active role of women in the courtly education, as for instance Eduard Wechssler has described it? High-placed women supposedly demanded a civilized, restrained mode of behavior from the clerics, knights, and entertainers who surrounded them, and in this way implanted courtly ideals into the unruly throngs of knights. There is to be sure Geoffrey of Monmouth's observation about the *facetae mulieres* at the court of King Arthur, who denied their affection to any man who had not proved himself three times in battle. This gives an interesting point of comparison with the courtly lady of romance and lyric, but hardly a confirmation of woman's role in the process of civilizing. The sources tell us much about courtly education, and they do not show woman as a mediator of it. But they tell us little about the motives impelling knights to seek such an education. It may well be that courtliness won the favor of women no less than that of rulers, and that this consideration urged a courtly education on young knights who were both amorous and ambitious.

‹›

A study of courtliness from the Latin sources will invariably lead to the German imperial courts. It is fairly evident that these courts had a central role to play in the formation and transmission of courtesy in

Europe. Their members were the bearers of what I called earlier the most important civilizing force in Europe since ancient Rome. The existence of an imperial tradition of court manners with classical models has been obscured by some assumptions that are firmly rooted in the social, political, and intellectual history of France and Germany from the high Middle Ages to the present. The first of these is quite simply the notion that the history of courtesy is inseparable from the history of vernacular courtly literature. Here no signs pointed to Germany; there were no literary sources prior to French courtly literature that might have indicated the presence of a sophisticated court etiquette there. That is, the only such source was the Latin *Ruodlieb*, but literary historians were content to see this as an anomaly, expressing perhaps the courtliness of the Benedictine who wrote it, not that of the court it celebrated. But *Ruodlieb* is anything but an anomaly. It is a highly original work which mirrors the high stage of moral, ethical and social sophistication attained at the imperial court, probably that of Henry III. If any of the fine scholars who studied the Provencal and Old French vocabularies of courtesy had looked to the Latin for models and analogues, they would have found themselves reverting constantly to German sources which often predate the vernacular ones. The central ethical-social concepts of courtesy, *curialitas, urbanitas, facetia, elegantia morum*, and so forth, are highly approachable; access to them is gained by a stratagem no more ingenious than leafing through Du Cange and the indices to the *Scriptores* series of the *Monumenta Germaniae Historica*. But this simple stratagem could only appear as a waste of time as long as vernacular courtly literature was seen as the starting point of the study of courtly ideals in Europe. But now it should be apparent that this literature relates to medieval courtliness as effect to cause and that to regard vernacular literature as the original mediator of courtesy is a distortion comparable to an argument that waves have their origin in the white water that appears at their crests, not in the long swells which precede and push them up.

Another hindrance to approaching medieval courtesy as a social and historical reality is the network of nationalistic prejudices surrounding the subject. Any time French-German literary and cultural relations are at issue, the questions stand in the shadow of the assumption that all influences flowed from west to east. To express it pointedly: a good many Frenchmen are persuaded or can be persuaded that whatever is elegant, urbane, courtly, and refined in Germany must have been imported from France. The corresponding prejudice in Germany has it that whatever is effeminate, overrefined, and unmanly in Germany derives from French influence. The influence exercised by the lyric and narrative poetry of France on Germany at the turn of the twelfth to the thirteenth century lends itself to understanding within these conventional categories. The dependence of Germany on France is an uncontestable fact of literary history. This fact has colored our understanding of the cultural relations between the two lands prior to the birth of courtly literature and created a blind spot in our perception of the early history of courtesy. We have seen that the reform abbot of Gorze complained loudly and bitterly against the importation of "French frivolities" that are sapping the honor and manhood of the empire. What more could nationalistic French historians ask for in the way of proving the early dependency of Germany on France; what more could German historians hope for in the way of reconfirming the age-old tendency of the French to corrupt the Germans? Siegfried's letter strikes the same chord as Wagner's Hans Sachs at the end of *Meistersinger*:

> . . . Welschen Dunst mit welschem Tand
> sie pflanzen uns in deutsches Land.

And even a great, critical scholar like Reto Bezzola could see in Siegfried of Gorze's letter the opposition of "l'esprit germanique" to "l'esprit du monde roman" (*Origines* 1:283), referring the reader to Steindorff's *Jahrbücher des deutschen Reiches unter Heinrich III.* as his authority! The German and the "Welscher" agree on the interpretation of the letter, even though both of them knew that Ralph Glaber had couched the same protest against Provencal influence on France in very nearly the same terms. Is this a case of "l'esprit germanique" speaking out of the mouth of an eleventh century French historian? Of course not. What Siegfried of Gorze and Ralph Glaber have in common is not any nationalistic spirit, but their devotion to the church reform and the antagonism to worldly ways that this produced. Both took it upon themselves to correct the ways of laymen, using fixed orthodox formulae. Provence was just a handy whipping boy. For Saxo Grammaticus, Germany was to serve the same purpose. Any marriage of a monarch with a foreign queen was likely to provoke the *topos*, "foreign ways are corrupting the upright customs of our ancient ancestors."

The modern perception of the cultural relations between Germany and France is strongly colored by the dichotomy, German "Kultur" versus French "civilisation." Art, music, philosophy, the abstract and the mystical, are the province of the Germans; the elegant civil life, to which the arts stand in a subservient position, that of the French. This dichotomy has played a dubious role in the intellectual history of these two lands. It came to its sharpest point during the first world war and in the tortured pages of Thomas Mann's *Betrachtungen eines Unpolitischen*. Mann represented Germany as the land of Luther, of Protestantism; the task of the Germans is "protest," rebellion against a shallow and corrupting French civilization. The spirit of that work is diffused broadly into the thinking of literary and intellectual historians on the interrelationships of Germany and France: the spiritualized intellectuality (*Geistigkeit*) of Germany began with Meister Eckhart, continued in Luther, pietism, and romanticism, and ended in the catastrophe of Fascism. French civilization begins in the medieval courts and continues through the age of Absolutism; its social and political sophistication expresses itself in courtly literature, in Classicism and the Enlightenment, and in the social novel. Politics and statesmanship are not the province of the Germans; on the contrary, they are failures at it, and two horrendous wars attest to that failure. But they are unsurpassable in the realm of music and philosophy. This dichotomy is set forth for us again by Hans Sachs further on in that same final aria:

> . . . zerging in Dunst
> das heil'ge röm'sche Reich,
> uns bliebe gleich
> die heil'ge deutsche Kunst!

"Even if the Holy Roman Empire dissolved into smoke, we would still possess, unchanged, holy German art!" These are dreadful lines on several accounts: to the nation that can be consoled in this way through the permanence of art, political cataclysm on the broadest scale might appear tolerable. And seen from the perspective of the late twentieth century, they take on the character of a bold and self-confident expression of a national tragic flaw. The lines are striking also for reversing the formula of civilization put forward at the beginning of this study: civilizations arise when culture willingly serves society, when artists, artisans, and warriors willingly subject themselves to a social and political order. But Hans Sachs', or Wagner's, sentiments send the social and political order to perdition and shield the artist in celestial isolation from the results. The role of the artist in romanticism generally is not a civilizing one; just the opposite. It is to emancipate the Promethean, and the subversion of a tyrannical or perverse or outdated political order can appear as a devout goal. But to the Germans the isolation of the aesthetic realm meant more than to the French and the English. And it had more prominent spokesmen. It was Nietzsche who so admired Wagner's claim that before his art civilization would dissipate "like fog before the sun."

The German empire in the earlier Middle Ages has no place within this model of German intellectual history. Its intellectual foundations presupposed a fruitful cooperation between Germany and Italian/ French traditions. A sense of the cultural antagonism between France and Germany existed mainly in the mind of reactionary reform monks. The civilizing trends of the period were the result of a multilayered collaboration between the political order and the order of culture. Germany was the country from which the impulses to civilizing emerged and spread.

The courtliness and urbanity of the imperial courts and their civilizing role in Europe are radically at odds with the conventional model of modern German intellectual history and have remained obscure in part because of it. I hope that this study will to some extent loosen the hold of this fixed idea on our notions of the origins and spread of courtliness in Europe.

But I would be sorry if my work were seen as speaking within the categories of that frame of thought. I am not arguing, "Not France but Germany was the birthplace of courtliness and European civilization!" I only conjure these sentiments at the end in order to exorcise them. The German imperial courts provided the social context in which an ideal of the Roman senator could be reborn and reshaped. The presupposition for this rebirth was the idea of *renovatio imperii Romani*. The architects of medieval courtesy were Germans, Frenchmen, and Italians. But it took a ruler of political foresight and vision like Otto I, and a cosmopolitan and liberal figure like Otto III, open to bold ideas and to the influence of antiquity, to form and cement the alliance between imperial politics and a system of education in which the civilizing forces of the period were called forth and nourished.

Notes

Introduction

1. *Vita Sancti Brunonis archiepiscopi Coloniensis auctore Ruotgero*, chaps. 5–6, *LB*, pp. 186–88.

2. Here I am following Josef Fleckenstein, "Königshof und Bischofschule unter Otto dem Grossen," *AKG* 38 (1956): 38–62.

3. Elias, *Über den Prozess der Zivilisation: Soziogenetische und psychogenetische Untersuchungen*, 2 vols., 2d ed., Suhrkamp Taschenbuch Wissenschaft, vols. 158–59 (1969; reprint, Frankfurt: Suhrkamp, 1979). There is now an English translation by Edmund Jephcott: *The Civilizing Process* (New York: Urizen, 1978). References here are to the 1979 German edition.

4. "Theory of Civilizing" refers to the epitome of Elias's ideas in the "Entwurf zu einer Theorie der Zivilisation," *Prozess* 2:312–454.

5. I take the term "literature of civilization" from Gary Schmidgall, *Shakespeare and the Courtly Aesthetic* (Berkeley and Los Angeles: University of California Press, 1981), p. 72 ff.

6. Cited here from *The Book of the Courtier*, translated by Charles S. Singleton (Garden City, N.Y.: Doubleday, 1959), pp. 295–96 (4.11). Castiglione's source was Plato, *Protagoras* 320C ff.

7. Singleton renders "giustizia e vergogna" as "justice and shame." But *vergogna* is closer to classical Latin *verecundia* than to the modern sense. Here surely it means regard for propriety, respectfulness, delicacy, tactfulness, the unwillingness to give offense. The phrase in the *Protagoras* is αἰδῶ τε καὶ δίκην, "respect and justice." Cf. Cicero's discussion of *iustitia et verecundia*: "Iustitiae partes sunt non violare homines, verecundiae non offendere" (*De officiis* 1.99). The latter is the essence of *decorum*.

8. See Frederick Barnard, "Culture and Civilization," in *Dictionary of the History of Ideas*, edited by Philip Wiener (New York: Charles Scribner's Sons, 1973), 1:613–21.

9. Cicero issues a warning against the lure of studies for the ruler which reads like an abstract of the moving forces behind *The Tempest*. See *De officiis* 1.157–58.

10. On Byzantine court ceremonial, see Arnold Toynbee, *Constantine Porphyrogenitus and his World* (London: Oxford University Press, 1973), p. 190 ff. On Japanese, see Ivan Morris, *The World of the Shining Prince: Court Life in Ancient Japan* (New York: Alfred A. Knopf, 1964; reprint, 1972), p. 154 ff.

11. This is the striking discovery of Daniel Javitch, *Poetry and Courtliness in Renaissance England* (Princeton, N.J.: Princeton University Press, 1978).

12. This is the approach of the very engaging work by Winfried Christ, *Rhetorik und Roman: Untersuchungen zu Gottfrieds von Strassburg Tristan und Isold*, Deutsche Studien, vol. 31 (Meisenheim am Glan: Hain, 1977).

13. Erich Köhler, "Einige Thesen zur Literatursoziologie," *GRM*, n.s., 24 (1974): 259.

14. See the discussion of the term *curialis* in John W. Baldwin, *Masters, Princes and Merchants: The Social Views of Peter the Chanter and His Circle* (Princeton, N.J.: Princeton University Press, 1970), 1: 175 ff.

15. "Bonus . . . esset Remensis archiepiscopatus, si non missas inde cantari oporteret." Quoted by Guibert of Nogent, *De vita sua* 1: 11, PL 156:853D.

Chapter 1: The Courtier Bishop

1. Hincmar of Reims, *De ordine palatii*, edited and translated by Thomas Gross and Rudolf Schieffer, 2d ed., MGH, Fontes iuris Germanici antiqui, vol. 3 (Hannover: Hahn, 1980). See the studies by Josef Fleckenstein, "Die Struktur des Hofes Karls des Grossen im Spiegel von Hinkmars *De ordine palatii*," *Zeitschrift des Aachener Geschichtsvereins* 83 (1976): 5–22, and "Karl der Grosse und sein Hof," in *Karl der Grosse: Lebenswerk und Nachleben*, vol. 1, *Persönlichkeit und Geschichte*, edited by Helmut Beumann, pp. 24–50 (Düsseldorf: Schwann, 1967). For a study of the sources on court structure and administration in the Middle Ages, see Paul Kirn, "Die mittelalterliche Staatsverwaltung als geistesgeschichtliches Problem," *HV* 27 (1932): 523–48.

2. See Paul Schubert, "Die Reichshofämter und ihre Inhaber bis um die Wende des 12. Jahrhunderts," *MIÖG* 34 (1913): 427–501.

3. Gilbert of Mons, *La Chronique de Gislebert de Mons*, edited by Leon Vanderkindere (Brussels: Kiessling, 1904), pp. 334–43. See Schubert, "Die Reichshofämter," pp. 498–99, for the importance of family influence in retaining court office.

4. The standard work on the court chapel is Josef Fleckenstein, *Die Hofkapelle der deutschen Könige*, 2 vols, MGH, Schriften 16:1–2 (Stuttgart: Hiersemann, 1959–66). Of the rich literature on the chapel, I will only cite those works to which I refer directly: Siegfried Görlitz, *Beiträge zur Geschichte der königlichen Hofkapelle im Zeitalter der Ottonen und Salier bis zum Beginn des Investiturstreites*, Historisch-Diplomatische Forschungen, vol. 1 (Weimar: Böhlau, 1936); Hans-Walter Klewitz, "Cancellaria: Ein Beitrag zur Geschichte des geistlichen Hofdienstes," *DA* 1 (1937): 44–79 (reprinted in Klewitz, *Ausgewählte Aufsätze zur Kirchen- und Geistesgeschichte des Mittelalters*, pp. 13–48 [Aalen: Scientia, 1971]). On the episcopal chapel: Siegfried Haider, *Das bischöfliche Kapellanat, I: Von den Anfängen bis in das 13. Jahrhundert*, MIÖG suppl. vol. 25 (Vienna and Cologne: Böhlau, 1977). See the review article by Stefan Weinfurter, "Zum bischöflichen Kapellanat und seiner Bedeutung für Köln: Bemerkungen zu einer Neuerscheinung über die Bischofskapelle," *AKG* 60 (1978): 203–12. See also Haider on the beginnings of the papal chapel, "Zu den Anfängen der päpstlichen Kapelle," *MIÖG* 87 (1979): 38–70. On the chapel of Friedrich II, see Hans Martin Schaller, "Die staufische Hofkapelle im Königreich Sizilien," *DA* 11 (1954–55): 462–505; idem, "Kanzlei und Hofkapelle Kaiser Friedrichs II.," *Annali dell' Istituto storico italo-germanico in Trento: Jahrbuch des italienisch-deutschen Instituts in Trient* 2 (1976): 75–116.

5. As Klewitz showed in "Cancellaria."

6. Cf. Fleckenstein, *Hofkapelle* 1:30, 40–42. Schaller, "Staufische Hofkapelle," p. 462: "Dieser Verband, exemt gegenüber der kirchlichen Hierarchie, immun gegenüber der staatlichen Verwaltung, frei von Steuern und Abgaben, war eine nach besonderem Recht lebende Gemeinschaft, die anscheinend durch eine Art Vasallitätsverhältnis zwischen den Kapellänen und dem Herrscher gekennzeichnet war." On the cultural role of the chapel, see Siegfried Haider, "Zum Verhältnis von Kapellanat und Geschichtsschreibung im Mittelalter," in *Geschichtsschreibung und geistiges Leben im Mittelalter: Festschrift für Heinz Löwe zum 65. Geburtstag*, edited by K. Hauck and H. Mordek, pp. 102–38 (Vienna and Cologne: Böhlau, 1978).

7. On these developments, see Albert Hauck, *Kirchengeschichte Deutschlands*, 3d ed. (Leipzig: Hinrichs, 1906), 3:28 ff.; Edgar N. Johnson, *The Secular Activities of the German Episcopate, 919–1024*, University of Nebraska Studies, vol. 30 (Lincoln, Neb.: University of Nebraska Press, 1932), p. 67 ff.; Fleckenstein, *Hofkapelle* 2:50 ff., 111 ff.; also the extensive survey of research by Oskar Köhler, "Die Ottonische Reichskirche: Ein Forschungsbericht," in *Adel und Kirche: Gerd Tellenbach zum 65. Geburtstag*, edited by Josef Fleckenstein, pp. 141–204 (Freiburg: Herder, 1968), see esp. p. 173 ff.

8. Robert Benson, *The Bishop Elect: A Study in Medieval Ecclesiastical Office* (Princeton, N.J.: Princeton University Press, 1968).

9. Fleckenstein, *Hofkapelle* 2:114.

10. Hans-Walter Klewitz, "Königtum, Hofkapelle und Domkapitel im 10. und 11. Jahrhundert," originally in *AUF* 16 (1939): 102–56; cited here from the reprint (Darmstadt: Wissenschaftliche Buchgesellschaft, 1960), p. 14.

11. Fleckenstein, *Hofkapelle* 2:50 ff.

12. Petrus Damiani, *Contra clericos aulicos*, PL 145:472C.

13. Cf. Hatto Kallfelz's introduction to *LB*, p. 4.

14. Friedrich Heer, *Die Tragödie des heiligen Reiches* (Stuttgart: Kohlhammer, 1952), pp. 9–81. The only good study specifically concerned with the representation of bishops in the *vitae* is Oskar Köhler, *Das Bild des geistlichen Fürsten in den Viten des 10. 11. und 12. Jahrhunderts*, Abhandlungen zur mittleren und neueren Geschichte, vol. 77 (Berlin: Verlag für Staatswissenschaften und Geschichte, 1935). See also the article by Karl Bosl, "Geistliche Fürsten," in *LThK* 4:619–22, 2d ed. (Freiburg: Herder, 1960). A valuable study of a major figure from the episcopal milieu in France is Peter von Moos's *Hildebert von Lavardin 1056–1133: Humanitas an der Schwelle des höfischen Zeitalters*, Pariser historische Studien, vol. 3 (Stuttgart: Hiersemann, 1965). Studies of the depiction of character and personality in the Middle Ages regularly draw on the episcopal *vitae*. E.g., Robert Teuffel, *Individuelle Persönlichkeitsschilderung in den deutschen Geschichtswerken des 10. und 11. Jahrhunderts*, BKMR, vol. 12 (Leipzig: Teubner, 1914; reprint, Hildesheim: Gerstenberg, 1974). An interesting work which leans heavily on the *vitae* is Paul Kirn, *Das Bild des Menschen in der Geschichtsschreibung von Polybios bis Ranke* (Göttingen: Vandenhoeck & Ruprecht, 1955).

15. Stendhal, *The Charterhouse of Parma*, translated by Margaret Shaw (Harmondsworth: Penguin, 1978), p. 129.

16. See, for example, Hippolyte Delehaye, *The Legends of the Saints*, translated by D. Attwater (New York: Fordham University Press, 1962).

17. See Friedrich Lotter, "Methodisches zur Gewinnung historischer Erkenntnisse aus hagiographischen Quellen," *HZ* 229 (1979): 310.

18. This can easily be observed by comparing the portrait of the courtier bishop prior to assuming office with the descriptions of the same man in the funeral orations or eulogies that frequently end the *vita*. On the division of the personality depiction into two types, see Friedrich Lotter, *Die Vita Brunonis des Ruotger: Ihre historiographische und ideengeschichtliche Stellung*, Bonner historische Forschungen, vol. 9 (Bonn: Rohrscheid, 1958), p. 28 ff.

19. On Benno's court service, see Heinrich Spier, "Benno II. von Osnabrück am Goslarer Königshof," *Harzzeitschrift* 7 (1955): 57–67. For a general characterization of Benno in contrast to the orthodox model of a bishop, see R. W. Southern, *Western Society and the Church in the Middle Ages*, The Pelican History of the Church, vol. 2 (Grand Rapids, Mich.: Erdmans, 1970), pp. 181–83.

20. *Vita Bennonis II. episcopi Osnabrugensis auctore Norberto abbate Iburgensis*, chap. 8, *LB*, p. 388.

21. Herbord (full ref., see below n. 34, item 3), p. 7: "ne ob eius dileccionem rem non vere auxisse videamur."

22. See Anselm of Havelberg, verse prologue to his *vita* of Adalbert II of Mainz, Bibl. rer. germ. 3:569, ll. 33–39.

23. Gertrud Simon, "Untersuchungen zur Topik der Widmungsbriefe mittelalterlicher Geschichtsschreiber bis zum Ende des 12. Jahrhunderts. II. Teil," *Archiv für Diplomatik* 5–6 (1959–60): 100.

24. On this aspect see Oskar Köhler, *Das Bild*, p. 73.

25. *Vita Adalberonis II. Mettensis episcopi*, MGH, SS 4:661, ll. 23–24; Gunther of Bamberg, MGH, SS 12:230, ll. 11–12; Lampert of Hersfeld, *Annalen*, edited by O. Holder-Egger, and translated by Adolf Schmidt with commentary by W. D. Fritz, AQDG, vol. 13 (Berlin: Rütten & Loening, 1957), p. 104 (1065).

26. *Vita Sancti Norberti archiepiscopi Magdeburgensis (Vita A)*, *LB*, p. 452; Philip of Heinsberg, MGH, SS 24:345, l. 16.

27. *Vita Sancti Oudalrici episcopi Augustani auctore Gerhardo*, edited by G. Waitz, *LB*, pp. 56 and 56–58.

28. ". . . monachum et hominem aspectu deformem Maguntinensi praesidere de-

dignantes deridebant" (*Vulculdi vita Bardonis archiepiscopi Mogunti*, Bibl. rer. germ. 3:525). Cf. Oskar Köhler's commentary, *Bild*, p. 73. A "boorish knight" (*miles stolidus*) murmured against Wolfgang of Regensburg that he was a "ragged and despicable fellow" (*Othloni vita Sancti Wolfkangi episcopi*, edited by G. Waitz, chap. 21, MGH, SS 4:535, l. 43 ff).

29. *Translatio Annonis archiepiscopi*, edited by R. Koepke, chap. 3, MGH, SS 11:516.

30. On the education of bishops and chaplains, see Haider, *Das bischöfliche Kapellanat*, pp. 274 ff., 335 ff.

31. *Vita Sancti Bernwardi episcopi Hildesheimensis auctore Thangmaro*, chap. 1, *LB*, p. 275; Wazo of Liège, *Gesta episcoporum Leodiensium*, edited by R. Koepke, MGH, SS 7:210, l. 30.

32. Cf. Fleckenstein, "Karl der Grosse und sein Hof," p. 42.

33. See Matthaeus Rothenhaeusler, "'Honestas morum': Eine Untersuchung zu cap. 73,3 der Regula S. Benedicti," in *Studia Benedictina in memoriam gloriosi ante saecula XIV transitus S.P. Benedicti*, Studia Anselmiana philosophica, theologica, fasc. 18–19, pp. 127–56 (Rome: Libreria Vaticana, 1947).

34. New editions of the *vitae* of Otto of Bamberg have appeared in recent years, edited by Jan Wikarjak and Kazimier Liman, and published in Warsaw by Państwowe and Wydawn: (1) The Monk of Prüfening (ca. 1140–46): *Sancti Ottonis episcopi Babenbergensis vita Prieflingensis*, MGH, n.s., vol. 7, fasc. 1 (1966); (2) Ebo of Michelsberg (ca. 1151–59): *Ebonis vita Sancti Ottonis episcopi Babenbergensis*, n.s., vol. 7, fasc. 2 (1969); and (3) Herbord of Michelsberg (1159): *Herbordi dialogus de vita Sancti Ottonis episcopi Babenbergensis*, n.s., vol. 7, fasc. 3 (1974). On these now standard editions, see the review articles by Jürgen Petersohn, "Bemerkungen zu einer neuen Ausgabe der Viten Ottos von Bamberg, 1. Prüfening Vita und Ebo," *DA* 27 (1971): 175–94; and "Bemerkungen . . . 2. Herbords Dialog," *DA* 33 (1977): 546–59.

35. *Vita Priefl.* l.3, p. 7: "his artibus cunctorum sibi sapientium concivit affectum . . . ut ipsi illius terre pontifices . . . morum elegantiam mirarentur."

36. *Gesta ep. Leod.*, chap. 25, MGH, SS 7:203, ll. 1–2: "admodum omni morum elegantia insignitus."

37. *Das Leben des Bischofs Meinwerk von Paderborn*, edited by F. Tenckhoff, MGH, SS rer. germ in us. schol., vol. 59 (Hannover: Hahn, 1921), chap. 5, p. 7.

38. *Vita Sancti Licinii episcopi Andegavensis auctore Marbodo*, PL 171:1496A: "Quem rex Clotarius, cum propter sanguinis propinquitatem, tum propter egregiae formae dignitatem ac morum elegantiam quae in adolescente eminebant, libens suscepit . . . inter amicos habere coepit, dignum plane cognitum, cum quo de magnis rebus, et regni administratione tractaret." Cf. Marbod, *Vita S. Gualteri*, PL 171:1567: (as a young man at school) "ingenii singularis vivacitas et elegans suavitas morum latere non potuit."

39. *Vita Altmanni episcopi Pataviensis*, edited by W. Wattenbach, chap. 40, MGH, SS 12:241, l. 31 ff.

40. *Ex Vita Sancti Udalrici priorensis Cellensis*, edited by R. Wilmans, *Vita posterior*, MGH, SS 12:254, ll. 25–26.

41. *Saxonis Gesta Danorum*, edited by J. Olrik and H. Raeder (Copenhagen: Levin & Munksgaard, 1931), 1:230–31 (VIII, x, 1). Italics are mine.

42. *Vita Heriberti archiepiscopi Coloniensis auctore Lantberto*, MGH, SS 4:742, ll. 17–18; Conrad I of Constance, *Vita Chounradi Constantiensis episcopi, Vita prior auctore Oudoscalco*, MGH, SS 4:431, ll. 45–46.

43. On the forces that shape the values within the *familia* of a ruler, see Norbert Elias, *Die höfische Gesellschaft: Untersuchungen zur Soziologie des Königtums und der höfischen Aristokratie*, 4th ed., Soziologische Texte, vol. 54 (Darmstadt and Neuwied: Luchterhand, 1979), pp. 188–90.

44. Marcel Proust, *The Guermantes Way*, translated by C. K. Scott Moncrieff (New York: Random House, 1952), pp. 40–41. Italics are mine.

45. Otto of Freising, *Gesta Friderici* 3.19, edited by G. Waitz, 3d ed., MGH, SS rer. germ. in us. schol., vol. 46 (Hannover and Leipzig: Hahn, 1912; reprint, Hannover, 1978), p. 190.

46. See Gerald of Wales, *De principis instructione liber*, edited by George F. Warner (London: Eyre & Spottiswoode, 1891), RS 92:8:9 ff. (1.2).

47. Two examples: Peter of Blois composed an imaginary dialogue between the abbot of Bonneval and Henry II, the former assuaging the king's anger at his sons with many arguments against wrath and vengefulness (PL 207:975–88). Thomasin of Zirclaere has a long dissertation on the virtue of *senfter muot*, *Der Wälsche Gast des Thomasin von Zirclaria*, edited by Heinrich Rückert, DNL, vol. 30 (Quedlinburg and Leipzig: Basse, 1852), l. 6859 ff. The *Ruodlieb* poet considered the mitigation of the king's anger a courtier's duty. He has the king praise Ruodlieb: "A quo [i.e., Ruodlieb] sum numquam minimam commotus in iram, / Quin irascentem me mitem reddit ut agnum" (*The Ruodlieb: Linguistic Introduction, Latin Text and Glossary*, edited by Gordon B. Ford, Jr. [Leiden: Brill, 1966], 5:406–7).

48. Cf. Elias, *Die höfische Gesellschaft*, p. 186.

49. Cited here from *The Life of Ailred of Rievaulx by Walter Daniel*, edited and translated by F. M. Powicke (New York: Oxford University Press, 1951), chap. 2, p. 2; chap. 3, p. 5 ff. The work dates ca. 1170.

50. The *miles stolidus* seems to be a regular antagonist of the court cleric. See above, n. 28.

51. David Lloyd, *State Worthies: or, The Statesmen and Favourites of England from the Reformation to the Revolution: Their Prudence and Policies, Successes and Miscarriages, Advancements and Falls* (London: J. Robson, 1766), 1:32.

52. Cf. Castiglione, *Il Libro del Cortegiano*, edited by Bruno Maier, 2d ed. (Turin: Unione Tipografico-Editrice Torinese, 1964), p. 198 (2.7), trans. Singleton, pp. 97–98.

53. *Vita S. Hugonis*, PL 166:1167A–B. The work dates before 1120, probably ca. 1117.

54. See also *Cortegiano* 1.28, 2.7. On *sprezzatura* see Erich Loos, *Baldassare Castigliones "Libro del Cortegiano": Studien zur Tugendauffassung des Cinquecento*, Analecta Romanica, vol. 2 (Frankfurt: Klostermann, 1955), p. 116 ff.; Joseph Mazzeo, "Castiglione's Courtier: The Self as a Work of Art," in his *Renaissance and Revolution: The Remaking of European Thought* (New York: Pantheon, 1965), pp. 145.

55. *Vita Burchardi episcopi*, edited by G. Waitz, MGH, SS 4:833, l. 35 ff.

56. *Vita Arnoldi archiepiscopi Moguntini*, edited by Ph. Jaffé, Bibl. rer. germ. 3:608.

57. Cf. Hauck, *Kirchengeschichte* 31, and Weinfurter, "Zum Bischöflichen Kapellanat" (above, n.4), p. 205.

58. Kunibert of Cologne (d. 648), *vita* second half of the 9th century. The miraculous selection of a bishop is perfectly common in chronicles from the period 10th–12th century. Thietmar of Merseburg has a miracle to relate for practically every episcopal election. Perhaps some genre consideration excluded the miraculous selection from the *vitae*?

59. On Otto's relationships with his chaplains, see Fleckenstein, *Hofkapelle* 2:110–11. On Tammo and the emperor, see Percy Ernst Schramm, *Kaiser, Rom und Renovatio: Studien zur Geschichte des römischen Erneuerungsgedankens vom Ende des karolingischen Reiches bis zum Investiturstreit*, 2d ed. (Darmstadt: Gentner, 1957), 1:111.

60. *Materials for the History of Thomas Becket, Archbishop of Canterbury*, edited by James Craigie Robertson (London: Longman, 1875–77), RS 67:3:237.

61. *Vita Chunradi archiepiscopi Salisburgensis*, MGH, SS 25:245, l. 35 ff.

62. See the discussion of the scene by R. W. Southern, *Western Society and the Church*, p. 183.

63. On the importance of this work, see Southern, *Western Society and Church*, pp. 172–73; and Heinz Hürten, "Gregor der Grosse und der mittelalterliche Episkopat," *ZfK* 73 (1962): 16–41. Hürten shows that the transformation of the bishop into "Reichsfürst" under the Ottos was directly contrary to Gregory's model (p. 17 ff.). He also questions Oskar Köhler's idea that Gregory's call for a balance of worldly and spiritual duties of the bishop was a guiding force in the *vitae*; the influence of the orthodox model in the period was practically nonexistent (pp. 19–20, 40–41). See also Hürten's article, "Die Verbindung von geistlicher und weltlicher Gewalt als Problem in der Amtsführung des mittelalterlichen deutschen Bischofs," *ZfK* 82 (1971): 16–28.

Chapter 2: Otto of Bamberg

1. For recent work on Otto, see Jürgen Petersohn, "Probleme der Otto-Viten und ihrer Interpretation: Bemerkungen im Anschluss an eine Neuerscheinung," *DA* 27 (1971): 314–72; and "Otto von Bamberg und seine Biographen: Grundformen und Entwicklung des Ottobildes im hohen und späten Mittelalter," *Zeitschrift für bayerische Landesgeschichte* 43 (1980): 3–27.

2. *Quadrilogus*, chap. 2, PL 190:346 ff.

3. "Fitque inter episcopum et comitem de tantae indolis iuvene religiosa concertatio, ut uterque pro morum gratia illum sibi adoptare intenderet" (*Vita Bern.*, chap. 2, *LB*, p. 278). See above, p. 33.

4. "optimatibus terrae illius in brevi est cognitus et honestissima contentione decertatus, cuius potissimum dominio subesse deberet" (*Vita Ben.*, chap. 5, *LB*, p. 380); and, "Hac itaque caeterisque, quas in eo diximus sitas, virtute conspicuus exteris quoque potentibus et dominis fama vulgante coepit esse expetibilis" (chap. 9, p. 390).

5. See Petersohn, "Otto und seine Biographen," p. 15. Herbord apparently belonged to a more liberal faction.

Chapter 3: Criticism of the Court

1. Klewitz, "Königtum, Hofkapelle und Domkapitel," p. 38, n. 5.

2. See *Vita Brun.* chap. 23, *LB*, pp. 212–14.

3. The term "court satirists" was coined by E. R. Curtius, *European Literature and the Latin Middle Ages*, translated by Willard R. Trask (New York: Harper, 1963), p. 537.

4. Specifically on the literature of court criticism, see Claus Uhlig, *Hofkritik im England des Mittelalters und der Renaissance: Studien zu einem Gemeinplatz der europäischen Moralistik*, Quellen und Forschungen zur Sprach- und Kulturgeschichte der germanischen Völker, n.s., vol. 56 (Berlin and New York: De Gruyter, 1973). Also Peter Dronke, "Peter of Blois and Poetry at the Court of Henry II," *Mediaeval Studies* 38 (1976): 185–235; Rolf Köhn, "'Militia curialis': Die Kritik am geistlichen Hofdienst bei Peter von Blois und in der lateinischen Literatur des 9.–12. Jahrhunderts," in *Miscellanea Mediaevalia 12: Soziale Ordnungen im Selbstverständnis des Mittelalters*, edited by Z. Zimmermann, pp. 227–55 (Berlin and New York: De Gruyter, 1979); C. Stephen Jaeger, "The Court Criticism of MHG Didactic Poets: Social Structures and Literary Conventions," *Monatshefte* 74 (1982): 398–409. For the Renaissance and after, Pauline M. Smith, *The Anti-Courtier Trend in Sixteenth-Century French Literature*, Travaux d'humanisme et Renaissance, vol. 84 (Geneva: Droz, 1966); Helmuth Kiesel, *"Bei Hof, bei Höll": Untersuchungen zur literarischen Hofkritik von Sebastian Brant bis Friedrich Schiller*, Studien zur deutschen Literatur, vol. 60 (Tübingen: Niemeyer, 1979). On the historical and social circumstances within which court criticism flourished at the court of Henry II, see Gunnar Stollberg, *Die soziale Stellung der intellektuellen Oberschicht im England des 12. Jahrhunderts*, Historische Studien, vol. 427 (Lübeck: Matthiessen, 1973); and Egbert Türck, *Nugae curialium: Le Règne d'Henri II Plantagenet (1154–1189) et l'éthique politique*, Hautes Études médiévales et modernes, vol. 28 (Geneva: Droz, 1977).

5. *Benzonis episcopi Albensis ad Heinricum IV imperatorem libri VII*, edited by K. Pertz, MGH, SS 11:599, l. 44.

6. John of Salisbury, *Iohannis Saresberiensis episcopi Carnotensis policratici sive de nugis curialium et vestigiis philosophorum libri VIII*, edited by Clemens C. I. Webb, 2 vols. (Oxford: Clarendon, 1909), 2:168–69 (7.18).

7. Uhlig, *Hofkritik*, pp. 46–47, takes John's many quotations from Terence to diminish the value of his court criticism as historical documentation. But the corroboration of the historicity at least of the ethical values under attack takes the weight from Uhlig's healthy reservation.

8. *Le Traité Eruditio regum et principum de Guibert de Tournai*, edited by A. de Poorter, Les Philosophes Belges, vol. 9 (Louvain: Institut supérieur de philosophie de l'université, 1914), p. 54 (ep. 2, chap. 10).

9. *Aeneae Silvii de curialium miseriis epistola*, edited by Wilfred P. Mustard (Baltimore and London: Johns Hopkins University Press, 1928).

10. PL 207:42–51. See Uhlig, *Hofkritik*, p. 99 ff.

11. "Dialogus inter dehortantem a curia et curialem," st. 7, in Peter Dronke, ed., "Peter of Blois and Poetry at the Court of Henry II," *Mediaeval Studies* 38 (1976): 208.

12. *Brunos Buch vom Sachsenkrieg*, edited by Hans-Eberhard Lohmann, MGH, Deutsches Mittelalter: Kritische Studientexte des Reichsinstituts für ältere deutsche Geschichtskunde, vol. 2 (Leipzig: Hiersemann, 1937), pp. 16–22 (chaps. 5–15).

13. Cited in *Quellen zur deutschen Verfassungs-, Wirtschafts- und Sozialgeschichte bis 1250*, edited by L. Weinrich, AQDG, vol. 32 (Darmstadt: Wissenschaftliche Buchgesellschaft, 1977), pp. 100–102 (*Wormser Hofrecht*, art. 30).

14. Gerald of Wales, *De princ. inst.*, prol., RS 21:8:lvii. See Hans Walther, *Lateinische Sprichwörter und Sentenzen des Mittelalters in alphabetischer Anordnung* (Göttingen: Vandenhoeck & Ruprecht, 1963), 1:576, #4757 ff. For some observations on this word play, see Baldwin, *Masters, Princes and Merchants*, 1.178.

15. Walter Map, *De nugis curialium*, ed. M. R. James, Anecdota Oxoniensia 14 (Oxford: Clarendon, 1914), p. 10 (1.10); John of Salisbury, *Vita Thomae*, chap. 7; RS 67:2:403–5.

16. *Pii Secundi Pontificis Maximi Commentarii rerum memorabilium, quae temporibus suis contigerunt* (Frankfurt: Officiana Aubriana, 1614), pp. 8–9 (bk. 1).

17. Johannes de Hauvilla, *Architrenius*, edited by Paul Schmidt (Munich: Fink, 1974), 4.325 ff.

18. *Anonym. I*, RS 67:4:12.

19. L. 1437 ff. Cited from the edition by Roland E. Pepin, "The *Entheticus* of John of Salisbury: A Critical Text," *Traditio* 31 (1975): 127–93, here p. 181.

20. The number of variations on "leave the court" in Walther's collection of proverbs is significant (see *Sprichwörter und Sentenzen* 1:201, no. 1761 ff). Both Uhlig and Kiesel set the proverb at the beginning of their studies as a kind of motto of court criticism. Kiesel includes a number of variations on the theme from the Renaissance and after.

21. *Plutarch's Lives*, translated by Bernadotte Perrin, The Loeb Classical Library (London and New York: Heinemann, Putnams, 1917), p. 13 (*Life of Agesilaus* 5.3).

22. My thanks to Peter von Moos for pointing out this medieval misunderstanding.

23. *Vita Chunradi archiepiscopi Salisburgensis*, chap. 3, MGH, SS 11:64.

Chapter 4: Adalbert of Bremen

1. "si tam diversi hominis diversam hystoriam diverso themate compaginans, cum non potui breviter aut dilucide, ut ars precipit, omnem operam dedi, ut scriberem veraciter, secundum quod scientia et opinio se habet in hac parte" (Adam von Bremen, *Hamburgische Kirchengeschichte*, edited by Bernhard Schmeidler, 3d ed., MGH, SS rer. germ. in us. schol., vol. 2 [Hannover and Leipzig: Hahn, 1917; reprint 1977], chap. 70, p. 218). The work is in four books; the biography of Adalbert takes up all of book 3. All references here are to the chapters of the third book. There is a good modern English translation: Adam of Bremen, *History of the Archbishops of Hamburg-Bremen*, translated and with an introduction and notes by Francis J. Tschan, Records of Civilization, Sources and Studies, vol. 53 (New York: Columbia University Press, 1959).

2. Paul Kirn, *Das Bild des Menschen*, p. 119 ff. Georg Misch, *Geschichte der Autobiographie* (Frankfurt: Schulte-Bulmke, 1959), vol. 3, fasc. 2, pt. 1, pp. 168–214. See especially the terse and eloquent article by Edgar N. Johnson, "Adalbert of Hamburg-Bremen: A Politician of the Eleventh Century," *Speculum* 9 (1934): 147–79.

3. Cf. Misch, *Autobiographie*, pp. 168–69.

4. Fleckenstein, *Hofkapelle* 2:256–57.

5. Cf. Lampert, *Annales*, p. 134 (1072): "has in eo virtutes nimium in oculis hominum insolentia et iactantiae levitas obfuscabat." Bruno of Merseburg, *Sax. bell.*, chap. 2, p. 14: "sic typho superbiae turgidus, ut nec in saeculari nobilitate nec in sancta conversatione quemquam putaret sibi aequalem."

6. *Chron. Laureshamense*, MGH, SS 21:413, l. 38 ff. (1056); cited in Johnson, "Adalbert," p. 167.

7. On Adalbert's plans for a patriarchate of the North, see Johnson, "Adalbert," p. 154 ff.

8. See chap. 1, pp. 143–44: "Igitur narrationis initium tale faciam, ut statim ex moribus eius possint omnia cognosci."

9. See Johnson, "Adalbert," pp. 162–71.

10. Bruno of Merseburg accuses Adalbert of instructing the young king to "do whatever your heart desires; only be careful that on the day of your death, you return to true faith" (*Sax. bell.*, chap. 5, p. 16).

11. Adam adapted the general frame, "Quid nunc prosunt . . ." from Lucan, *Pharsalia* 4.799 ff.

12. This is Misch's approach (see above, n. 2).

Chapter 5: The Defense of the Courtier

1. "Teachers of the world" is also a possible translation of *professores mundi*, though the meaning "teacher" for *professor*, present in classical Latin, was not prominent in the Middle Ages. In any case, Peter of Blois places them parallel to martyrs and disciples. Hence the primary sense was probably "men who make the world their creed."

2. See the commentary in Gottfried von Strassburg, *Tristan*, edited by R. Bechstein and revised by Peter Ganz, Deutsche Klassiker des Mittelalters, n.s., vol. 4 (Wiesbaden: Brockhaus, 1978), 1:292–93.

3. Ganz and Bechstein refer to Publilius Syrus, "Sententiae" 315: "miserrima est fortuna, quae inimico caret." The defiant stance apparently did not appeal to the medieval mentality. I find no echo of this proverb in Walther's collection.

4. On Joseph in the Middle Ages, see Manfred Derpmann, *Die Josephgeschichte: Auffassung und Darstellung im Mittelalter*, Beihefte zum Mittellateinischen Jahrbuch, vol. 13 (Düsseldorf: Henn, 1974).

5. Saint Ambrose, *Sancti Ambrosii Mediolanensis episcopi De officiis ministrorum libri tres*, esp. 2.16–17, PL, 16:123 ff.

6. *Verbum abbreviatum*, chap. 55, PL 205:169. Cf. Baldwin, *Masters, Princes and Merchants*, pp. 175–204.

7. The best available edition is *Johannis Lemovicensis, Abbatis de Zirc 1208–1218 Opera Omnia*, edited Constantin Horváth, 3 vols. (Vesprém, Hungary: Egyházmegyei Könyvnyomda, 1932). The *Somnium Pharaonis* is in 1:71–126.

8. This is possibly an echo of Gerald of Wales, *De princ. inst.* 1.21, RS 21:8:147: "Gloriosior est accelerata quam morosa victoria." See ibid., pp. 146–49, for a large dossier on the advantages of early death. But the motivations are Christian, orthodox ones. Honor gained in state service as consolation for an early death seems to be the contribution of Johannes.

9. Wilhelm Berges, *Die Fürstenspiegel des hohen und späten Mittelalters*, MGH, Schriften, vol. 2 (Leipzig: Hiersemann, 1938; reprint, 1952), contains numerous references in passing to Johannes. See index.

10. Cf. Fulgentius, *Mythologies* 2:8. Baudri of Bourgeuil, *Carmen* 216, ll. 697–98: "Illecebras mundi quoniam sapientia transit, / At Sirenarum neglegit intuitum"; and 1058–59: "Innocuus sollers Scillam pertransit Ulixes / Nam mundi rabiem transit homo sapiens." *The Commentary on the First Six Books of the Aeneid of Vergil Commonly Attributed to Bernardus Silvestris*, edited by Julian Jones and Elizabeth Jones (Lincoln, Neb., and London: University of Nebraska Press, 1977), p. 22, l. 5: "socii Ulixis, i.e. socii sapientis . . ."; and p. 105, ll. 5–6: "Intrant mentes, virtus scilicet et sapientia, quod intelligimus per Menelaum et Ulixem."

11. See the discussion in W. B. Stanford, *The Ulysses Theme: A Study in the Adaptability of a Traditional Hero* (Oxford: Blackwell, 1968), p. 284.

12. Cf. Cicero, *De officiis* 1.113.

13. Edmond Faral, *Les Arts poétiques du XIIe et du XIIIe siècle* (Paris: Champion, 1924), p. 120 ff.; see pp. 123–25 for the portrait of Ulysses.

14. See the commentary by Hennig Brinkmann, *Zu Wesen und Form mittelalterlicher Dichtung* (Halle/Saale: Niemeyer, 1928), p. 60, and his observation, n. 1: "Ulixes fällt / etwas heraus."

15. The context is confusing because there is an abrupt shift in l. 31. Previously the subject had been the chambers of Ulysses' mind. At l. 31 we are back to the man himself, and "outer man" is puzzling, since it seems to continue the logic of the preceding: first the man's mind, now the outer man. The new translation by Roger P. Parr (Matthew of Vendôme, *Ars versificatoria* [Milwaukee: Marquette University Press, 1981], p. 32), prefers to follow this apparent logic: "It [i.e., *rationis apex*] exceeds nature in power, and the inner man is the / Trusted teacher of the outer man." But this translation causes insoluble problems. It must be Ulysses himself, not his reason, who outdoes in virtue what has been given him by nature (l. 31), and he himself, not his reason, surpasses in manners the human norm (l. 33). L. 31 sounds a new theme. Likewise Ulysses himself must be the "faithful *vassal*," not teacher, of the "outer man," meaning here men in their worldly relations with each other. (The term "inner man" is Pauline. See Rom. 7:22 and Eph. 3:16. But the biblical context is of no importance here.)

16. See the edition by P. G. Schmidt, "'Causa Aiacis et Ulixis I–II': Zwei ovidianische Streitgedichte des Mittelalters," *Mittellateinisches Jahrbuch* 1 (1964): 100–32.

17. See ibid., p. 103 ff. on the poets' adaptation of Ovid; see also ibid., pp. 100–101 for a description of the manuscripts.

18. *Carmina Burana* 92, "De Phyllide et Flora," st. 30. On the cleric's laziness, ibid., sts. 15, 16, 17, 39.

19. See Schmidt, "'Causa Aiacis,'" pp. 108–9.

20. *Ulrichi Hutteni Opera*, edited by Eduard Böcking (Leipzig: Teubner, 1860), 4:48.

Chapter 6: From Court Ideal to Literary Ideal

1. See the works by Siegfried Haider on the episcopal chapel (above, chap. 1, n. 4), and on the papal chapel, "Zu den Anfängen der päpstlichen Kapelle," *MIÖG* 87 (1979): 38–70.

2. Görlitz calls service in the royal chapel "das höchste erstrebenswerte Ziel jedes jungen Geistlichen" (*Königliche Hofkapelle*, p. 26). This may overstate the case a little, but it certainly is true that the standards of the royal chapel must have been widely influential.

3. Two formulations of the type outside the genre of bishop's *vita* are Phillip of Harvengt's letter to a former friend and schoolmate, now bishop, Epistle 13, PL 203:97–119, and Henry of Huntingdon, *Epistola ad Walterum de mundi contemptu, sive de episcopis et viris illustribus sui temporis*, PL 195:979 ff. See esp. the description of Simon, Deacon of Huntingdon, son of the king's chancellor and a man "regaliter enutritus": (while still a youth) "in summam regis amicitiam et curiales dignitates mox provectus est. Erat autem celer ingenio, clarus eloquio, forma venustus, gratia coruscus, aetate junior, prudentia senilis" (983B).

4. The bride expedition, as I mentioned earlier, is itself a literary motif, and it is probable that literature influenced this depiction of the bishop's life. But then diplomatic expeditions were part and parcel of the duties of the court cleric.

5. For a more detailed discussion, see my article, "The Barons' Intrigue in Gottfried's *Tristan*: Notes Towards a Sociology of Fear in Court Society," *JEGP* 83 (1984): 46–66.

6. The Latin passages are cited above in chaps. 3 and 4. The MHG is from Hugo von Trimberg, *Der Renner*, edited by Gustav Ehrismann, BLVS, vol. 247 (Tübingen: Litt. Verein, 1908), 1:728, and refers to the fears and anxiety produced by life at court.

7. See for instance Loos, "*Libro del Cortegiano*," pp. 171–73; Mazzeo, "Castiglione's Courtier, p. 133; Ernest Barker, "The Education of the English Gentleman in the 16th Century," in his *Traditions of Civility: Eight Essays* (Cambridge: Cambridge University Press, 1948), p. 124; Ruth Kelso, *The Doctrine of the English Gentleman in the Sixteenth Century*, University of Illinois Studies in Language and Literature, vol. 14 (Urbana: University of Illinois Press, 1929), p. 70.

8. *Secretum Secretorum: Nine English Versions*, edited by M. A. Manzaloni, EETS, vol. 276 (Oxford: Oxford University Press, 1977), 1:79–80.

9. For an extensive list of such tracts, see Kelso, *Doctrine of the English Gentleman*, pp. 169–277.

Chapter 7: Ancient Urbanity and the Spirit of Revival

1. See Jean Frappier's insistence on the distinction between courtesy and romantic love in "Vues sur les conceptions courtoises dans les littératures d'oc et d'oïl au XIIe siècle," *Cahiers de civilisation médiévale* 2 (1959): 136.

2. For two recent surveys of research on the origins and nature of courtesy and courtly love, see Ursula Liebertz-Grün, *Zur Soziologie des "amour courtois": Umrisse der Forschung*, Beihefte zum Euphorion, vol. 10 (Heidelberg: Winter, 1977); and Roger Boase, *The Origin and Meaning of Courtly Love: A Critical Study of European Scholarship* (Manchester: Manchester University Press; and Totowa, N.J.: Rowman & Littlefield, 1977). Boase's work is less a "critical study of European scholarship" than a plea for Arabic origins. The perspective promised in the title is further skewed by his ignoring German scholarship.

There are good studies of the Provencal and OF vocabulary of courtesy, though there is hardly more than a mention of the corresponding Latin terms in any of them. See Hans Krings, "Die Geschichte des Wortschatzes der Höflichkeit im Französischen," Diss., Bonn, 1961. Glyn S. Burgess, *Contribution à l'étude du vocabulaire pré-courtois*, Publications romanes et françaises, vol. 110 (Geneva: Droz, 1970). Glynnis M. Cropp, *Le Vocabulaire courtois des troubadours de l'époque classique*, Publications romanes et françaises, vol. 135 (Geneva: Droz, 1975). With the exception of Werner Schrader's *Studien über das Wort höfisch in der mhd. Dichtung* (Würzburg: Triltsch, 1935), the studies of MHG concentrate on the loan words from OF. See Felix Piquet, *De vocabulis quae in duodecimo saeculo et in tertii decimi principio a Gallis Germani assumpserint* (Paris: Leroux, 1898). Hugo Palander, "Der französische Einfluss auf die deutsche Sprache im 12. Jahrhundert," *Memoires de la Société Néophilologique de Helsinki* 3 (1902): 75–204, and 8 (1929): 1–310. Emil Öhmann, *Die MHD Lehnprägung nach altfranzösischem Vorbild* (Helsinki, 1951).

3. Gustav Ehrismann, "Die Grundlagen des ritterlichen Tugendsystems," *ZfdA* 56 (1919): 137–216; see also his *Geschichte der deutschen Literatur bis zum Ausgang des Mittelalters* (Munich: Beck, 1927), vol. 2, pt. 2/1, pp. 19–24. A number of studies connected with the controversy are conveniently collected in Günter Eifler, ed., *Ritterliches Tugendsystem*, WDF, vol. 56 (Darmstadt: Wissenschaftliche Buchgesellschaft, 1970).

4. E. R. Curtius, "Das 'Ritterliche Tugendsystem,'" *DVJS* 21 (1943): 343–68. Appears also in his *European Literature and the Latin Middle Ages*, pp. 519–37.

5. Edmond Faral, *Recherches sur les sources latines des contes et romans courtois du moyen âge* (Paris: Champion, 1913), pp. 194–95. Frappier, "Vues," p. 146 ff.

6. In this sketch of ancient urbanity I am following Henri Bléry, *Rusticité et urbanité romaines* (Paris: Belin, 1909); Karl Lammermann, "Von der attischen Urbanität und ihrer Auswirking in der Sprache," Diss., Göttingen, 1935. Edwin Ramage, *Urbanitas: Ancient Sophistication and Refinement*, University of Cincinnati Classical Studies, vol. 3 (Norman, Okla.: University of Oklahoma Press, 1973).

7. See S. L. Galpin, "Cortois and Vilain," Diss., Yale, 1905.

8. See *Phaidon* 116C–D; Lammermann, "Von der attischen Urbanität," p. 10.

9. Interesting for comparison with medieval notions of the civilizing power of love is an example given by Ramage, *Urbanitas* (pp. 16–17). In Achilles Tatius' *Leucippe and Clitophon* (ca. 300), an ungovernable young man, Callisthenes, is transformed under the influence of love from a loose, hot-tempered, and unscrupulous fellow into a polite, modest, discreet gentleman.

10. Cf. Robert Philippson, "Das Sittlichschöne bei Panaitios," *Philologus* 85, n.s., 39 (1930): 357–413. On the idea of *kalokagathia*, see Werner Jaeger, *Paideia: The Ideals of Greek Culture*, 2d ed., translated by Gilbert Highet (New York: Oxford University Press, 1960), 1:4 ff. Also, H. I. Marrou, *A History of Education in Antiquity*, translated by George Lamb (Madison, Wis.: University of Wisconsin Press, 1956), pp. 43–45.

11. Cicero, *De officiis*, edited and translated by Walter Miller, Loeb Classical Library, vol. 30 (Cambridge, Mass.: Harvard University Press, 1913), p. 101.

12. See *De oratore* 2.67: "Socratem opinor in hac ironia dissimulantiaque longe lepore et humanitate omnibus praestitisse. Genus est perelegans et cum gravitate salsum cumque oratoriis dictionibus tum urbanis sermonibus accommodatum. Et hercule omnia haec, quae a me de facetiis disputantur, non maiora forensium actionum quam omnium sermonum condimenta sunt."

13. See Albrecht Dihle, "Antike Höflichkeit und christliche Demut," *Studi italiani di filologia classica* 26 (1952): 169–98.

14. "Sketchy" is the best word to describe available treatments of Cicero's influence on the Middle Ages. See Tadeusz Zielinski, *Cicero im Wandel der Jahrhunderte*, 2d ed. (Leipzig and Berlin: Teubner, 1908); Gerhard Traub, *Studien zum Einfluss Ciceros auf die höfische Moral*, Deutsches Werden, vol. 1 (Greifswald: Bamberg, 1933); and John C. Rolfe, *Cicero and his Influence* (New York: Cooper Square, 1963).

15. See the list of schoolbooks from the end of the twelfth century in C. H. Haskins, *Studies in the History of Medieval Science* (Cambridge, Mass.: Harvard University, 1924), p. 372: "Tullius de officiis utilissimus est."

16. An edition of the work by Saint Ambrose is in PL 16:23–184. On the relation of Ambrose's to Cicero's work see O. Hiltbrunner, "Die Schrift *De officiis ministrorum* des Heiligen Ambrosius und ihr Ciceronisches Vorbild," *Gymnasium* 71 (1964): 174–89. K. Zelzer, "Zur Beurteilung der Cicero-Imitation bei Ambrosius, *De officiis*," *Wiener Studien*, n.s., 11 (1977): 168–91: Friedrich Ohly, "Ausserbiblisch Typologisches zwischen Cicero, Ambrosius und Aelred von Rievaulx," *Schriften zur mittelalterlichen Bedeutungsforschung* (Darmstadt: Wissenschaftliche Buchgesellschaft, 1977), pp. 338–60.

17. *Martini episcopi Bracarensis opera omnia*, edited by Claude Barlow (New Haven: Yale University Press, 1950), pp. 236–50. Barlow's lengthy introduction to the work gives a clear picture of its influence. He lists many manuscripts from the eleventh century, from both Germany and France. Hildebert of Lavardin composed a verse adaptation of the work, the *Libellus de quatuor virtutibus vitae honestae*, PL 171:1055–64.

18. Hans Baron, "Cicero and the Roman Civic Spirit in the Middle Ages and the Early Renaissance," in *Lordship and Community in Medieval Europe: Selected Readings*, edited by F. L. Cheyette (New York: Holt, Rinehart & Winston, 1968), pp. 291–314. Revised from an essay first published in the *Bulletin of the John Rylands Library* 22 (1938): 72–97.

19. N. E. Nelson, "Cicero's *De officiis* in Christian Thought: 300–1300," in *Essays and Studies in English and Comparative Literature*, University of Michigan Publications in Language and Literature, vol. 10 (Ann Arbor: University of Michigan Press, 1933), pp. 59–160. On the eleventh century, see p. 88.

20. *Briefsammlungen der Zeit Heinrichs IV.*, edited by Carl Erdmann and Norbert Fickermann, MGH, Briefe der deutschen Kaiserzeit, vol. 5 (Weimar: Böhlau, 1950).

21. Carl Erdmann, *Studien zur Briefliteratur Deutschlands im 11. Jahrhundert*, MGH, Schriften, vol. 1 (Leipzig: Hiersemann, 1938), pp. 61, 104–5.

22. Cf. James Stuart Beddie, "Libraries in the Twelfth Century: Their Catalogues and Contents," in *Anniversary Essays in Mediaeval History by Students of C. H. Haskins* (Boston and New York: Houghton Mifflin, 1929), p. 12.

23. *Gesta ep. Leod.*, chap. 61, MGH, SS 7:226, l. 21 ff.: "Ita certe facinus, ad quod multa satellitum milia rapinis inhiantium impellebant fluctuantem regis animum, Deo inspirante dissuadere potuerunt longe positi unius hominis litterae." Cf. *De officiis*, 1.79.

24. For Erdmann's discussion of the poem, see his "Ein neues Zeugnis für die Renovatio-Gedanken unter Otto III," in *Forschungen zur politischen Ideenwelt des Frühmittelalters*, edited by Friedrich Baethgen (Berlin: Akademie, 1951), pp. 109–11. Also Josef Fleckenstein, "Bruns Dedikationsgedicht als Zeugnis der karolingischen Renovatio unter Otto d. Gr.: Zu Carl Erdmanns neuer und Wilhelm Wattenbachs alter Deutung," *DA* 11 (1954–55): 219–26; and Hans Martin Klinkenberg, "Noch einmal zu Brunos Dedikationsgedicht," *DA* 12 (1956): 197–200.

25. Curtius, *European Literature*, p. 254, n. 20. Curtius made a fairly casual refer-

ence which later commentators of Brun's poem have taken excessively seriously. To form an idea of the flexibility of meaning in the phrases *patres nostri, patres antiqui*, and *veteres patres*, see below, pp. 227–31.

26. Here I am following Schramm, *Kaiser, Rom und Renovatio*.

27. See Percy Ernst Schramm, *Kaiser, Könige und Päpste: Gesammelte Aufsätze zur Geschichte des Mittelalters* (Stuttgart: Hiersemann, 1969), 3:213–14.

28. *Die Chronik des Bischofs Thietmar von Merseburg*, edited by Robert Holtzmann, 2d ed., MGH, SS rer. germ., n.s., vol. 9 (Berlin: Weidmann, 1955), p. 184 (4.47).

29. Cf. Schramm, *Kaiser, Rom und Renovatio* 2:62 ff.

30. *Die Briefsammlung Gerberts von Reims*, edited by Fritz Weigle, MGH, Briefe der deutschen Kaiserzeit, vol. 2 (Berlin, Zürich, and Dublin: Weidmann, 1966), p. 222 (Ep. 186).

31. "in otio et negotio praeceptorum M. Tullii diligens fui executor" (Ep. 158, ed. Weigle, p. 187).

32. Karl Hauck, "Heinrich III und der Ruodlieb," *PBB* 70 (1948): 372–419.

33. See Karl Jordan, *Die Entstehung der römischen Kurie: Ein Versuch, mit Nachtrag, 1962*, Libelli, vol. 91 (Darmstadt: Wissenschaftliche Buchgesellschaft, 1962), pp. 26–27. Reprinted from *Zeitschrift der Savigny-Stiftung für Rechtsgeschichte*, vol. 59, Kanonische Abteilung 28 (1939), pp. 97–152. Jordan points out that there is a lacuna in the use of the word *curia* ca. 900–1050.

34. On literary life at the court of Henry III, see Reto Bezzola, *Les Origines et la formation de la littérature courtoise en occident (500–1200)*, 3 pts. in 5 vols. (Paris: Champion, 1958–63), 1:276 ff; Wattenbach and Holtzmann, *DGO* 1:13 ff.; and Karl Hauck, "Mittellateinische Literatur," in *Deutsche Philologie im Aufriss*, 2d ed., edited by Wolfgang Stammler (Berlin: Schmidt, 1960), 2:2599 ff.

35. *Ad Heinricum*, MGH, SS 11:591–681. On Benzo see Manitius, *Geschichte der lateinischen Literatur* 3:454–57; Schramm, *Kaiser, Rom und Renovatio*, 1:258 ff.

36. There are various testimonies to the idealizing of the Ottonian chapel. See, for example, Sigebert of Gembloux, *Vita Deoderici episcopi Mettensis auctore Sigeberto Gemblacensi*, MGH, SS 4:467, ll. 36–37: "Iure felicia dixerim Ottonis tempora, cum claris praesulibus et sapientibus viris res publica sit reformata."

37. This points to the dubious aspect of Benzo's work: it is unashamedly self-seeking and self-serving. It is, as much as anything, an advertisement for Benzo. He has been driven from his office by political opponents, and he seeks the emperor's help in regaining it.

38. See my *Medieval Humanism in Gottfried von Strassburg's "Tristan und Isolde"* (Heidelberg: Winter, 1977), pp. 14–15, 126–38.

Chapter 8: The Language of Courtesy

1. The orthodox position is described in detail above, chap. 3. The moderately conservative position is illustrated by the court service of Ulrich of Zell (see below, p. 152).

2. Herbert of Bosham has a long dissertation on the "two-fold grace" possessed by some men which permits them to serve God and the world, "Jerusalem and Babylon" at the same time. Examples are Joseph in Egypt and the subject of his biography, Thomas Becket. See *Vita Thomae* 2.1, RS 67:3:163.

3. *Habitus* is not easy to render exactly here. In ML generally, and in Herbord's own usage, it means "way of living," "manner of conduct," and at the same time "dress." Here it seems to me that "dress" is consistent with *in cibo aut potu* (though *sermo* and *gestus* may equally argue for "way of living"), and that this rendering is more consistent with the *officia exterioris hominis*.

4. See M.-D. Chenu, "Disciplina," *Revue des sciences philosophiques et theologiques* 25 (1936): 686–92; and W. Dürig, "*Disciplina*: Eine Studie zur Bedeutung des Wortes in der Sprache der Liturgie und der Väter" *Sacris Erudiri* 4 (1952): 245–79.

5. See *Confessiones* 3.1.1: "elegans et urbanus esse gestiebam abundanti vanitate"— PL 32:683.

6. See Helena Gamer, "Studien zum Ruodlieb," *ZfdA* 88 (1957–58): 253.

7. *Sigebotonis vita Paulinae*, edited by I. R. Dietrich, MGH, SS 30:2:920, ll. 34 ff.

8. Joachim Bumke, *Mäzene im Mittelalter: Die Gönner und Auftraggeber der höfischen Literatur in Deutschland 1150–1300* (Munich: Beck, 1979), p. 85–86.

9. Gustav Ehrismann, "Die Grundlagen des ritterlichen Tugendsystems," *ZfdA* 56 (1919): 137–216; cited here from the reprint in *Ritterliches Tugendsystem*, edited by Günter Eifler, Wege der Forschung, vol. 56 (Darmstadt: Wissenschaftliche Buchgesellschaft, 1970), on *zuht-decorum*, p. 15, n. 18.

10. "Stans Puer ad mensam," in *The Babees Book, The Bokes of Nurture etc.*, edited by Frederick Furnivall, p. 26, EETS, o.s., vol. 32 (London: Trübner, 1868; reprint, New York, 1969).

11. Cf. Chrétien, *Lancelot* 596: "cortois et bien apris"; *Yvain* 5484: "mout est bele et bien aprise." Cf. Galpin, *Cortois and Vilain*, pp. 78–80.

12. "Imperial tradition" is Bezzola's term ("la tradition imperiale"), the subtitle for the first part of his *Les Origines*. It refers to court traditions in general; his special focus is on literary productivity.

13. *The Ecclesiastical History of Orderic Vitalis*, edited and translated by Marjorie Chibnall, 6 vols., Oxford Mediaeval Texts (Oxford: Oxford University Press, 1969–80), 2:224 (*Hist. eccl.* 4).

14. *Glossaria Latina iussu academiae Britannicae edita*, vol. 1, *Glossarium Ansileubi sive librum glossarum*, edited by W.-M. Lindsay et al (Paris: Société anonyme d'édition "Les Belles Lettres," 1926), p. 198 (*eliganter*), p. 231 (*facetus*).

15. *Glossarium latinum bibliothecae Parisinae antiquissimum*, edited by G. F. Hildebrand (Göttingen: Dieterich, 1854), p. 125.

16. Papias, *Vocabulista* (Venice: Philippus de Pincis Mantuanus, 1496; reprint, Torino, 1966), pp. 103, 365.

17. *Liber epistularum Guidonis de Basochis*, edited by Herbert Adolfsson, Acta Universitatis Stockholmiensis, Studia Latina Stockholmiensia, vol. 18 (Stockholm: Almquist & Wiksell, 1969), p. 1 (ep. 1, l. 9 ff.).

18. The text of Sven Aggesen is printed in *Den Danske Rigslovgivning indtil 1400*, edited by Erik Kroman (Copenhagen: Munksgaard, 1971), pp. 8–34. For a discussion of the texts, see Thomas Riis, *Les institutions politiques centrales du Danemark, 1100–1332*, Odense University Studies in History and Social Sciences, vol. 46 (Odense: Odense University Press, 1977), pp. 31–47.

19. Cf. Lotter, "Historische Erkenntnisse," pp. 320 ff., 342.

20. Cf. R. Drögereit, "Die Vita Bernwardi und Thangmar," *Unsere Diözese in Vergangenheit und Gegenwart: Zeitschrift des Vereins für Heimatkunde im Bistum Hildesheim* 28 (1959): 2–46.

21. "Ästhetische Formkultur." See Bert Nagel, *Staufische Klassik: Deutsche Dichtung um 1200* (Heidelberg: Stiehm, 1977), pp. 69–162, esp. 74–75.

22. See Burgess, *Vocab. précourtois*, p. 114 (with reference to Frances Norwood): "*cointe* évoquait cette beauté recherchée qui résultait de l'éducation." See also Krings, *Wortschatz der Höflichkeit*, pp. 59–60.

23. *Gesta Friderici* 2.13, ed. Waitz, p. 116.

24. On the translation "courtly grace" for *domesticus lepor*, see the glosses in Niermeyer, *Med. Lat. Lex.*, pp. 347–48. The noun *domesticus* is synonymous with *curialis*, member of a royal household. The adjective could take on the same meaning of "courtly, suave, polite."

25. *Andreae Capellani Regii Francorum De amore libri tres*, edited by E. Trojel (Copenhagen: Gad, 1892; reprint, Munich, 1972), p. 127. Translation quoted (with certain liberties) from Andreas Capellanus, *The Art of Courtly Love*, translated by John J. Parry, Records of Civilization, Sources and Studies (New York: Columbia University Press, and Norton, 1969), p. 93.

26. *Gerhohi Praepositi Reichersbergensis Opera inedita II: Expositionis Psalmorum pars tertia et pars nona, tomus primus*, edited by Damian van den Eynde, Odulph van den Eynde, and Angelinus Rijmersdael, Spicilegium Pontificii Athenaei Antoniani, vol. 9 (Rome: Pontificium Athenaeum Antonianum, 1956), p. 52 ff.

27. *Anonymus Haserensis de episcopis Eichstetensibus,* chap. 22, MGH, SS 7:259–60. The incident is cited in Johnson, *Secular Activities,* pp. 242–43.

28. See the discussion of the scene in Von Moos, *Hildebert,* p. 149.

29. See Franz Bittner, "Studien zum Herrscherlob in der mittellateinischen Dichtung," (Diss., Würzburg, 1962), pp. 24–25.

30. See Gregory the Great, *Regula pastoralis,* 2.10, PL 77:44B ff. Also, Martin Heinzelmann, *Bischofsherrschaft in Gallien: Zur Kontinuität römischer Führungsschichten vom 4. bis zum 7. Jahrhundert: Soziale, prosopographische und bildungsgeschichtliche Aspekte,* Beihefte der Francia, vol. 5 (Zurich: Artemis, 1976), pp. 36, 38, 152 ff.; and K. L. Noethlichs, "Materialien zum Bischofsbild aus den spätantiken Rechtsquellen," *Jahrbuch für Antike und Christentum* 16 (1973): p. 33 ff.

31. *Chroniques des comtes d'Anjou et des seigneurs d'Amboise,* edited by Louis Halphen and René Poupardin, CTSEEH, vol. 48 (Paris: Picard, 1913), p. 177: "Fuit igitur mitis, gratus, benignissimi animi; in cives clemens, offensarum et injuriarum indultor fuit. Convicia sibi a multis illata audiens, patienter dissimulavit; omnibus universaliter . . . amabilis et jocundus exstitit."

32. In the new edition, *Des Minnesangs Frühling, unter Benutzung der Ausgaben von K. Lachmann, M. Haupt, F. Vogt und Carl v. Kraus,* edited by H. Moser and H. Tervooren, 36th ed. (Stuttgart: Hirzel, 1977), 1:315 (Reinmar 10.5). In the older edition, *MF* 163:5–12.

33. See Dihle, "Antike Höflichkeit und christliche Demut," p. 183.

34. See Reto Bezzola, *Les Origines,* 1:50–55, 76.

35. See Heinzelmann, *Bischofsherrschaft,* p. 163; Ernst Jerg, *Vir Venerabilis: Untersuchungen zur Titulatur der Bischöfe in den ausserkirchlichen Texten der Spätantike als Beitrag zur Deutung ihrer öffentlichen Stellung,* Wiener Beiträge zur Theologie, vol. 26 (Vienna: Herder, 1970), pp. 88, 96, 186 (*deo amabilis*).

36. Cf. Hartmann von Aue, *Iwein* 887–88: (Arthur is annoyed to see his knights spring up like servants when he enters the room because) "er waz in weizgot verre / baz geselle danne herre."

37. On the position of personal chaplain to the queen, see Fleckenstein, *Hofkapelle* 2:265–66.

38. The list is not to be taken as paradigmatic, but rather as the harsh condemnation of a conservative, strongly anti-curial monk. His source, the *Vita prior,* had compared the court of Henry III with that of Nebuchadnezzar (ibid., p. 251).

39. *Fundatio ecclesiae Hildesheimensis,* chap. 4, l. 1 ff., MGH, SS 30:2:945. On the text see *DGQ* 2:576. The passage is taken over by the Saxon annalist (MGH, SS 6:686).

40. These become standard formulations to describe the lavish court life. See Peter of Blois's poem "Dialogus inter dehortantem a curia et curialem," st. 4: "Tenent nos in curia / cultus delicacior, / cibus exquisicior / et laucior. . . ." Peter Dronke, "Peter of Blois and Poetry at the Court of Henry II," *Mediaeval Studies* 38 (1976): 207. King David of Scotland levied a three-year tax on all of his countrymen, "qui vellent habitare cultius, amiciri elegantius, pasci accuratius," *Willelmi Malmesbiriensis de gestis regum Anglorum,* edited by William Stubbs, 2 vols. (London: Eyre & Spottiswoode, 1887), 5:400 (RS 90:2:476).

41. *Chron. Hildesheimense,* chap. 16, MGH, SS 7:853.

42. See *Vita Godehardi episcopi Hildenesheimensis auctore Wolfherio posterior,* chap. 33, MGH, SS 11:215, ll. 51–52. "Qui tamen apud imperatorem et primates ad summum mundanae felicitatis apicem honorifice profecit."

43. See Gerald of Wales, *Expugnatio Hibernica,* edited by James F. Dimrock (London: Longmans, 1867), 2:16; RS 21, 5:338: "auri cupidus et curialiter ambitiosus."

44. See Köhn, "'Militia curialis,'" p. 246.

45. *Chronicon abbatiae Evesham,* edited by W. Dunn Macray (London: Longman, 1863), RS 29:199.

46. *Gesta episcoporum Halberstadensium,* edited by L. Weiland, MGH, SS 23:114, ll. 51–52.

47. Aegidius Columna, *De regimine principum* (Venice, 1498), 2.3.18 (chapter heading): "Quid est curialitas et quod decet ministros regum et principum curiales esse."

Konrad von Megenberg, freely adapting Aegidius' discourse on the courtliness of royal advisors, writes, "Dicamus itaque, quod ministri minores imperatoris duo in se debent habere milicie bona, videlicet curialitatem morum et armorum industriam. . . . Congruit igitur ministros Cesaris tanto curialiores esse, id est bonis moribus splendidiores, quanto curia eius sublimior est curiis omnium secularium miliciarum" *Ökonomik (Buch II)*, edited by Sabine Krüger, MGH, Staatsschriften des späteren Mittelalters 3:5 (Stuttgart: Hiersemann, 1977), p. 199 (*Yconomica* 2.4.12).

48. *Ecclesiastical History* 4:188–89 (*Hist. eccl.* 8.10).

49. "Das Liebesconcil in Remiremont," edited by W. Meyer, Nachrichten der Kgl. Gesellschaft der Wissenschaften zu Göttingen, Phil.-Hist. Kl. 1914 (Berlin, 1915), p. 11, ll. 70–73.

50. *Radulphi de Coggeshall chronicon anglicanum*, edited by J. Stephenson (London: Longman, 1875), RS 66:122.

51. See Krings, "Wortschatz," pp. 35–36; Cropp, "*Vocabulaire courtois*," pp. 97–98; and Reto Bezzola's discussion of the poem as representing the transformation of William's concept of Love, *Les Origines*, vol. 2, pt. 2, p. 306 ff.

52. The *Chanson de Roland*, as preserved in the Oxford text, was composed after 1086, and before the mid-twelfth century. For some notes on dating, see John Benton, "'Nostre Franceis n'unt talent d fuïr': The *Song of Roland* and the Enculturation of a Warrior Class," *Olifant* 6 (1979): 239–40, nn. 18, 32.

53. *Die religiösen Dichtungen des 11. und 12. Jahrhunderts*, edited by Friedrich Maurer (Tübingen: Niemeyer, 1970), 3:289 (*Priesterleben* 17.14). Cf. Schrader, *Studien über das Wort "höfisch,"* p. 4 ff.

54. *Isidori Hispalensis episcopi etymologiarum sive originum libri XX*, edited by W. M. Lindsay (Oxford: Clarendon, 1911), bk. 10, p. 95.

55. William of Malmesbury, *Gesta reg. angl.* 4.312, RS 90:2:367.

56. The traditions of humor in the Middle Ages and the ambivalent reception of humor in medieval Christianity are traced and analysed by Joachim Suchomski, "*Delectatio*" und "*utilitas*": *Ein Beitrag zum Verständnis mittelalterlicher komischer Literatur*, Bibliotheca Germanica, vol. 18 (Bern and Munich: Francke, 1975).

57. *De consideratione* 3.13.22, in *S. Bernardi Opera*, edited by J. Leclerq and H. M. Rochais (Rome: Editiones Cistercienses, 1963), 3:430.

58. *De principis instructione* 1.11, RS 21:8:42: "'Quid distat inter Scotum et sotum?' . . . Cui Alquinus tale facetum quidem et eodem schemate periculosum tamen et exasperans . . . responsum dedit, 'Tabula tantum.'"

59. Castiglione devotes a long section of the *Libro del Cortegiano* to *facezie* (2.42–83). See Burckhardt's chapter "Ridicule and Wit" in *Civilization of the Renaissance in Italy*. Also the article by G. Luck, "'Vir facetus': A Renaissance Ideal," *Studies in Philology* 55 (1958): 107–21.

60. If there is anything to credit in the awful picture of Henry's court painted by his clerical opponents (the author of the *Vita Chunradi* was among them, as was Konrad himself), then such an ambiguous summons must have in fact been very ominous. Cf. Bruno of Merseburg's story of Henry's secretary Conrad, "iuvenis nobilitate et moribus insignis," summoned by the king and enjoined to make the journey accompanied by only a single squire. He was ambushed while under way and murdered, and the cause was never known (*Saxonicum bellum*, chap. 11, p. 19).

61. Cf. Walter Map's story of a knight assassinated on a hunt, *De nugis curialium*, vol. 1, fasc. 12, pp. 16–17. Also Gottfried, *Tristan* 5362 ff., and *Nibelungenlied*, sts. 972–1001.

62. Konrad von Würzburg, *Der trojanische Krieg*, edited by Adelbert von Keller, BLVS 44 (Stuttgart: Litterarischer Verein, 1858), l. 22018.

63. Walther von Wartburg, *Französisches etymologisches Wörterbuch: Eine Darstellung des galloromanischen Sprachschatzes* (Leipzig and Berlin: Teubner, 1934), 3:354.

64. C. Stephen Jaeger, *Medieval Humanism*, pp. 151–52; D. H. Green, *Irony in the Medieval Romance* (Cambridge and New York: Cambridge University Press, 1979), p. 359 ff.

65. *Historia regum Britanniae,* chap. 154, edited by Edmond Faral, *La Légende arthurienne: Etudes et documents,* Bibliothèque de l'école des hautes études 257 (Paris: Champion, 1929), 3:238.

66. Wace translates Geoffrey's *facetia* with *curteisie; faceta mulier* with *curteise dame. Le Roman de Brut de Wace,* edited by Ivor Arnold (Paris: Société des anciens textes français, 1940), 2.10493 ff., 10511 ff.

67. Edition by A. Morel-Fatio, in *Romania* 15 (1886): 224–35. See the commentary by Ingeborg Glier, *Artes amandi: Untersuchung zu Geschichte, Überlieferung und Typologie der deutschen Minnereden,* MTU 34 (Munich: Beck, 1971), pp. 18–20.

68. See the collection of tracts in *Der deutsche Facetus,* edited by Carl Schroeder, Palaestra 86 (Berlin: Mayer & Müller, 1911).

69. *Benedicti Regula,* edited by Rudolph Hanslik, CSEL 75 (Vienna: Hoelder-Pichler-Tempsky, 1960), p. 151 (64.15).

70. Gamer, "Studien zum Ruodlieb," p. 250.

71. Cf. Lotter, "Erkenntnisse," p. 323.

72. There is some echo in the monastic life apparently. Cf. Smaragd's comment on the Benedictine Rule, PL 102:890A ff. (chap. 53): "omnibus hilarem te ostende." But the social context of this quality in the tenth to twelfth century cannot have been the monastic life, contrary to Christian Götte, *Das Menschen- und Herrscherbild des rex major im 'Ruodlieb',* Medium Aevum, vol. 34 (Munich: Fink, 1981), p. 19, who quotes Smaragd and the Benedictine Rule as background to the atmosphere of cheery conviviality in *Ruodlieb.*

73. On *amicitia* as an ideal of the Carolingian court, see Fleckenstein, "Der Hof Karls des Grossen," p. 43.

74. See Ch. Camproux, "La Joie civilisatrice chez les Troubadours," *La Table Ronde* 97 (1957): 64–69. Alexander J. Denomy, "Jois Among the Early Troubadours: Its Meaning and Possible Source," *Mediaeval Studies* 13 (1951): 177–217. H.-W. Eroms, *"Vreude" bei Hartmann von Aue,* Medium Aevum, vol. 20 (Munich: Fink, 1970), pp. 24 ff., 54 ff., 131 ff.

75. Cf. Hartmann, *Erec* 1801; Gottfried, *Tristan* 536 ff. Telling also are the running polemics against "Epicureans" at court in John of Salisbury's *Policraticus,* mentioned earlier (1.4). Cf. esp. the following passage: "Siquidem Epicurus et totus grex sodalium eius vitam beatam asserit quae semper tanta iocunditate letatur ut tristitiae et perturbationis non interveniat vel tenuis motus. . . . Caro siquidem opinata est . . . quod amore iocisque nil est iocundius" (7.15, ed. Webb, 2:154).

76. *De gradibus humilitatis et superbiae* 12.40; *Opera* 3.46.

77. *Das Geschichtswerk des Otto Morena und seiner Fortsetzer über die Taten Friedrichs I. in der Lombardei,* edited by Ferdinand Güterbock, MGH, SS rer. germ., n.s., vol. 7 (Berlin: Weidmann, 1930; reprint, 1964), p. 167–70. I have shortened the passage, omitting some portraits and favoring references to ethical virtues, social graces, and physical beauty, omitting warrior virtues and the many repetitions.

78. *Civilitas* is of course more important in the civil life of the sixteenth century than in the Middle Ages, as Krings asserts (*Wortschatz,* pp. 147–90), but I believe he underestimates its importance in the twelfth century.

79. See Gerald of Wales' dissertation on this virtue, *De principis instructione* 1.3, RS:21:8:12–13.

80. One aspect I will only mention in passing but which I encountered several times is "courtliness" as a musical term. John of Affligem, in his *De musica cum tonario,* edited by J. Smits van Waesberghe, Corpus scriptorum de musica, vol. 1 (Rome: American Institute of Musicology, 1950), p. 117 (chap. 18), lists *curialitas* as one of the modes of music. The only hint about the nature of this mode is his comment, "Aliosque namque *morosa et curialis* vagatio . . . delectat" (p. 109, chap. 16). Saint Bernard of Clairvaux is accused by an enemy of having composed in his youth "cantiunculas mimicas et urbanos modulos" (PL 178:1857).

81. Frappier, "Vues," p. 135. Frappier is trying to combat the tendency of literary historians to disregard the social aspect altogether. But of these two aspects, the social and literary, the latter is the latecomer.

Chapter 9: The Clerical Rebellion Against Courtliness

1. See Archibald R. Lewis, *The Development of Southern French and Catalan Society, 718–1050* (Austin, Texas: University of Texas Press, 1965), pp. 123–24, 391 ff.

2. Cf. Bezzola's detailed treatment, *Les Origines*, vol. 2, pt. 2, pp. 243–326.

3. See R. William Leckie, *The Passage of Dominion: Geoffrey of Monmouth and the Periodization of Insular History in the Twelfth Century* (Toronto: University of Toronto Press, 1981), p. 60.

4. Raoul Glaber, *Les Cinq Livres de ses histoires (900–1044)*, edited by Maurice Prou. CTSEEH, vol. 1 (Paris: Picard, 1886), pp. 89–90 (*Historiae* 3.9.40).

5. William was something like a mentor to Ralph (Manitius, *Geschichte der lateinischen Literatur* 2:350). Ralph wrote a *vita* of William (PL 142:701–20). Both men were strict adherents of the Cluny reform.

6. An edition of the letter in Wilhelm von Giesebrecht, *Geschichte der deutschen Kaiserzeit*, 5th ed. (Leipzig: Duncker & Humblot, 1885), 2:714–18, here p. 718.

7. Cf. Bezzola, *Les Origines* 1:282. Marie Bulst-Thiele, *Kaiserin Agnes*, BKMR, vol. 52 (Leipzig and Berlin: Teubner, 1933), pp. 3–4. Of the numerous references given here to evidence of French influence under Henry III, only two actually confirm the phenomenon: the letter of Siegfried of Gorze and the *Sermones* of Amarcius Sextus.

8. *Hist. eccl.* 8.10, ed. Chibnall, 4:186.

9. See ibid. 6.11, ed. Chibnall, 6:60 ff. Henry I and his court are chided for wearing long hair, *femineo more.* They lose their manly strength in imitating women. Here also the customs are related to amatory practice, since they are said to grow their beards long (!) for fear of pricking their mistresses with short bristles when they kiss.

10. *Gesta reg. angl.* 4.314, ed. Stubbs, RS 90:2:369–70. The work was finished by 1120 but reworked twice by 1140. Cf. Manitius 3.470.

11. *Hist. nov.* 1.453, ed. Stubbs, RS 90:2:530–31. The custom was so offensive that the Council of Rouen in 1096 denied the sacraments to any long-haired layman. Cf. *Hist. eccl.* 9.3, ed. Chibnall, 5:22.

12. On Gebhard, see Fleckenstein, *Hofkapelle* 2:79, 113–14.

13. *Thietmar Merseburgensis episcopi chronicon*, edited by Robert Holtzmann, 2d ed., MGH, SS rer. germ. n.s., vol. 9 (Berlin: Weidmann, 1955), p. 270 (5.43).

14. *Visio quinta*, PL 146:357–59.

15. Here I am following Albert Hauck, *Kirchengeschichte Deutschlands*, 4th ed. (Leipzig: Hinrich, 1913), 4:357–69.

16. *Die religiösen Dichtungen des 11. und 12. Jahrhunderts*, edited by Friedrich Maurer (Tübingen: Niemeyer, 1970), 3:263–64 (*Priesterleben*, 4.10 ff.). On "Heinrich von Melk" see the article by Peter-Erich Neuser in the 2d edition of the *Verfasser-Lexikon*. Whoever he was, he lived in the Bavarian-Austrian area.

17. On Saxo see Manitius, 3.502–7. See esp. the introduction by Hilda Ellis Davidson to her commentary on the new translation by Peter Fisher: Saxo Grammaticus, *The History of the Danes: Books I–IX* (Cambridge, and Totowa, N.J.: D. S. Brewer and Rowman & Littlefield, 1980), 2:1–14 (with extensive bibliography).

18. Books 1–9 treat legendary material; books 10–16 are concerned with the historical period. The latter are supposed to have been written first. Interest in Saxo has concentrated almost exclusively on the antiquarian, on the survival of pagan themes and motifs in books 1–9. But Saxo is an important witness to the Latin vocabulary of courtesy and to the contemporary reception of the phenomenon. On his Latin, see Franz Blatt, *Saxonis Gesta Danorum: Tomus II: Index verborum* (Copenhagen: Munksgaard, 1957), vols. 5–13 (Danish). Reprinted in German translation as "Einleitung zu einem Wörterbuch über die Latinität Saxos," in *Mittellateinische Philologie: Beiträge zur Erforschung der mittelalterlichen Latinität*, edited by Alf Önnerfors, WDF, vol. 292 (Darmstadt: Wiss. Buchges., 1975), pp. 242–60.

19. Anti-courtly passages in Saxo besides those discussed in text: V, iii, 14, p. 117; XIII, v, 4, pp. 349–50; XIV, ix, 1, p. 387. The list is not exhaustive.

20. The persistence of this constellation is interesting: a king marries a foreign queen who brings with her the perversities of her countrymen. Cf. Robert the Pious

and Constance; Henry III and Agnes; here Ingellus and the daughter of the Saxon Svertingus.

21. *The Nine Books of the Danish History of Saxo Grammaticus*, translated by Oliver Elton (London: Norroena Society, 1905), 2:392–93.

22. See *Gesta Danorum* XIII, v, 4, p. 349; XIV, ix, 1, p. 387; XIV, lii, 1, p. 502.

23. See Jan de Vries, "Die Starkadsaga," in De Vries, *Kleine Schriften*, edited by K. Heeroma and A. Kylstra (Berlin: De Gruyter, 1965), pp. 20–36; originally in *GRM* 36 (1955): 281–97.

24. *Gesta Danorum* VI, ix, 4, p. 171: "Aulici risu populi lacessor / . . . / aspero carpor sale, dum loquaci / mordeor ausu." This scene is a good example of courtiers' exercising what Petrus Damiani calls *mordax eloquentia* (PL 144:258C). Cf. the reception of Hagen and Dancwart in Island in *Nibelungenlied*, st. 430,1: "Die zît wart disen recken in gelfe vil gedreut."

25. Cf. the advice of *Facetus*: the lover should pick out the woman who pleases him most, then "Hanc firmis oculis ridentibus intueatur" (153). When he finds her alone, "Huc veniat ludens, cantet suspiria miscens" (161). He communicates with her through signs: "Nutibus et signis sepe loquatur ei" (192).

26. See Dietrich Kralik, "Passau im Nibelungenlied," *Österreichische Akademie der Wissenschaften, Phil.-Hist. Kl. Anzeiger*, vol. 87 (1950), nr. 20, pp. 451–70.

27. See Bert Nagel, *Das Nibelungenlied: Stoff, Form, Ethos* (Frankfurt: Hirschgraben, 1965), pp. 156–204.

28. Cited from the edition, *Das Nibelungenlied*, edited by Karl Bartsch and Helmut de Boor, 18th ed. (Wiesbaden: Brockhaus, 1965).

29. For more detailed arguments see my article, "The Nibelungen Poet and the Clerical Rebellion Against Courtesy," in *Spectrum Medii Aevi: Essays in Early German Literature in Honor of George Fenwick Jones*, edited by William C. McDonald, Göppinger Arbeiten zur Germanistik, vol. 362 (Göppingen: Kümmerle, 1983), pp. 177–205.

30. The term is that of Orderic Vitalis. In the speech of Bp. Serlo of Séez chiding Henry I of England and his retinue (see n. 9, above), the bishop urges the king to rouse "useful anger" in himself ("utiliter irascere"—ed. Chibnall, 6:62).

Chapter 10: Courtliness in the Chronicles

1. See Curtius, *European Literature*, pp. 178–79.

2. Cf. the counsel of the god of love in *Roman de la Rose* 2099 ff.

3. See Painter, *French Chivalry*, p. 28: Chivalric ideals "grew out of their own cultural tradition and function in society. These ideals developed in the mind of the miles or chevalier, hence are properly called 'Chivalric.'" Marc Bloch, *Feudal Society*, translated by L. A. Manyon (Chicago: University of Chicago Press, 1968), p. 317: "It [chivalric conduct] was superimposed on rules of conduct evolved at an earlier date as the spontaneous expression of class consciousness . . . [it] constituted above all a class code of noble and 'courteous' people." Cf. Ehrismann, *Gesch. d. deut. Lit.* 2.1, p. 19: "Der neue ritterliche Geist hat einen neuen, veredelten Menschentypus geschaffen, der sich durch feinere Gesittung erhob über den altmodischen gewalttätigen Recken."

4. Hans Patze, "Adel und Stifterchronik: Frühformen territorialer Geschichtsschreibung im hochmittelalterlichen Reich," *Blätter für deutsche Landesgeschichte* 100 (1964): 8–81; 101 (1965): 67–128.

5. An example is the *vita* of Godfrey of Cappenberg, *Vita Godefridi comitis Capenbergensis*, edited by Ph. Jaffé, MGH, SS 12:513–30.

6. Excluding such earlier tribal histories as Jordanes on the Goths, Paulus Diaconus on the Lombards, and Widukind on the Saxons.

7. Helgaud de Fleury, *Vie de Robert le Pieux*, edited and translated by Robert-Henri Bautier and Gilette Labory, Sources d'histoire médiévale, vol. 1 (Paris: Éditions du CNRS, 1965), p. 60 (chap. 2).

8. William of Jumièges, *Gesta Normannorum ducum*, PL 149:779–910. Cf. Manitius 3.440 ff.

9. Cf. Robert of Torigni's description of Henry I of England: "vir pluribus virtutibus

praeditus, justitiae ac pacis sector, religionis amator, iniquorum et furum ferven-tissimus punitor, inimicorum suorum non solum excellentium principum et comitum, verum et nominatissimorum regum felicissimus triumphator" (8.10, PL 149:886C).

10. Guillaume de Poitiers, *Histoire de Guillaume le conquérant*, edited and translated by R. Foureville, Les Classiques de l'histoire de France au moyen âge, vol. 23 (Paris: Société d'édition "Les Belles Lettres," 1952), pp. 12–14 (chap. 6).

11. PL 149:1093–1210. Manitius 3.457 ff.

12. An interesting formulation that recurs in this work is *miles elegantissimus*. (1186B and 1189C). The adjective accords with nothing else in his description of knights, and no passage allows us to formulate its meaning. Still he evidently had a refined conception of an excellent knight.

13. *Chroniques des comtes d'Anjou et des seigneurs d'Amboise*, edited by Louis Halphen and René Poupardin, CTSEEH, vol. 48 (Paris: Picard, 1913).

14. See Alfred Jeanroy, *La Poésie lyrique des Troubadours* (Toulouse and Paris: Didier, 1934), 1:84; Bezzola, *Les Origines*, vol. 2, pt. 2, p. 463 ff.

15. Cf. Karl Bosl, "Leitbilder und Wertvorstellungen des Adels von der Merowinger-zeit bis zur Höhe der feudalen Gesellschaft," *Sitzungsberichte der Bayerischen Akademie der Wissenschaften, Phil.-Hist. Kl.* (1974), no. 5 (Munich: Bayerische Akademie der Wissenschaften und Beck, 1974).

16. On Jean de Marmoutier, see Bezzola, *Les Origines*, vol. 2, pt. 2, pp. 329–34.

17. Urban T. Holmes, *A History of Old French Literature from the Origins to 1300*, 2d ed. rev. (New York: Russell & Russell, 1962), p. 165 ff. He dates *Erec* before 1162; *Cligès* ca. 1162; *Lancelot* ca. 1166; *Yvain* 1169.

18. Cf. Claude Luttrell, *The Creation of the First Arthurian Romance: A Quest* (London: Arnold, 1974), esp. pp. 26–46; and Tony Hunt, "Redating Chrétien de Troyes," *BBSIA* 30 (1978): 209–37.

19. Bezzola, *Les Origines*, vol. 3, pt. 1, pp. 150–98.

20. See Arno Borst's characterization in "Das Rittertum im Hochmittelalter: Idee und Wirklichkeit," in *Das Rittertum im Mittelalter*, edited by Arno Borst, WDF, vol. 349 (Darmstadt: Wissenschaftliche Buchgesellschaft, 1976), pp. 212–46.

21. Lambert of Ardres, *Historia comitum Ghisnensium*, edited by I. Heller, MGH, SS 24:603, l. 39 ff. (chap. 90).

22. Joachim Bumke, *Studien zum Ritterbegriff im 12. und 13. Jahrhundert*, 2d ed., Beihefte zum Euphorion, vol. 1 (Heidelberg: Winter, 1964), pp. 147–48.

23. *Recherches sur les sources latines des contes et romans courtois du moyen âge* (Paris: Champion, 1913), p. 195.

24. An extreme position on this point is taken by D. W. Robertson and John Benton in their essays in *The Meaning of Courtly Love*, edited by F. X. Newman, Papers of the First Annual Conference of the Center for Medieval and Early Renaissance Studies, State University of New York at Binghamton (Albany, N.Y.: State University of New York Press, 1968). See the answer of Jean Frappier, "Sur un procès fait á l'amour cour-tois," in his *Amour courtois et table ronde*, Publications romanes et françaises, vol. 126 (Geneva: Droz, 1973), pp. 145–93.

Chapter 11: Instructing the Laity in Courtesy

1. See Jean de Marmoutier, *Chroniques des comtes d'Anjou*, pp. 184–85.

2. Cf. S. Painter, *French Chivalry*, pp. 28–64; J. Huizinga, *The Waning of the Middle Ages: A Study of the Forms of Life, Thought and Art in France and the Netherlands in the 14th and 15th Century* (London: Arnold, 1955), pp. 56–94.

3. These enforcing mechanisms are sharply analyzed by Elias, *Prozess* 2:397–409.

4. *Die Werke Wipos*, edited by Harry Bresslau, 3d ed., MGH, SS rer. germ. in us. schol., vol. 61 (Hannover and Leipzig: Hahn, 1915; reprint, 1977), p. 10 (*Gesta Chuonradi*, chap. 1). On the formulation *litterae et mores* in Hildebert, see Von Moos, *Hildebert*, p. 24 ff.

5. Cf. Philippe Delhaye, "L'Enseignement de la philosophie morale au XIIe siècle," *Mediaeval Studies* 11 (1949): 77–95; cited here from the reprint in German under the title

"Moralphilosophischer Unterricht im 12. Jahrhundert," in *Ritterliches Tugendsystem*, pp. 301–40.

6. William of Conches in his commentary on Boethius' Consolation of Philosophy, cited in Delhaye, "L'Enseignement," p. 302, n. 4.

7. *De septem septenis*, PL 199:949A. Cited in Delhaye, "L'Enseignment," p. 303, n. 6.

8. Margaret Gibson, *Lanfranc of Bec* (Oxford: Clarendon, 1978), p. 19.

9. Hincmar, *De ordine palatii*, p. 80–81, l. 451 ff.: "Alter ordo per singula ministeria in discupilis congruebat, qui a magistro suo singuli adhaerentes et honorificabant et honorificabantur." Cf. Franz Brunhölzl, "Der Bildungsauftrag der Hofschule," in *Karl der Grosse*, vol. 2, *Das Geistige Leben*, edited by Bernhard Bischoff (Düsseldorf: Schwann, 1965), pp. 28–41.

10. See Rosamund McKittrick, "The Palace School of Charles the Bald," in *Charles the Bald: Court and Kingdom*, edited by Margaret Gibson and Janet Nelson, pp. 385–400, BAR International Series, vol. 101 (Oxford: BAR, 1981). See also, on the debate about an Ottonian court school, Fleckenstein, "Königshof und Bischofschule," p. 40 ff.

11. *Vie de Bouchard le vénérable, comte de Vendôme, de Corbeil, de Melun et de Paris*, edited by Ch. Bourel de la Roncière, CTSEEH, vol. 13 (Paris: Picard, 1892), p. 5.

12. James W. Thompson, *The Literacy of the Laity in the Middle Ages*, University of California Publications in Education, vol. 9 (Berkeley and Los Angeles: University of California Press, 1939; reprint, New York, 1963). Herbert Grundmann, "Litteratus-Illitteratus: Der Wandel einer Bildungsnorm vom Altertum zum Mittelalter," in *Ausgewählte Aufsätze*, pp. 1–66, Schriften der MGH 25:3 (Stuttgart: Hiersemann, 1978). (First appeared in *AKG* 40 [1958]: 1–65.) H. G. Richardson and G. O. Sayles, *The Governance of Mediaeval England from the Conquest to Magna Carta* (Edinburgh: Edinburgh University Press, 1963), pp. 265–84 ("Statecraft and Learning"). Ralph V. Turner, "The *Miles Literatus* in Twelfth- and Thirteenth-Century England: How Rare a Phenomenon?" *AHR* 83 (1978): 928–45.

13. This describes the state of education, for instance, of Henry the Lion and Baldwin II of Guines. Cf. Thompson, *Literacy*, pp. 141f., 99.

14. *Tetralogus* 190 ff.; *Die Werke Wipos*, p. 81. On the passage see Thompson, *Literacy*, pp. 60–61, 90–91; Grundmann, "Litteratus-Illitteratus," p. 50.

15. Matthew Paris, *Historia Anglorum (Historia minor)*, edited by Frederic Madden, RS 44: 1 (London: Longman, 1866), p. 316.

16. *Heinrichs von Meissen, des Frauenlobes, Leiche, Sprüche, Streitgedichte und Lieder*, edited by Ludwig Etmüller, DNL, vol. 16 (Quedlinburg and Leipzig: Basse, 1843), p. 141 (Spruch 244.6 ff).

17. *The Medieval French Roman d'Alexandre*, edited by Milan S. La Du, Elliott Monographs, no. 36 (Princeton, N.J.: Princeton University Press, 1937; reprint, New York, 1965), p. 4, l. 48 ff. My thanks to Alexander Cizek for pointing out the passage to me.

18. "Quid Dione valeat et amoris deus, / primus novit clericus et instruxit meus" ("De Phyllide et Flora," st. 41). Likewise in the "Love Council of Remiremont," Elizabeth de Falcon on clerics: "Inest curialitas clericis et probitas" (ed. Meyer, l. 73). And in the OF love debate "Le jugement d'amour," ed. Faral, *Les Sources*, p. 257, l. 142 ff: "Que clers set plus de cortoisie / Et que miex doit avoir amie / Ke autre gent, ne chevalier / Ne sevent vaillant un denier / Enviers clerc qui d'amor s'envoise."

19. *Lancelot: Nach der Heidelberger Pergamenthandschrift pal. germ. 147*, edited by Reinhold Kluge, DTM, vol. 42 (Berlin: Akademie, 1948), 1:20, ll. 35–36. My thanks to Ingrid Hahn for this reference. On the episode in the Vulgate cycle, see Jean Frappier, "L'Institution de Lancelot dans le Lancelot en Prose," in *Mélanges de philologie romane et de littérature médiévale offerts à Ernest Hoepffner*, pp. 267–78 (Paris: Les Belles Lettres, 1949); reprinted in Frappier, *Amour courtois et table ronde*, pp. 169–79.

20. *Moralitas* is a common Latin term in the twelfth century for moral instruction. The author of the *Moralium dogma philosophorum* refers to Seneca as "ille moralitatis eruditor elegantissimus" (Proeemium, p. 5). W. T. H. Jackson pointed out the concept in Boethius' treatise on music, where the harmonizing and humanizing effect of music is said to serve *moralitas* (*PMLA* 77 [1962]: 370.) But the context in which it occurs in *Tristan* is moral instruction, not music. Since it is common in this sense in Latin in the

twelfth century, this must be taken to be its immediate reference in Gottfried's poem.

21. Alexander Neckam, *De naturis rerum*, edited by T. Wright, RS 34 (London: Longman, 1863), p. 312 (2.175).

22. "Der heimliche Bote," in *Mittelhochdeutsche Übungsstücke*, edited by H. Meyer-Benfey, pp. 30–32 (Halle: Niemeyer, 1909). Helmut De Boor, *Die höfische Literatur: Vorbereitung, Blüte, Ausklang: 1170–1250* (Munich: Beck, 1964), p. 394, dates the work 1180–90. More recently Ingeborg Glier, *Artes amandi*, p. 18 ff, dates it 1170–80.

23. Gustav Ehrismann, "Phaset," *ZfdA* 64 (1927): 301–6.

24. See Thompson, *Literacy*, p. 133.

25. Cf. Marbod's *Vita Gualterii*, PL 171:1567B: "Cum enim post tenerae educationem infantiae, sicut plerique nobilium liberi solent, in studium litterarum missus est." And his *Vita Licinii*, PL 171:1495C: "post prima elementa, sicut liberi nobilium solent, in disciplinam litterariam datus [est]." Note the present tense throughout. It was a current custom.

26. Cf. Wipo's statement that the Germans, in constrast to Italians, considered it "vacuum et turpe" for nonclerics to receive an education (*Tetralogus*, 199 ff.) Cf. Thompson, *Literacy*, p. 90 ff.

27. Ep. 16, PL 203:147–51. See Thompson, *Literacy*, pp. 139–40.

28. Ep. 17, PL 203:151–56. See Thompson, *Literacy*, pp. 143–44. One of the persistent themes of this letter is that Henry should honor and cultivate the learned clerics at his court and should constantly draw gifted men to court.

29. There are some observations on the duty of correction in Georges Duby, *The Three Orders: Feudal Society Imagined*, translated by Arthur Goldhammer (Chicago and London: University of Chicago Press, 1978), pp. 257–58. It is prominent among the prescriptions in Gregory's *Regula pastoralis* 2.4, PL 77:30–32; and 2.6, PL 77:34 ff.

30. Peter of Blois, *Dialogus inter regem Henricum II et abbatem Bonaevallensem*, PL 207:975–88.

31. Cf. Diploma of Henry V: "Si ecclesias deo dicatas amplificare et sublimare intendimus, antecessorum nostrorum regum ac imperatorum morem exequimur" (25 March 1121), *Monumenta Boica* (Munich: Cota, 1831), 29:1:240, #445. Dipl. of Lothar III: "Divinis et salutaribus sanctarum scripturarum erudimur documentis, et antecessorum nostrorum admonemur exemplis, ut aecclesias dei summa devotione ac benignitate ditemus . . ." (5 April 1130, *Mon. Boi.* 29:1:255, #455.)

32. See Gertrud Simon, "Untersuchungen zur Topik der Widmungsbriefe mittelalterlicher Geschichtsschreiber bis zum Ende des 12. Jahrhunderts: Zweiter Teil," *Archiv für Diplomatik* 5 (1959): 102–3.

33. "Ad edificationem sanctimonie et propagationem virtutis et fortitudinis incentivum veterum fuit patrum industria ante oculos hominum sui temporis proponere, qui, vel prudentia perspicaces vel justitia severi vel fortitudine insuperabiles vel modestia circumfusi, probitatis quodam speciali radio coruscant, quatenus ad eorum normam, si quid prava enormasset consuetudo, in melius reformarent et quod melior conversatio tenuerat ad eorum speculum roborassent" (ed. Halphen, pp. 172–73).

34. *Annales Stederburgenses*, ad annum 1194, MGH SS 16:230, ll. 37 ff. Cf. MGH, SS 9:29, ll. 17–18: "Et vita [sic] veterum Nosset per scripta priorum, / Atque statum miserum [sic] Per mores sciret eorum." Cf. Thompson, *Literacy*, pp. 113–14.

35. *Gesta Frid. Cont.* 4.86, ed. Waitz, p. 344: "Scripturas et antiquorum regum gesta sedule perquirit."

36. William of Tyre, *Historia* 16.2; *Recueil des historiens des croisades: Historiens occidentales* (Paris: Imprimerie royale, 1844), 1:705–6. Cited in Thompson, *Literacy*, p. 158, n. 120.

37. MGH, SS 22:22, l. 13 ff.: "in puerorum scolis facias lectitari; cum sit honestius istorias et naturas regum et imperatorum, quibus mundus instruitur et ornatur, animo pueri legentis imprimere, quam fabulas Choridonis vel pecudes Melibei memorie commendare."

38. See Paul Zumthor on the evolution of romance in *Grundriss der romanischen Literaturen des Mittelalters IV: 1: Le Roman jusqu'à la fin du XIIIe siècle*, edited by Jean Frappier and Reinhold R. Grimm (Heidelberg: Winter, 1978), p. 60 ff.

39. Cf. Gertrud Simon, "Untersuchungen II," p. 99.

40. *Le Roman de Rou de Wace*, edited by A. J. Holden, Société des anciens textes français, vol. 2 (Paris: Picard, 1970), p. 309, l. 8 ff.

41. See M. T. Clanchy, *From Memory to Written Record: England, 1066–1307* (London: Arnold, 1979). See especially Brian Stock, *The Implications of Literacy: Written Language and Models of Interpretation in the Eleventh and Twelfth Centuries* (Princeton: Princeton University Press, 1983). This important book only came to my attention shortly before my manuscript went to the printer.

42. On Gerold's collection and the *Chanson de Guillaume*, see Bezzola, *Les Origines* 2:491 ff.

43. Cf. Carl Erdmann, "'Fabulae curiales': Neues zum Spielmannsgesang und zum Ezzo-Liede," *ZfdA* 73 (1936): 87–98.

44. Luttrell's study places beyond doubt Chrétien's high learning and his familiarity with humanist ideas current in the cathedral schools. Cf. Alexandre Micha, "Chrétien de Troyes," in *GRLMA*, IV:1:231–32.

45. The participation of clerics in the writing of courtly lyric has also been underestimated. See the correction to this picture in Joachim Bumke, *Ministerialität und Ritterdichtung: Umrisse der Forschung* (Munich: Beck, 1976).

46. Frappier, "Vues," p. 146. For other, earlier observations on the role of clerics, see Faral, *Les Sources*, pp. 194–95; Jeanroy gives a skewed view of their role, partly because of his dogged and unconvincing opposition to the views of Brinkmann. See *La Poésie lyrique* 1:76 ff. See also Moshe Lazar, *Amour courtois et "Fin Amors" dans la littérature du XIIe siècle*, Bibliothèque française et romane: Etudes littéraires, vol. 8 (Paris: Klincksieck, 1964), pp. 11 ff., 15.

47. In Gottfried's prologue, an acrostic spells out the name *DIETERICH*, possibly a reference to his patron, otherwise unidentified.

48. Elias points out that "ideals" arise when rules of behavior that have a practical application in one class are transferred to another class in which the practical necessity of these forms no longer exists. *Prozess* 2:482, n. 134.

Chapter 12: Courtliness in the Romance

1. See *De nugis curialium* 1.12, pp. 16–17.

2. Hugo Kuhn was the first to point out the many similarities between *Tristan* and *Nibelungenlied*, in his "Tristan, Nibelungenlied, Artusstruktur," Sitzungsberichte der bayerischen Akademie der Wissenschaften, Phil.-Hist. Klasse (1973), no. 5.

3. "[Monet Honestas ut] . . . Interius sibimet ut pauci vivat et extra / Ut plures, intus sibi vivens, pluribus extra; / . . . ut omnibus omnis / Pareat . . ." (Alain de Lille, *Anticlaudianus: Texte critique avec une introduction et des tables*, edited by R. Bossuat [Paris: Vrin, 1955], p. 163 [7.215–18]). Quoted here from Alan of Lille, *Anticlaudianus or the Good and Perfect Man*, translated and with a commentary by James J. Sheridan (Toronto: Pontifical Institute, 1973), p. 180. The lines are loosely adapted from Seneca, *Epist. Moral. ad Lucilium* 5.2–3: "Intus omnia dissimilia sint, frons populo nostra conveniat."

4. See Joan M. Ferrante, *The Conflict of Love and Honor: The Medieval Tristan Legend in France, Germany and Italy*, De proprietatibus litterarum, Series practica no. 78 (The Hague and Paris: Mouton, 1973), p. 11: The dominant theme of Arthurian romance is "the development of the individual toward his proper place in society."

5. Gert Kaiser has interpreted Iwein's education in much the same way, in his *Textauslegung und gesellschaftliche Selbstdeutung: Die Artusromane Hartmanns von Aue*, 2d ed. (Wiesbaden: Athenaion, 1978). But he places this development very directly against the background of the rise of the ministerial class, for which he was criticised by Ursula Peters, Hedda Ragotzky, and Volker Schupp. I agree that the civilizing tendency evident in *Iwein* cannot be restricted to a particular class within the lower nobility.

6. Here I am relying on Schrader, *Studien zum Wort "höfisch"*, but particularly on Hubert Heinen's forthcoming study "The Concepts *hof*, *hövesch*, and the Like in Hartmann's *Iwein*." My thanks to Professor Heinen for allowing me to read the Ms. prior to publication.

7. On the question of dating and the relative chronology of Hartmann's works, see Peter Wapnewski, *Hartmann von Aue*, 7th ed., Sammlung Metzler, vol. 17 (Stuttgart: Metzler, 1979), p. 16 ff.

8. Erich Auerbach, for instance, sees him as "a true knight," and "a true knight, one of the elect." *Mimesis: The Representation of Reality in Western Literature*, translated by Willard Trask (Garden City, N.Y.: Doubleday, 1957), p. 118. He is speaking of Chrétien's figure, it is true, and Hartmann has placed the knight's negative side in sharper profile. But his inspiration was Chrétien.

9. There is some controversy about the interpretation put forward here, which is basically that of Wapnewski (*Hartmann von Aue*, p. 76 ff.). It has been suggested that the phrase "âne zuht" is to be understood to mean "wildly, in an undisciplined way." See Paul Salmon, "'Âne zuht': Hartmann von Aue's Criticism of Iwein," *Modern Language Review* 69 (1974): 556–61, and Christian Gellinek, "Iwein's Duel and Laudine's Marriage," in *The Epic in Medieval Society: Aesthetic and Moral Values*, edited by Harald Scholler (Tübingen: Niemeyer, 1977), pp. 226–39. Granting Salmon's point that "âne zuht" *can* have a meaning other than moral, it need not be understood in that secondary sense in the scene in question. Granting also Gellinek's point that the battle is fair and honorable, we are not obliged to see its end partaking of those qualities because its beginning does. The ideal of mercy shown to a vanquished enemy (cf. *Parzival* 171.25 ff.)—no minor item within Hartmann's values—is violated in that scene. Wapnewski points out that Iwein's adventures in the second half of the romance aim at showing the hero's attainment and exercise of mercifulness, *erbermde*, and it is certainly the discourteous and inhumane act of pursuing Ascalon to finish him off and have something to show his fellows which is being expunged in those events. On balance, the arguments for interpreting the pursuit of Ascalon as a violation of humanity outweigh those which minimize Iwein's moral guilt.

10. References are to *Wolfram von Eschenbach*, edited by Albert Leitzmann, 7th ed. rev. Wilhelm Deinert, 3 vols., ATB, vols. 12–14 (Tübingen: Niemeyer, 1961–65).

11. See Ursula Hennig,, "Die Gurnemanzlehren und die unterlassene Frage Parzivals," *PBB* 97 (Tübingen, 1975): 312–32.

12. *Kiusche* is a rich concept in Wolfram, not restricted to the sense of sexual abstinence.

13. Schrader, *Studien*, p. 41.

Conclusion

1. See Southern, *Society and Church*, p. 198 ff.

BIBLIOGRAPHY

Primary Sources

Biographical works are generally entered under the name of the subject followed by (*Vita*) or (*Gesta*).

Acerbus Morena. *Das Geschichtswerk des Otto Morena und seiner Fortsetzer über die Taten Friedrichs I. in der Lombardei.* MGH, SS rer. germ., n.s., vol. 7. Berlin: Weidmann, 1930.

Adalbero II of Metz (*Vita*). *Vita Adalberonis II. Mettensis episcopi.* MGH, SS 4:658–72.

Adalbert of Hamburg-Bremen (*Vita*). See Adam of Bremen.

Adalbert II of Mainz (*Vita*). *Anselmi Havelbergensis vita Adelberti II Moguntini.* Edited by Ph. Jaffé. Bibl. rer. germ. 3:565–603.

Adalbert of Prague (*Vita*). *Vita Sancti Adalberti episcopi.* MGH, SS 4:574–612. *Vita antiquior auctore Iohanne Canapario,* pp. 581–95. *Vita secunda auctore Brunone archiepiscopo,* pp. 595–612.

Adam of Bremen. *Hamburgische Kirchengeschichte.* Edited by Bernhard Schmeidler. 3d ed. MGH, SS rer. germ. in us. schol., vol. 2. Hannover and Leipzig: Hahn, 1917. Reprint. 1977.

Aegidius Columna. *De regimine principum.* Venice, 1498.

Aeneae Silvii de curialium miseriis epistola. Edited by Wilfred P. Mustard. Baltimore and London: Johns Hopkins University Press, 1928.

Ailred of Rievaulx (*Vita*). *The Life of Ailred of Rievaulx by Walter Daniel.* Edited and translated by F. M. Powicke. New York and Oxford: Oxford University Press, 1951.

Albero of Trier (*Gesta*). *Gesta Alberonis archiepiscopi Treverensis auctore Balderico.* LB, pp. 543–617. Reprint from MGH, SS 8:243–60.

Alexander Neckham. *De naturis rerum.* Edited by T. Wright. RS 34. London: Longman, 1863.

Altmann of Passau (*Vita*). *Vita Altmanni episcopi Pataviensis.* Edited by W. Wattenbach. MGH, SS 12:226–43.

Ambrose, Saint. *Sancti Ambrosii Mediolanensis episcopi De officiis ministrorum libri tres.* PL 16:23–184.

Andreae Capellani Regii Francorum De amore libri tres. Edited by E. Trojel. Copenhagen: Gad, 1892. Reprint. 1972.

Annales Hildesheimenses. Edited by G. Waitz. MGH, SS rer. germ., vol. 8. Hannover: Hahn, 1878.

Annalista Saxo. Edited by G. Waitz. MGH, SS 6:542–777.

Anno of Cologne (*Vita*). *Vita Annonis archiepiscopi Coloniensis*. Edited by R. Koepke. MGH, SS 11:462–515.
Translatio Annonis archiepiscopi. Edited by R. Koepke. MGH, SS 11: 514–18.
Vita Annonis Minor: Die jüngere Annovita. Edited by M. Mittler. Siegburger Studien, vol. 10. Siegburg: Respublica, 1975.
Anonymus Haserensis de episcopis Eichstetensibus. MGH, SS 7:253–66.
Anselm of Liège. *Gesta episcoporum Leodiensium*. Edited by R. Koepke. MGH, SS 7:189–234.
Anselm of Lucca (*Vita*). *Vita Anselmi episcopi Lucensis auctore Bardone presbytero*. Edited by R. Wilmans. MGH, SS 12:1–35.
Vita metrica Sancti Anselmi Lucensis episcopi auctore Rangerio Lucensi. Edited by E. Sackur; G. Schwartz; and B. Schmeidler. MGH, SS 30:2:1152–1307.
Arnold of Mainz (*Vita*). *Vita Arnoldi archiepiscopi Moguntini*. Edited by Ph. Jaffé. Bibl. rer. germ. 3:604–75.
Arnulf of Soissons (*Vita*). *Hariulfi Aldenburgensis abbatis Vita Sancti Arnulfi Suessionensis episcopi*. PL 174:1375–1438.
Balderich of Liège (*Vita*). *Vita Balderici episcopi Leodiensis auctore monacho Sancti Iacobi Leodiensis*. MGH, SS 4:724–38.
Bardo of Mainz (*Vita*). *Vulculdi vita Bardonis archiepiscopi Moguntini*. Edited by Ph. Jaffé. Bibl. rer. germ. 3:521–29.
Baldrinus Burgulianus. *Carmina*. Edited by Karlheinz Hilbert. Heidelberg: Winter, 1979.
Baudri of Bourgeuil. *Vita Sancti Hugonis Rothomagensis episcopi auctore Baldrico Dolensi*. PL 166:1163–72.
Becket, Thomas (*Vitae*). *Materials for the History of Thomas Becket, Archbishop of Canterbury*. Edited by James Craigie Robertson. RS 67, vols. 1–3. London: Longman, 1875–77.
Bernard of Parma (*Vita*). *Vitae prima et secunda Sancti Bernardi episcopi Parmensis*. Edited by P. E. Schramm. MGH, SS 30:2. *Vita prima*, pp. 1316–23. *Vita secunda*, pp. 1323–27.
Benno II of Osnabrück (*Vita*). *Vita Bennonis II. episcopi Osnabrugensis auctore Norberto abbate Iburgensi*. LB, pp. 363–441. Reprint from MGH, SS 30:2:869–92.
Benzo of Alba. *Benzonis episcopi Albensis ad Heinricum IV imperatorem libri VII*. Edited by K. Pertz. MGH, SS 11:591–681.
Bernward of Hildesheim (*Vita*). *Vita Sancti Bernwardi episcopi Hildesheimensis auctore Thangmaro*. LB, pp. 263–361. Reprint from MGH, SS 4:754–82.
Briefsammlungen der Zeit Heinrichs IV. Edited by Carl Erdmann and Norbert-Fickermann. MGH, Briefe der deutschen Kaiserzeit, vol. 5. Weimar: Böhlau, 1950.
Brun of Cologne (*Vita*). *Vita Sancti Brunonis archiepiscopi Coloniensis auctore Ruotgero*. LB, pp. 169–259. Reprint from *Ruotgers Lebensbeschreibung des Erzbischofs Bruno von Köln*. Edited by Irene Ott. MGH, SS rer. germ. n.s., vol 10. Weimar: Böhlaus Nachfolger, 1951.
Bruno of Merseburg. *Brunos Buch vom Sachsenkrieg*. Edited by Hans-Eberhard Lohmann. MGH, Deutsches Mittelalter: Kritische Studientexte des Reichsinstituts für ältere deutsche Geschichtskunde, vol. 2. Leipzig: Hiersemann, 1937.
Burckhard of Vendôme (*Vita*). Eudes de St. Maure (Odo Fossatensis). *Vie de*

Bouchard le vénérable, comte de Vendôme, de Corbeil, de Melun et de Paris. Edited by Ch. Bourel de la Roncière. CTSEEH, vol. 13. Paris: Picard, 1892.

Burchard of Worms (*Vita*). *Vita Burchardi episcopi.* Edited by G. Waitz. MGH, SS 4:829–46.

Carmina Burana, mit Benutzung der Vorarbeiten Wilhelm Meyers. Kritisch herausgegeben von Alfons Hilka und Otto Schumann. 2 vols. Heidelberg: Winter, 1930–41.

Castiglione, Baldesar. *Il Libro del Cortegiano.* Edited by Bruno Maier. 2d ed. Turin: Unione Tipografico-Editrice Troinese, 1964.

———. *The Book of the Courtier.* Translated by Charles S. Singleton. Garden City, N.Y.: Doubleday, 1959.

Chrétien de Troyes. *Erec et Enide.* Edited by Mario Roques. CFMA, vol. 80. Paris: Champion, 1963.

———. *Cligès.* Edited by E. A. Micha. CFMA, vol. 84. Paris: Champion, 1957.

———. *Le Chevalier au lion (Yvain).* Edited by Mario Roques. CFMA, vol. 89. Paris: Champion, 1960.

———. *Le Roman de Perceval ou le conte du graal.* 2d ed. Edited by W. Roach. Textes littéraires français, vol. 71. Geneva: Droz; and Paris: Minard, 1959.

Chronicon abbatiae Evesham. Edited by W. Dunn Macray. RS 29. London: Longman, 1863.

Chronica episcoporum ecclesiae Merseburgensis. Edited by Roger Wilmans. MGH, SS 10:157–212.

Chronicon episcoporum Hildesheimensium. MGH, SS 7:845–73.

Chroniques des comtes d'Anjou et des seigneurs d'Amboise. Edited by Louis Halphen and René Poupardin. CTSEEH, vol 48. Paris: Picard, 1913.

Cicero. *De officiis.* Edited and translated Walter Miller. Loeb Classical Library, vol. 30. Cambridge, Mass: Harvard University Press, 1913.

Conrad I of Constance (*Vita*). *Vita Chounradi Constantiensis episcopi.* MGH, SS vol. 4.
  Vita prior auctore Oudoscalco, pp. 430–36.
  Vita altera auctore anonymo, pp. 436–45.

Conrad of Pfullingen (*Vita*). *Vita et passio Conradi archiepiscopi Treverensis auctore Theoderico.* MGH, SS 8:212–19.

Conrad I of Salzburg (*Vita*). *Vita Chunradi archiepiscopi Salisburgensis.* MGH, SS 11:62–77.

Dieterich of Metz (*Vita*). *Vita Deoderici episcopi Mettensis auctore Sigeberto Gemblacensi.* MGH, SS 4:461–83.

Dudo of Saint Quentin. *De moribus et actis primorum Normanniae ducum.* PL 141:607–758.

Eberhard I of Salzburg (*Vita*). *Vita Sancti Eberhardi archiepiscopi Salzburgensis.* MGH, SS 4:77–84.

Gundechari liber pontificalis Eichstetensis. MGH, SS 7:239–50.
  Ottonis et aliorum continuationes, pp. 250–53.

Eichstatt, Bishops of (*Gesta*). See *Anonymus Haserensis.*

Eraclius of Liège (*Vita*). *Vita Evracli Leodiensium episcopi auctore Reinero.* MGH, SS 20:561–65.

"Facetus." Edited by A. Morel-Fatio. *Romania* 15 (1886): 224–35.

Fundatio ecclesiae Hildensemensis. Edited by A. Hofmeister. MGH, SS 30:2: 939–46.

Gaufred of Malaterra. *De rebus gestis Rogerii regis Sicilii, Liber de acquisitione regni Siciliae, Calabriae, Apuliae et insulae Siciliae, per gloriosum principem Robertum Guiscardem et fratres de Normannia venientes.* PL 149:1094–1210.

Geoffrey of Monmouth. *Historia regum Britanniae.* Edited by Edmond Faral. In *La Légende arthurienne: Études et documents.* Bibliothèque de l'école des hautes études, vol. 257. Paris: Champion, 1929.

Gerald of Wales. *De principis instructione liber.* Edited by George F. Warner. RS 92, vol. 8. London: Eyre & Spottiswoode, 1891.

Gerhard of Toul (*Vita*). *Vita Sancti Gerardi episcopi Tullensis auctore Widrico.* Edited by G. Waitz. MGH, SS 4:490–505.

Gerhoh of Reichersberg. *Liber de aedificio Dei, seu de studio et cura disciplinae ecclesiasticae.* PL 194:1187–1336.

Gesta episcoporum Halberstadensium. Edited by L. Weiland. MGH, SS 23:73–123.

Gesta episcoporum Leodiensium. See Anselm of Liège.

Gesta episcoporum Mettensium. Edited by G. Waitz. MGH, SS 10:531–51.

Gesta episcoporum Tullensium. Edited by G. Waitz. MGH, SS 8:631–48.

Gesta Hammaburgensis ecclesiae pontificum. See Adam of Bremen.

Gesta pontificum Cameracensium. Edited by V. C. Bethmann. MGH, SS 7:393–525.

Gilbert of Mons. *La Chronique de Gislebert de Mons.* Edited by Léon Vanderkindere. Brussels: Kiessling, 1904.

Glossaria Latina iussu academiae Britannicae edita. Vol. 1, *Glossarium Ansileubi sive librum glossarum.* Edited by W. M. Lindsay et al. Paris: Société anonyme d'édition "Les Belles Lettres," 1926.

Glossarium latinum bibliothecae Parisinae antiquissimum. Edited by G. F. Hildebrand. Göttingen: Dieterich, 1854.

Godehard of Hildesheim (*Vita*). *Vita Godehardi episcopi Hildeneesheimensis auctore Wolfherio.* MGH, SS 11. *Vita prior*, pp. 167–96. *Vita posterior*, pp. 196–218.

Godfrey of Cappenberg (*Vita*). *Vita Godefridi comitis Capenbergensis.* Edited by Ph. Jaffé. MGH, SS 12:513–30.

Gottfried von Strassburg. *Tristan und Isold.* Edited by Friedrich Ranke. 11th ed. Dublin and Zurich: Weidmann, 1967.

Gregory the Great. *Regulae pastoralis liber ad Joannem episcopum civitatis Ravennae.* PL 77:13–128.

Guibert de Tournai. *Le Traité Eruditio regum et principum de Guibert de Tournai.* Edited by A. de Poorter. Les Philosophes Belges, vol 9. Louvain: Institut supérieur de philosophie de l'université, 1914.

Guido de Basochis. *Liber epistularum Guidonis de Basochis.* Edited by Herbert Adolfsson. Acta Universitatis Stockholmiensis, Studia Latina Stockholmiensia, vol. 18. Stockholm: Almquist & Wiksell, 1969.

Guillaume de Lorris: *Le Roman de la rose.* Vol. 1. Edited by Félix Lecoy. CFMA, vol. 92. Paris: Champion, 1965.

Guillaume de Poitiers. *Histoire de Guillaume le conquérant.* Edited and translated by R. Foureville. Les Classiques de l'histoire de France au moyen âge, vol. 23. Paris: Société d'édition "Les Belles Lettres," 1952.

Hartmann von Aue. *Erec.* Edited by Albert Leitzmann. 3d ed. rev. Ludwig Wolf. ATB, vol. 39. Tübingen: Niemeyer, 1963.

———. *Iwein.* Edited by Benecke and Lachmann. 7th ed. rev. L. Wolf. Berlin: De Gruyter, 1968.

"Der heimliche Bote." In *Mittelhochdeutsche Übungsstücke*. Edited by H. Meyer-Benfey, pp. 30–32. Halle: Niemeyer, 1909.

Helgaud de Fleury. *Vie de Robert le Pieux*. Edited and translated by Robert-Henri Bautier and Gilette Labory. Sources d'histoire médiévale, vol. 1. Paris: Editions du CNRS, 1965.

Henry of Huntingdon. *Epistola ad Walterum de mundi contemptu, sive de episcopis et viris illustribus sui temporis*. PL 195:979–990.

Herbert of Bosham. See Becket, Thomas.

Heribert of Cologne. (*Vita*). *Vita Heriberti archiepiscopi Coloniensis auctore Lantberto*. MGH, SS 4:739–53.

———. Dinter, Peter. *Rupert von Deutz, Vita Heriberti: Kritische Edition mit Kommentar und Untersuchungen*. Bonn: Röhrscheid, 1976.

Hildebert of Lavardin. *Sancti Hugonis abbatis Cluniacensis vita*. PL 159:857–94.

Hincmar of Rheims. *De ordine palatii*. Edited and translated by Thomas Gross and Rudolf Schieffer. 2d ed. MGH, Fontes iuris Germanici antiqui, vol. 3. Hannover: Hahn, 1980.

Hugh of Cluny. (*Vita*). See Hildebert of Lavardin.

Isidore of Seville. *Isidori Hispalensis episcopi etymologiarum sive originum libri XX*. Edited by W. M. Lindsay. 2 vols. Oxford: Clarendon, 1911.

John of Salisbury. *Iohannis Saresberiensis episcopi Carnotensis policratici sive de nugis curialium et vestigiis philosophorum libri VIII*. Edited by Clemens C. I. Webb. 2 vols. Oxford: Clarendon, 1909.

John of Limoges. *Johannis Lemovicensis, abbatis de Zirc 1208–1218 opera omnia*. Edited by Constantin Horváth. 3 vols. Vesprém, Hungary: Egyházmegyei Konyvnyomda, 1932.

Lambert of Ardres. *Historia comitum Ghisnensium*. Edited by I. Heller. MGH, SS 24:550–642.

Lampert of Hersfeld. *Annalen*. Edited by O. Holder-Egger. Translated by Adolf Schmidt with commentary by W. D. Fritz. AQDG, vol. 13. Berlin: Rütten & Loening, 1957.

"Das Liebesconcil in Remiremont." Edited by W. Meyer. Nachrichten der Kgl. Gesellschaft der Wissenschaften zu Göttingen, Phil.-Hist. Kl. 1914. Berlin: Weidmann, 1915.

Lietbert of Cambrai (*Vita*). *Vita Lietberti episcopi Cameracensis auctore Rodulfo monacho*. Edited by A. Hofmeister. MGH, SS 30:2:838–66.

Marbod of Rennes. *Vita Sancti Licinii episcopi Andegavensis auctore Marbodo*. PL 171:1493–1504.

———. *Vita Sancti Magnobodi Andegavensis episcopi auctore Marbodo*. PL 171:1547–62.

———. *Vita Sancti Gualterii seu Gauterii abbatis et canonici Stirpensis in dioecesi Galliarum Lemovicensi auctore Marbodo*. PL 171:1565–76.

Martini episcopi Bracarensis opera omnia. Edited by Claude Barlow. New Haven: Yale University Press, 1950.

Meinwerk of Paderborn (*Vita*). *Das Leben des Bischofs Meinwerk von Paderborn*. Edited by F. Tenckhoff. MGH, SS rer. germ. in us. schol., vol. 59. Hannover: Hahn, 1921.

Das Moralium dogma philosophorum des Guillaume de Conches: Lateinisch, altfranzösisch und mittelniederfränkisch. Edited by John Holmberg. Leipzig: Harrassowitz et al., 1929.

Das Nibelungenlied. Edited by Karl Bartsch and Helmut De Boor. 18th ed. Wiesbaden: Brockhaus, 1965.

Norbert of Xanten (*Vita*). *Vita Sancti Norberti archiepiscopi Magdeburgensis (Vita A)*. LB, pp. 443–541. Reprint from R. Wilmans, ed., MGH, SS 12:663–703.

Orderic Vitalis. *The Ecclesiastical History of Orderic Vitalis*. Edited and translated by Marjorie Chibnall. 6 vols. Oxford Medieval Texts. Oxford: Oxford University Press, 1969–80.

Otto of Bamberg (*Vita*). *Sancti Ottonis episcopi Babenbergensis vita Prieflingensis*. Edited by Jan Wikarjak and Kazimierz Liman. MPH, n.s., vol. 7, fasc. 1. Warsaw: Państwowe Wydawn, 1966.

Ebonis vita Sancti Ottonis episcopi Babenbergensis. Edited by Jan Wikarjak and Kazimierz Liman. MPH, n.s., vol. 7, fasc. 2. Warsaw: Państwowe Wydawn, 1969.

Herbordi dialogus de vita Sancti Ottonis episcopi Babenbergensis. Edited by Jan Wikarjak and Kazimierz Liman. MPH, n.s., vol. 7, fasc. 3. Warsaw: Państwowe Wydawn, 1974.

Otto of Freising. *Gesta Friderici*. Edited by G. Waitz. 3d ed. MGH, SS rer. germ. in us. schol., vol. 46. Hannover and Leipzig: Hahn, 1912. Reprint. Hannover, 1978.

Papias. *Vocabulista*. Venice: Philippus de Pincis Mantuanus, 1496. Reprint. Torino, 1966.

Paulina of Zell (*Vita*). *Sigebotonis vita Paulinae*. Edited by I. R. Dieterich. MGH, SS 30:2:909–38.

Peter of Blois. *Opera Omnia*. PL, vol. 207.

Petrus Damiani: *Sancti Petri Damiani S.R.E. cardinalis episcopi Ostiensis, ordinis Sancti Benedicti, e congregatione Fontis-Avellanae opera omnia*. PL, vols. 144, 145.

Radulphus Glaber. *Raoul Glaber, Les cinq livres de ses histoires*. Edited by Maurice Prou. CTSEEH, vol. 1. Paris: Picard, 1886.

Rahewin. See Otto of Freising.

Reginardus of Liège (*Vita*). *Vita Reginardi episcopi Leodiensis auctore Reinero*. Edited by W. Arndt. MGH, SS 20:571–78.

Die religiösen Dichtungen des 11. und 12. Jahrhunderts. Edited by Friedrich Maurer. 3 vols. Tübingen: Niemeyer, 1970.

The Ruodlieb: Linguistic Introduction, Latin Text and Glossary. Edited by Gordon B. Ford, Jr. Leiden: Brill, 1966.

Saxo Grammaticus. *Saxonis Gesta Danorum*. Edited by J. Olrik and H. Raeder. Copenhagen: Levin & Munksgaard, 1931.

———. *The History of the Danes: Books I–IX*. Translated by Peter Fisher with introduction by Hilda Ellis Davidson. 2 vols. Cambridge: D. S. Brewer; and Totowa, N.J.: Rowman & Littlefield, 1980.

———. *Danorum regum heroumque historia Books X–XVI: The Text of the First Edition with Translation and Commentary in Three Volumes*. Translated by Eric Christiansen. BAR International Series, vols. 84 and 118 (i and ii). Oxford: BAR, 1980–81.

Sextus Amarcius. *Sexti Amarcii Galli Piostrati sermonum libri IV*. Edited by M. Manitius. Leipzig: Teubner, 1888.

Sichard of Cremona. *Sicardi episcopi Cremonensis Cronica*. Edited by O. Holder-Egger. MGH, SS 31:22–183.

Sigebert of Gembloux. See Dieterich of Metz. (*Vita*.)

Thietmar of Merseburg. *Die Chronik des Bischofs Thietmar von Merseburg*. Edited by Robert Holtzmann. 2d ed. MGH, SS rer. germ., n.s., vol 9. Berlin: Weidmann, 1955.

Thomasin of Zirclaere. *Der Wälsche Gast des Thomasin von Zirclaria.* Edited by Heinrich Rückert. DNL, vol. 30. Quedlinburg and Leipzig: Basse, 1852.

Ulrich of Augsburg (*Vita*). *Vita Sancti Oudalrici episcopi Augustani auctore Gerhardo.* Edited by G. Waitz. LB, pp. 35–167. Reprint from MGH, SS 4, pp. 377–419.

Ulrich of Zell. (*Vita*). *Ex vita Sancti Udalrici priorensis Cellensis.* Edited by R. Wilmans. MGH, SS 12. *Vita prior,* pp. 251–53. *Vita posterior,* pp. 253–67.

Wace. *Le Roman de Brut de Wace.* Edited by Ivor Arnold. 2 vols. Paris: Société des anciens textes français, 1938, 1940.

———. *Le Roman de Rou de Wace.* Edited by A. J. Holden. Société des anciens textes français, vols. 1–3. Paris: Picard, 1970–73.

Walter Map. *De nugis curialium.* Edited by M. R. James. Anecdota Oxoniensia, vol. 14. Oxford: Clarendon, 1914.

Wernher of Merseburg (*Vita*). *Vita Wernheri episcopi Merseburgensis.* Edited by R. Wilmans. MGH, SS 12:244–48.

William of Jumièges. *Gesta Normannorum ducum.* PL 149:779–910.

William of Malmesbury: *Willelmi Malmesburiensis libri tres de vita Sancti Wulfstani.* PL 179:1733–72.

———. *Willelmi Malmesbiriensis de gestis regum Anglorum.* Edited by William Stubbs. 2 vols. London: Eyre & Spottiswoode, 1887. RS 90.

William of Poitiers. See Guillaume de Poitiers.

Wipo. *Die Werke Wipos.* Edited by Harry Bresslau. 3d ed. MGH, SS rer. germ. in us. schol., vol. 61. Hannover and Leipzig: Hahn, 1915. Reprint. 1977.

Wireker, Nigel. *Contra curiales et officiales clericos.* In *The Anglo-Latin Satirical Poets and Epigrammatists of the Twelfth Century,* edited by Thomas Wright. London: Longman, 1872. RS 59:1:146–230.

Wolbodo of Liège (*Vita*). *Vita Wolbodonis episcopi Leodiensis auctore Reinero.* Edited by W. Arndt. MGH, SS 20:565–71.

Wolfgang of Regensburg (*Vita*). *Othloni vita Sancti Wolfkangi episcopi.* Edited by G. Waitz. MGH, SS 4:521–42.

Wolfram von Eschenbach. *Parzival.* Edited by Albert Leitzmann. ATB, vols. 12–14. Tübingen: Niemeyer, 1961–65.

Secondary Sources

Anton, H. H. *Fürstenspiegel und Herrscherethos in der Karolingerzeit.* Bonner historische Forschungen, vol. 32. Bonn: Röhrscheid, 1968.

Auer, Leopold. "Der Kriegsdienst des Klerus unter den sächsischen Kaisern, I." *MIÖG* 79 (1971): 316–407. *MIÖG* 80 (1972): 48–70.

Baldwin, John W. *Masters, Princes and Merchants: The Social Views of Peter the Chanter and His Circle.* 2 vols. Princeton, N.J.: Princeton University Press, 1970.

Barker, Ernest. *Traditions of Civility: Eight Essays.* Cambridge: Cambridge University Press, 1948.

Baron, Hans. "Cicero and the Roman Civic Spirit in the Middle Ages and the Early Renaissance." In *Lordship and Community in Medieval Europe: Se-*

lected Readings, edited by F. L. Cheyette, pp. 291–314. New York: Holt, Rinehart & Winston, 1968. Originally in *Bulletin of the John Rylands Library* 22 (1938): 72–97.

Beinlich, J. "Die Persönlichkeit Erzbischofs Adalbert von Bremen." Diss., Greifswald, 1918.

Benson, Robert. *The Bishop Elect: A Study in Medieval Ecclesiastical Office.* Princeton, N.J.: Princeton University Press, 1968.

Benton, John. "The Court of Champagne as a Literary Center." *Speculum* 36 (1961): 551–91.

———. "'Nostre Franceis n'unt talent de fuïr': The *Song of Roland* and the Enculturation of a Warrior Class," *Olifant* 6 (1979): 237–58.

Berges, Wilhelm. *Die Fürstenspiegel des hohen und späten Mittelalters.* MGH, Schriften, vol. 2. Leipzig: Hiersemann, 1938. Reprint. 1952.

Bertram, Adolf. *Geschichte des Bistums Hildesheim.* 3 vols. Hildesheim: Lax, 1899–1925.

Bezzola, Gian Andri. *Das Ottonische Kaisertum in der französischen Geschichtsschreibung des 10. und beginnenden 11. Jahrhunderts.* Veröffentlichungen des Instituts für österreichische Geschichtsforschung, vol. 18. Graz and Cologne: Böhlau, 1956.

Bezzola, Reto. *Les Origines et la formation de la littérature courtoise en occident (500–1200).* 3 pts. in 5 vols. Paris: Champion, 1958–63.

Bittner, Franz. "Studien zum Herrscherlob in der mittellateinischen Dichtung." Diss., Würzburg, 1962.

Blatt, Franz. *Saxonis Gesta Danorum, Tomus II: Index Verborum.* Copenhagen: Levin & Munksgaard, 1957.

———. "Einleitung zu einem Wörterbuch über die Latinität Saxos." In *Mittellateinische Philologie: Beiträge zur Erforschung der mittelalterlichen Latinität*, edited by Alf Önnerfors, pp. 242–60. WDF, vol. 292. Darmstadt: Wissenschaftliche Buchgesellschaft, 1975.

Bléry, Henri. *Rusticité et urbanité romaines.* Paris: Belin, 1909.

Bloch, Marc. *Feudal Society.* Translated by L. A. Manyon. Chicago: University of Chicago Press, 1968.

Boase, Roger. *The Origin and Meaning of Courtly Love: A Critical Study of European Scholarship.* Manchester: Manchester University Press; and Totowa, N.J.: Rowman & Littlefield, 1977.

Bonadeo, A. "Function and Purpose of the Courtier in Castiglione." *Philological Quarterly* 50 (1971): 36–46.

Born, Lester K. "The Perfect Prince: 13th and 14th Century Ideals." *Speculum* 3 (1928): 470–504.

Borst, Arno. "Das Rittertum im Hochmittelalter: Idee und Wirklichkeit." In *Das Rittertum im Mittelalter*, edited by Arno Borst. WDF, vol. 349. Darmstadt: Wissenschaftliche Buchgesellschaft, 1976. Pp. 212–46.

Bosl, Karl. "Der 'aristokratische Charakter' europäischer Staats- und Sozialentwicklung: Prolegomena zu einer allgemeinen Verfassungsgeschichte." *Hist. Jb.* 74 (1955): 631–42.

———. "Geistliche Fürsten." In *LthK* 4:619–22. 2d ed. Freiburg: Herder, 1960.

———. "Der Adelsheilige: Idealtypus und Wirklichkeit, Gesellschaft und Kultur im merowingerzeitlichen Bayern des 7. und 8. Jahrhunderts." In *Speculum Historiale: Geschichte im Spiegel von Geschichtsschreibung und Geschichtsdeutung: Festschrift Johannes Spörl*, edited by C. Bauer et al., pp. 167–87. Freiburg and Munich: Alber, 1965.

————. "Leitbilder und Wertvorstellungen des Adels von der Merowingerzeit bis zur Höhe der feudalen Gesellschaft." Sitzungsberichte der Bayerischen Akademie der Wissenschaft, Phil.-Hist. Kl., 1974, no. 5. Munich: Bayerische Akademie der Wissenschaft and Beck, 1974.

Braun, Werner. *Studien zum Ruodlieb: Ritterideal, Erzählstruktur und Darstellungsstil.* Quellen und Forschungen zur Sprach- und Kulturgeschichte der germanischen Völker, n.s., vol. 7. Berlin: De Gruyter, 1962.

Brinkmann, Hennig. *Zu Wesen und Form mittelalterlicher Dichtung.* Halle/Saale: Niemeyer, 1928.

————. *Entstehungsgeschichte des Minnesangs.* Halle: Niemeyer, 1926.

Brühl, Carlrichard. "Die Sozialstruktur des deutschen Episkopats im 11. und 12. Jahrhundert." In *Le istituzione ecclesiastiche della Societas Christiana dei secoli XI–XII: diocesi, pievi e parrocchie: atti della sesta settimana internazionale di studio, Milano, 1–7 settembre, 1974*, pp. 42–56. Milan: Vita e Pensiero, 1977.

Brunhölzl, Franz. "Der Bildungsauftrag der Hofschule." In *Karl der Grosse: Lebenswerk und Nachleben*; vol. 2, *Geistiges Leben*, edited by B. Bischoff, pp. 28–41. Düsseldorf: Schwann, 1965.

————. "Zum Ruodlieb." *DVJS* 39 (1965): 506–22.

Bulst-Thiele, Marie. *Kaiserin Agnes.* BKMR, vol. 52. Leipzig and Berlin: Teubner, 1933.

Bumke, Joachim. *Ministerialität und Ritterdichtung: Umrisse der Forschung.* Munich: Beck, 1976.

————. *Studien zum Ritterbegriff im 12. und 13. Jahrhundert.* 2d ed. Beihefte zum Euphorion, vol. 1. Heidelberg: Winter, 1976.

————. *Mäzene im Mittelalter: Die Gönner und Auftraggeber der höfischen Literatur in Deutschland 1150–1300.* Munich: Beck, 1979.

Burgess, Glynn S. *Contribution à l'étude du vocabulaire pré-courtois.* Publications romanes et françaises, vol. 110. Geneva: Droz, 1970.

Camproux, Ch. "La Joie civilatrice chez les troubadours." *La Table ronde* 97 (1957): 64–69.

Christ, Winfried. *Rhetorik und Roman: Untersuchungen zu Gottfrieds von Strassburg Tristan und Isold.* Deutsche Studien, vol. 31. Meisenheim am Glan: Hain, 1977.

Clanchy, M. T. *From Memory to Written Record: England, 1066–1307.* London: Arnold, 1979.

Cropp, Glynnis M. *Le Vocabulaire courtois des troubadours de l'époque classique.* Publications romanes et françaises, vol. 135. Geneva: Droz, 1975.

Curtius, Ernst Robert. *European Literature and the Latin Middle Ages.* Translated by Willard R. Trask. New York: Harper, 1963.

De Boor, Helmut. *Die höfische Literatur: Vorbereitung, Blüte, Ausklang: 1170–1250: Geschichte der deutschen Literatur.* Vol. 2. Munich: Beck, 1964.

Dehio, Georg. *Geschichte des Erzbistums Hamburg-Bremen bis zum Ausgang der Mission.* Berlin: Hertz, 1877.

Delehaye, Hippolyte. *The Legends of the Saints.* Translated by D. Attwater. New York: Fordham University Press, 1962.

Delhaye, Philippe. "Une adaption du 'de officiis' au XIIe siècle: Le *Moralium dogma philosophorum.*" *RTAM* 16 (1949): 227–58; 17 (1950): 5–28.

————. "L'Enseignement de la philosophie morale au XIIe siècle." *Mediaeval Studies* 11 (1949): 77–95. Reprinted in German under the title "Moralphilosophischer Unterricht im 12. Jahrhundert." In *Ritterliches Tugend-*

system, edited by Günter Eifler, pp. 301–40. WDF, vol 56. Darmstadt: Wissenschaftliche Buchgesellschaft, 1970.

Denomy, A. J. "Courtly Love and Courtliness." *Speculum* 28 (1953): 44–63.

———. "Jois Among the Early Troubadours: Its Meaning and Possible Source." *Mediaeval Studies* 13 (1951): 177–217.

Derpmann, Manfred. *Die Josephsgeschichte: Auffassung und Darstellung im Mittelalter.* Beihefte zum Mittellateinischen Jahrbuch, vol. 13. Düsseldorf: Henn, 1974.

Diefenbach, Lorenz. *Glossarium Latino-Germanicum mediae et infimae Aetatis.* Frankfurt: Baer, 1857.

Dihle, Albrecht. "Antike Höflichkeit und christliche Demut." *Studi italiani di filologia classica* 26 (1952): 169–90.

Drögereit, R. "Die Vita Bernwardi und Thangmar." *Unsere Diözese in Vergangenheit und Gegenwart: Zeitschrift des Vereins für Heimatkunde im Bistum Hildesheim* 28 (1959): 2–46.

Dronke, Peter. *Medieval Latin and the Rise of the European Love Lyric.* 2 vols. 2d ed. Oxford: Clarendon, 1968.

———, ed. "Peter of Blois and Poetry at the Court of Henry II." *Mediaeval Studies* 38 (1976): 185–235.

Duby, Georges. *The Three Orders: Feudal Society Imagined.* Translated by Arthur Goldhammer. Chicago and London: University of Chicago Press, 1978.

Dupin, H. *La Courtoisie au moyen âge.* Paris: Picard, 1931.

Egenter, R. "Bischofsstand und bischöfliches Ethos nach dem heiligen Thomas von Aquin." In *Episcopus: Studien über das Bischofsamt: M. Kardinal von Faulhaber zum 80. Geburtstag,* pp. 164–84. Regensburg: Gregorius, 1949.

Ehrismann, Gustav. "Die Grundlagen des ritterlichen Tugendsystems." *ZfdA* 56 (1919): 137–216.

———. "Phaset." *ZfdA* 64 (1927): 301–6.

———. *Geschichte der deutschen Literatur bis zum Ausgang des Mittelalters.* Munich: Beck, 1972.

Eichler, Sigurd. "Studien über die 'maze': Ein Beitrag zur Begriffs- und Geistesgeschichte der höfischen Kultur." Diss. Bonn, 1941. Bonner Beiträge zur deutschen Philologie, vol. 13.

Eifler, Günter, ed. *Ritterliches Tugendsystem.* WDF, vol. 56. Darmstadt: Wissenschaftliche Buchgesellschaft, 1970.

Elias, Norbert. *Über den Prozess der Zivilisation: Soziogenetische und psychogenetische Untersuchungen.* 2 vols. 2d ed. Suhrkamp Taschenbuch Wissenschaft, vols. 158–59. 1969. Reprint. Frankfurt: Suhrkamp, 1979.

———. *Die höfische Gesellschaft: Untersuchungen zur Soziologie des Königtums und der höfischen Aristokratie.* 4th ed. Soziologische Texte, vol. 54. Darmstadt and Neuwied: Luchterhand, 1979.

Erdmann, Carl. "Die Bamberger Domschule im Investiturstreit." *Zeitschrift für Bayerische Landesgeschichte* 9 (1936): 1–46.

———. "'Fabulae curiales': Neues zum Spielmannsgesang und zum Ezzo-Liede." *ZfdA* 73 (1936): 87–98.

———. *Studien zur Briefliteratur Deutschlands im 11. Jahrhundert.* MGH, Schriften, vol. 1. Leipzig: Hiersemann, 1938.

———. *Forschungen zur politischen Ideenwelt des Frühmittelalters.* Edited by Friedrich Baethgen. Berlin: Akademie, 1951.

Faral, Edmond. *Recherches sur les sources latines des contes et romans courtois du moyen âge.* Paris: Champion, 1913.

———. *Les Arts poétiques du XIIe siècle.* Paris: Champion, 1924.

Ferrante, Joan M. "*Cortes amor* in Medieval Texts." *Speculum* 55 (1980): 686–95.

Fleckenstein, Josef. "Königshof und Bischofschule unter Otto dem Grossen." *AKG* 38 (1956): 38–62.

———. *Die Hofkapelle der deutschen Könige.* 2 vols. MGH, Schriften, vol. 16/1 & 2. Stuttgart: Hiersemann, 1959–66.

———. "Karl der Grosse und sein Hof." In *Karl der Grosse: Lebenswerk und Nachleben*; vol. 1, *Persönlichkeit und Geschichte*, edited by Helmut Beumann, pp. 24–50. Düsseldorf: Schwann, 1967.

———. "Die Struktur des Hofes Karls des Grossen im Spiegel von Hinkmars *De ordine palatii.*" *Zeitschrift des Aachener Geschichtsvereins* 83 (1976): 5–22.

Flitner, Wilhelm. *Die Geschichte der abendländischen Lebensformen.* Munich: Piper, 1967.

Frank, Karl S. "Vom Kloster als scola dominici servitii zum Kloster ad servitium Imperii." *Studien und Mitteilungen zur Geschichte des Benediktinerordens* 91 (1980): 80–97.

Frappier, Jean. "L'Institution de Lancelot dans le Lancelot en Prose." In *Mélanges de philologie romane et de littérature médiévale offerts à Ernest Hoepffner*, pp. 269–78. Paris: Les Belles Lettres, 1949. Reprinted in Frappier, *Amour courtois et table ronde*, pp. 169–79.

———. "Vues sur les conceptions courtoises dans les littératures d'oc et d'oïl au XIIe siècle." *Cahiers de civilisation médiévale* 2 (1959): 135–56.

———. *Le Roman breton: Les origines de la légende Arthurienne: Chrétien de Troyes.* Paris: Centre de documentation universitaire, 1964.

———. "Sur un procès fait à l'amour courtois." In *Amour courtois et table ronde.* Publications romanes et françaises, vol. 126. Geneva: Droz, 1973.

Frappier, Jean, and Reinhold R. Grimm. *Grundriss der romanischen Literaturen des Mittelalters IV: 1, Le Roman jusqu'à la fin du XIIIe siècle.* Heidelberg: Winter, 1978.

Galpin, S. M. "Cortois and Vilain." Diss. Yale University, 1905.

Gamer, Helena M. "Studien zum Ruodlieb." *ZfdA* 88 (1957–58): 249–66.

Ganz, Peter. "Der Begriff des 'Höfischen' bei den Germanisten." In *Wolfram Studien IV*, edited by W. Schröder. Berlin: Schmidt, 1977.

Gebauer, J. *Geschichte der Stadt Hildesheim.* 2 vols. Hildesheim and Leipzig: Lax, 1922.

Giesebrecht, Wilhelm von. *Geschichte der deutschen Kaiserzeit.* 6 vols. in 8. 5th ed. Leipzig: Duncker & Humblot, 1877–95.

Glauche, G. *Schullektüre im Mittelalter: Entstehung und Wandlungen des Lektürekanons bis 1200 nach den Quellen dargestellt.* Münchener Beiträge zur Mediävistik und Renaissance-Forschung, vol. 5. Munich: Arbeo, 1970.

Glier, Ingeborg. *Artes amandi: Untersuchung zu Geschichte, Überlieferung und Typologie der deutschen Minnereden.* MTU, vol. 34. Munich: Beck, 1971.

Görlitz, Siegfried. *Beiträge zur Geschichte der königlichen Hofkapelle im Zeitalter der Ottonen und Salier bis zum Beginn des Investiturstreites.* Historisch-Diplomatische Forschungen, vol. 1. Weimar: Böhlau, 1936.

Götte, Christian. *Das Menschen- und Herrscherbild des rex major im "Ruodlieb": Studien zur Ethik und Anthropologie im "Ruodlieb".* Medium Aevum, vol 34. Munich: Fink, 1981.

Goez, Werner. *Translatio imperii: Ein Beitrag zur Geschichte des Geschichtsdenkens im Mittelalter und in der früheren Neuzeit.* Tübingen: Mohr, 1958.

Green, D. H. *Irony in the Medieval Romance.* Cambridge and New York: Cambridge University Press, 1979.

Green, Richard Firth. *Poets and Princepleasers: Literature and the English Court in the Late Middle Ages.* Toronto: University of Toronto Press, 1980.

Gruenter, Rainer. "Der Favorit: Das Motiv der höfischen Intrige in Gotfrids Tristan: Ein Vortrag." *Euphorion* 58 (1964): 113–28.

Grundmann, Herbert. "Litteratus-Illitteratus: Der Wandel einer Bildungsnorm vom Altertum zum Mittelalter." In his *Ausgewählte Aufsätze,* pp. 1–66. MGH, Schriften, 25:3. Stuttgart: Hiersemann, 1978.

Haider, Siegfried. *Das bischöfliche Kapellanat, I: Von den Anfängen bis in das 13. Jahrhundert.* MIÖG, suppl. vol. 25. Vienna and Cologne: Böhlau, 1977.

———. Zum Verhältnis von Kapellanat und Geschichtsschreibung im Mittelalter. In *Geschichtsschreibung und geistiges Leben im Mittelalter: Festschrift für Heinz Löwe zum 65. Geburtstag,* edited by K. Hauck and H. Mordek, pp. 102–38. Vienna and Cologne: Böhlau, 1978.

———. "Zu den Anfängen der päpstlichen Kapelle." *MIÖG* 87 (1979): 38–70.

Hampe, Karl. "Der Kulturwandel um die Mitte des 12. Jahrhunderts." *AKG* 21 (1931): 129–50.

Hanning, R. W. "The Social Significance of 12th Century Chivalric Romance." *Mediaevalia et Humanistica,* n.s., 3 (1972): 3–29.

Hauck, Albert. *Kirchengeschichte Deutschlands.* Vol 3. 3d ed. Leipzig: Hinrichs, 1906.

Hauck, Karl. "Heinrich III. und der Ruodlieb." *PBB* 70 (1948): 372–419.

———. "Mittellateinische Literatur." In *Deutsche Philologie im Aufriss,* 2d ed., edited by Wolfgang Stammler, 2:2555–624. 2d ed. Berlin: Schmidt, 1960.

Haug, Walter. "Höfische Idealität und heroische Tradition im Nibelungenlied." In *Colloquio italo-germanico sul tema: I Nibelunghi,* pp. 35–50. Rome: Accademia Nazionale dei Lincei, 1974.

Hausmann, Friedrich. *Reichskanzlei und Hofkapelle unter Heinrich V und Konrad III.* MGH, Schriften, vol. 14. Stuttgart: Hiersemann, 1956.

Heer, Friedrich. *Die Tragödie des heiligen Reiches.* Stuttgart: Kohlhammer, 1952.

Heinzelmann, Martin. *Bischofsherrschaft in Gallien: Zur Kontinuität römischer Führungsschichten vom 4. bis zum 7. Jahrhundert: Soziale, prosopographische und bildungsgeschichtliche Aspekte.* Beihefte der Francia, vol. 5. Zurich: Artemis, 1976.

Hertling, L. "Der mittelalterliche Heiligentypus nach den Tugendkatalogen." *Zeitschrift für Aszese und Mystik* 8 (1933): 260–68.

Hofer, Stefan. *Chrétien de Troyes: Leben und Werk des altfranzösischen Epikers.* Graz: Böhlau, 1954.

Hoffmann, H. "Politik und Kultur im Ottonischen Reichskirchensystem: Zur Interpretation der Vita Brunonis." *Rheinische Vierteljahrsblätter* 22 (1957): 31–55.

Holmes, Urban T. *A History of Old French Literature from the Origins to 1300.* 2d ed. rev. New York: Russell & Russell, 1962.

Hoyler, August. *Gentleman-Ideal und Gentleman-Erziehung mit besonderer Berücksichtigung der Renaissance. Erziehungsgeschichtliche Untersuchungen,* vol. 1. Leipzig: Meiner, 1933.

Hürten, Heinz. "Gregor der Grosse und der mittelalterliche Episkopat." *ZfK* 73 (1962): 16–41.

―――. "Die Verbindung von geistlicher und weltlicher Gewalt als Problem in der Amtsführung des mittelalterlichen deutschen Bischofs." *ZfK* 82 (1971): 16–28.

Hug, Wolfgang. "Elemente der Biographie im Hochmittelalter: Untersuchungen zu Darstellungsform und Geschichtsbild der Viten vom Ausgang der Ottonen bis in die Anfänge der Stauferzeit." Diss., Munich, 1957.

Hunt, Tony. "Redating Chrétien de Troyes." *BBSIA* 30 (1978): 209–37.

Jackson, W. T. H. "Der Streit zwischen miles und clericus." *ZdfA* 85 (1954–55): 293–303.

Jaeger, C. Stephen. *Medieval Humanism in Gottfried von Strassburg's "Tristan und Isolde."* Heidelberg: Winter, 1977.

―――. "The Court Criticism of MHG Didactic Poets: Social Structures and Literary Conventions." *Monatshefte* 74 (1982): 398–409.

―――. "The Barons' Intrigue in Gottfried's *Tristan*: Notes Towards a Sociology of Fear in Court Society." *JEGP* 83 (1984): 46–66.

―――. "The Nibelungen Poet and the Clerical Rebellion against Courtesy." *Spectrum Medii Aevi: Essays in Early German Literature in Honor of George Fenwick Jones*, edited by W. C. McDonald, pp. 177–205. Göppinger Arbeiten zur Germanistik, vol. 362. Göppingen: Kümmerle, 1983.

―――. "The Courtier Bishop in Vitae from the Tenth to the Twelfth Century." *Speculum* 58 (1983): 291–325.

Jaeger, Werner. *Paideia: The Ideas of Greek Culture.* 2d ed. Translated by Gilbert Highet. New York: Oxford University Press, 1960.

Javitch, Daniel. *Poetry and Courtliness in Renaissance England.* Princeton, N.J.: Princeton University Press, 1978.

Jeanroy, Alfred. *La Poésie lyrique des Troubadours.* 2 vols. Toulouse and Paris: Didier, 1934.

Jenal, Georg. *Erzbischof Anno II. von Köln (1056–75) und sein politisches Wirken: Ein Beitrag zur Geschichte der Reichs- und Territorialpolitik im 11. Jahrhundert.* 2 vols. Monographien zur Geschichte des Mittelalters, vol. 8/i & ii. Stuttgart: Hiersemann, 1974–75.

Jerg, Ernst. *Vir Venerabilis: Untersuchungen zur Titulatur der Bischöfe in den ausserkirchlichen Texten der Spätantike als Beitrag zur Deutung ihrer öffentlichen Stellung.* Wiener Beiträge zur Theologie, vol. 26. Vienna: Herder, 1970.

Johnson, Edgar N. *The Secular Activities of the German Episcopate, 919–1024.* University of Nebraska Studies, vol. 30. Lincoln, Neb.: University of Nebraska Press, 1932.

―――. "Adalbert of Hamburg-Bremen: A Politician of the Eleventh Century." *Speculum* 9 (1934): 147–79.

Jordan, Karl. *Die Entstehung der römischen Kurie: Ein Versuch, mit Nachtrag, 1962.* Libelli, vol. 91. Darmstadt: Wissenschaftliche Buchgesellschaft, 1962.

Kästner, Hannes. *Harfe und Schwert: Der höfische Spielmann bei Gottfried von Strassburg.* Untersuchungen zur deutschen Literaturgeschichte, vol. 30. Tübingen: Niemeyer, 1981.

Kaiser, Reinhold. *Bischofsherrschaft zwischen Königtum und Fürstenmacht: Studien zur bischöflichen Stadtherrschaft im westfränkisch-französischen Reich im frühen und hohen Mittelalter*. Pariser historische Studien, vol. 17. Bonn: Röhrscheid, 1981.

Keller, Hagen. "Zur Struktur der Königsherrschaft im karolingischen und nachkarolingischen Italien: Der *consiliarius regis* in den italienischen Königsdiplomen des 9. und 10. Jahrhunderts." *Quellen und Forschungen aus italienischen Archiven und Bibliotheken* 47 (1967): 123–223.

Kelso, Ruth. *The Doctrine of the English Gentlemen in the Sixteenth Century, with a Bibliographical List of Treatises on the Gentleman and Related Subjects Published in Europe to 1625*. University of Illinois Studies in Language and Literature, vol. 14. Urbana, Ill.: University of Illinois Press, 1929.

Kiesel, Helmuth. *"Bei Hof, bei Höll": Untersuchungen zur literarischen Hofkritik von Sebastian Brant bis Friedrich Schiller*. Studien zur deutschen Literatur, vol. 60. Tübingen: Niemeyer, 1979.

Kilgour, Reymond L. *The Decline of Chivalry as Shown in the French Literature of the Late Middle Ages*. Harvard Studies in Romance Languages, vol. 12. Cambridge, Mass.: Harvard University Press, 1937; reprint, Gloucester, Mass., 1966.

Kirn, Paul. "Die mittelalterliche Staatsverwaltung als geistesgeschichtliches Problem." *HV* 27 (1932): 523–48.

———. *Das Bild des Menschen in der Geschichtsschreibung von Polybios bis Ranke*. Göttingen: Vandenhoeck & Ruprecht, 1955.

Kleinschmidt, Erich. *Herrscherdarstellung: Zur Disposition mittelalterlichen Aussageverhaltens untersucht an Texten über Rudolf I. von Habsburg*. Biblioteca Germanica, vol. 17. Bern and Munich: Francke, 1974.

Klewitz, Hans-Walter. "Cancellaria: Ein Beitrag zur Geschichte des geistlichen Hofdienstes." *DA* 1 (1937): 44–79. Reprinted in Klewitz, *Ausgewählte Aufsätze zur Kirchen- und Geistesgeschichte des Mittelalters*, pp. 13–48. Aalen: Scientia, 1971.

———. "Königtum, Hofkapelle und Domkapitel im 10. und 11. Jahrhundert." *AUF* 16 (1939): 102–56. Reprint. Darmstadt: Wissenschaftliche Buchgesellschaft, 1960.

Knapp, Fritz Peter. "Bemerkungen zum 'Ruodlieb.'" *ZfdA* 104 (1975): 189–204.

Köhler, Erich. *Ideal und Wirklichkeit in der höfischen Epik: Studien zur Form der frühen Artus- und Graldichtung*. 2d ed. Beihefte zur Zeitschrift für romanische Philologie, vol. 97. Tübingen: Niemeyer, 1970.

———. "Einige Thesen zur Literatursoziologie." *GRM*, n.s., 24 (1974): 257–64.

Köhler, Oskar. *Das Bild des geistlichen Fürsten in den Viten des 10., 11., und 12. Jahrhunderts*. Abhandlungen zur mittleren und neueren Geschichte, vol. 77. Berlin: Verlag für Staatswissenschaften und Geschichte, 1935.

———. "Die Ottonische Reichskirche: Ein Forschungsbericht." In *Adel und Kirche: Gerd Tellenbach zum 65. Geburtstag*, edited by Josef Fleckenstein, pp. 141–204. Freiburg: Herder, 1968.

Köhn, Rolf. "'Militia curialis': Die Kritik am geistlichen Hofdienst bei Peter von Blois und in der lateinischen Literatur des 9.–12. Jahrhunderts." In *Miscellanea Mediaevalia 12: Soziale Ordnungen im Selbstverständnis des Mittelalters*, edited by A. Zimmermann, pp. 227–57. Berlin and New York: De Gruyter, 1979.

Kolb, Herbert. "Der Hof und die Höfischen: Bemerkungen zu Gottfried von Strassburg." *ZfdA* 106 (1977): 236–52.

Krings, Hans. "Die Geschichte des Wortschatzes der Höflichkeit im Französischen." Diss., Bonn, 1961.

Kurth, Godefroid. *Notger de Liège et la civilisation au Xe siècle.* 2 vols. Paris: Picard, 1905.

Lammermann, Karl. "Von der attischen Urbanität und ihrer Auswirkung in der Sprache." Diss., Göttingen, 1935.

Lazar, Moshe. *Amour courtois et "Fin Amors" dans la littérature du XIIe siècle.* Bibliothèque française et romane: Etudes littéraires, vol. 8. Paris: Klincksieck, 1964.

Leckie, R. William, Jr. *The Passage of Dominion: Geoffrey of Monmouth and the Periodization of Insular History in the Twelfth Century.* Toronto: University of Toronto Press, 1981.

Legge, M. Dominica. *Anglo-Norman Literature and Its Background.* Oxford: Clarendon, 1963.

———. "La 'Courtoisie' en anglo-normand." In *Orbis mediaevalis: Mélanges de langue et de littérature offerts à Reto Raduolf Bezzola à l'occasion de son quatre-vingtième anniversaire,* edited by G. Güntert et al., pp. 235–39. Bern: Francke, 1978.

Lejeune, Rita. "Le Rôle littéraire d'Aliénor d'Aquitaine et de sa famille." *Cultura Neolatina* 14 (1954): 5–57.

Lewis, Archibald R. *The Development of Southern French and Catalan Society, 718–1050.* Austin, Tex.: University of Texas Press, 1965.

Liebertz-Grün, Ursula. *Zur Soziologie des "amour courtois": Umrisse der Forschung.* Beihefte zur Zeitschrift Euphorion, vol. 10. Heidelberg: Winter, 1977.

Liebeschütz, Hans. "Das 12. Jahrhundert und die Antike." *AKG* 35 (1953): 247–71.

Lippelt, Helmut. *Thietmar von Merseburg: Reichsbischof und Chronist.* Mitteldeutsche Forschungen, vol. 72. Cologne and Vienna: Böhlau, 1973.

Loos, Erich. *Baldassare Castigliones "Libro del Cortegiano": Studien zur Tugendauffassung des Cinquecento.* Analecta Romanica, vol. 2. Frankfurt: Klostermann, 1955.

Lotter, Friedrich. *Die Vita Brunonis des Ruotger: Ihre historiographische und ideengeschichtliche Stellung.* Bonner historische Forschungen, vol. 9. Bonn: Rohrscheid, 1958.

———. "Zu den Anredeformen und ehrenden Epitheta der Bischöfe in Spätantike und frühem Mittelalter." *DA* 27 (1971): 514–17.

———. *Severinus von Noricum: Legende und historische Wirklichkeit.* Monographien zur Geschichte des Mittelalters, vol. 12. Stuttgart: Hiersemann, 1976.

———. "Methodisches zur Gewinnung historischer Erkenntnisse aus hagiographischen Quellen." *HZ* 229 (1979): 298–356.

Lüntzel, Hermann. *Geschichte der Diözese und Stadt Hildesheim.* 2 vols. Hildesheim: Gerstenberg, 1858.

Luck, G. "'Vir facetus': A Renaissance Ideal." *Studies in Philology* 55 (1958): 107–21.

Luttrell, Claude. *The Creation of the First Arthurian Romance: A Quest.* London: Arnold, 1974.

Maitre, Léon. *Les Ecoles épiscopales et monastiques en occident avant les universités.* Paris: Picard; Ligué:Abbaye St. Martin, 1924.

Manitius, Max. *Geschichte der lateinischen Literatur des Mittelalters.* Handbuch der Altertumswissenschaft 9:2:2–3. Munich: Beck, 1923–31.

Marrou, H. I. *A History of Education in Antiquity*. Translated by George Lamb. Madison, Wis.: University of Wisconsin Press, 1956.

Mazzeo, Joseph. "Castiglione's *Courtier*: The Self as a Work of Art." In his *Renaissance and Revolution: The Remaking of European Thought*, pp. 131–60. New York: Pantheon, 1965.

McKittrick, Rosamund. "The Palace School of Charles the Bald." In *Charles the Bald: Court and Kingdom*, edited by Margaret Gibson and Janet Nelson, pp. 385–400. BAR International Series, vol. 101. Oxford: BAR, 1981.

Meier, Rudolf. *Die Domkapitel zu Goslar und Halberstadt in ihrer persönlichen Zusammensetzung im Mittelalter*. Veröffentlichungen des Max-Planck-Instituts für Geschichte, vol. 5. Göttingen: Vandenhoeck & Ruprecht, 1967.

Misch, Georg. *Geschichte der Autobiographie*. Vol. 3, pt. 1. Frankfurt: Schulte, Bulmke, 1959.

Mitterauer, Michael. "Studium und Fürstendienst im hochmittelalterlichen Österreich." Prüfungsarbeit, Institut für österreichische Geschichtsforschung, Vienna. Photocopy.

———. "Magister Heinricus phisicus, Protonotar Herzog Leopolds VI." *Jahrbuch des Stiftes Klosterneuburg*, n.s., 3 (1963): 49–61.

Mohr, Wolfgang. "Wandel des Menschenbildes in der mittelalterlichen Dichtung." *Wirkendes Wort*, 1. Sonderheft (1953): 37–48.

Moos, Peter von. *Hildebert von Lavardin 1056–1133: Humanitas an der Schwelle des höfischen Zeitalters*. Pariser historische Studien, vol. 3. Stuttgart: Hiersemann, 1965.

Morris, Colin. "Zur Verwaltungsethik: Die Intelligenz des 12. Jahrhunderts im politischen Leben." *Saeculum* 24 (1973): 241–50.

———. *The Discovery of the Individual, 1050–1200*. New York: Harper, 1973.

Müller, Heribert. *Heribert, Kanzler Ottos III. und Erzbischof von Köln*. Veröffentlichungen des Kölner Geschichtsvereins, vol. 33. Cologne: Wamper, 1977.

Nelson, N. E. "Cicero's *De officiis* in Christian Thought: 300–1300." In *Essays and Studies in English and Comparative Literature*, pp. 59–160. University of Michigan Publications in Language and Literature, vol. 10. Ann Arbor: University of Michigan Press, 1933.

Noethlichs, K. L. "Materialien zum Bischofsbild aus den spätantiken Rechtsquellen." *Jahrbuch für Antike und Christentum* 16 (1973): 28–59.

Norwood, Frances. "Aperçu sur le vocabulaire de la beauté dans *Erec et Enide*." *Bulletin des jeunes Romanistes* 4 (1961): 26–30.

———. "Etude des termes designants la beauté dans la littérature courtoise française du XIIe siècle." Diss., Manchester, 1963.

Noyes, Gertrud. *A Bibliography of Courtesy and Conduct Books in 17th Century England*. New Haven: Tuttle, Morehouse & Taylor, 1937.

Oediger, F. W. *Die Regesten der Erzbischöfe von Köln im Mittelalter*. Publikationen der Gesellschaft für Rheinische Geschichtskunde, vol 21. Bonn: Hanstein, 1954–61.

Öhmann, Emil. *Die Mittelhochdeutsche Lehnprägung nach altfranzösischem Vorbild*. Helsinki, 1951.

Painter, Sidney. *French Chivalry: Chivalric Ideas and Practices in Mediaeval France*. Ithaca, N.Y.: Cornell University Press, 1967.

Palander, Hugo. "Der französische Einfluss auf die deutsche Sprache im 12.

Jahrhundert." *Memoires de la Société Néophilologique de Helsinki* 3 (1902): 75–204; 8 (1929): 1–310.

Patze, Hans. "Adel und Stifterchronik: Frühformen territorialer Geschichtsschreibung im hochmittelalterlichen Reich." *Blätter für deutsche Landesgeschichte* 100 (1964): 8–81; 101 (1965): 67–128.

Payen, Jean-Charles. *Les Origines de la courtoisie dans la littérature française médiévale.* Paris: Centre de documentation universitaire, 1966–68. 2 vols.

Peters, Ursula. "Fürstenhof und höfische Dichtung: Der Hof Hermanns von Thüringen als literarisches Zentrum." Konstanzer Universitätsreden, no. 113. Konstanz: Universitätsverlag, 1981.

Petersohn, Jürgen. "Probleme der Otto-Viten und ihrer Interpretation: Bemerkungen im Anschluss an eine Neuerscheinung." *DA* 27 (1971): 314–72.

———. "Bemerkungen zu einer neuen Ausgabe der Viten Ottos von Bamberg, 1. Prüfening Vita und Ebo." *DA* 27 (1971): 175–94.

———. "Bemerkungen . . . 2. Herbords Dialog." *DA* 33 (1977): 546–59.

———. "Otto von Bamberg und seine Biographen: Grundformen und Entwicklung des Ottobildes im hohen und späten Mittelalter." *Zeitschrift für bayerische Landesgeschichte* 43 (1980): 3–27.

Philippson, Robert. "Das Sittlichschöne bei Panaitios." *Philologus* 85, n.s., 39 (1930): 357–413.

Piquet, Felix. *De vocabulis quae in duodecimo saeculo et in tertii decimi principio a Gallis Germani assumpserunt.* Paris: Leroux, 1898.

Prestage, Edgar, ed. *Chivalry: A Series of Studies to Illustrate its History and Significance and Civilizing Influence.* London: Paul, Treach, Trubner, 1928.

Prinz, Friedrich. *Klerus und Krieg im früheren Mittelalter: Untersuchungen zur Rolle der Kirche beim Aufbau der Königsherrschaft.* Monographien zur Geschichte des Mittelalters, vol. 2. Stuttgart: Hiersemann, 1971.

———. "Die bischöfliche Stadtherrschaft im Frankenreich vom 5. bis zum 7. Jahrhundert." *HZ* 217 (1973): 1–35.

Ramage, Edwin. *Urbanitas: Ancient Sophistication and Refinement.* University of Cincinnati Classical Studies, vol. 3. Norman, Okla.: University of Oklahoma Press, 1973.

Rand, E. K. *Cicero in the Courtroom of St. Thomas.* Milwaukee: Marquette University Press, 1946.

Raynaud de Lage, Guy. "'Courtois' et 'courtoisie' dans le *Roman de Thèbes.*" In his *Les Premiers Romans français et autres études littéraires et linguistiques,* pp. 211–16. Publications romanes et françaises, vol. 138. Geneva: Droz, 1976.

Reilly, Bernard. "The Court Bishops of Alfonso VII of Leon-Castilla, 1147–1157." *Mediaeval Studies* 36 (1974): 67–78.

Renardy, Ch. "Les Ecoles liégoises du XIe et XIIe siècle: Leur évolution." *Revue Belge de philologie et d'histoire* 57 (1979): 309–28.

Richardson, H. G., and G. O. Sayles. *The Governance of Mediaeval England from the Conquest to Magna Carta.* Edinburgh: Edinburgh University Press, 1963.

Riis, Thomas. *Les Institutions politiques centrales du Danemark, 1100–1332.* Odense University Studies in History and Social Sciences, vol. 46. Odense: Odense University Press, 1977.

Rocher, Daniel. *Thomasin von Zerklaere: Der Welsche Gast, 1215–1216.* 2 vols. Lille: University of Lille; Paris: Champion, 1977.

Rolfe, John C. *Cicero and his Influence.* New York: Cooper Square, 1963.

Rothenhaeusler, Matthaeus. "'Honestas morum': Eine Untersuchung zu cap. 73,3 der Regula S. Benedicti." In *Studia Benedictina in memoriam gloriosi ante saecula XIV transitus S. P. Benedicti*, pp. 127–56. Studia Anselmiana philosophica, theologica, fasc. 18–19. Rome: Libreria Vaticana, 1947.

Salamon, L. B. "The Courtier and the Scholemaster." *Comparative Literature* 25 (1973): 17–36.

Schalk, Fritz. "Zur romanischen Wortgeschichte I: Mediocritas." *RF* 64 (1952): 263–303.

Schaller, Hans Martin. "Die staufische Hofkapelle im Königreich Sizilien." *DA* 11 (1954–55): 462–505.

———. "Kanzlei und Hofkapelle Kaiser Friedrichs II." *Annali dell' Istituto storico italo-germanico in Trento: Jahrbuch des italienisch-deutschen Instituts in Trient* 2 (1976): 75–116.

Schmeidler, B. "Anti-asketische Äusserungen aus Deutschland im 11. und beginnenden 12. Jahrhundert." In *Kultur und Universalgeschichte: Walter Goetz zu seinem 60. Geburtstag*, pp. 35–52. Leipzig and Berlin: Teubner, 1927.

Schmidgall, Gary. *Shakespeare and the Courtly Aesthetic.* Berkeley and Los Angeles: University of California Press, 1981.

Schmidt, P. G. "'Causa Aiacis et Ulixis I–II': Zwei ovidianische Streitgedichte des Mittelalters." *Mittellateinisches Jahrbuch* 1 (1964): 100–132.

Schneider, Johannes. *Die Vita Heinrici IV. und Sallust: Studien zu Stil und Imitatio in der mittellateinischen Prosa.* Deutsche Akademie zu Berlin, Schriften der Sektion für Altertumswissenschaft, vol. 49. Berlin: Akademie, 1965.

Schramm, Percy Ernst. *Kaiser, Rom und Renovatio: Studien zur Geschichte des römischen Erneuerungsgedankens vom Ende des karolingischen Reiches bis zum Investiturstreit.* 2 vols. 2d ed. Darmstadt: Gentner, 1957.

———. *Kaiser, Könige und Päpste: Gesammelte Aufsätze zur Geschichte des Mittelalters.* 5 vols. Stuttgart: Hiersemann, 1969.

Schrader, Werner. *Studien über das Wort höfisch in der mittelhochdeutschen Dichtung.* Würzburg: Triltsch, 1935.

Schubert, Paul. "Die Reichshofämter und ihre Inhaber bis um die Wende des 12. Jahrhunderts." *MIÖG* 34 (1913): 427–501.

Smith, Pauline M. *The Anti-Courtier Trend in Sixteenth-Century French Literature.* Travaux d'humanisme et Renaissance, vol. 84. Geneva: Droz, 1966.

Sneyders de Vogel, K. "L'Education d'Alexandre le Grand." *Neophilologus* 28 (1942–43): 161–71.

Southern, R. W. *Western Society and the Church in the Middle Ages.* Pelican History of the Church, vol. 2. Grand Rapids, Mich.: Erdmans, 1970.

Specht, F. A. *Geschichte des Unterrichtswesens in Deutschland von den ältesten Zeiten bis zur Mitte des 13. Jahrhunderts.* Stuttgart: Cotta, 1885.

Spier, Heinrich, "Benno II. von Osnabrück am Goslarer Königshof." *Harzzeitschrift* 7 (1955): 57–67.

Stanton, Donna C. *The Aristocrat as Art: A Study of the Honnête Homme and the Dandy in Seventeenth- and Nineteenth-Century French Literature.* New York: Columbia University Press, 1980.

Stock, Brian. *The Implications of Literacy: Written Language and Models of Interpretation in the Eleventh and Twelfth Centuries.* Princeton: Princeton University Press, 1983.

Stollberg, Gunnar. *Die soziale Stellung der intellektuellen Oberschicht im England des 12. Jahrhunderts.* Historische Studien, vol. 427. Lübeck: Matthiesen, 1973.

Suchomski, Joachim. *"Delectatio" und "utilitas": Ein Beitrag zum Verständnis mittelalterlicher komischer Literatur.* Bibliotheca Germanica, vol. 18. Bern and Munich: Francke, 1975.

Teuffel, Robert. *Individuelle Persönlichkeitsschilderung in den deutschen Geschichtswerken des 10. und 11. Jahrhunderts.* BKMR, vol. 12. Leipzig: Teubner, 1914. Reprint. Hildesheim: Gerstenberg, 1974.

Thompson, James W. *The Literacy of the Laity in the Middle Ages.* University of California Publications in Education, vol. 9. Berkeley and Los Angeles: University of California Press, 1939. Reprint. New York, 1963.

Traub, Gerhard. *Studien zum Einfluss Ciceros auf die höfische Moral.* Deutsches Werden, vol. 1. Greifswald: Bamberg, 1933.

Türck, Egbert. *Nugae curialium: Le règne d'Henri II Plantagenet (1154–1189) et l'éthique politique.* Hautes Études médiévales et modernes, vol. 28. Geneva: Droz, 1977.

Turner, Ralph V. "The *Miles Literatus* in Twelfth- and Thirteenth-Century England: How Rare a Phenomenon?" *AHR* 83 (1978): 928–45.

Uhlig, Claus. *Hofkritik im England des Mittelalters und der Renaissance: Studien zu einem Gemeinplatz der europäischen Moralistik.* Quellen und Forschungen zur Sprach- und Kulturgeschichte der germanischen Völker, n.s., vol. 56. Berlin and New York: De Gruyter, 1973.

Vogt, Hilde. *Die literarische Personenschilderung des frühen Mittelalters.* BKMR, vol. 53. Hildesheim: Gerstenberg, 1934.

Wais, Kurt. "Chevalerie et courtoisie en tant que créateurs de rapports sociaux dans la littérature du moyen âge." In *Actes du VIe congrès de l'association internationale de littérature comparée,* pp. 297–302. Stuttgart: Bieber, 1975.

Walther, Hans. *Lateinische Sprichwörter und Sentenzen des Mittelalters in alphabetischer Anordnung,* 5 vols. Göttingen: Vandenhoeck & Ruprecht, 1963.

Wattenbach, W.; R. Holtzmann; and F. J. Schmale. *Deutschlands Geschichtsquellen im Mittelalter: Die Zeit der Sachsen und Salier.* 2 vols. Cologne and Graz: Böhlau, 1967.

Wechssler, Eduard. *Das Kulturproblem des Minnesangs: Studien zur Vorgeschichte der Renaissance.* Halle: Niemeyer, 1909.

Weinfurter, Stefan. "Zum bischöflichen Kapellanat und seiner Bedeutung für Köln: Bemerkungen zu einer Neuerscheinung über die Bischofskapelle." *AKG* 60 (1978): 203–12.

Weise, Georg. "Vom Menschenideal und Modewörtern der Gotik und der Renaissance." *DVJS* 14 (1936): 171–222.

West, Constance B. *Courtoisie in Anglo-Norman Literature.* Oxford: Blackwell, 1938.

Wettstein, Jacques. *Mezura: L'Idéal des troubadours: Son essence et ses aspects.* Zurich: Leemann, 1945.

Zelzer, K. "Zur Beurteilung der Cicero-Imitation bei Ambrosius, *De officiis.*" *Wiener Studien,* n.s., 11 (1977): 168–91.

Zielinski, Tadeusz. *Cicero im Wandel der Jahrhunderte.* 2d ed. Leipzig and Berlin: Teubner, 1908.

Zoepf, Ludwig. *Das Heiligenleben im 10. Jahrhundert.* BKMR, vol. 1. Leipzig and Berlin: Teubner, 1908.

INDEX

THE MIDDLE AGES
Edward Peters, *General Editor*

Christian Society and the Crusades, 1198–1229. Sources in Translation, including The Capture of Damietta by Oliver of Paderborn. Edited by Edward Peters

The First Crusade: The Chronicle of Fulcher of Chartres and Other Source Materials. Edited by Edward Peters

Love in Twelfth-Century France. John C. Moore

The Burgundian Code: The Book of Constitutions or Law of Gundobad and Additional Enactments. Translated by Katherine Fischer Drew

The Lombard Laws. Translated, with an Introduction, by Katherine Fischer Drew

From St. Francis to Dante: Translations from the Chronicle of the Franciscan Salimbene (1221–1288). G. G. Coulton

The Duel and the Oath. Parts I and II of Superstition and Force. Henry Charles Lea. Introduction by Edward Peters

The Ordeal. Part III of Superstition and Force. Henry Charles Lea

Torture. Part IV of Superstition and Force. Henry Charles Lea

Witchcraft in Europe, 1110–1700: A Documentary History. Edited by Alan C. Kors and Edward Peters

The Scientific Achievement of the Middle Ages. Richard C. Dales

History of the Lombards. Paul the Deacon. Translated by William Dudley Foulke

Monks, Bishops, and Pagans: Christian Culture in Gaul and Italy, 500–700. Edited, with an Introduction, by Edward Peters

The World of Piers Plowman. Edited and translated by Jeanne Krochalis and Edward Peters

Felony and Misdemeanor: A Study in the History of Criminal Law. Julius Goebel, Jr.

Women in Medieval Society. Edited by Susan Mosher Stuard

The Expansion of Europe: The First Phase. Edited by James Muldoon

Laws of the Alamans and Bavarians. Translated, with an Introduction, by Theodore John Rivers

Law, Church, and Society: Essays in Honor of Stephan Kuttner. Edited by Robert Somerville and Kenneth Pennington

The Fourth Crusade: The Conquest of Constantinople, 1201–1204. Donald E. Queller

The Magician, the Witch, and the Law. Edward Peters

Daily Life in the World of Charlemagne. Pierre Riché. Translated, with an Introduction, by Jo Ann McNamara

Repression of Heresy in Medieval Germany. Richard Kieckhefer

The Royal Forests of Medieval England. Charles R. Young

Popes, Lawyers, and Infidels: The Church and the Non-Christian World, 1250–1550. James Muldoon

Heresy and Authority in Medieval Europe. Edited, with an Introduction, by Edward Peters